SCIENCE RELIGION AND REALITY

SCIENCE RELIGION AND REALITY

ARTHUR JAMES, EARL OF BALFOUR, O.M., F.R.S.

BRONISLAW MALINOWSKI, Ph.D., D.Sc.

CHARLES SINGER, M.D., D.Litt.

ANTONIO ALIOTTA, D.Phil.

ARTHUR S. EDDINGTON, M.A., F.R.S.

JOSEPH NEEDHAM, M.A.

JOHN W. OMAN, D.Phil., D.D.

WILLIAM BROWN, M.A., M.D., D.Sc.

CLEMENT C. J. WEBB, M.A., LL.D.

WILLIAM RALPH INGE, D.D., LL.D.

EDITED BY

JOSEPH NEEDHAM

KENNIKAT PRESS
Port Washington, N. Y./London

SCIENCE RELIGION AND REALITY

First published in 1925
Reissued in 1970 by Kennikat Press
Library of Congress Catalog Card No: 70-108706
SBN 8046-0926-8

Manufactured by Taylor Publishing Company   Dallas, Texas

ESSAY AND GENERAL LITERATURE INDEX REPRINT SERIES

EDITORIAL COMMITTEE

Two extravagances : to exclude Reason, to admit only Reason.—

BLAISE PASCAL

MY thanks are due to all those who have helped in the preparation of this book. I am particularly indebted to Michael Oakeshott, of Caius College, Cambridge, to whom must be ascribed many valuable suggestions concerning the general scheme and marshalling of the book as a whole. Further I take delight in acknowledging the continual inspiration which those who know Sir Frederick Hopkins, F.R.S., are ever accustomed to receive from him. Finally, I thank my wife for all the assistance she has given me.

J. N.

Cambridge, 1925

CONTENTS

INTRODUCTION
BY LORD BALFOUR

I

I HAVE been honoured by a request to write a brief Introduction
to the present volume of "Essays on Science and Religion." With
some diffidence I accepted the responsibility—not because the
essays themselves stand in need of either praise or commentary,
but because I value the association with the distinguished essayists
who are here contributing to this old and famous discussion.

It must, of course, be admitted that discussions may be old and
famous without on that account having more than a historic
interest. The issues they deal with may be dead and buried. Only
students who delight in contemplating the mutations of human
beliefs may think it worth while to give them decent sepulture with
all the honours of a learned epitaph ; the rest of the world forget
that they have ever been. Such cases indeed are fewer than might
have been supposed. Even where death seems to be complete,
where no smallest trace of some once famous theory appears to
survive, a fragment of it will reappear generations later as part of
the living tissue of the most advanced speculation [1] But in the
case of science and religion the main theme has never wholly lost
its interest, and each generation insists on resurveying the subject
from its own particular point of view.

When I was asked to contribute this Introduction I vaguely
remembered a work published fifty-two years ago by Dr. Draper,
entitled "The Conflict between Science and Religion." His
volume, which went through many editions, was one of a very
respectable series of scientific handbooks, called the International
Science Series. It was composed in a most pessimistic vein. He
supposed the Western world to be on the edge of an intellectual
revolution, catastrophic in its suddenness, incalculable in its results.
The collision between science and religion, rendered acute by the
then recent Vatican Council, could end, he thought, only in
one way. Educated mankind would suddenly awake and find

---

[1] See a very curious example of this in Mr. Needham's essay in this
book, p. 252.

themselves in a world from which religion had been finally expelled by the sciences born of rational research. Though not (as I suppose) himself embarrassed by any form of religious dogma, he was too cautious a man to regard the prospect without some disquiet. But the disease (he thought) was far advanced ; he knew of no remedy ; all he could do, therefore, was to warn his readers of a peril he foresaw but was unable to avert ; and this he did.

Half a century has passed since Dr. Draper wrote, and religion is still with us. Not only so, but, so far as I can judge, its relations to science are more satisfactory at the end of this period than they were at the beginning. And this is certainly not·because science has been stationary. There has never been a period in which its progress has been more startling, in which its discoveries have been of wider scope or more fundamental significance. Nor do I believe (though here I am on more uncertain ground) that the deeper side of religion has suffered any eclipse, at least among thinking people, during these eventful years. In such circumstances, it is not perhaps surprising that the most interesting characteristic of Dr. Draper's volume of 1873 is its total *want* of interest for readers in 1925. If it met the needs of anxious inquirers fifty years ago, how greatly has our intellectual climate changed ! How irrelevant to the wider issues of science and religion are the particular incidents, medieval in date or medieval in spirit, on which he chiefly dwells. In the present volume, at least, little is said about them, either directly or by implication.

II

This observation must not be taken to mean that the following essays are written in support of any general scheme of belief common to all the writers. Few of them have seen the work of their fellow-authors. None have modified their views to fit them into any prearranged pattern. That, in these circumstances, different and sometimes incompatible points of view should be presented to the reader is inevitable. But few readers, I imagine, will regard this as a defect.

So far as I personally am concerned, I assume that my business is to express in the briefest outline how I regard the subject-matter on which we are all of us engaged. Let me then take as my point of departure an observation incidentally made in the first of the following essays by Dr. Malinowski. He tells us, in a most interesting account of his researches in Melanesia, that among the peoples he visited there was no conflict between religion and science, that their relations were not so much competitive as complementary—religion being called in to fill the gap left vacant by primitive science in the world-outlook of these undeveloped races. A function similar in kind it has no doubt performed at many stages of culture. Where explanation was desired for some interesting event, or class of events, and no "natural" explanation presented itself, a "supernatural" one was invoked to supply the want ; and it inevitably followed that as the knowledge of Nature grew, and with it the number of events for which a natural explanation could be found, the sphere of science increased, and the sphere officially claimed for religion correspondingly diminished. Often indeed the victory was a silent one, gained without noise or strife, and scarcely realised either by victor or vanquished. But it has not always been so. Sometimes the retiring party has fought a determined rearguard action against overwhelming odds, and then the world has been called on to witness that conflict between religion and science to which so much importance has been attached.

And certainly its importance cannot easily be exaggerated if we proceed on the assumption that science and religion are alternative methods of explaining the universe, between which we are being called upon, with ever-increasing insistence, to make our choice. If this be indeed the fact, the catastrophe foretold by Dr. Draper may really be imminent, and we may after all be nearing the time when the conflict between science and religion will automatically end with the extinction of the weaker combatant.

But the assumption is wholly without warrant. No doubt mankind have frequently explained natural events by the action of supernatural powers. But I find it difficult to believe that at any stage of culture deities were invented merely to account for particular kinds of experience, as the ether has been invented by modern physicists to account for certain electro-magnetic phenomena. Doubtless, since deities were available, they were often thus used. But I should suppose that, in spite of appearances to the contrary, primitive religions were no more rooted in a purely scientific desire for causal explanations than is the belief of a modern theologian in a Deity immanent in every phase of nature.

III

However this may be, there can be no doubt that the modern man looks to science and not to religion to explain the world of sense which lies about him. How then, so far as he is concerned, can there be any cause of conflict between science and religion ? If there be no world but the world revealed in sense experience, so much the worse for religion. But science has nothing to complain of. If, on the other hand, there *be* another world, how is science injured, provided always it be left in undisturbed possession of its own territory ? Peace in circumstances like these should surely be easy of attainment.

Now I believe that as a matter of fact peace on these terms is far commoner than we are sometimes apt to suppose. Through long periods of recorded history there has been little deserving the name of a conflict between science and religion. Their frontiers were too far apart. The claims of science were still too modest, those of religion were still too vague, to make collision easy. So that the disputes which really stirred the theological world were either those dividing sect from sect, or those dividing philosophy from religion. Even now, in a world where so much has changed, there are, I suspect, countless persons sincerely accepting both religion and science who never trouble themselves about any of the incompatibilities, real or imaginary, which, in the opinion of more contentious intellects, separate the two.

IV

Putting these easy-going, but not ill-advised, persons on one side, can we determine the period at which the growth of science first brought it into effective collision with the religious views authoritatively held (for example) in Western Europe ? In the third of the following essays Dr. Singer reminds us that during the Middle Ages there was neither growth in science, nor conflict between science and religion. Over what, then, did the first direct collision occur ? We might naturally suppose that it was occasioned by the great Copernican reconstruction of astronomy, the most important first-fruits of the new scientific era. And to this the ecclesiastical condemnation of Galileo no doubt gives much support. Nevertheless, I cannot help thinking that its immediate effects may easily be exaggerated. The shock to familiar beliefs inflicted by the new theory was doubtless great. Everything that mankind had ever said about sun and stars, day and night, or the revolving year, was couched (as most of it still is) in geocentric terminology. On this subject the literature of every country, sacred and secular, used the language of the market-place. And the language of the market-place was in perfect accord with what seemed to be the plain teaching of uncontradicted observation. We must not therefore be surprised that the posthumous gift of Copernicus to science was an occasion of stumbling to learned and simple alike. But I am not aware, that in Protestant countries at least, where there was certainly no inclination to underrate the verbal authority of Scripture, it raised any very serious religious difficulties. It might, perhaps, have done so if the substitution of the sun for the earth as the centre of our system had obviously involved a complete change in our whole estimate of astronomical magnitudes. But Copernicus only described motions ; measurements of mass, size and distance belong to a later age. And it was not, I suppose, till the discoveries of Newton had begun to bear their full fruit that the material insignificance of our planet in the celestial scheme was brought home to the most sluggish imagination. So it came about that when men at last realised that events, which they regarded as of infinite spiritual importance, had in fact occurred on the most insignificant of cosmic theatres, this result had been so gradually reached that adjustment to the new point of view presented no insuperable difficulties to religious thought.

V

It seems clear indeed that such difficulties as there are belong not so much to the sphere of thought as to the sphere of emotion. They are rather aesthetic than rational ; and it is only in some mood of aesthetic sentiment that we can do them justice. Let us then conceive ourselves to be gazing on a clear and quiet night upon the unveiled glory of the heavens, striving to form some adequate representation of the greatness and splendour of the innumerable suns which, crowded though they seem, lie far removed from each other and from us in the unsounded depths of space. And then, when imagination wearies of the effort, let us consider the petty planet which for the moment is our home, and

recall the tremendous events of which in the Christian story it is
alleged to have been the scene.   Surely in the mood which this
experience naturally provokes, the contrast between the conclusions
of science and the doctrines of religion, though it may leave our
reason unperplexed, must somewhat disturb our feelings.

Before, however, we treat this as more than a passing sense of
discord, it would be well to ask what science really has to tell us
about the " heavenly host," which man has always looked at with
awe and often with adoration.   Whence comes the glory of the
stars ?   What are they in their essential nature ?

The answer of science to these questions seems sufficiently
explicit.   The glory of the stars is the joint product of our mental
constitution, our nervous system, our eyes, and certain electro-
magnetic happenings whose effects are conveyed to us from the
remotest parts of space through the ether by which we are surrounded.   The orbs of heaven, apart from our perception of them,
consist of incredibly minute electric charges thinly scattered
through the vast and vacant [1] areas, which, in the language of sense
perception, we describe as stars.   Now it is open to anyone to say
that he deems these sparse collections of ultra-microscopic entities
as in themselves more interesting and impressive than the spectacular splendours which have moved the wonder and the worship
of countless generations of his ancestors.   There is much to be
said for his view.   But, however interesting and impressive they
may be, it is obviously absurd to regard their " glories " as so
remote and inaccessible, framed on so immeasurable a scale, so
independent of man's earthly destinies, that we should shrink from
the idea that in the general scheme of things (if there be one) the
dwellers on earth could by comparison count for much.   For,
after all, it is to us who dwell on earth that these glories owe their
being.   If we are nothing, they are nothing.   They are born of
our terrestrial sensibilities.   They have no separate existence.
They are not the independent characteristics of the material
object itself.   Such independent characteristics do indeed exist ;
mass, for example, and motion.   But among them we ought not
to count the " glory of the heavens," nor ought we to belittle the
earthly conditions without which no trace of that glory could ever
have existed.

It may be objected that reflections like these, if they have any

[1] Vacant as here used means, of course, empty of matter.

validity at all, must affect our admiration, not merely of Sirius and Orion, but of all things beautiful, whether they be suns or flowers. Perhaps so. I am not, however, here concerned with the general theory of aesthetics, but only with the question whether there is, or is not, any emotional incongruity between the character of the material universe as displayed by science, and the spiritual importance of the events which are believed by the adherents of more than one great religion to have occurred upon our planet. If aesthetic problems have incidentally been raised, it is no present business of mine. Here I am only dealing with religion and science.

Again, there may be critics who think poorly of the theory of perception which I have assumed without discussion in the preceding paragraphs. How far this will meet the approval of my philosophic readers must depend, I suppose, upon their philosophy. I need only say that, to the best of my belief, it is the only one consistent with science as commonly understood, and therefore the only one relevant to my immediate argument.

VI

Most persons, however, who treat science as the enemy of religion are not thinking so much of these emotional antagonisms as of hard contradictions about matters of fact. In their view science gives one account of what has been or is, and religion gives another. Since both alternatives cannot be true, on which (they ask) should we pin our faith? Having stated the question in these general terms, they perhaps condescend to particulars. Taking for illustration the collection of ancient books held sacred in the West, they inquire whether we are really to believe that the world was created some six thousand years ago, that the work of creation was accomplished in six days, that life, human and subhuman, was almost exterminated by a flood, that springing afresh from the surviving remnant, mankind repeopled the earth, became divided in race and language, and finally produced, among many mighty nations, a small people whose history, plentifully seasoned with marvels, has profoundly modified the religious history of the world.

Now evidently summaries of this type treat the Bible as if it professed to be (among other things) a textbook of cosmology and history, with the advantage over other textbooks of being inspired and therefore infallible. I will not inquire into the merits of this theory. It is not likely to be held by any readers of this volume, whatever be their views either on science or religion. Inspired, in the opinion of the present writer, the Bible certainly is. Infallible in the sense commonly attributed to that word, it certainly is not. It neither provides, nor, in the nature of things, could provide, faultless anticipations of sciences still unborn. If by a miracle it had provided them, without a miracle they could not have been understood. Its authors belonged each to his own time and country ; speaking their language, sharing their errors, seeing nature through their eyes. And if their spiritual insight has in so many cases made them teachers for all time, science has no cause of complaint. Genius is beyond its jurisdiction.

It may, perhaps, be urged that while this way of considering the historic parts of the Bible restores the living interest so nearly smothered by the uncritical devotion of earlier generations, it does not touch the real dispute between science and religion. This turns (it will be said) upon allegations of fact which are too inconsistent with the known course of nature for the sciences to accept, and too essential a part of its creed for Christianity to surrender. Neither party can afford either to abandon its position or to explain it away. The natural and the supernatural, science and superstition here come into irreconcilable conflict. Compromise is impossible. The battle, whatever be the issue, must be fought to a finish.

This way of looking at things seems to be neither good philosophy, nor good theology, nor good science. Yet I own to feeling a certain reluctance in discussing it—so wearisome is the controversy with which it is historically connected, so ingrained are the confusions on which it rests. But evidently it cannot be wholly avoided if we are to take account of the intellectual considerations which have embarrassed and still embarrass the relations of science and religion. For among all these, none, I suppose, have produced a greater effect in modern times than those which depend on the contrast which is drawn between the natural and the supernatural, or on the credibility or incredibility of miraculous occurrences.

VII

Let us then consider, in the first place, some points on which all men are agreed. No one practically doubts that the world in which we live possesses a certain kind and measure of regularity. Every expectation that we entertain, every action that we voluntarily perform, implies the belief. The most fantastic fairy tale requires it as a background ; there are traces of it even in our dreams.

Again, we are all at one in treating with suspicion any statement which, in our judgement, is inconsistent with the " sort of way things happen " in the world as we conceive it. It seems to us more probable that this or that witness should be mistaken or mendacious, than that the wonders to which he testified should be true. If we have no antecedent ground for thinking him a liar, we probably accept his statements when he confines his narrative to the familiar or the commonplace ; when he deals in marvels we begin to doubt ; when his marvels become too marvellous we frankly disbelieve—though well aware (if we be men of sense) that what is exceedingly marvellous may nevertheless be true.

Such, roughly speaking, has been, and is, the general procedure of mankind. But evidently it is ill-suited to satisfy historians, philosophers, or men of science. It lacks precision. It rests on no clear principles. It depends too obviously on personal predilections. We seek a criterion of credibility more objective and more fundamental. We should like to know, for example, whether there is any sort of event which is inherently impossible, any sort of statement which, without being self-contradictory, may always be pronounced untrue.

This question will, to many high authorities, seem capable of the simplest answer. Unbroken experience (they will tell us) establishes the uniformity of nature, and it is the uniformity of nature which makes inferences from experience possible. Were this disturbed by miraculous occurrences the very foundations of science would be shaken. On broad general grounds therefore " miracles " must be treated in this scientific age as intrinsically incredible. They never have happened, and they never can happen. Many excellent people have indeed professed to see them, and we need not doubt their veracity. But illusion is easy, credulity is limitless, and there is nothing in their testimony which can absolve us from the plain duty of purifying or rejecting every narrative in which a taint of the "miraculous" can be detected.

VIII

In spite of its apparent precision all this is very loose talk, raising more questions than it answers.

What, for example, is meant by the uniformity of nature? About the course of nature we know little ; yet surely we know enough to make us hesitate to call it uniform. Phase follows phase in a perpetual flow ; but every phase is unique. Nature, as a whole, neither repeats itself, nor (according to science) can possibly repeat itself. Why, then, when we are considering it as a whole, should we describe it as uniform?

Perhaps it will be said that amidst all this infinite variety some fixed rules are always obeyed. Matter (for example) always gravitates to matter. Energy is never either created or destroyed. May we not—nay *must* we not—extend yet further this conception of unbroken regularity, and accept the view that nature, if not uniform as a whole, is nevertheless compounded of uniformities, of causal sequences, endlessly repeated, which collectively illustrate and embody the universal reign of unalterable law? Were any of these causal sequences to fail, we should no doubt be faced with a " miracle " ; but such an event (it is urged) would violate all experience, and it need not be seriously considered.

IX

Now this has always seemed to me a most unsatisfactory theory. It throws upon experience a load of responsibility which experience is quite unable to bear. No doubt, as I have already pointed out, the whole conduct of life depends upon our assuming, instinctively or otherwise, that the kind of thing which has happened once, will, under more or less similar circumstances, be likely to happen again. But this assumption, whether instinctive or reflective, whether wisely acted on or unwisely, supplies a very frail foundation for the speculative structure sometimes based upon it. Can it be denied, for example, that nature, uncritically observed, seems honeycombed with irregularities, that the wildest excesses of credulity may arise not from ignoring experience, but from refusing to correct it, that the most ruthless editing is required to force the uncensored messages we receive from the external world into the ideal mould which satisfies our individual convictions ?

But what is this ideal mould ? We sometimes talk as if by the help of Scientific Method or Inductive Logic we could map out all reality into a scheme of well-defined causes indissolubly connected with well-defined effects, together forming sequences whose recurrence in different combinations constitutes the changing pattern of the universe.

But can such hopes be realised ? In the world of concrete fact nothing occurs through the action of a single cause, nor yet through the simple co-operation of many causes, each adding its own unqualified contribution to the total effect, as we picture horse helping horse to draw a loaded dray. Our world is a much more complicated affair. Sequences are never exactly repeated. Causes can never be completely isolated. Their operation is never unqualified. Fence round your laboratory experiments with what precautions you will, no two of them will ever be performed under exactly the same conditions. For the purpose in hand the differences may be negligible. With skilled observers they commonly are. But the differences exist, and they must certainly modify, however imperceptibly, the observed result.

X

It seems evident from considerations like these that no argument directly based on mere experience can be urged either for or against the possibility of " miracles." Common-sense looks doubtfully upon anything out of the common ; and science follows suit. But this is very different from the speculative assertion that, since " miracles " are a violation of natural law, their occurrence must be regarded as impossible. The intrusion of an unexpected and perhaps anomalous element into the company of more familiar factors in world development may excite suspicion, but it does not of necessity violate anything more important than our preconceived expectations.

I think it will be found that those who most vehemently reject this way of regarding the world are unconsciously moved not by their knowledge of scientific laws, but by preference for a particular scientific ideal. They are persuaded that if only we had the right kind of knowledge and adequate powers of calculation, we should be able to explain the whole contents of possible experience by applying mathematical methods to certain simple data. They refuse to believe that this calculable " Whole " can suffer interference at the hands of any incalculable power. They find no room in the close-knit tissue of the world process, as they conceive it, for any arbitrary element to find lodgment. They have a clear notion of what science ought to be, and that notion is incompatible with the " miraculous."

XI

Now it is certainly true that, so far as Nature is concerned, the idea of a calculable " whole " is one which makes a most powerful appeal to most of us. And it is also true that remote as we are from its attainment, the science of our own day has made, and is making, marvellous advances towards it. We now know that the units of which the material universe is built are of only two kinds, and strictly conform to one or other of two patterns. We know approximately their size and their mass. We know a good deal about their motions and their powers of radiation. We know that they repel members of their own class and attract members of the other ; we know that they constitute the essence of all that interests the physicist, the astronomer, the chemist ; of all the objects which are valued for their beauty ; of all the physiological devices through which organic life becomes possible, and mind becomes cognisant of matter. In spite of our almost limitless ignorance of details, in spite of the unbridged chasms which still divide one branch of scientific knowledge from another, these discoveries do certainly dangle before our eyes with a new brilliancy, the idea of a cosmic flow of calculable events depending on measurable conditions, and (in theory at least) amenable to mathematical treatment.

XII

The conception of a material universe, overwhelming in its complexity and its splendour, yet potentially susceptible of complete explanation by the actions and reactions of two very minute

and simple kinds of electrical sub-atom, is, without doubt, extraordinarily fascinating. From the early days of scientific philosophy or (if you prefer it) of philosophical science, thinkers have
been hungering after some form of all-embracing atomism. They
have now apparently reached it (so far as matter is concerned) by
the way of observation and experiment—truly a marvellous
performance. Yet the very lucidity of the new conceptions
helps to bring home to us their essential insufficiency as a theory
of the universe. They may be capable of explaining the constitution and behaviour of inanimate objects. They may go
some (as yet unmeasured) distance towards explaining organic
life. But they certainly cannot explain mind. No man really
supposes that he personally is nothing more than a changing group
of electrical charges, so distributed that their relative motions
enable or compel them in their collective capacity to will, to hope,
to love, to think, perhaps to discuss themselves as a physical multiplicity, certainly to treat themselves as a mental unity. No creed
of this kind can ever be extracted by valid reasoning from the sort
of data which the physics either of the present or the future can
possibly supply.

The truth is that the immense advances which in modern
times have been made by mechanical or quasi-mechanical explanations of the material world have somewhat upset the mental
balance of many thoughtful persons who approach the problems
of reality exclusively from the physical side. It is not that they
formulate any excessive claims to knowledge. On the contrary,
they often describe themselves as agnostics. Nevertheless they
are apt unconsciously to assume that they already enjoy a good
bird's-eye view of what reality *is*, combined with an unshaken
assurance about what it is *not*. They tacitly suppose that every
discovery, if genuine, will find its place within the framework
of a perfected physics, and, if it does not, may be summarily
dismissed as mere superstition.

XIII

After all, however, superstition may be negative as well as
positive, and the excesses of unbelief may be as extravagant as
those of belief. Doubtless the universe, as conceived by men
more primitive than ourselves, was the obscure abode of strange

deities. But what are we to say about a universe reduced without remainder to collections of electric charges radiating energy through a hypothetical ether ? Thus to set limits to reality must always be the most hazardous of speculative adventures. To do so by eliminating the spiritual is not only hazardous but absurd. For if we are directly aware of anything, it is of ourselves as personal agents ; if anything can be proved by direct experiment it is that we can, in however small a measure, vary the " natural " distribution of matter and energy. We can certainly act on our environment, and as certainly our action can never be adequately explained in terms of entities which neither think, nor feel, nor purpose, nor know. It constitutes a spiritual invasion of the physical world :—it is a miracle.

XIV

To me therefore it seems that in the present state of our knowledge or (if you prefer it) of our ignorance, we have no choice but to acquiesce provisionally in an unresolved dualism. Our experience has a double outlook. The first we may call material. It brings us face to face with such subjects as electricity, mass, motion, force, energy, and with such manifestations of energy as ethereal radiation The second is spiritual. The first deals with objects which are measurable, calculable, capable (up to a point) of precise definition. The second deals with the immeasurable, the incalculable, the indefinable and (let me add) the all-important. The first touches the fundamentals of science ; the second is intimately connected with religion. Yet different as they seem, both are real. They belong to the same universe ; they influence each other ; somewhere and somehow they must be in contact along a common frontier.

But where is that frontier to be drawn ? And how are we to describe the relation between these co-terminous provinces of reality ? This is perhaps a question for metaphysics rather than for religion or science ; and some day, perhaps, metaphysics may provide us with a satisfying answer. In the meanwhile, I may conclude this Introduction at a less ambitious level—concerning myself rather with the relations between religion and science in the practice of life, than with any high problems of speculative philosophy.

XV

I suggest then that in scientific research it is a wise procedure to press "mechanical" theories of the material world to their utmost limits. Were I, for example, a biologist I should endeavour to explain all the phenomena under investigation in terms of matter and motion. I should always be searching for what could be measured and calculated, however confident I might be that in some directions at least the hopeless limitations of such a view would very rapidly become apparent.

In the practice of life, on the other hand, and in the speculation of philosophy, we are free to move within wider horizons. In forming our estimate of the sort of beliefs which may properly be regarded as rationally acceptable, we ought not to be limited by mechanistic pre-suppositions, however useful these may be in our investigations of nature. We are spiritual beings, and must take account of spiritual values. The story of man is something more than a mere continuation of the story of matter. It is different in kind. If we cannot calculate the flow of physical events, that is because our knowledge of natural processes is small, and our power of calculation feeble. If we cannot calculate the course of human history, that is because (among other reasons) it is inherently incalculable. No two specimens of humanity exactly resemble each other, or live in circumstances that are exactly comparable. The so-called "repetitions" of history are never more than vague resemblances. The science of history therefore, if there be one, is something quite different from (say) the science of physics. And this is true even when history is wholly divorced from religion. But when it is considered in a different setting, when man is regarded as a spiritual agent in a world under spiritual guidance, events of spiritual significance cannot be wholly judged by canons of criticism which seem sufficient for simpler cases. Unexampled invasions of the physical sphere by the spiritual are not indeed to be lightly believed. But they are certainly not to be rejected merely because historians cannot bring themselves to accept the "miraculous."

XVI

This point of view, for those who are prepared to take it, may help to eliminate some of the chief causes of conflict between science and religion. In times not far distant there were men devoted to religion who blundered ignorantly into science, and men devoted to science who meddled unadvisedly with religion. Theologians found their geology in Genesis ; materialists supposed that reality could be identified with the mechanism of matter. Neither procedure is to be commended ; nor is it by these paths that the unsolved riddle of the universe can best be approached. A science which declares itself incompatible with religion, a religion which deems itself a substitute for science, may indulge in controversies as interminable as they are barren. But there is a better way ; and the writers of the following essays, each by his own methods, each from his own point of view, have ably endeavoured to pursue it.

(Note :—Some of the more controversial portions of this Introduction have been dealt with at greater length in my Gifford Lectures, 1914 and 1923.)

MAGIC SCIENCE AND RELIGION
BY BRONISLAW MALINOWSKI

CONTENTS

I

PRIMITIVE MAN AND HIS RELIGION

THERE are no peoples however primitive without religion and magic. Nor are there, it must be added at once, any savage races lacking either in the scientific attitude or in science, though this lack has been frequently attributed to them. In every primitive community, studied by trustworthy and competent observers, there have been found two clearly distinguishable domains, the Sacred and the Profane ; in other words, the domain of Magic and Religion and that of Science.

On the one hand there are the traditional acts and observances, regarded by the natives as sacred, carried out with reverence and awe, hedged round with prohibitions and special rules of behaviour. Such acts and observances are always associated with beliefs in supernatural forces, especially those of magic, or with ideas about beings, spirits, ghosts, dead ancestors, or gods. On the other hand, a moment's reflection is sufficient to show that no art or craft however primitive could have been invented or maintained, no organised form of hunting, fishing, tilling, or search for food could be carried out without the careful observation of natural process and a firm belief in its regularity, without the power of reasoning and without confidence in the power of reason ; that is, without the rudiments of science.

The credit of having laid the foundations of an anthropological study of religion belongs to Edward B. Tylor. In his well-known theory he maintains that the essence of primitive religion is animism, the belief in spiritual beings, and he shows how this belief has originated in a mistaken but consistent interpretation of dreams, visions, hallucinations, cataleptic states, and similar phenomena. Reflecting on these, the savage philosopher or theologian was led to distinguish the human soul from the body. Now the soul obviously continues to lead an existence after death, for it appears in dreams, haunts the survivors in memories and in visions and apparently influences human destinies.

Thus originated the belief in ghosts and the spirits of the dead, in immortality and in a nether world. But man in general, and primitive man in particular, has a tendency to imagine the outer world in his own image. And since animals, plants, and objects move, act, behave, help man or hinder him, they also must be endowed with souls or spirits. Thus animism, the philosophy and the religion of primitive man, had been built up from observations and by inferences, mistaken but comprehensible in a crude and untutored mind.

Tylor's view of primitive religion, important as it was, was based on too narrow a range of facts, and it made early man too contemplative and rational. Recent fieldwork, done by specialists, shows us the savage interested rather in his fishing and gardens, in tribal events and festivities than brooding over dreams and visions, or explaining " doubles " and cataleptic fits, and it reveals also a great many aspects of early religion which cannot be possibly placed in Tylor's scheme of animism.

The extended and deepened outlook of modern anthropology finds its most adequate expression in the learned and inspiring writings of Sir James Frazer. In these he has set forth the three main problems of primitive religion with which present-day anthropology is busy : magic and its relation to religion and science ; totemism and the sociological aspect of early faith ; the cults of fertility and vegetation. It will be best to discuss these subjects in turn.

Frazer's " Golden Bough," the great codex of primitive magic, shows clearly that animism is not the only, nor even the dominating belief in primitive culture. Early man seeks above all to control the course of nature for practical ends, and he does it directly, by rite and spell, compelling wind and weather, animals and crops to obey his will. Only much later, finding the limitations of his magical might, does he in fear or hope, in supplication or defiance, appeal to higher beings ; that is, to demons, ancestor-spirits or gods. It is in this distinction between direct control on the one hand and propitiation of superior powers on the other that Sir James Frazer sees the difference between religion and magic. Magic, based on man's confidence that he can dominate nature directly, if only he knows the laws which govern it magically, is in this akin to science. Religion, the confession of human impotence in certain matters, lifts man above the magical level, and later on maintains its independence side by side with science, to which magic has to succumb.

This theory of magic and religion has been the starting-point of most modern studies of the twin subjects. Professor Preuss in Germany, Dr. Marett in England, and MM. Hubert et Mauss in France have independently set forth certain views, partly in criticism of Frazer, partly following up the lines of his inquiry. These writers point out that similar as they appear, science and magic differ yet radically. Science is born of experience, magic made by tradition. Science is guided by reason and corrected by observation, magic, impervious to both, lives in an atmosphere of mysticism. Science is open to all, a common good of the whole community, magic is occult, taught through mysterious initiations, handed on in a hereditary or at least in a very exclusive filiation. While science is based on the conception of natural forces, magic springs from the idea of a certain mystic, impersonal power, which is believed in by most primitive peoples. This power, called *mana* by some Melanesians, *arungquiltha* by certain Australian tribes, *wakan, orenda, manitu* by various American Indians, and nameless elsewhere, is stated to be a well-nigh universal idea found wherever magic flourishes. According to the writers just mentioned we can find among the most primitive peoples and throughout the lower savagery a belief in a supernatural, impersonal force, moving all those agencies which are relevant to the savage and causing all the really important events in the domain of the sacred. Thus *mana*, not animism, is the essence of "pre-animistic religion," and it is also the essence of magic, which is thus radically different from science.

There remains the question, however, what is *mana*, this impersonal force of magic supposed to dominate all forms of early belief? Is it a fundamental idea, an innate category of the primitive mind, or can it be explained by still simpler and more fundamental elements of human psychology or of the reality in which primitive man lives ? The most original and important contribution to these problems is given by the late Professor Durkheim, and it touches the other subject, opened up by Sir James Frazer : that of totemism and of the sociological aspect of religion.

Totemism, to quote Frazer's classical definition, " is an intimate relation which is supposed to exist between a group of kindred people on the one side and a species of natural or artificial objects on the other side, which objects are called the totems of the human group." Totemism thus has two sides : it is a mode of social grouping and a religious system of beliefs and practices. As religion, it expresses primitive man's interest in his surroundings, the desire to claim an affinity and to control the most important objects : above all, animal or vegetable species, more rarely useful inanimate objects, very seldom man-made things. As a rule species of animals and plants used for staple food or at any rate edible or useful or ornamental animals are held in a special form of " totemic reverence " and are tabooed to the members of the clan which is associated with the species and which sometimes performs rites and ceremonies for its multiplication. The social aspect of totemism consists in the subdivision of the tribe into minor units, called in anthropology *clans, gentes, sibs,* or *phratries.*

In totemism we see therefore not the result of early man's speculations about mysterious phenomena, but a blend of a utilitarian anxiety about the most necessary objects of his surroundings, with some preoccupation in those which strike his imagination and attract his attention, such as beautiful birds, reptiles and dangerous animals. With our knowledge of what could be called the totemic attitude of mind, primitive religion is seen to be nearer to reality and to the immediate practical life interests of the savage, than it appeared in its " animistic " aspect emphasised by Tylor and the earlier anthropologists.

By its apparently strange association with a problematic form of social division, I mean the clan system, totemism has taught anthropology yet another lesson : it has revealed the importance of the sociological aspect in all the early forms of cult. The savage depends upon the group with whom he is in direct contact both for practical co-operation and mental solidarity to a far larger extent than does civilised man. Since—as can be seen in totemism, magic, and many other practices—early cult and ritual are closely associated with practical concerns as well as with mental needs, there must exist an intimate connection between social organisation and religious belief. This was understood already by that pioneer of religious anthropology, Robertson Smith, whose principle that primitive religion " was essentially an affair of the community rather than of individuals " has become a *Leitmotiv* of modern research. According to Professor Durkheim, who has put these views most forcibly, " the religious " is identical

with " the social." For " in a general way . . . a society has
all that is necessary to arouse the sensation of the Divine in minds,
merely by the power that it has over them ; for to its members
it is what a God is to its worshippers." [1] Professor Durkheim
arrives at this conclusion by the study of totemism, which he
believes to be the most primitive form of religion. In this the
" totemic principle " which is identical with *mana* and with " the
God of the clan . . . can be nothing else than the clan itself." [2]

These strange and somewhat obscure conclusions will be
criticised later, and it will be shown in what consists the grain
of truth they undoubtedly contain and how fruitful it can be. It
has borne fruit, in fact, in influencing some of the most important
writings of mixed classsical scholarship and anthropology, to
mention only the works of Miss Jane Harrison and Mr. Cornford.

The third great subject introduced into the Science of Religion
by Sir James Frazer is that of the cults of vegetation and fertility.
In " The Golden Bough," starting from the awful and mysterious
ritual of the wood divinities at Nemi, we are led through an
amazing variety of magical and religious cults, devised by man to
stimulate and control the fertilising work of skies and earth and
of sun and rain, and we are left with the impression that early
religion is teeming with the forces of savage life, with its young
beauty and crudity, with its exuberance and strength so violent
that it leads now and again to suicidal acts of self-immolation.
The study of " The Golden Bough " shows us that for primitive
man death has meaning mainly as a step to resurrection, decay as
a stage of re-birth, the plenty of autumn and the decline of winter
as preludes to the revival of spring. Inspired by these passages
of " The Golden Bough " a number of writers have developed,
often with greater precision and with a fuller analysis than by
Frazer himself, what could be called the *vitalistic* view of religion.
Thus Mr. Crawley in his " Tree of Life," M. van Gennep in
his " Rites de Passage," and Miss Jane Harrison in several works,
have given evidence that faith and cult spring from the crises of
human existence, " the great events of life, birth, adolescence,
marriage, death . . . it is about these events that religion
largely focusses." [3] The tension of instinctive need, strong
emotional experiences, lead in some way or other to cult and belief.

[1] *The Elementary Forms of the Religious Life*, p. 206.
[2] *Ibid*.   [3] J. Harrison, *Themis*, p. 42.

" Art and Religion alike spring from unsatisfied desire." [1]   How much truth there is in this somewhat vague statement and how much exaggeration we shall be able to assess later on.

There are two important contributions to the theory of primitive religion which I mention here only, for they have some-how remained outside the main current of anthropological interest. They treat of the primitive idea of one God and of the place of morals in primitive religion respectively.   It is remarkable that they have been and still are neglected, for are not these two questions first and foremost in the mind of anyone who studies religion, however crude and rudimentary it may be ?   Perhaps the explanation is in the preconceived idea that " origins " must be very crude and simple and different from the " developed forms," or else in the notion that the " savage " or " primitive " is really savage and primitive !

The late Andrew Lang indicated the existence among some Australian natives of the belief in a tribal All-Father, and the Rev. Pater Wilhelm Schmidt has adduced much evidence proving that this belief is universal among all the peoples of the simplest cultures and that it cannot be discarded as an irrelevant fragment of mythology, still less as an echo of missionary teaching.   It looks, according to Pater Schmidt, very much like an indication of a simple and pure form of early monotheism.

The problem of morals as an early religious function was also left on one side, until it received an exhaustive treatment, not only in the writings of Pater Schmidt but also and notably in two works of outstanding importance : the " Origin and Development of Moral Ideas " of Professor E. Westermarck, and " Morals in Evolution " of Professor L. T. Hobhouse.

I is not easy to summarise concisely the trend of anthropolo-gical studies in our subject.   On the whole it has been towards an increasingly elastic and comprehensive view of religion.   Tylor had still to refute the fallacy that there are primitive peoples without religion.   To-day we are somewhat perplexed by the discovery that to a savage all is religion, that he perpetually lives in a world of mysticism and ritualism.   If religion is co-extensive with " life " and with " death " into the bargain, if it arises from all " collective " acts and from all " crises in the individual's existence," if it comprises all savage " theory " and covers all his

[1] J. Harrison, *Themis*, p. 44.

"practical concerns"—we are led to ask, not without dismay : What remains outside it, what is the world of the "profane" in primitive life ? Here is a first problem into which modern anthropology, by the number of contradictory views, has thrown some confusion, as can be seen even from the above short sketch. We shall be able to contribute towards its solution in the next section.

Primitive religion, as fashioned by modern anthropology, has been made to harbour all sorts of heterogeneous beings. At first reserved in animism for the solemn figures of ancestral spirits, ghosts and souls, besides a few fetishes, it had gradually to admit the thin, fluid, ubiquitous *mana* ; then, like Noah's Ark, it was with the introduction of totemism loaded with beasts, not in pairs but in shoals and species, joined by plants, objects, and even manufactured articles ; then came human activities and concerns and the gigantic ghost of the Collective Soul, Society Divinised. Can there be any order or system put into this medley of apparently unrelated objects and principles ? This question will occupy us in the third section.

One achievement of modern anthropology we shall not question : the recognition that magic and religion are not merely a doctrine or a philosophy, not merely an intellectual body of opinion, but a special mode of behaviour, a pragmatic attitude built up of reason, feeling, and will alike. It is a mode of action as well as a system of belief, and a sociological phenomenon as well as a personal experience. But with all this, the exact relation between the social and the individual contributions to religion is not clear, as we have seen from the exaggerations committed on either side. Nor is it clear what are the respective shares of emotion and reason. All these questions will have to be dealt with by future anthropology, and it will be possible only to suggest solutions and indicate lines of argument in this short essay.

II

RATIONAL MASTERY BY MAN OF HIS SURROUNDINGS

The problem of primitive knowledge has been singularly neglected by anthropology. Studies on savage psychology were exclusively confined to early religion, magic and mythology. Only recently the work of several English, German, and French writers, notably the daring and brilliant speculations of Professor Lévy-

Bruhl, gave an impetus to the student's interest in what the savage does in his more sober moods. The results were startling indeed : Professor Lévy-Bruhl tells us, to put it in a nutshell, that primitive man has no sober moods at all, that he is hopelessly and completely immersed in a mystical frame of mind. Incapable of dispassionate and consistent observation, devoid of the power of abstraction, hampered by "a decided aversion towards reasoning," he is unable to draw any benefit from experience, to construct or comprehend even the most elementary laws of nature. "For minds thus orientated there is no fact purely physical." Nor can there exist for them any clear idea of substance and attribute, cause and effect, identity and contradiction. Their outlook is that of confused superstition, "pre-logical," made of mystic "participations" and "exclusions." I have here summarised a body of opinion, of which the brilliant French sociologist is the most decided and competent spokesman, but which numbers, besides, many anthropologists and philosophers of renown.

But there are also dissenting voices. When a scholar and anthropologist of the measure of Professor J. L. Myres entitles an article in *Notes and Queries* " Natural Science," and when we read there that the savage's " knowledge based on observation is distinct and accurate," we must surely pause before accepting primitive man's irrationality as a dogma. Another highly competent writer, Dr. A. A. Goldenweiser, speaking about primitive " discoveries, inventions and improvements "—which could hardly be attributed to any pre-empirical or pre-logical mind—affirms that "it would be unwise to ascribe to the primitive mechanic merely a passive part in the origination of inventions. Many a happy thought must have crossed his mind, nor was he wholly unfamiliar with the thrill that comes from an idea effective in action." Here we see the savage endowed with an attitude of mind wholly akin to that of a modern man of science !

To bridge over the wide gap between the two extreme opinions current on the subject of primitive man's reason, it will be best to resolve the problem into two questions.

First, has the savage any rational outlook, any rational mastery of his surroundings, or is he, as M. Lévy-Bruhl and his school maintain, entirely " mystical " ? The answer will be that every primitive community is in possession of a considerable store of knowledge, based on experience and fashioned by reason.

The second question then opens : Can this primitive knowledge be regarded as a rudimentary form of science or is it, on the contrary, radically different, a crude empiry, a body of practical and technical abilities, rules of thumb and rules of art having no theoretical value ? This second question, epistemological rather than belonging to the study of man, will be barely touched upon at the end of this section and a tentative answer only will be given.

In dealing with the first question, we shall have to examine the "profane" side of life, the arts, crafts and economic pursuits, and we shall attempt to disentangle in it a type of behaviour, clearly marked off from magic and religion, based on empirical knowledge and on the confidence in logic. We shall try to find whether the lines of such behaviour are defined by traditional rules, known, perhaps even discussed sometimes, and tested. We shall have to inquire whether the sociological setting of the rational and empirical behaviour differs from that of ritual and cult. Above all we shall ask, do the natives distinguish the two domains and keep them apart, or is the field of knowledge constantly swamped by superstition, ritualism, magic or religion ?

Since in the matter under discussion there is an appalling lack of relevant and reliable observations, I shall have largely to draw upon my own material, mostly unpublished, collected during a few years' field-work among the Melanesian and Papuo-Melanesian tribes of Eastern New Guinea and the surrounding archipelagoes. As the Melanesians are reputed, however, to be specially magic-ridden, they will furnish an acid test of the existence of empirical and rational knowledge among savages living in the age of polished stone.

These natives, and I am speaking mainly of the Melanesians who inhabit the coral atolls to the N.E of the main island, the Trobriand Archipelago and the adjoining groups, are expert fishermen, industrious manufacturers and traders, but they rely mainly on gardening for their subsistence. With the most rudimentary implements, a pointed digging-stick and a small axe, they are able to raise crops sufficient to maintain a dense population and even yielding a surplus, which in olden days was allowed to rot unconsumed, and which at present is exported to feed plantation hands. The success in their agriculture depends—besides the excellent natural conditions with which they are favoured—upon their extensive knowledge of the classes of the soil, of the various cultivated plants, of the mutual adaptation of these two factors, and, last not least, upon their knowledge of the importance of accurate and hard work. They have to select the soil and the seedlings, they have appropriately to fix the times for clearing and burning the scrub, for planting and weeding, for training the vines of the yam-plants. In all this they are guided by a clear knowledge of weather and seasons, plants and pests, soil and tubers, and by a conviction that this knowledge is true and reliable, that it can be counted upon and must be scrupulously obeyed.

Yet mixed with all their activities there is to be found magic, a series of rites performed every year over the gardens in rigorous sequence and order. Since the leadership in garden work is in the hands of the magician, and since ritual and practical work are intimately associated, a superficial observer might be led to assume that the mystic and the rational behaviour are mixed up, that their effects are not distinguished by the natives and not distinguishable in scientific analysis. Is this so really?

Magic is undoubtedly regarded by the natives as absolutely indispensable to the welfare of the gardens. What would happen without it no one can exactly tell, for no native garden has ever been made without its ritual, in spite of some thirty years of European rule and missionary influence and well over a century's contact with white traders. But certainly various kinds of disaster, blight, unseasonable droughts and rains, bush-pigs and locusts, would destroy the unhallowed garden made without magic.

Does this mean, however, that the natives attribute all the good results to magic? Certainly not. If you were to suggest to a native that he should make his garden mainly by magic and scamp his work, he would simply smile on your simplicity. He knows as well as you do that there are natural conditions and causes, and by his observations he knows also that he is able to control these natural forces by mental and physical effort. His knowledge is limited, no doubt, but as far as it goes it is sound and proof against mysticism. If the fences are broken down, if the seed is destroyed or has been dried or washed away, he will have recourse not to magic, but to work, guided by knowledge and reason. His experience has taught him also, on the other hand, that in spite of all his forethought and beyond all his efforts there are agencies and forces which one year bestow unwonted and unearned benefits of fertility, making everything run smooth and well, rain and sun appear at the right moment, noxious insects remain in abeyance, the harvest yield a superabundant crop ; and another year again the same agencies bring ill-luck and bad chance, pursue him from beginning till end and thwart all his most strenuous efforts and his best-founded knowledge. To control these influences and these only he employs magic.

Thus there is a clear-cut division : there is first the well-known set of conditions, the natural course of growth, as well as the ordinary pests and dangers to be warded off by fencing and weeding. On the other hand there is the domain of the un-accountable and adverse influences, as well as the great unearned increment of fortunate coincidence. The first conditions are coped with by knowledge and work, the second by magic.

This line of division can also be traced in the social setting of work and ritual respectively. Though the garden magician is, as a rule, also the leader in practical activities, these two functions are kept strictly apart. Every magical ceremony has its distinctive name, its appropriate time and its place in the scheme of work, and it stands out of the ordinary course of activities completely. Some of them are ceremonial and have to be attended by the whole community, all are public in that it is known when they are going to happen and anyone can attend them. They are performed on selected plots within the gardens and on a special corner of this plot. Work is always tabooed on such occasions, sometimes only while the ceremony lasts, sometimes for a day or two. In his lay character the leader and magician directs the work, fixes the dates for starting, harangues and exhorts slack or careless gardeners. But the two rôles never overlap or interfere : they are always clear, and any native will inform you without hesitation whether the man acts as magician or as leader in garden work.

What has been said about gardens can be paralleled from any one of the many other activities in which work and magic run side by side without ever mixing. Thus in canoe-building empirical knowledge of material, of technology, and of certain principles of stability and hydrodynamics, function in company and close association with magic, each yet uncontaminated by the other.

For example, they understand perfectly well that the wider the span of the outrigger the greater the stability yet the smaller the resistance against strain. They can clearly explain why they have to give this span a certain traditional width, measured in fractions of the length of the dug-out. They can also explain, in rudimentary but clearly mechanical terms, how they have to behave in a sudden gale, why the outrigger must be always on the weather side, why the one type of canoe can and the other cannot beat. They have, in fact, a whole system of principles of sailing, embodied in a complex and rich terminology, traditionally handed on and obeyed as rationally and consistently as is modern science by modern sailors. How could they sail otherwise under eminently dangerous conditions in their frail primitive craft ?

But even with all their systematic knowledge, methodically applied, they are still at the mercy of powerful and incalculable tides, sudden gales during the monsoon season and unknown reefs. And here comes in their magic, performed over the canoe during its construction, carried out at the beginning and in the course of expeditions and resorted to in moments of real danger. If the modern seaman, entrenched in science and reason, provided with all sorts of safety appliances, sailing on steel-built steamers, if even he has a singular tendency to superstition—which does not rob him of his knowledge or reason, nor make him altogether pre-logical—can we wonder that his savage colleague, under much more precarious conditions, holds fast to the safety and comfort of magic ?

An interesting and crucial test is provided by fishing in the Trobriand Islands and its magic. While in the villages on the inner Lagoon fishing is done in an easy and absolutely reliable manner by the method of poisoning, yielding abundant results without danger and uncertainty, there are on the shores of the open sea dangerous modes of fishing and also certain types in which the yield greatly varies according to whether shoals of fish appear beforehand or not. It is most significant that in the Lagoon fishing, where man can rely completely upon his knowledge and skill, magic does not exist, while in the open-sea fishing, full of danger and uncertainty, there is extensive magical ritual to secure safety and good results.

Again, in warfare the natives know that strength, courage, and agility play a decisive part. Yet here also they practise magic to master the elements of chance and luck.

Nowhere is the duality of natural and supernatural causes divided by a line so thin and intricate, yet, if carefully followed up, so well marked, decisive, and instructive, as in the two most

fateful forces of human destiny : health and death. Health to
the Melanesian is a natural state of affairs and, unless tampered with,
the human body will remain in perfect order. But the natives
know perfectly well that there are natural means which can affect
health and even destroy the body. Poisons, wounds, burns, falls,
are known to cause disablement or death in a natural way. And
this is not a matter of private opinion of this or that individual,
but it is laid down in traditional lore and even in belief, for there
are considered to be different ways to the nether world for those
who died by sorcery and those who met " natural " death. Again,
it is recognised that cold, heat, overstrain, too much sun, overeating, can all cause minor ailments, which are treated by natural
remedies such as massage, steaming, warming at a fire and certain
potions. Old age is known to lead to bodily decay and the
explanation is given by the natives that very old people grow weak,
their oesophagus closes up, and therefore they must die.

But besides these natural causes there is the enormous domain
of sorcery and by far the most cases of illness and death are ascribed
to this. The line of distinction between sorcery and the other
causes is clear in theory and in most cases of practice, but it must
be realised that it is subject to what could be called the personal
perspective. That is, the more closely a case has to do with the
person who considers it, the less will it be " natural," the more
" magical." Thus a very old man, whose pending death will be
considered natural by the other members of the community, will
be afraid only of sorcery and never think of his natural fate.
A fairly sick person will diagnose sorcery in his own case, while
all the others might speak of too much betel nut or overeating or
some other indulgence.

But who of us really believes that his own bodily infirmities
and the approaching death is a purely natural occurrence, just an
insignificant event in the infinite chain of causes ? To the most
rational of civilised men health, disease, the threat of death, float
in a hazy emotional mist, which seems to become denser and more
impenetrable as the fateful forms approach. It is indeed astonishing that "savages " can achieve such a sober, dispassionate outlook in
these matters as they actually do.

Thus in his relation to nature and destiny, whether he tries
to exploit the first or to dodge the second, primitive man recognises
both the natural and the supernatural forces and agencies, and he

tries to use them both for his benefit. Whenever he has been taught by experience that effort guided by knowledge is of some avail, he never spares the one or ignores the other. He knows that a plant cannot grow by magic alone, or a canoe sail or float without being properly constructed and managed, or a fight be won without skill and daring. He never relies on magic alone, while, on the contrary, he sometimes dispenses with it completely, as in fire-making and in a number of crafts and pursuits. But he clings to it, whenever he has to recognise the impotence of his knowledge and of his rational technique.

I have given my reasons why in this argument I had to rely principally on the material collected in the classical land of magic, Melanesia. But the facts discussed are so fundamental, the conclusions drawn of such a general nature, that it will be easy to check them on any modern detailed ethnographic record. Comparing agricultural work and magic, the building of canoes, the art of healing by magic and by natural remedies, the ideas about the causes of death in other regions, the universal validity of what has been established here could easily be proved. Only, since no observations have methodically been made with reference to the problem of primitive knowledge, the data from other writers could be gleaned only piecemeal and their testimony though clear would be indirect.

I have chosen to face the question of primitive man's rational knowledge directly : watching him at his principal occupations, seeing him pass from work to magic and back again, entering into his mind, listening to his opinions. The whole problem might have been approached through the avenue of language, but this would have led us too far into questions of logic, semasiology, and theory of primitive languages. Words which serve to express general ideas such as *existence, substance,* and *attribute, cause* and *effect,* the *fundamental* and the *secondary* ; words and expressions used in complicated pursuits like sailing, construction, measuring and checking ; numerals and quantitative descriptions, correct and detailed classifications of natural phenomena, plants and animals— all this would lead us exactly to the same conclusion : that primitive man can observe and think, and that he possesses, embodied in his language, systems of methodical though rudimentary knowledge.

Similar conclusions could be drawn from an examination of

those mental schemes and physical contrivances which could be described as diagrams or formulas. Methods of indicating the main points of the compass, arrangements of stars into constellations, co-ordination of these with the seasons, naming of moons in the year, of quarters in the moon—all these accomplishments are known to the simplest savages. Also they are all able to draw diagrammatic maps in the sand or dust, indicate arrangements by placing small stones, shells, or sticks on the ground, plan expeditions or raids on such rudimentary charts. By co-ordinating space and time they are able to arrange big tribal gatherings and to combine vast tribal movements over extensive areas.[1] The use of leaves, notched sticks, and similar aids to memory is well known and seems to be almost universal. All such " diagrams " are means of reducing a complex and unwieldy bit of reality to a simple and handy form. They give man a relatively easy mental control over it. As such are they not—in a very rudimentary form no doubt—fundamentally akin to developed scientific formulas and " models," which are also simple and handy paraphrases of a complex or abstract reality, giving the civilised physicist mental control over it ?

This brings us to the second question : Can we regard primitive knowledge, which, as we found, is both empirical and rational, as a rudimentary stage of science, or is it not at all related to it ? If by science be understood a body of rules and conceptions, based on experience and derived from it by logical inference, embodied in material achievements and in a fixed form of tradition and carried on by some sort of social organisation—then there is no doubt that even the lowest savage communities have the beginnings of science, however rudimentary.

Most epistemologists would not, however, be satisfied with such a " minimum definition " of science, for it might apply to the rules of an art or craft as well. They would maintain that the rules of science must be laid down explicitly, open to control by experiment and critique by reason. They must not only be rules of practical behaviour, but theoretical laws of knowledge. Even accepting this stricture, however, there is hardly any doubt that many of the principles of savage knowledge are scientific in this sense. The native shipwright knows not only practically of buoyancy, leverage, equilibrium, he has to obey these laws not

---

[1] *Cf.* the writer's *Argonauts of the Western Pacific*, chap. xvi.

only on water, but while making the canoe he must have the principles in his mind. He instructs his helpers in them. He gives them the traditional rules, and in a crude and simple manner, using his hands, pieces of wood, and a limited technical vocabulary, he explains some general laws of hydrodynamics and equilibrium. Science is not detached from the craft, that is certainly true, it is only a means to an end, it is crude, rudimentary, and inchoate, but with all that it is the matrix from which the higher developments must have sprung.

If we applied another criterion yet, that of the really scientific attitude, the disinterested search for knowledge and for the understanding of causes and reasons, the answer would certainly not be in a direct negative. There is, of course, no widespread thirst for knowledge in a savage community, new things such as European topics bore them frankly and their whole interest is largely encompassed by the traditional world of their culture. But within this there is both the antiquarian mind passionately interested in myths, stories, details of customs, pedigrees, and ancient happenings, and there is also to be found the naturalist, patient and painstaking in his observations, capable of generalisation and of connecting long chains of events in the life of animals, and in the marine world or in the jungle. It is enough to realise how much European naturalists have often learned from their savage colleagues to appreciate this interest found in the native for nature. There is finally among the primitives, as every field-worker well knows, the sociologist, the ideal informant capable with marvellous accuracy and insight to give the *raison d'être*, the function, and the organisation of many a simpler institution in his tribe.

Science, of course, does not exist in any uncivilised community as a driving power, criticising, renewing, constructing. Science is never consciously made. But on this criterion, neither is there law, nor religion, nor government among savages.

The question, however, whether we should call it *science* or only *empirical and rational knowledge* is not of primary importance in this context. We have tried to gain a clear idea as to whether the savage has only one domain of reality or two, and we found that he has his profane world of practical activities and rational outlook besides the sacred region of cult and belief. We have been able to map out the two domains and to give a more detailed description of the one. We must now pass to the second.

III

LIFE, DEATH, AND DESTINY IN EARLY FAITH AND CULT

We pass now to the domain of the *sacred*, to religious and magical creeds and rites. Our historical survey of theories has left us somewhat bewildered with the chaos of opinions and with the jumble of phenomena. While it was difficult not to admit into the enclosure of religion one after the other, spirits and ghosts, totems and social events, death and life, yet in the process religion seemed to become a thing more and more confused, both an all and a nothing. It certainly cannot be defined by its subject-matter in a narrow sense, as "spirit worship," or as "ancestor cult," or as the "cult of nature." It includes animism, animatism, totemism, and fetishism, but it is not any one of them exclusively. The *ism* definition of religion in its origins must be given up, for religion does not cling to any one object or class of objects, though incidentally it can touch and hallow all. Nor, as we have seen, is religion identical with Society or the Social, nor can we remain satisfied by a vague hint that it clings to life only, for death opens perhaps the vastest view on to the other world. As an "appeal to higher powers," religion can only be distinguished from magic and not defined in general, but even this view will have to be slightly modified and supplemented.

The problem before us is, then, to try to put some order into the facts. This will allow us to determine somewhat more precisely the character of the domain of the *Sacred* and mark it off from that of the *Profane*. It will also give us an opportunity to state the relation between magic and religion.

1. *The Creative Acts of Religion*

It will be best to face the facts first and, in order not to narrow down the scope of the survey, to take as our watchword the vaguest and most general of indices : " Life." As a matter of fact, even a slight acquaintance with ethnological literature is enough to convince anyone that in reality the physiological phases of human life, and, above all, its crises, such as conception, pregnancy, birth, puberty, marriage, and death, form the nuclei of numerous rites and beliefs. Thus beliefs about conception, such as that in reincarnation, spirit-entry, magical impregnation, exist in one form or another in almost every tribe, and they are often associated with rites and observances. During pregnancy the expectant mother has to keep certain taboos and undergo ceremonies, and her husband shares at times in both. At birth, before and after, there are various magical rites to prevent dangers and undo sorcery, ceremonies of purification, communal rejoicings and acts of presentation of the new-born to higher powers or to the community. Later on in life the boys and, much less frequently, the girls have to undergo the often protracted rites of initiation, as a rule shrouded in mystery and marred by cruel and obscene ordeals.

Without going any further, we can see that even the very beginnings of human life are surrounded by an inextricably mixed-up medley of beliefs and rites. They seem to be strongly attracted by any important event in life, to crystallise round it, surround it with a rigid crust of formalism and ritualism—but to what purpose ? Since we cannot define cult and creed by their objects, perhaps it will be possible to perceive their function.

A closer scrutiny of the facts allows us to make from the outset a preliminary classification into two main groups. Compare a rite carried out to prevent death in childbed with another typical custom, a ceremony in celebration of a birth. The first rite is carried out as a means to an end, it has a definite practical purpose which is known to all who practise it and can be easily elicited from any native informant. The post-natal ceremony, say a presentation of a new-born or a feast of rejoicing in the event, has no purpose : it is not a means to an end but an end in itself. It expresses the feelings of the mother, the father, the relatives, the whole community, but there is no future event which this ceremony foreshadows, which it is meant to bring about or to prevent. This difference will serve us as a *prima facie* distinction between magic and religion. While in the magical act the underlying idea and aim is always clear, straightforward, and definite, in the religious ceremony there is no purpose directed towards a subsequent event. It is only possible for the sociologist to establish the function, the sociological *raison d'être* of the act. The native can always state the end of the magical rite, but he will say of a religious ceremony that it is done because such is the usage, or because it has been ordained, or he will narrate an explanatory myth.

In order to grasp better the nature of primitive religious ceremonies and their function, let us analyse the ceremonies of initiation. They present right through the vast range of their occurrence certain striking similarities. Thus the novices have to undergo a more or less protracted period of seclusion and preparation. Then comes initiation proper, in which the youth, passing through a series of ordeals, is finally submitted to an act of bodily mutilation : at the mildest, a slight incision or the knocking out of a tooth ; or, more severe, circumcision ; or, really cruel and dangerous, an operation such as the sub-incision practised in some Australian tribes. The ordeal is usually associated with the idea of the death and rebirth of the initiated one, which is sometimes enacted in a mimetic performance. But besides the ordeal, less conspicuous and dramatic, but in reality more important, is the second main aspect of initiation : the systematic instruction of the youth in sacred myth and tradition, the gradual unveiling of tribal mysteries and the exhibition of sacred objects.

The ordeal and the unveiling of tribal mysteries are usually believed to have been instituted by one or more legendary ancestors or culture-heroes, or by a Superior Being of superhuman character. Sometimes he is said to swallow the youths, or to kill them, and then to restore them again as fully initiated men. His voice is imitated by the hum of the bull-roarer to inspire awe in the uninitiated women and children. Through these ideas initiation brings the novice into relationship with higher powers and personalities, such as the Guardian Spirits and Tutelary Divinities of the North American Indians, the Tribal All-Father of some Australian Aborigines, the Mythological Heroes of Melanesia and other parts of the world. This is the third fundamental element, besides ordeal and the teaching of tradition, in the rites of passing into manhood.

Now what is the sociological function of these customs, what part do they play in the maintenance and development of civilisation ? As we have seen, the youth is taught in them the sacred traditions under most impressive conditions of preparation and ordeal and under the sanction of Supernatural Beings—the light of tribal revelation bursts upon him from out of the shadows of fear, privation, and bodily pain.

Let us realise that in primitive conditions tradition is of supreme value for the community and nothing matters as much as the conformity and conservatism of its members. Order and civilisation can be maintained only by strict adhesion to the lore and knowledge received from previous generations. Any laxity in this weakens the cohesion of the group and imperils its cultural outfit to the point of threatening its very existence. Man has not yet devised the extremely complex apparatus of modern science which enables him nowadays to fix the results of experience into imperishable moulds, to test it ever anew, gradually to shape it into more adequate forms and enrich it constantly by new additions. The primitive man's share of knowledge, his social fabric, his customs and beliefs, are the invaluable yield of devious experience of his forefathers, bought at an extravagant price and to be maintained at any cost. Thus, of all his qualities, truth to tradition is the most important, and a society which makes its tradition sacred has gained by it an inestimable advantage of power and permanence. Such beliefs and practices, therefore, which put a halo of sanctity round tradition and a supernatural stamp upon it, will have a " survival value " for the type of civilisation in which they have been evolved.

We may, therefore, lay down the main function of initiation ceremonies : they are a ritual and dramatic expression of the supreme power and value of tradition in primitive societies ; they also serve to impress this power and value upon the minds of each generation, and they are at the same time an extremely efficient means of transmitting tribal lore, of ensuring continuity in tradition and of maintaining tribal cohesion.

We still have to ask : What is the relation between the purely physiological fact of bodily maturity which these ceremonies mark, and their social and religious aspect ? We see at once that religion does something more, infinitely more, than the mere " sacralising of a crisis of life." From a natural event it makes a social transition, to the fact of bodily maturity it adds the vast conception of entry into manhood with its duties, privileges, responsibilities, above all with its knowledge of tradition and the communion with sacred things and beings. There is thus a creative element in the rites of religious nature. The act establishes not only a social event in the life of the individual but also a spiritual metamorphosis, both associated with the biological event but transcending it in importance and significance.

Initiation is a typically religious act, and we can see clearly here how the ceremony and its purpose are one, how the end is realised in the very consummation of the act. At the same time we can see the function of such acts in society in that they create mental habits and social usages of inestimable value to the group and its civilisation.

Another type of religious ceremony, the rite of marriage, is also an end in itself in that it creates a supernaturally sanctioned bond, superadded to the primarily biological fact : the union of man and woman for lifelong partnership in affection, economic community, the procreation and rearing of childrer. This union, monogamous marriage, has always existed in human societies— so modern anthropology teaches in the face of the older fantastic hypotheses of "promiscuity" and "group marriage." By giving monogamous marriage an imprint of value and sanctity, religion offers another gift to human culture. And that brings us to the consideration of the two great human needs of propagation and nutrition.

2. *Providence in Primitive Life*

Propagation and nutrition stand first and foremost among the vital concerns of man. Their relation to religious belief and practice has been often recognised and even over-emphasised. Especially sex has been, from some older writers up to the psycho-analytic school, frequently regarded as the main source of religion. In fact, however, it plays an astonishingly insignificant part in religion, considering its force and insidiousness in human life in general. Besides love magic and the use of sex in certain magical performances—phenomena not belonging to the domain of religion —there remain to be mentioned here only acts of licence at harvest festivities or other public gatherings, the facts of temple prostitution and, at the level of barbarism and lower civilisation, the worship of phallic divinities. Contrary to what one would expect, in savagery sexual cults play an insignificant rôle. It must also be remembered that acts of ceremonial licence are not mere indulgence, but that they express a reverent attitude towards the forces of generation and fertility in man and nature, forces on which the very existence of society and culture depends. Religion, the permanent source of moral control, which changes its incidence but remains eternally vigilant, has to turn its attention to these forces, at first drawing them merely into its sphere, later on submitting them to repression, finally establishing the ideal of chastity and the sanctification of askesis.

When we pass to nutrition, the first thing to be noted is that eating is for primitive man an act surrounded by etiquette, special prescriptions and prohibitions, and a general emotional tension to a degree unknown to us. Besides the magic of food, designed to make it go a long way, or to prevent its scarcity in general—and we do not speak here at all of the innumerable forms of magic associated with the procuring of food—food has also a conspicuous rôle in ceremonies of a distinctly religious character. First-fruit offerings of a ritual nature, harvest ceremonies, big seasonal feasts in which crops are accumulated, displayed, and, in one way or another, sacralised, play an important part among agricultural peoples. Hunters, again, or fishers celebrate a big catch or the opening of the season of their pursuit by feasts and ceremonies at which food is ritually handled, the animals propitiated or worshipped. All such acts express the joy of the community, their sense of the great value of food, and religion through them consecrates the reverent attitude of man towards his daily bread.

To primitive man, never, even under the best conditions, quite free from the threat of starvation, abundance of food is a primary condition of normal life. It means the possibility of looking beyond the daily worries, of paying more attention to the remoter, spiritual aspects of civilisation. If we thus consider that food is the main link between man and his surroundings, that by receiving it he feels the forces of destiny and providence, we can see the cultural, nay, biological importance of primitive religion in the sacralisation of food. We can see in it the germs of what in higher types of religion will develop into the feeling of dependence upon Providence, of gratitude, and of confidence in it.

Sacrifice and communion, the two main forms in which food is ritually ministered, can be now beheld in a new light against the background of man's early attitude of religious reverence towards the providential abundance of food. That the idea of giving, the importance of the exchange of gifts in all phases of social contact, plays a great rôle in sacrifice seems—in spite of the unpopularity of this theory nowadays—unquestionable in view of the new knowledge of primitive economic psychology.[1] Since

---

[1] *Cf.* the writer's *Argonauts of the Western Pacific*, 1923, and the article on "Primitive Economics" in the *Economic Journal*, 1921; as well as Professor Rich. Thurnwald's memoir on "Die Gestaltung der Wirtschaftsentwicklung aus ihren Anfängen heraus" in *Erinnerungsgabe für Max Weber*, 1923.

the giving of gifts is the normal accompaniment of all social intercourse among primitives, the spirits who visit the village, or the demons who haunt some hallowed spot, or divinities when approached, are given their due, their share sacrificed from the general plenty, as any other visitors or persons visited would be. But underlying this custom there is a still deeper religious element. Since food is to the savage the token of the beneficence of the world, since plenty gives him the first, the most elementary, inkling of Providence, by sharing in food sacrificially with his spirits or divinities the savage shares with them in the beneficial powers of his Providence already felt by him but not yet comprehended. Thus in primitive societies the roots of sacrificial offerings are to be found in the psychology of gift, which is to them communion in beneficent abundance.

The sacramental meal is only another expression of the same mental attitude, carried out in the most appropriate manner by the act by which life is retained and renewed—the act of eating. But this ritual seems to be extremely rare among lower savages, and the sacrament of communion, prevalent at a level of culture when the primitive psychology of eating is no more, has by then acquired a different symbolic and mystical meaning. Perhaps the only case of sacramental eating, well attested and known with some detail, is the so-called " totemic sacrament " of the Central Australian tribes, and this seems to require a somewhat more special interpretation.

3. *Man's Selective Interest in Nature*

This brings us to the subject of totemism, briefly defined in the first section. As may have been seen, the following questions have to be asked about totemism. First, why does a primitive tribe select for its totems a limited number of species, primarily animals and plants; and on what principles is this selection made? Secondly, why is this selective attitude expressed in beliefs of affinity, in cults of multiplication, above all in the negative injunctions of totemic taboos, and again in injunctions of ritual eating, as in the Australian " totemic sacrament "? Thirdly and finally, why with the subdivision of nature into a limited number of selected species does there run parallel a subdivision of the tribe into clans correlated with the species?

The above outlined psychology of the primitive attitude towards food and its abundance and our principle of man's practical and pragmatic outlook lead us directly to an answer. We have seen that food is the primary link between the primitive and providence. And the need of it and the desire for its abundance have led man to economic pursuits, collecting, hunting, fishing, and they endow these pursuits with varied and tense emotions. A number of animal and vegetable species, those which form the staple food of the tribe, dominate the interests of the tribesmen. To primitive man nature is his living larder, to which—especially at the lowest stages of culture—he has to repair directly in order to gather, cook, and eat when hungry. The road from the wilderness to the savage's belly and consequently to his mind is very short, and for him the world is an indiscriminate background against which there stand out the useful, primarily the edible, species of animals or plants. Those who have lived in the jungle with savages, taking part in collecting or hunting expeditions, or who have sailed with them over the lagoons, or spent moonlit nights on sandbanks waiting for the shoals of fish or for the appearance of turtle, know how keen and selective is the savage's interest, how it clings to the indications, trails, and to the habits and peculiarities of his quarry, while it yet remains quite indifferent to any other stimuli. Every such species which is habitually pursued forms a nucleus round which all the interests, the impulses, the emotions of a tribe tend to crystallise. A sentiment of social nature is built round each species, a sentiment which naturally finds its expression in folk-lore, belief, and ritual.

It must also be remembered that the same type of impulse which makes small children delight in birds, take a keen interest in animals, and shrink from reptiles, places animals in the front rank of nature for primitive man. By their general affinity with man—they move, utter sounds, manifest emotions, have bodies and faces like him—and by their superior powers—the birds fly in the open, the fishes can swim under water, reptiles renew their skins and their life and can disappear in the earth—by all this the animal, the intermediate link between man and nature, often his superior in strength, agility, and cunning, usually his indispensable quarry, assumes an exceptional place in the savage's view of the world.

The primitive is deeply interested in the appearance and

properties of beasts ; he desires to have them and, therefore, to control them as useful and edible things ; sometimes he admires and fears them. All these interests meet and, strengthening each other, produce the same effect: the selection, in man's principal preoccupations, of a limited number of species, animal first, vegetable in the second place, while inanimate or man-made things are unquestionably but a secondary formation, an introduction by analogy, of objects which have nothing to do with the substance of totemism.

The nature of man's interest in the totemic species indicates also clearly the type of belief and cult to be there expected. Since it is the desire to control the species, dangerous, useful, or edible, this desire must lead to a belief in special power over the species, affinity with it, a common essence between man and beast or plant. Such a belief implies, on the one hand, certain considerations and restraints—the most obvious being a prohibition to kill and to eat ; on the other hand, it endows man with the supernatural faculty of contributing ritually to the abundance of the species, to its increase and vitality.

This ritual leads to acts of magical nature, by which plenty is brought about. Magic, as we shall see presently, tends in all its manifestations to become specialised, exclusive and departmental and hereditary within a family or clan. In totemism the magical multiplication of each species would naturally become the duty and privilege of a specialist, assisted by his family. The families in course of time become clans, each having its headman as the chief magician of its totem. Totemism in its most elementary forms, as found in Central Australia, is a system of magical co-operation, a number of practical cults, each with its own social basis but all having one common end : the supply of the tribe with abundance. Thus totemism in its sociological aspect can be explained by the principles of primitive magical sociology in general. The existence of totemic clans and their correlation with cult and belief is but an instance of departmental magic and of the tendency to inheritance of magical ritual by one family. This explanation, somewhat condensed as it is, attempts to show that, in its social organisation, belief, and cult, totemism is not a freakish outgrowth, not a fortuitous result of some special accident or constellation, but the natural outcome of natural conditions.

Thus we find our questions answered : man's selective interest in a limited number of animals and plants and the way in which this interest is ritually expressed and socially conditioned appear as the natural result of primitive existence, of the savage's spontaneous attitudes towards natural objects and of his prevalent occupations. From the survival point of view, it is vital that man's interest in the practically indispensable species should never abate, that his belief in his capacity to control them should give him strength and endurance in his pursuits and stimulate his observation and knowledge of the habits and natures of animals and plants. Totemism appears thus as a blessing bestowed by religion on primitive man's efforts in dealing with his useful surroundings, upon his " struggle for existence." At the same time it develops his reverence for those animals and plants on which he depends, to which he feels in a way grateful, and yet the destruction of which is a necessity to him. And all this springs from the belief of man's affinity with those forces of nature upon which he mainly depends. Thus we find a moral value and a biological significance in totemism, in a system of beliefs, practices, and social arrangements which at first sight appears but a childish, irrelevant, and degrading fancy of the savage.

4. *Death and the Reintegration of the Group*

Of all sources of religion, the supreme and final crisis of life— death—is of the greatest importance. Death is the gateway to the other world in more than the literal sense. According to most theories of early religion, a great deal, if not all, of religious inspiration has been derived from it—and in this orthodox views are on the whole correct. Man has to live his life in the shadow of death, and he who clings to life and enjoys its fullness must dread the menace of its end. And he who is faced by death turns to the promise of life. Death and its denial—Immortality—have always formed, as they form to-day, the most poignant theme of man's forebodings. The extreme complexity of man's emotional reactions to life finds necessarily its counterpart in his attitude to death. Only what in life has been spread over a long space and manifested in a succession of experiences and events is here at its end condensed into one crisis which provokes a violent and complex outburst of religious manifestations.

Even among the most primitive peoples, the attitude at death is infinitely more complex and, I may add, more akin to our own, than is usually assumed. It is often stated by anthropologists that the dominant feeling of the survivors is that of horror at the corpse and of fear of the ghost. This twin attitude is even made by no less an authority than Wilhelm Wundt the very nucleus of all religious belief and practice. Yet this assertion is only a half-truth, which means no truth at all. The emotions are extremely complex and even contradictory; the dominant elements, love of the dead and loathing of the corpse, passionate attachment to the personality still lingering about the body and a shattering fear of the gruesome thing that has been left over, these two elements seem to mingle and play into each other. This is reflected in the spontaneous behaviour and in the ritual proceedings at death. In the tending of the corpse, in the modes of its disposal, in the post-funerary and commemorative ceremonies, the nearest relatives, the mother mourning for her son, the widow for her husband, the child for the parent, always show some horror and fear mingled with pious love, but never do the negative elements appear alone or even dominant.

The mortuary proceedings show a striking similarity throughout the world. As death approaches, the nearest relatives in any case, sometimes the whole community, forgather by the dying man, and dying, the most private act which a man can perform, is transformed into a public, tribal event. As a rule, a certain differentiation takes place at once, some of the relatives watching near the corpse, others making preparations for the pending end and its consequences, others again performing perhaps some religious acts at a sacred spot. Thus in certain parts of Melanesia the real kinsmen must keep at a distance and only relatives by marriage perform the mortuary services, while in some tribes of Australia the reverse order is observed.

As soon as death has occurred, the body is washed, anointed and adorned, sometimes the bodily apertures are filled, the arms and legs tied together. Then it is exposed to the view of all, and the most important phase, the immediate mourning, begins. Those who have witnessed death and its sequel among savages and who can compare these events with their counterpart among other uncivilised peoples must be struck by the fundamental similarity of the proceedings. There is always a more or less conventionalised and dramatised outburst of grief and wailing in sorrow, which often passes among savages into bodily lacerations and the tearing of hair. This is always done in a public display and is associated with visible signs of mourning, such as black or white daubs on the body, shaven or dishevelled hair, strange or torn garments.

The immediate mourning goes on round the corpse. This, far from being shunned or dreaded, is usually the centre of pious attention. Often there are ritual forms of fondling or attestations of reverence. The body is sometimes kept on the knees of seated persons, stroked and embraced. At the same time these acts are usually considered both dangerous and repugnant, duties to be fulfilled at some cost to the performer. After a time the corpse has to be disposed of. Inhumation with an open or closed grave ; exposure in caves or on platforms, in hollow trees or on the ground in some wild desert place ; burning or setting adrift in canoes—these are the usual forms of disposal.

This brings us to perhaps the most important point, the twofold contradictory tendency, on the one hand to preserve the body, to keep its form intact, or to retain parts of it ; on the other hand the desire to be done with it, to put it out of the way, to annihilate it completely. Mummification and burning are the two extreme expressions of this two-fold tendency. It is impossible to regard mummification or burning or any intermediate form as determined by mere accident of belief, as a historical feature of some culture or other which has gained its universality by the mechanism of spread and contact only. For in these customs is clearly expressed the fundamental attitude of mind of the surviving relative, friend or lover, the longing for all that remains of the dead person and the disgust and fear of the dreadful transformation wrought by death.

One extreme and interesting variety in which this double-edged attitude is expressed in a gruesome manner is sarco-cannibalism, a custom of partaking in piety of the flesh of the dead person. It is done with extreme repugnance and dread and usually followed by a violent vomiting fit. At the same time it is felt to be a supreme act of reverence, love, and devotion. In fact it is considered such a sacred duty that among the Melanesians of New Guinea, where I have studied and witnessed it, it is still performed in secret, although severely penalised by the white Government. The smearing of the body with the fat of the dead, prevalent in Australia and Papuasia is, perhaps, but a variety of this custom.

In all such rites, there is a desire to maintain the tie and the parallel tendency to break the bond. Thus the funerary rites are considered as unclean and soiling, the contact with the corpse as defiling and dangerous, and the performers have to wash, cleanse their body, remove all traces of contact, and perform ritual lustrations. Yet the mortuary ritual compels man to overcome the repugnance, to conquer his fears, to make piety and attachment triumphant, and with it the belief in a future life, in the survival of the spirit.

And here we touch on one of the most important functions of religious cult. In the foregoing analysis I have laid stress on the direct emotional forces created by contact with death and with the corpse, for they primarily and most powerfully determine the behaviour of the survivors. But connected with these emotions and born out of them, there is the idea of the spirit, the belief in the new life into which the departed has entered. And here we return to the problem of animism with which we began our survey of primitive religious facts. What is the substance of a spirit, and what is the psychological origin of this belief ?

The savage is intensely afraid of death, probably as the result of some deep-seated instincts common to man and animals. He does not want to realise it as an end, he cannot face the idea of complete cessation, of annihilation. The idea of spirit and of spiritual existence is near at hand, furnished by such experiences as are discovered and described by Tylor. Grasping at it, man reaches the comforting belief in spiritual continuity and in the life after death. Yet this belief does not remain unchallenged in the complex, double-edged play of hope and fear which sets in always in the face of death. To the comforting voice of hope, to the intense desire of immortality, to the difficulty, in one's own case, almost the impossibility, of facing annihilation there are opposed powerful and terrible forebodings. The testimony of the senses, the gruesome decomposition of the corpse, the visible disappearance of the personality—certain apparently instinctive suggestions of fear and horror seem to threaten man at all stages of culture with some idea of annihilation, with some hidden fears and forebodings. And here into this play of emotional forces, into this supreme dilemma of life and final death, religion steps in, selecting the positive creed, the comforting view, the culturally valuable belief in immortality, in the spirit independent of the body, and in the continuance of life after death. In the various ceremonies at death, in commemoration and communion with the departed, and worship of ancestral ghosts, religion gives body and form to the saving beliefs.

Thus the belief in immortality is the result of a deep emotional revelation, standardised by religion, rather than a primitive philosophic doctrine. Man's conviction of continued life is one of the supreme gifts of religion, which judges and selects the better of the two alternatives suggested by self-preservation—the hope of continued life and the fear of annihilation. The belief in spirits is the result of the belief in immortality. The substance of which the spirits are made is the full-blooded passion and desire for life, rather than the shadowy stuff which haunts his dreams and illusions. Religion saves man from a surrender to death and destruction, and in doing this it merely makes use of the observations of dreams, shadows, and visions. The real nucleus of animism lies in the deepest emotional fact of human nature, the desire for life.

Thus the rites of mourning, the ritual behaviour immediately after death, can be taken as pattern of the religious act, while the belief in immortality, in the continuity of life and in the nether world, can be taken as the prototype of an act of faith. Here, as in the religious ceremonies previously described, we find self-contained acts, the aim of which is achieved in their very performance. The ritual despair, the obsequies, the acts of mourning, express the emotion of the bereaved and the loss of the whole group. They endorse and they duplicate the natural feelings of the survivors ; they create a social event out of a natural fact. Yet, though in the acts of mourning, in the mimic despair of wailing, in the treatment of the corpse and in its disposal, nothing ulterior is achieved, these acts fulfil an important function and possess a considerable value for primitive culture.

What is this function ? The initiation ceremonies we have found fulfil theirs in sacralising tradition ; the food cults, sacrament and sacrifice bring man into communion with providence, with the beneficent forces of plenty ; totemism standardises man's practical, useful attitude of selective interest towards his surroundings. If the view here taken of the biological function of religion is true, some such similar rôle must also be played by the whole mortuary ritual.

The death of a man or woman in a primitive group, consisting of a limited number of individuals, is an event of no mean importance. The nearest relatives and friends are disturbed to the depth of their emotional life. A small community bereft of a member, especially if he be important, is severely mutilated. The whole event breaks the normal course of life and shakes the moral foundations of society. The strong tendency on which we have insisted in the above description : to give way to fear and horror, to abandon the corpse, to run away from the village, to destroy all the belongings of the dead one—all these impulses exist, and if given way to would be extremely dangerous, disintegrating the group, destroying the material foundations of primitive culture. Death in a primitive society is, therefore, much more than the removal of a member. By setting in motion one part of the deep forces of the instinct of self-preservation, it threatens the very cohesion and solidarity of the group, and upon this depends the organisation of that society, its tradition, and finally the whole culture. For if primitive man yielded always to the disintegrating impulses of his reaction to death, the continuity of tradition and the existence of material civilisation would be made impossible.

We have seen already how religion, by sacralising and thus standardising the other set of impulses, bestows on man the gift of mental integrity. Exactly the same function it fulfils also with regard to the whole group. The ceremonial of death which ties the survivors to the body and rivets them to the place of death, the beliefs in the existence of the spirit, in its beneficent influences or malevolent intentions, in the duties of a series of commemorative or sacrificial ceremonies—in all this religion counteracts the centrifugal forces of fear, dismay, demoralisation, and provides the most powerful means of reintegration of the group's shaken solidarity and of the re-establishment of its morale.

In short, religion here assures the victory of tradition and culture over the mere negative response of thwarted instinct.

With the rites of death we have finished the survey of the main types of religious acts. We have followed the crises of life as the main guiding thread of our account, but as they presented themselves we also treated the side issues, such as totemism, the cults of food and of propagation, sacrifice and sacrament, the commemorative cults of ancestors and the cults of the spirits. To one type already mentioned we still have to return—I mean, the seasonal feasts and ceremonies of communal or tribal character—and to the discussion of this subject we proceed now.

IV

THE PUBLIC AND TRIBAL CHARACTER OF PRIMITIVE CULTS

The festive and public character of the ceremonies of cult is a conspicuous feature of religion in general. Most sacred acts happen in a congregation ; indeed, the solemn conclave of the faithful united in prayer, sacrifice, supplication, or thanksgiving is the very prototype of a religious ceremony. Religion needs the community as a whole so that its members may worship in common its sacred things and its divinities, and society needs religion for the maintenance of moral law and order.

In primitive societies the public character of worship, the give-and-take between religious faith and social organisation, is at least as pronounced as in higher cultures. It is sufficient to glance over our previous inventory of religious phenomena to see that ceremonies at birth, rites of initiation, mortuary attentions to the dead, burial, the acts of mourning and commemoration, sacrifice and totemic ritual, are one and all public and collective, frequently affecting the tribe as a whole and absorbing all its energies for the time being. This public character, the gathering together of big numbers, is especially pronounced in the annual or periodical feasts held at times of plenty, at harvest or at the height of the hunting or fishing season. Such feasts allow the people to indulge in their gay mood, to enjoy the abundance of crops and quarry, to meet their friends and relatives, to muster the whole community in full force, and to do all this in a mood of happiness and harmony. At times during such festivals visits of the departed take place : the spirits of ancestors and dead relatives return and receive offerings and sacrificial libations, mingle with the survivors in the acts of cult and in the rejoicings of the feast. Or the dead, even if they do not actually revisit the suvivors, are commemorated by them, usually in the form of ancestor cult. Again, such festivities being frequently held embody the ritual of garnered crops and other cults of vegetation. But whatever the other issues of such festivities, there can be no doubt that religion

demands the existence of seasonal, periodical feasts with a big concourse of people, with rejoicings and festive apparel, with an
abundance of food, and with relaxation of rules and taboos. The
members of the tribe come together, and they relax the usual
restrictions, especially the barriers of conventional reserve in social
and in sexual intercourse. The appetites are provided for, indeed
pandered to, and there is a common participation in the pleasures, a
display to everyone of all that is good, the sharing of it in a universal
mood of generosity. To the interest in plenty of material goods
there is joined the interest in the multitude of people, in the
congregation, in the tribe as a body.

With these facts of periodical festive gathering a number of
other distinctly social elements must be ranged : the tribal character
of almost all religious ceremonies, the social universality of moral
rules, the contagion of sin, the importance of sheer convention and
tradition in primitive religion and morals, above all the identification of the whole tribe as a social unit with its religion ; that is,
the absence of any religious sectarianism, dissension, or heterodoxy
in primitive creed.

1. *Society as the Substance of God*

All these facts, especially the last one, show that religion is
a tribal affair, and we are reminded of the famous dictum of
Robertson Smith, that primitive religion is the concern of the
community rather than of the individual. This exaggerated
view contains a great deal of truth, but, in science, to recognise
where the truth lies, on the one hand, and to unearth it and bring it
fully to light, on the other, are by no means the same. Robertson
Smith did not do much more in this matter, in fact, than set
forth the important problem : why is it that primitive man
performs his ceremonies in public ? What is the relation between
society and the truth revealed by religion and worshipped in it ?

To these questions, some modern anthropologists, as we
know, give a trenchant, apparently conclusive, and exceedingly
simple answer. Professor Durkheim and his followers maintain
that religion is social, for all its Entities, its God or Gods, the Stuff
all things religious are made of, are nothing more nor less than
Society divinised.

This theory seems very well to explain the public nature of
cult, the inspiration and comfort drawn by man, the social animal,

from congregation, the intolerance shown by religion, especially in its early manifestations, the cogency of morals and other similar facts. It also satisfies our modern democratic bias, which in social science appears as a tendency to explain all by "collective" rather than by "individual" forces. This, the theory which makes *vox populi vox Dei* appear as a sober, scientific truth, must surely be congenial to modern man.

Yet, upon reflection, critical misgivings, and very serious ones at that, arise. Everyone who has experienced religion deeply and sincerely knows that the strongest religious moments come in solitude, in turning away from the world, in concentration and in mental detachment, and not in the distraction of a crowd. Can primitive religion be so entirely devoid of the inspiration of solitude ? No one who knows savages at first-hand or from a careful study of literature will have any doubts. Such facts as the seclusion of novices at initiation, their individual, personal struggles during the ordeal, the communion with spirits, divinities, and powers in lonely spots, all these show us primitive religion frequently lived through in solitude. Again, as we have seen before, the belief in immortality cannot be explained without the consideration of the religious frame of mind of the individual, who faces his own pending death in fear and sorrow. Primitive religion does not entirely lack its prophets, seers, soothsayers and interpreters of belief. All such facts, though they certainly do not prove that religion is exclusively individual, make it difficult to understand how it can be regarded as *the Social* pure and simple.

And again, the essence of morals, as opposed to legal or customary rules, is that they are enforced by conscience. The savage does not keep his taboo for fear of social punishment or of public opinion. He abstains from breaking it partly because he fears the direct evil consequences flowing from the will of a divinity, or from the forces of the sacred, but mainly because his personal responsibility and conscience forbid him doing it. The forbidden totem animal, incestuous or forbidden intercourse, the tabooed action or food, are directly abhorrent to him. I have seen and felt savages shrink from an illicit action with the same horror and disgust with which the religious Christian will shrink from the committing of what he considers sin. Now this mental attitude is undoubtedly due in part to the influence of society, in so far as the particular prohibition is branded as horrible and disgusting by tradition. But it works in the individual and through forces of the individual mind. It is, therefore, neither exclusively social nor individual, but a mixture of both.

Professor Durkheim tries to establish his striking theory that Society is the raw material of Godhead by an analysis of primitive tribal festivities. He studies especially the seasonal ceremonies of the Central Australians. In these "the great collective effervescence during the periods of concentration" causes all the phenomena of their religion, and "the religious idea is born out of their effervescence." Professor Durkheim lays thus the emphasis on emotional ebullition, on exaltation, on the increased power which every individual feels when part of such a gathering. Yet but a little reflection is sufficient to show that even in primitive societies the heightening of emotions and the lifting of the individual out of himself are by no means restricted to gatherings and to crowd phenomena. The lover near his sweetheart, the daring adventurer conquering his fears in the face of real danger, the hunter at grips with a wild animal, the craftsman achieving a masterpiece, whether he be savage or civilised, will under such conditions feel altered, uplifted, endowed with higher forces. And there can be no doubt that from many of these solitary experiences where man feels the forebodings of death, the pangs of anxiety, the exaltation of bliss, there flows a great deal of religious inspiration. Though most ceremonies are carried out in public, much of religious revelation takes place in solitude.

On the other hand there are in primitive societies collective acts with as much effervescence and passion as any religious ceremony can possibly have, yet without the slightest religious colouring. Collective work in the gardens, as I have seen it in Melanesia, when men become carried away with emulation and zest for work, singing rhythmic songs, uttering shouts of joy and slogans of competitive challenge, is full of this "collective effervescence." But it is entirely profane, and society which "reveals itself" in this as in any other public performance assumes no divine grandeur or godlike appearance. A battle, a sailing regatta, one of the big tribal gatherings for trading purposes, an Australian lay-corrobboree, a village brawl, are all from the social as well as from the psychological point of view essentially examples of crowd effervescence. Yet no religion is generated on any of these occasions. Thus the *collective* and the *religious*, though impinging on each other, are by no means coextensive, and while a great deal of belief and religious inspiration must be traced back to solitary experiences of man, there is much concourse and effervescence which has no religious meaning nor religious consequence.

If we extend yet further the definition of "society" and regard it as a permanent entity, continuous through tradition and culture, each generation brought up by its predecessor and moulded into its likeness by the social heritage of civilisation—can we not regard then Society as the prototype of Godhead ? Even thus the facts of primitive life will remain rebellious to this theory. For tradition comprises the sum-total of social norms and customs, rules of art and knowledge, injunctions, precepts, legends and myths, and part of this only is religious, while the rest is essentially profane. As we have seen in the second section of this essay, primitive man's empirical and rational knowledge of nature, which is the foundation of his arts and crafts, of his economic enterprises and of his constructive abilities, forms an autonomous domain of social tradition. Society as the keeper of lay tradition, of the profane, cannot be the religious principle or Divinity, for the place of this latter is within the domain of the sacred only. We have found, moreover, that one of the chief tasks of primitive religion, especially in the performance of initiation ceremonies and tribal mysteries, is to sacralise the religious part of tradition. It is clear, therefore, that religion cannot derive all its sanctity from that source which itself is made sacred by religion.

It is in fact only by a clever play on words and by a double-edged sophistication of the argument that "society" can be identified with the Divine and the Sacred. If, indeed, we set equal the *social* to the *moral* and widen this concept so that it covers all belief, all rules of conduct, all dictates of conscience ; if, further, we personify the Moral Force and regard it as a Collective Soul, then the identification of Society with Godhead needs not much dialectical skill to be defended. But since the moral rules are only one part of the traditional heritage of man, since morality is not identical with the Power or Being from which it is believed to spring, since finally the metaphysical concept of "Collective Soul" is barren in anthropology, we have to reject the sociological theory of religion.

To sum up, the views of Durkheim and his school cannot be accepted. First of all, in primitive societies religion arises to a great extent from purely individual sources. Secondly, society as a crowd is by no means always given to the production of religious beliefs or even to religious states of mind, while collective effervescence is often of an entirely secular nature. Thirdly, tradition, the sum-total of certain rules and cultural achievements, embraces, and in primitive societies keeps in a tight grip, both Profane and Sacred. Finally, the personification of society, the conception of a " Collective Soul," is without any foundation in fact, and is against the sound methods of social science.

2. The Moral Efficiency of Savage Beliefs

With all this, in order to do justice to Robertson Smith, Durkheim, and their school, we have to admit that they have brought out a number of relevant features of primitive religion. Above all, by the very exaggeration of the sociological aspect of primitive faith they have set forth a number of most important questions : Why are most religious acts in primitive societies performed collectively and in public ? What is the part of society in the establishment of the rules of moral conduct ? Why are not only morality but also belief, mythology, and all sacred tradition compulsory to all the members of a primitive tribe ? In other words, why is there only one body of religious beliefs in each tribe, and why is no difference of opinion ever tolerated ?

To give an answer to these questions we have to go back to our survey of religious phenomena, to recall some of our conclusions there arrived at, and especially to fix our attention upon the technique by which belief is expressed and morals established in primitive religion.

Let us start with the religious act par excellence, the ceremonial of death. Here the call to religion arises out of an individual crisis, the death which threatens man or woman. Never does an individual need the comfort of belief and ritual so much as in the sacrament of the viaticum, in the last comforts given to him at the final stage of his life's journey—acts which are well-nigh universal in all primitive religions. These acts are directed against the overwhelming fear, against the corroding doubt, from which the savage is no more free than the civilised man. These acts confirm his hope that there is a hereafter, that it is not worse than present life ; indeed, better. All the ritual expresses that belief, that emotional attitude which the dying man requires, which is the greatest comfort he can have in his supreme conflict. And this affirmation has behind it weight of numbers and the pomp of solemn ritual. For in all savage societies, death, as we have seen, compels the whole community to forgather, to attend to the dying, and to carry out the duties towards him. These duties do not, of course, develop any emotional sympathy with the dying— this would lead merely to a disintegrating panic. On the contrary, the line of ritual conduct opposes and contradicts some of the strongest emotions to which the dying man might become a prey. The whole conduct of the group, in fact, expresses the hope of salvation and immortality ; that is, it expresses only one among the conflicting emotions of the individual.

After death, though the main actor has made his exit, the tragedy is not at an end. There are the bereaved ones, and these, savage or civilised, suffer alike, and are thrown into a dangerous mental chaos. We have given an analysis of this already, and found that, torn between fear and piety, reverence and horror, love and disgust, they are in a state of mind which might lead to mental disintegration. Out of this, religion lifts the individual by what could be called spiritual co-operation in the sacred mortuary rites. We have seen that in these rites there is expressed the dogma of continuity after death, as well as the moral attitude towards the departed. The corpse, and with it the person of the dead one, is a potential object of horror as well as of tender love. Religion confirms the second part of this double attitude by making the dead body into an object of sacred duties. The bond of union between the recently dead and the survivors is maintained, a fact of immense importance for the continuity of culture and for the safe keeping of tradition. In all this we see that the whole community carries out the biddings of religious tradition, but that these are again enacted for the benefit of a few individuals only, the bereaved ones, that they arise from a personal conflict and are a solution of this conflict. It must also be remembered that what the survivor goes through on such an occasion prepares him for his own death. The belief in immortality, which he has lived through and practised in the case of his mother or father, makes him realise more clearly his own future life.

In all this we have to make a clear distinction between the belief and the ethics of the ritual on the one hand, and on the other the means of enforcing them, the technique by which the individual is made to receive his religious comfort. The saving belief in spiritual continuity after death is already contained in the individual mind ; it is not created by society. The sum-total of innate tendencies, known usually as " the instinct of self-preservation," is at the root of this belief. The faith in immortality is, as we have seen, closely connected with the difficulty of facing one's own annihilation or that of a near and beloved person. This tendency makes the idea of the final disappearance of human personality odious, intolerable, socially destructive. Yet this idea and the fear of it always lurk in individual experience, and religion can remove it only by its negation in ritual.

Whether this is achieved by a Providence directly guiding human history, or by a process of natural selection in which a culture which evolves a belief and a ritual of immortality will survive and spread—this is a problem of theology or metaphysics. The anthropologist has done enough when he has shown the value of a certain phenomenon for social integrity and for the continuity of culture. In any case we see that what religion does in this matter is to select one out of the two alternatives suggested to man by his instinctive endowment.

This selection once made, however, society is indispensable for its enactment. The bereaved member of the group, himself overwhelmed by sorrow and fear, is incapable of relying on his own forces. He would be unable by his single effort to apply the dogma to his own case. Here the group steps in. The other members, untouched by the calamity, not torn mentally by the metaphysical dilemma, can respond to the crisis along the lines dictated by the religious order. Thus they bring consolation to the stricken one and lead him through the comforting experiences of religious ceremony. It is always easy to bear the misfortunes—of others, and the whole group, in which the majority are untouched by the pangs of fear and horror, can thus help the afflicted minority. Going through the religious ceremonies, the bereaved emerges changed by the revelation of immortality, communion with the beloved, the order of the next world. Religion commands in acts of cult, the group executes the command.

But, as we have seen, the comfort of ritual is not artificial, not manufactured for the occasion. It is but the result of the two conflicting tendencies which exist in man's innate emotional reaction to death : the religious attitude consists merely in the selection and ritual affirmation of one of these alternatives—the hope in a future life. And here the public concourse gives the emphasis, the powerful testimony to the belief. Public pomp and ceremony take effect through the contagiousness of faith, through the dignity of unanimous consent, the impressiveness of collective behaviour. A multitude enacting as one an earnest and dignified ceremony invariably carries away even the disinterested observer, still more the affected participant.

But the distinction between social collaboration as the only technique necessary for the enactment of a belief on the one hand, and the creation of the belief or self-revelation of society on the other, must be emphatically pointed out. The community proclaims a number of definite truths and gives moral comfort to its members, but it does not give them the vague and empty assertion of its own divinity.

In another type of religious ritual, in the ceremonies of initiation, we found that the ritual establishes the existence of some power or personality from which tribal law is derived, and which is responsible for the moral rules imparted to the novice. To make the belief impressive, strong, and grandiose, there is the pomp of the ceremony and the hardships of preparation and ordeal. An unforgettable experience, unique in the life of the individual, is created, and by this he learns the doctrines of tribal tradition and the rules of its morality. The whole tribe is mobilised and all its authority set in motion to bear witness to the power and reality of the things revealed.

Here again, as at the death, we have to do with a crisis in the individual life, and a mental conflict associated with it. At puberty, the youth has to test his physical power, to cope with his sexual maturity, to take up his place in the tribe. This brings him promises, prerogatives, and temptations, and at the same time imposes burdens upon him. The right solution of the conflict lies in his compliance with tradition, in his submission to the sexual morality of his tribe and to the burdens of manhood, and that is accomplished in the ceremonies of initiation.

The public character of these ceremonies avails both to establish the greatness of the ultimate law-giver and to achieve homogeneity and uniformity in the teaching of morals. Thus they become a form of condensed education of a religious character. As in all schooling, the principles imparted are merely selected, fixed, emphasised out of what there is in the individual endowment. Here again publicity is a matter of technique, while the contents of what is taught are not invented by society but exist in the individual.

In other cults again, such as harvest festivals, totemic gatherings, first-fruit offerings and ceremonial display of food, we find religion sacralising abundance and security and establishing the attitude of reverence towards the beneficent forces without. Here again the publicity of the cult is necessary as the only technique suitable for the establishment of the value of food, accumulation and abundance. The display to all, the admiration of all, the rivalry between any two producers, are the means by which value is created. For every value, religious and economic, must possess universal currency. But here again we find only the selection and emphasis of one of the two possible individual reactions. Accumulated food can either be squandered or preserved. It can either be an incentive to immediate heedless consumption and light-hearted carelessness about the future, or else it can stimulate man to devising means of hoarding the treasure and of using it for culturally higher purposes. Religion sets its stamp on the culturally valuable attitude and enforces it by public enactment.

The public character of such feasts subserves another sociologically important function. The members of every group which forms a cultural unit must come in contact with each other from time to time, but besides its beneficent possibility of strengthening social ties, such contact is also fraught with the danger of friction. The danger is greater when people meet in times of stress, dearth, and hunger, when their appetite is unsatisfied and their sexual desires ready to flare up. A festive tribal gathering at times of plenty, when everyone is in a mood of harmony with nature and consequently with each other, takes on, therefore, the character of a meeting in a moral atmosphere. I mean an atmosphere of general harmony and benevolence. The occurrence of occasional licence at such gatherings and the relaxation of the rules of sex and of certain strictures of etiquette are probably due to the same course. All motives for quarrel and disagreement must be eliminated or else a big tribal gathering could not peacefully come to an end. The moral value of harmony and goodwill is thus shown to be higher than the mere negative taboos which curb the principal human instincts. There is no virtue higher than charity, and in primitive religions as well as in higher it covers a multitude of sins ; nay, it outweighs them.

It is, perhaps, unnecessary to go in detail over all the other types of religious acts. Totemism, the religion of the clan, which affirms the common descent from or affinity with the totemic animal, and claims the clan's collective power to control its supply and impresses upon all the clan members a joint totemic taboo and a reverential attitude towards the totemic species, must obviously culminate in public ceremonies and have a distinctly social character. Ancestor cult, the aim of which is to unite into one band of worshippers the family, the sib or the tribe, must bring them together in public ceremonies by its very nature, or else it would fail to fulfil its function. Tutelary spirits of local groups, tribes, or cities ; departmental gods ; professional or local divinities must one and all—by their very definition—be worshipped by village, tribe, town, profession, or body politic.

In cults which stand on the border-line between magic and religion, such as the Intichuma ceremonies, public garden rites, ceremonies of fishing and hunting, the necessity of performance in public is obvious, for these ceremonies, clearly distinguishable from any practical activities which they inaugurate or accompany, are yet their counterpart. To the co-operation in practical enterprise there corresponds the ceremony in common. Only by uniting the group of workers in an act of worship do they fulfil their cultural function.

In fact, instead of going concretely into all the types of religious ceremony, we might have established our thesis by an abstract argument : since religion centres round vital acts, and since all these command public interest of joint co-operative groups, every religious ceremony must be public and carried out by groups. All crises of life, all important enterprises, arouse the public interest of primitive communities, and they have all their ceremonies, magical or religious. The same social body of men which unites for the enterprise or is brought together by the critical event performs also the ceremonial act. Such an abstract argument, however, correct though it be, would not have allowed us to get a real insight into the mechanism of public enactment of religious acts such as we have gained by our concrete description.

3. *Social and Individual Contributions in Primitive Religion*

We are forced therefore to the conclusion that publicity is the indispensable technique of religious revelation in primitive communities, but that society is neither the author of religious truths, nor still less its self-revealed subject. The necessity of the public *mise en scène* of dogma and collective enunciation of moral truths is due to several causes. Let us sum them up.

First of all, social co-operation is needed to surround the unveiling of things sacred and of supernatural beings with solemn grandeur. The community whole-heartedly engaged in performing the forms of the ritual creates the atmosphere of homogeneous belief. In this collective action, those who at the moment least need the comfort of belief, the affirmation of the truth, help along those who are in need of it. The evil, disintegrating forces of destiny are thus distributed by a system of mutual insurance in spiritual misfortune and stress. In bereavement, at the crisis of puberty, during impending danger and evil, at times when prosperity might be used well or badly—religion standardises the right way of thinking and acting and society takes up the verdict and repeats it in unison.

In the second place, public performance of religious dogma is indispensable for the maintenance of morals in primitive communities. Every article of faith, as we have seen, wields a moral influence. Now morals, in order to be active at all, must be universal. The endurance of social ties, the mutuality of services and obligations, the possibility of co-operation, are based in any society on the fact that every member knows what is expected of him ; that, in short, there is a universal standard of conduct. No rule of morals can work unless it is anticipated and unless it can be counted upon. In primitive societies, where law, as enforced by judgements and penalties, is almost completely absent, the automatic, self-acting moral rule is of the greatest importance for forming the very foundations of primitive organisation and culture. This is possible only in a society where there is no private teaching of morals, no personal codes of conduct and honour, no ethical schools, no differences of moral opinion. The teaching of morals must be open, public, and universal.

Thirdly and finally, the transmission and the conservation of sacred tradition entails publicity, or at least collectiveness of performance. It is essential to every religion that its dogma should be considered and treated as absolutely inalterable and inviolable. The believer must be firmly convinced that what he is led to accept as truth is held in safe keeping, handed on exactly as it has been received, placed above any possibility of falsification or alteration. Every religion must have its tangible, reliable safeguards by which the authenticity of its tradition is guaranteed. In higher religions, we know the extreme importance of the authenticity of holy writings, the supreme concern about the purity of the text and the truth of interpretation. The native races have to rely on human memory. Yet, without books or inscriptions, without bodies of theologians, they are not less concerned about the purity of their texts, not less well safeguarded against alteration and misstatement. There is only one factor which can prevent the constant breaking of the sacred thread : the participation of a number of people in the safe-keeping of tradition. The public enactment of myth among certain tribes, the official recitals of sacred stories on certain occasions, the embodiment of parts of belief in sacred ceremonies, the guardianship of parts of tradition given to special bodies of men : secret societies, totemic clans, highest-age grades—all these are means of safeguarding the doctrine of primitive religions. We see that wherever this doctrine is not quite public in the tribe there is a special type of social organisation serving the purpose of its keeping.

These considerations explain also the orthodoxy of primitive religions, and excuse their intolerance. In a primitive community, not only the morals but also the dogmas have to be identical for all members. As long as savage creeds had been regarded as idle superstitions, as make-belief, as childish or diseased fancies, or at best crude philosophic speculations, it was difficult to understand why the savage clung to them so obstinately, so faithfully. But once we see that every canon of the savage's belief is a live force to him, that his doctrine is the very cement of social fabric—for all his morality is derived from it, all his social cohesion and his mental composure—it is easy to understand that he cannot afford to be tolerant. And it is clear also that once you begin to play ducks and drakes with his "superstitions," you destroy all his morality, without much chance of giving him another instead.

We see thus clearly the need for the prominently overt and collective nature of religious acts and for the universality of moral principles, and we also realise clearly why th's is much more prominent in primitive religions than in civilised ones. Public participation and social interest in matters religious are thus explicable by clear, concrete, empirical reasons, and there is no room for an Entity, revealing itself in artful disguise to its worshippers, mystified and misled in the very act of revelation. The fact is that the social share in religious enactment is a condition necessary but not sufficient, and that without the analysis of the individual mind, we cannot take one step in the understanding of religion.

At the beginning of our survey of religious phenomena, in Section III, we have made a distinction between magic and religion ; later on in the account, however, we left the magical rites completely on one side, and to this important domain of primitive life we have now to return.

V

THE ART OF MAGIC AND THE POWER OF FAITH

Magic—the very word seems to reveal a world of mysterious and unexpected possibilities ! Even for those who do not share in that hankering after the occult, after the short-cuts into " esoteric truth," this morbid interest, nowadays so freely ministered to by stale revivals of half-understood ancient creeds and cults, dished up under the names of " theosophy," " spiritism " or " spiritualism," and various pseudo-" sciences," -ologies and -isms—even for the clear scientific mind the subject of magic has a special attraction. Partly perhaps because we hope to find in it the quintessence of primitive man's longings and of his wisdom—and that, whatever it might be, is worth knowing Partly because " magic " seems to stir up in everyone some hidden mental forces, some lingering hopes in the miraculous, some dormant beliefs in man's mysterious possibilities. Witness to this is the power which the words *magic, spell, charm, to bewitch* and *to enchant*, possess in poetry, where the inner value of words, the emotional forces which they still release, survive longest and are revealed most clearly.

Yet when the sociologist approaches the study of magic, there where it still reigns supreme, where even now it can be found fully developed—that is, among the stone-age savages of to-day— he finds to his disappointment an entirely sober, prosaic, even clumsy art, enacted for purely practical reasons, governed by crude and shallow beliefs, carried out in a simple and monotonous technique. This was already indicated in the definition of magic given above when in order to distinguish it from religion we described it as a body of purely practical acts, performed as a means to an end. Such also we have found it when we tried to disentangle it from knowledge and from practical arts, in which it is so strongly enmeshed, superficially so alike that it requires some effort to distinguish the essentially different mental attitude and the specifically ritual nature of its acts. Primitive magic—every field anthropologist knows it to his cost—is extremely monotonous and unexciting, strictly limited in its means of action, circumscribed in its beliefs, stunted in its fundamental assumptions. Follow one rite, study one spell, grasp the principles of magical belief, art and sociology in one case, and you will know not only all the acts of the tribe, but, adding a variant here and there, you will be able to settle as a magical practitioner in any part of the world yet fortunate enough to have faith in that desirable art.

1. *The Rite and the Spell*

Let us have a look at a typical act of magic, and choose one which is well known and generally regarded as a standard performance—an act of black magic. Among the several types which we meet in savagery, witchcraft by the act of pointing the magical dart is, perhaps, the most widespread of all. A pointed bone or a stick, an arrow or the spine of some animal, is ritually, in a mimic fashion, thrust, thrown, or pointed in the direction of the man to be killed by sorcery. We have innumerable recipes in the oriental and ancient books of magic, in ethnographic descriptions and tales of travellers, of how such a rite is performed. But the emotional setting, the gestures and expressions of the sorcerer during the performance, have been but seldom described. Yet these are of the greatest importance. If a spectator were suddenly transported to some part of Melanesia and could observe the sorcerer at work, not perhaps knowing exactly what he was looking at, he might think that he had either to do with a lunatic or else he would guess that here was a man acting under the sway of uncontrolled anger. For the sorcerer has, as an essential part of the ritual performance, not merely to point the bone dart at his victim, but with an intense expression of fury and hatred he has to thrust it in the air, turn and twist it as if to bore it in the wound, then pull it back with a sudden jerk. Thus not only is the act of violence, of stabbing, reproduced, but the passion of violence has to be enacted.

We see thus that the dramatic expression of emotion is the essence of this act, for what is it that is reproduced in it? Not its end, for the magician would in that case have to imitate the death of the victim, but the emotional state of the performer, a state which closely corresponds to the situation in which we find it and which has to be gone through mimetically.

I could adduce a number of similar rites from my own experience, and many more, of course, from other records. Thus, when in other types of black magic the sorcerer ritually injures or mutilates or destroys a figure or object symbolising the victim, this rite is, above all, a clear expression of hatred and anger. Or when in love magic the performer has really or symbolically to grasp, stroke, fondle the beloved person or some object representing her, he reproduces the behaviour of a heart-sick lover who has lost his common sense and is overwhelmed by passion. In war magic, anger, the fury of attack, the emotions of combative passion, are frequently expresssed in a more or less direct manner. In the magic of terror, in the exorcism directed against powers of darkness and evil, the magician behaves as if himself overcome by the emotion of fear, or at least violently struggling against it. Shouts, brandishing of weapons, the use of lighted torches, form often the substance of this rite. Or else in an act, recorded by myself, to ward off the evil powers of darkness, a man has ritually to tremble, to utter a spell slowly as if paralysed by fear. And this fear gets hold also of the approaching sorcerer and wards him off.

All such acts, usually rationalised and explained by some principle of magic, are *prima facie* expressions of emotion. The substances and paraphernalia used in them have often the same significance. Daggers, sharp-pointed lacerating objects, evil-smelling or poisonous substances, used in black magic ; scents, flowers, inebriating stimulants, in love magic; valuables, in economic magic—all these are associated primarily through emotions and not through ideas with the end of the respective magic.

Besides such rites, however, in which a dominant element serves to express an emotion, there are others in which the act does forecast its result, or, to use Sir James Frazer's expression, the rite imitates its end. Thus, in the black magic of the Melanesians recorded by myself, a characteristic ritual way of winding-up the spell is for the scorerer to weaken the voice, utter a death-rattle, and fall down in imitation of the rigor of death. It is, however, not necessary to adduce any other examples, for this aspect of magic and the allied one of contagious magic has been brilliantly described and exhaustively documented by Frazer. Sir James has also shown that there exists a special lore of magical substances based on affinities, relations, on ideas of similarity and contagion, developed with a magical pseudo-science.

But there are also ritual proceedings in which there is neither imitation nor forecasting nor the expression of any special idea or emotion. There are rites so simple that they can be described only as an immediate application of magical virtue, as when the performer stands up and, directly invoking the wind, causes it to rise. Or again, as when a man conveys the spell to some material substance which afterwards will be applied to the thing or person to be charmed. The material objects used in such ritual are also of a strictly appropriate character—substances best fitted to receive, retain, and transmit magical virtue, coverings designed to imprison and preserve it until it is applied to its object.

But what is the magical virtue which figures not only in the last-mentioned type of act but in every magical rite ? For whether it be an act expressing certain emotions or a rite of imitation and foreshadowing or an act of simple casting, one feature they have always in common : the force of magic, its virtue, must always be conveyed to the charmed object. What is it ? Briefly, it is always the power contained in the spell, for, and this is never sufficiently emphasised, the most important element in magic is the spell. The spell is that part of magic which is occult, handed over in magical filiation, known only to the practitioner. To the natives knowledge of magic means knowledge of spell, and in an analysis of any act of witchcraft it will always be found that the ritual centres round the utterance of the spell. The formula is always the core of the magical performance.

The study of the texts and formulas of primitive magic reveals that there are three typical elements associated with the belief in magical efficiency. There are, first, the phonetic effects, imitations of natural sounds, such as the whistling of the wind, the growling of thunder, the roar of the sea, the voices of various animals. These sounds symbolise certain phenomena and thus are believed to produce them magically. Or else they express certain emotional states associated with the desire which is to be realised by means of the magic.

The second element, very conspicuous in primitive spells, is the use of words which invoke, state, or command the desired aim. Thus the sorcerer will mention all the symptoms of the disease which he is inflicting, or in the lethal formula he will describe the end of his victim. In healing magic the wizard will give word-pictures of perfect health and bodily strength. In economic magic the growing of plants, the approach of animals, the arrival of fish in shoals are depicted. Or again the magician uses words and sentences which express the emotion under the stress of which he works his magic, and the action which gives expression to this emotion. The sorcerer in tones of fury will have to repeat such verbs as " I break—I twist—I burn—I destroy," enumerating with each of them the various parts of the body and internal organs of his victim. In all this we see that the spells are built very much on the same pattern as the rites and the words selected for the same reasons as the substances of magic

Thirdly there is an element in almost every spell to which there is no counterpart in ritual. I mean the mythological allusions, the references to ancestors and culture heroes from whom this magic has been received. And that brings us to perhaps the most important point in the subject, to the traditional setting of magic.

2. The Tradition of Magic

Tradition, which, as we have several times insisted, reigns supreme in primitive civilisation, gathers in great abundance round magical ritual and cult. In the case of any important magic we invariably find the story accounting for its existence. Such a story tells when and where it entered the possession of man, how it became the property of a local group or of a family or clan. But such a story is not the story of its origins. Magic never " originated," it never has been made or invented. All magic simply " was " from the beginning an essential adjunct of all such things and processes as vitally interest man and yet elude his normal rational efforts. The spell, the rite, and the thing which they govern are coeval.

Thus, in Central Australia, all magic existed and has been inherited from the *alcheringa* times, when it came about like everything else. In Melanesia all magic comes from a time when humanity lived underground and when magic was a natural knowledge of ancestral man. In higher societies magic is often derived from spirits and demons, but even these, as a rule, originally received and did not invent it. Thus the belief in the primeval natural existence of magic is universal. As its counterpart we find the conviction that only by an absolutely unmodified immaculate transmission does magic retain its efficiency. The slightest alteration from the original pattern would be fatal. There is, then, the idea that between the object and its magic there exists an essential nexus. Magic is the quality of the thing, or rather, of the relation between man and the thing, for though never man-made it is always made for man. In all tradition, in all mythology, magic is always found only in the possession of man and through the knowledge of man or man-like being. It implies the performing magician quite as much the thing to be charmed and the means of charming. It is part of the original endowment of primeval humanity, of the *mura-mura* or *alcheringa* of Australia, of the subterrestrial humanity of Melanesia, of the people of the magical Golden Age all the world over.

Magic is not only human in its embodiment, but also in its subject-matter : it refers principally to human activities and states, hunting, gardening, fishing, trading, love-making, disease, and death. It is not directed so much to nature as to man's relation to nature and to the human activities which affect it. Moreover, the effects of magic are usually conceived not as a product of nature influenced by the charm, but as something specially magical, something which nature cannot produce, but only the power of magic. The graver forms of disease, love in its passionate phases, the desire for a ceremonial exchange and other similar manifestations in the human organism and mind, are the direct product of the spell and rite. Magic is thus not derived from an observation of nature or knowledge of its laws, it is a primeval possession of man to be known only through tradition and affirming man's autonomous power of creating desired ends.

Thus, the force of magic is not a universal force residing everywhere, flowing where it will or it is willed to. Magic is the one and only specific power, a force unique of its kind, residing exclusively in man, let loose only by his magical act, gushing out with his voice, conveyed by the casting forth of the rite.

It may be here mentioned that the human body, being the receptacle of magic and the channel of its flow, must be submitted to various conditions. Thus the magician has to keep all sorts of taboos, or else the spell might be injured, especially as in certain parts of the world, in Melanesia for instance, the spell resides in the magician's belly, which is the seat of memory as well as of food. When necessary it is summoned up to the larynx, which is the seat of intelligence, and thence sent forth by the voice, the main organ of the human mind. Thus, not only is magic an essentially human possession, but it is literally and actually enshrined in man and can be handed on only from man to man, according to very strict rules of magical filiation, initiation, and instruction. It is thus never conceived as a force of nature, residing in things, acting independently of man, to be found out and learned by him, by any of those proceedings by which he gains his ordinary knowledge of nature.

3. *Mana and the Virtue of Magic*

The obvious result of this is that all the theories which lay *mana* and similar conceptions at the basis of magic are pointing altogether in the wrong direction. For if the virtue of magic is exclusively localised in man, can be wielded by him only under very special conditions and in a traditionally prescribed manner, it certainly is not a force such as the one described by Dr. Codrington : "This *mana* is not fixed in anything and can be conveyed in almost anything." Mana also "acts in all ways for good and evil . . . shows itself in physical force or in any kind of power and excellence which a man possesses." Now it is clear that this force as described by Codrington is almost the exact opposite of the magical virtue as found embodied in the mythology of savages, in their behaviour, and in the structure of their magical formulas. For the real virtue of magic, as I know it from Melanesia, is fixed only in the spell and in its rite, and it cannot be "conveyed in" anything, but can be conveyed only by its strictly defined procedure. It never acts "in all ways," but only in ways specified by tradition. It never shows itself in physical force, while its effects upon the powers and excellences of man are strictly limited and defined.

And again, the similar conception found among the North American Indians cannot have anything to do with the specialised concrete virtue of magic. For of the *wakan* of the Dakota we read "all life is *wakan*. So also is everything which exhibits power, whether in action, as the winds and drifting clouds, or in passive endurance, as the boulder by the wayside . . . It embraces all mystery, all secret power, all divinity." Of the *orenda*, a word taken from the Iroquois, we are told : "This potence is held to be the property of all things . . . the rocks, the waters, the tides, the plants and the trees, the animals and man, the wind and the storms, the clouds and the thunders and the lightnings . . . by the inchoate mentality of man, it is regarded as the efficient cause of all phenomena, all the activities of his environment."

After what has been established about the essence of magical power, it hardly needs emphasising that there is little in common between the concepts of the *mana* type and the special virtue of magical spell and rite. We have seen that the key-note of all magical belief is the sharp distinction between the traditional force of magic on the one hand and the other forces and powers with which man and nature are endowed. The conceptions of the *wakan, orenda,* and *mana* class which include all sorts of forces and powers, besides that of magic, are simply an example of an early generalisation of a crude metaphysical concept such as is found in several other savage words also, extremely important for our knowledge of primitive mentality but, as far as our present data go, opening only a problem as to the relation between the early concepts of "force," "the supernatural," and "the virtue of magic." It is impossible to decide, with the summary information at our disposal, what is the primary meaning of these compound concepts : that of physical force and that of supernatural efficiency. In the American concepts the emphasis seems to be on the former, in the Oceanic on the latter. What I want to make clear is that in all the attempts to understand native mentality it is necessary to study and describe the types of behaviour first and to explain their vocabulary by their customs and their life. There is no more fallacious guide of knowledge than language, and in anthropology the "ontological argument" is specially dangerous.

It was necessary to enter into this problem in detail, for the theory of *mana* as the essence of primitive magic and religion has been so brilliantly advocated and so recklessly handled that it must be realised first that our knowledge of the *mana*, notably in Melanesia, is somewhat contradictory, and especially that we have hardly any data at all showing just how this conception enters into religious or magical cult and belief.

One thing is certain : magic is not born of an abstract conception of universal power, subsequently applied to concrete cases. It has undoubtedly arisen independently in a number of actual situations. Each type of magic, born of its own situation and of the emotional tension thereof, is due to the spontaneous flow of ideas and the spontaneous reaction of man. It is the uniformity of the mental process in each case which has led to certain universal features of magic and to the general conceptions which we find at the basis of man's magical thought and behaviour. It will be necessary to give now an analysis of the situations of magic and the experiences which they provoke.

4. *Magic and Experience*

So far we have been dealing mainly with native ideas and with native views of magic. This has led us to a point where the savage simply affirms that magic gives man the power over certain things. Now we must analyse this belief from the point of view of the sociological observer. Let us realise once more the type of situation in which we find magic. Man, engaged in a series of practical activities, comes to a gap ; the hunter is disappointed by his quarry, the sailor misses propitious winds, the canoe-builder has to deal with some material of which he is never certain that it will stand the strain, or the healthy person suddenly feels his strength failing. What does man do naturally under such conditions, setting aside all magic, belief and ritual ? Forsaken by his knowledge, baffled by his past experience and by his technical skill, he realises his impotence. Yet his desire grips him only the more strongly ; his anxiety, his fears and hopes, induce a tension in his organism which drives him to some sort of activity. Whether he be savage or civilised, whether in possession of magic or entirely ignorant of its existence, passive inaction, the only thing dictated by reason, is the last thing in which he can acquiesce. His nervous system and his whole organism drive him to some substitute activity. Obsessed by the idea of the desired end, he sees it and feels it. His organism reproduces the acts suggested by the anticipations of hope, dictated by the emotion of passion so strongly felt.

The man under the sway of impotent fury or dominated by thwarted hate spontaneously clenches his fist and carries out imaginary thrusts at his enemy, muttering imprecations, casting words of hatred and anger against him. The lover aching for his unattainable or irresponsive beauty sees her in his visions, addresses her, and entreats and commands her favours, feeling himself accepted, pressing her to his bosom in his dreams. The anxious fisherman or hunter sees in his imagination the quarry enmeshed in the nets, the animal attained by the spear ; he utters their names, describes in words his visions of the magnificent catch, he even breaks out into gestures of mimic representation of what he desires. The man lost at night in the woods or the jungle, beset by superstitious fear, sees around him the haunting demons, addresses them, tries to ward off, to frighten them, or shrinks from them in fear, like an animal which attempts to save itself by feigning death.

These reactions to overwhelming emotion or obsessive desire are natural responses of man to such a situation, based on a universal psycho-physiological mechanism. They engender what could be called extended expressions of emotion in act and in word, the threatening gestures of impotent anger and its maledictions, the spontaneous enactment of the desired end in a practical impasse, the passionate fondling gestures of the lover, and so on. All these spontaneous acts and spontaneous words make man forecast the images of the wished-for results, or express his passion in uncontrollable gestures, or break out into words which give vent to desire and anticipate its end.

And what is the purely intellectual process, the conviction formed during such a free outburst of emotion in words and deeds ? First there surges a clear image of the desired end, of the hated person, of the feared danger or ghost. And each image is blended with its specific passion, which drives us to assume an active attitude towards that image. When passion reaches the breaking point at which man loses control over himself, the words which he utters, his blind behaviour, allow the pent-up physiological tension to flow over. But over all this outburst presides the image of the end. It supplies the motive-force of the reaction, it apparently organises and directs words and acts towards a definite purpose. The substitute action in which the passion finds its vent, and which is due to impotence, has subjectively all the value of a real action, to which emotion would, if not impeded, naturally have led.

As the tension spends itself in these words and gestures the obsessing visions fade away, the desired end seems nearer satisfaction, we regain our balance, once more at harmony with life. And we remain with a conviction that the words of malediction and the gestures of fury have travelled towards the hated person and hit their target ; that the imploration of love, the visionary embraces, cannot have remained unanswered, that the visionary attainment of success in our pursuit cannot have been without a beneficial influence on the pending issue. In the case of fear, as the emotion which has led us to frenzied behaviour gradually subsides, we feel that it is this behaviour that has driven away the terrors. In brief, a strong emotional experience which spends itself in a purely subjective flow of images, words, and acts of behaviour, leaves a very deep conviction of its reality, as if of some practical and positive achievement, as if of something done by a power revealed to man. This power, born of mental and physiological obsession, seems to get hold of us from outside, and to primitive man, or to the credulous and untutored mind of all ages, the spontaneous spell, the spontaneous rite, and the spontaneous belief in their efficiency must appear as a direct revelation from some external and no doubt impersonal sources.

When we compare this spontaneous ritual and verbiage of overflowing passion or desire with traditionally fixed magical ritual and with the principles embodied in magical spells and substances, the striking resemblance of the two products shows that they are not independent of each other. Magical ritual, most of the principles of magic, most of its spells and substances, have been revealed to man in those passionate experiences which assail him in the impasses of his instinctive life and of his practical pursuits, in those gaps and breaches left in the ever-imperfect wall of culture which he erects between himself and the besetting temptations and dangers of his destiny. In this I think we have to recognise not only one of the sources but the very fountainhead of magical belief.

To most types of magical ritual, therefore, there corresponds a spontaneous ritual of emotional expression or of a forecast of the desired end. To most features of magical spell, to the commands, invocations, metaphors, there corresponds a natural flow of words, in malediction, in entreaty, in exorcism, and in the descriptions of unfulfilled wishes. To every belief in magical efficiency there can be laid in parallel one of those illusions of subjective experience, transient in the mind of the civilised rationalist, though even there never quite absent, but powerful and convincing to the simple man in every culture, and, above all, to the primitive savage mind.

Thus the foundations of magical belief and practice are not taken from the air, but are due to a number of experiences actually lived through, in which man receives the revelation of his power to attain the desired end. We must now ask : What is the relation between the promises contained in such experience and their fulfilment in real life? Plausible though the fallacious claims of magic might be to primitive man, how is it that they have remained so long unexposed ?

The answer to this is that, first, it is a well-known fact that in human memory the testimony of a positive case always over-shadows the negative one. One gain easily outweighs several losses. Thus the instances which affirm magic always loom far more conspicuously than those which deny it. But there are other facts which endorse by a real or apparent testimony the claims of magic. We have seen that magical ritual must have originated from a revelation in a real experience. But the man who from such an experience conceived, formulated, and gave to his tribesmen the nucleus of a new magical performance—acting, be it remembered, in perfect good faith—must have been a man of genius. The men who inherited and wielded his magic after him, no doubt always building it out and developing it, while believing that they were simply following up the tradition, must have been always men of great intelligence, energy, and power of enterprise. They would be the men successful in all emergencies. It is an empirical fact that in all savage societies magic and outstanding personality go hand in hand. Thus magic also coincides with personal success, skill, courage, and mental power. No wonder that it is considered a source of success.

This personal renown of the magician and its importance in enhancing the belief about the efficiency of magic are the cause of an interesting phenomenon : what may be called the *current mythology* of magic. Round every big magician there arises a halo made up of stories about his wonderful cures or kills, his catches, his victories, his conquests in love. In every savage society such stories form the backbone of belief in magic, for, supported as they are by the emotional experiences which everyone has had himself, the running chronicle of magical miracles establishes its claims beyond any doubt or cavil. Every eminent practitioner, besides his traditional claim, besides the filiation with his predecessors, makes his personal warrant of wonder-working.

Thus myth is not a dead product of past ages, merely surviving 's an idle narrative. It is a living force, constantly producing new phenomena, constantly surrounding magic by new testimonies. Magic moves in the glory of past tradition, but it also creates its atmosphere of ever-nascent myth. As there is the body of legends already fixed, standardised, and constituting the folk-lore of the tribe, so there is always a stream of narratives flowing freely from present-day occurrences, frequently similar in kind to those of the mythological time. Magic is the bridge between the golden age of primeval craft and the wonder-working power of to-day. Hence the formulas are full of mythical allusions, which, when uttered, unchain the powers of the past and cast them into the present.

With this we see also the rôle and meaning of mythology in a new light. Myth is not a savage speculation about origins of things born out of philosophic interest. Neither is it the result of the contemplation of nature—a sort of symbolical representation of its laws. It is the historical statement of one of those events which once for all vouch for the truth of a certain form of magic. Sometimes it is the actual record of a magical revelation coming directly from the first man to whom magic was revealed in some dramatic occurrence. More often it bears on its surface that it is merely a statement of how magic came into the possession of a clan or a community or a tribe. In all cases it is a warrant of its truth, a pedigree of its filiation, a charter of its claims to validity. And as we have seen, myth is the natural result of human faith, because every power must give signs of its efficiency, must act and be known to act, if people are to believe in its virtue. Every belief engenders its mythology, for there is no faith without miracles, and the main myth recounts simply the primeval miracle of the magic.

Myth, it may be added at once, can attach itself not only to

magic but to any form of social power or social claim.   It is used
always to account for extraordinary privileges or duties, for great
social inequalities, for severe burdens of rank, whether this be very
high or very low.   Also the beliefs and powers of religion are
traced to their sources by mythological accounts.   Religious myth,
however, is rather an explicit dogma, the belief in the nether
world, in creation, in the nature of divinities, spun out into a story.
Sociological myth, on the other hand, especially in primitive
cultures, is usually blended with legends about the sources of
magical power.   It can be said without exaggeration that the
most typical, most highly developed, mythology in primitive
societies is that of magic, and the function of myth is not to explain
but to vouch for, not to satisfy curiosity but to give confidence in
power, not to spin out yarns but to establish the validity of belief.
The deep connection between myth and cult, the pragmatic
function of myth in enforcing belief, has been so persistently
overlooked in favour of the ætiological or explanatory theory of
myth that it was necessary to dwell on this point.

5. *Magic and Science*

We have had to make a digression on mythology since we found
that myth is engendered by the real or imaginary success of witchcraft.   But what about its failures ?   With all the strength which
magic draws from the spontaneous belief and spontaneous ritual of
intense desire or thwarted emotion, with all the force given it by
the personal prestige, the social power and success common in the
magician and practitioner—still there are failures and breakdowns,
and we should vastly underrate the savage's intelligence, logic, and
grasp of experience if we assumed that he is not aware of it and
that he fails to account for it.

First of all, magic is surrounded by strict conditions : exact
remembrance of a spell, unimpeachable performance of the rite,
unswerving adhesion to the taboos and observances which shackle
the magician.   If any one of these is neglected, failure of
magic follows.   And then, even if magic be done in the most
perfect manner, its effects can be equally well undone : for
against every magic there can be also counter-magic.   If magic, as
we have shown, is begotten by the union of man's steadfast desire
with the wayward whim of chance, then every desire, positive or
negative, may—nay, must—have its magic.   Now in all his social

and worldly ambitions, in all his strivings to catch good fortune and trap propitious luck, man moves in an atmosphere of rivalry, of envy, and of spite. For luck, possessions, even health, are matters of degree and of comparison, and if your neighbour owns more cattle, more wives, more health, and more power than yourself, you feel dwarfed in all you own and all you are. And such is human nature that a man's desire is as much satisfied by the thwarting of others as by the advancement of himself. To this sociological play of desire and counter-desire, of ambition and spite, of success and envy, there corresponds the play of magic and counter-magic, or of magic white and black.

In Melanesia, where I have studied this problem at first-hand, there is not one single magical act which is not firmly believed to possess a counter-act which, when stronger, can completely annihilate its effects. In certain types of magic, as for instance that of health and disease, the formulas actually go in couples. A sorcerer who learns a performance by which to cause a definite disease will at the same time learn the formula and the rite which can annul completely the effects of his evil magic. In love, again, not only does there exist a belief that, when two formulas are performed to win the same heart, the stronger will override the weaker one, but there are spells uttered directly to alienate the affections of the sweetheart or wife of another. Whether this duality of magic is as consistently carried out all the world over as in the Trobriands it is difficult to say, but that the twin forces of white and black, of positive and negative, exist everywhere is beyond doubt. Thus the failures of magic can be always accounted for by the slip of memory, by slovenliness in performance or in observance of a taboo and, last not least, by the fact that someone else has performed some counter-magic.

We are now in a position to state more fully the relation between magic and science already outlined above. Magic is akin to science in that it always has a definite aim intimately associated with human instincts, needs, and pursuits. The magic art is directed towards the attainment of practical aims. Like the other arts and crafts, it is also governed by a theory, by a system of principles which dictate the manner in which the act has to be performed in order to be effective. In analysing magical spells, rites, and substances we have found that there is a number of general principles which govern them. Both science and magic develop a special technique. In magic, as in the other arts, man can undo what he has done or mend the damage which he has wrought. In fact, in magic the quantitative equivalents of black and white seem to be much more exact and the effects of witchcraft much more completely eradicated by counter-witchcraft than is possible in any practical art or craft. Thus both magic and science show certain similarities, and, with Sir James Frazer, we can appropriately call magic a pseudo-science.

And the spurious character of this pseudo-science is not hard to detect. Science, even as represented by the primitive knowledge of savage man, is based on the normal universal experience of everyday life, experience won in man's struggle with nature for his subsistence and safety, founded on observation, fixed by reason. Magic is based on specific experience of emotional states in which man observes not nature but himself, in which the truth is revealed not by reason but by the play of emotions upon the human organism. Science is founded on the conviction that experience, effort, and reason are valid ; magic on the belief that hope cannot fail nor desire deceive. The theories of knowledge are dictated by logic, those of magic by the association of ideas under the influence of desire. As a matter of empirical fact the body of rational knowledge and the body of magical lore are incorporated each in a different tradition, in a different social setting and in a different type of activity, and all these differences are clearly recognised by the savages. The one constitutes the domain of the profane ; the other, hedged round by observances, mysteries, and taboos, makes up half of the domain of the sacred.

6. *Magic and Religion*

Both magic and religion arise and function in situations of emotional stress : crises of life, lacunae in important pursuits, death and initiation into tribal mysteries, unhappy love and un-satisfied hate. Both magic and religion open up escapes from such situations and such impasses as offer no empirical way out except by ritual and belief into the domain of the supernatural. This domain embraces, in religion, beliefs in ghosts, spirits, the primitive forebodings of providence, the guardians of tribal mysteries ; in magic, the primeval force and virtue of magic. Both magic and religion are based strictly on mythological tradition, and they also both exist in the atmosphere of the miraculous, in a constant revelation of their wonder-working power. They both are surrounded by taboos and observances which mark off their acts from those of the profane world.

Now what distinguishes magic from religion ? We have taken for our starting-point a most definite and tangible distinction : we have defined, within the domain of the sacred, magic as a practical art consisting of acts which are only means to a definite end expected to follow later on ; religion as a body of self-contained acts being themselves the fulfilment of their purpose. We can now follow up this difference into its deeper layers. The practical art of magic has its limited, circumscribed technique : spell, rite, and the condition of the performer form always its trite trinity. Religion, with its complex aspects and purposes, has no such simple technique, and its unity can be seen neither in the form of its acts nor even in the uniformity of its subject-matter, but rather in the function which it fulfils and in the value of its belief and ritual. Again, the belief in magic, corresponding to its plain practical nature, is extremely simple. It is always the affirmation of man's power to cause certain definite effects by a definite spell and rite. In religion, on the other hand, we have a whole supernatural world of faith : the pantheon of spirits and demons, the benevolent powers of totem, guardian spirit, tribal all-father, the vision of the future life, create a second supernatural reality for primitive man. The mythology of religion is also more varied and complex as well as more creative. It usually centres round the various tenets of belief, and it develops them into cosmogonies, tales of culture-heroes, accounts of the doings of gods and demigods. In magic, important as it is, mythology is an ever-recurrent boasting about man's primeval achievements.

Magic, the specific art for specific ends, has in every one of its forms come once into the possession of man, and it had to be handed over in direct filiation from generation to generation. Hence it remains from the earliest times in the hands of specialists, and the first profession of mankind is that of a wizard or witch. Religion, on the other hand, in primitive conditions is an affair of all, in which everyone takes an active and equivalent part. Every member of the tribe has to go through initiation, and then himself initiates others. Everyone wails, mourns, digs the grave and commemorates, and in due time everyone has his turn in being mourned and commemorated. Spirits are for all, and everyone becomes a spirit. The only specialisation in religion—that is, early spiritualistic mediumism—is not a profession but a personal gift. One more difference between magic and religion is the play of black and white in witchcraft, while religion in its primitive stages has but little of the contrast between good and evil, between the beneficent and malevolent powers. This is due also to the practical character of magic, which aims at direct quantitative results, while early religion, though essentially moral, has to deal with fateful, irremediable happenings and supernatural forces and beings, so that the undoing of things done by man does not enter into it. The maxim that fear first made gods in the universe is certainly not true in the light of anthropology.

In order to grasp the difference between religion and magic and to gain a clear vision of the three-cornered constellation of magic, re'igion, and science, let us briefly realise the cultural function of each. The function of primitive knowledge and its value have been assessed already and indeed are not difficult to grasp. By acquainting man with his surroundings, by allowing him to use the forces of nature, science, primitive knowledge, bestows on man an immense biological advantage, setting him far above all the rest of creation. The function of religion and its value we have learned to understand in the survey of savage creeds and cults given above. We have shown there that religious faith establishes, fixes, and enhances all valuable mental attitudes, such as reverence for tradition, harmony with environment, courage and confidence in the struggle with difficulties and at the prospect of death. This belief, embodied and maintained by cult and ceremonial, has an immense biological value, and so reveals to primitive man truth in the wider, pragmatic sense of the word.

What is the cultural function of magic? We have seen that all the instincts and emotions, all practical activities, lead man into impasses where gaps in his knowledge and the limitations of his early power of observation and reason betray him at a crucial moment. Human organism reacts to this in spontaneous outbursts, in which rudimentary modes of behaviour and rudimentary beliefs in their efficiency are engendered. Magic fixes upon these beliefs and rudimentary rites and standardises them into permanent traditional forms. Thus magic supplies primitive man with a number of ready-made ritual acts and beliefs, with a definite mental and practical technique which serves to bridge over the dangerous gaps in every important pursuit or critical situation. It enables man to carry out with confidence his important tasks, to maintain his poise and his mental integrity in fits of anger, in the throes of hate, of unrequited love, of despair and anxiety. The function of magic is to ritualise man's optimism, to enhance his faith in the victory of hope over fear. Magic expresses the greater value for man of confidence over doubt, of steadfastness over vacillation, of optimism over pessimism.

Looking from far and above, from our high places of safety in developed civilisation, it is easy to see all the crudity and irrelevance of magic. But without its power and guidance early man could not have mastered his practical difficulties as he has done, nor could man have advanced to the higher stages of culture. Hence the universal occurrence of magic in primitive societies and its enormous sway. Hence do we find magic an invariable adjunct of all important activities. I think we must see in it the embodiment of the sublime folly of hope, which has yet been the best school of man's character.[1]

[1] *Bibliographical Note.* The most important works on Primitive Religion, Magic and Knowledge, referred to in the text, directly or implicitly, are : E. B. Tylor, *Primitive Culture*, 4th ed., 2 vols., 1903 ; J. F. McLennan, *Studies in Ancient History*, 1886 ; W. Robertson Smith, *Lectures on the Religion of the Semites*, 1889 ; A. Lang, *The Making of Religion*, 1889, and *Magic and Religion*, 1901. These, though out of date as regards material and some of their conclusions, are still inspiring and deserve study. Entirely fresh and representing the most modern points of view are the classical works of J. G. Frazer, *The Golden Bough*, 3rd ed., in 12 vols., 1911–14 (also abridged edition, 1 vol.) ; Totemism and Exogamy, 4 vols., 1910 ; *Folk-Lore in the Old Testament*, 3 vols., 1919 ; *The Belief in Immortality and the Worship of the Dead*, so far 3 vols., 1913–24. With Frazer's works should be read the two excellent contributions of E. Crawley, *The Mystic Rose*, 1902 (out of print, new edition forthcoming), and *The Tree of Life*, 1905. Also, on the subject of the history of morals, the two extremely important works : E. Westermarck, *The Origin and Development of the Moral Ideas*, 2 vols., 1905, and L. T. Hobhouse, *Morals in Evolution*, 2nd ed., 1915. Further : D. G. Brinton, *Religions of Primitive Peoples*, 1899 ; K. Th. Preuss, *Der Ursprung der Religion und Kunst*, 1904 (in " Globus," serially) ; R. R. Marett, *The Threshold of Religion*, 1909 ; H. Hubert et M. Mauss, *Mélanges d'Histoire des Religions*, 1909 ; A. van Gennep, *Les Rites de Passage*, 1909 ; J. Harrison, *Themis* (1910–2) ; I. King, *The Development of Religion*, 1910 ; W. Schmidt, *Der Ursprung der Gottesidee*, 1912 ; E. Durkheim, *Les Formes élémentaires de la Vie religieuse*, 1912 (also English translation) ; P. Ehrenreich, *Die Allgemeine Mythologie*, 1910 ; R. H. Lowie, *Primitive Religion*, 1925. An encyclopaedic survey of facts and opinions will be found in Wilh. Wundt's voluminous *Völkerpsychologie*, 1904 ff. ; J. Hastings' *Encyclopaedia of Religion and Ethics* is excellent and indispensable to the serious student. Primitive Knowledge in particular is discussed by

L. Lévy-Bruhl in *Les fonctions mentales dans les sociétées inférieures*, 1910 ; F. Boas, *The Mind of Primitive Man*, 1910 ; R. Thurnwald, *Psychologie des Primitiven Menschen*, in the *Handbuch der vergl. Psychol.*, edited by G. Kafka, 1922 ; A. A. Goldenweiser, *Early Civilization*, 1923. *Cf.* also R. H. Lowie, *Primitive Society*, 1920 ; and A. L. Kroeber, *Anthropology*, 1923. For fuller information upon the natives of Melanesia, who loom largely in the foregoing descriptions, *cf.* R. H. Codrington, *The Melanesians*, 1891 ; C. G. Seligman, *The Melanesians of British New Guinea*, 1910 ; R. Thurnwald, *Forschungen auf den Solomoinseln und Bismarckarchipel*, 2 vols., 1912, and *Die Gemeinde der Bánaro*, 1921 ; B. Malinowski, *The Natives of Mailu*, 1915 (in Trans. of the R. Soc. of S. Australia, vol. xxxix) ; *Baloma*, article in the Journ. of the R. Anthrop. Institute, 1916 ; *Argonauts of the Western Pacific*, 1922 ; and three articles in *Psyche*, III., 2 ; IV., 4 ; V., 3, 1923–5.

HISTORICAL RELATIONS
OF RELIGION AND SCIENCE
BY CHARLES SINGER

CONTENTS

1. Introduction

IN this chapter we are concerned with the history of the *relationship*, one to another, of two great departments of human activity. Our treatment will therefore need to be very different from what it would be if we were discussing either department separately. Looking back through history we can see that always and everywhere, since man attained the level of civilisation, there has been activity in both departments. Yet only under certain circumstances do the two sides of man's nature represented by these departments come to affect each other. It is often the case therefore that periods and movements that are of great importance for the history of religion as such, or for the history of science as such, may have very little significance for the end we have here in view ; while periods on which historians of science and historians of religion lay but scant stress may be of great importance for our purpose.

Apart from the necessarily imperfect character of a short sketch covering so vast a period of time, there is a certain respect in which such an account must perforce remain extremely unsatisfactory. It is impossible in such an historical account to treat any aspect of religion save its formal and external exhibition. Thus we shall be dealing with precisely that aspect which many will think the least important in the religious life. Yet it is only when religion expresses itself in formal and external fashion that it can be said to come into contact with the scientific standpoint. The reader must realise this limitation at the very outset and I would beg him to bear it in his mind throughout, as I have borne it in mine. Unless we accept such a limitation, the attempt on which we are embarked would involve no less than a history of the human heart. I do not believe it would be possible to write such a history, for the topic is unsuited to the historical method. Nor, if such a history could be written, would it have any clear relation to the development of scientific thought.

But I must draw my reader's attention to a further limitation which is not inherent in the method but is self-imposed. I am to discuss the historical development of the relations of religion and science. In doing this, within the space at my disposal, I shall not concern myself greatly with such solutions as have been propounded at various periods for the reconciliation of the two modes of thought. I shall merely seek to indicate how the two activities have diverged, approached, united, receded, or have run parallel to each other, or again, how they have crossed each other's paths and reinforced or injured each other during the passage of time. It is specially my intention to avoid any discussion of recent controversies or of modern attempts to heal such breaches as may exist between religion and science. The treatment of these must be the task of others. I therefore omit more modern and contemporary history, and there is the greater reason to do this because, as it seems to me, the position has not fundamentally altered for about two centuries. Moreover, many of the points of contact between religion and science are better brought out in the simpler atmosphere of ancient culture than in our own complex civilisation.

Lastly, consideration of space demands the omission of all details concerning the lives and characters of the protagonists of our story. We are concerned here only with the realm of thought.

2. *Primitive Man*

Until man reaches a certain level of civilisation he forms no clear idea of the world as a whole. In spite of the number and strangeness of his myths, in spite of the vast stress that he lays on ceremonial, in spite of the bizarre character of the beliefs that form the background of his magical practices—man on the " anthropological level " is yet intensely practical in all his aims and ideas. His actions are controlled by his immediate ends, the acquisition of food, the avoidance of disease, the production of offspring. For such purposes he must placate powers whose motives he hardly seeks to analyse. Still less does he seek nor is he able to attain any comprehensive view of the essential nature of these powers. As he emerges from the savage state, the poor attempts that he makes to express his views as to the nature of these higher powers are still almost incoherent. Man is as yet without any *system* either of philosophy or of religion in our sense of the words.

But has the savage any science ? He has certainly some of those elements which become at a later stage incorporated into the scientific mood. Even palaeolithic man, for instance, could observe and record with marvellous accuracy the form and habits of the beasts on which he preyed. Yet, despite these powers and aspirations, we cannot admit that man in the pre-civilised stages can be said to have the capacity that we call scientific.

Science involves, and must involve, something far more than the mere power to observe and record. It is true that much of scientific practice is little else than the systematic collection and record of observations, and our savage has perhaps in certain matters attained to the systematic stage. But behind the vast systematic collection of observations that occupies the main scientific effort throughout the ages there is a motive, an aspiration, that is absent from the savage mind. It is just that motive which makes science. The scientific motive is provided by a conscious faith in the existence of general laws underlying the multiplicity of phenomena. Science is the purposeful search for such general laws that can then be used to link together the observed phenomena. The savage has none of this faith, this aspiration. If he had, he would cast off his magic and cease to be a savage. This faith, we have said, is a thing consciously held. It is something moreover which is by no means necessarily implied when the savage resorts, as he often does, to reason. While many modern anthropologists are disposed to deny the existence of a pre-logical stage of human development, they must, we believe, admit a *pre-scientific stage*. Where there is no science or where science is not yet differentiated, we cannot hope to trace anything which concerns us here.[1]

3. *Early Religions*

Let us now glance at the religious practices and beliefs of the savage. We say religious *practices and beliefs* because on this level man cannot be said to profess *a* religion. We observe that

[1] I find that what I have written above concerning the absence of science among peoples on the anthropological level traverses statements in the previous essay. Dr. Malinowski regards science as a very early development. The difference between us is, however, almost entirely verbal. It is due to the fact that I have interpreted *science* as the self-conscious investigation of nature with the direct and avowed object of educing general laws. Such is science as we know it to-day and as the Greeks knew it. Dr. Malinowski, however, rightly considers that there are certain scientific elements even in the most primitive culture and it is these *elements* that he calls *science*. I should describe this early stage as *science in the making*. If the reader will bear these terminological differences in mind, he will perceive that there is little or no difference between Dr. Malinowski and myself.

the religious beliefs and practices of a savage tribe are seldom sharply marked off from those of neighbouring tribes, nor do the legends and beliefs of such peoples provide anything in the way of a complete explanation of life. An actual religious system implies a great mental advance from the savage state. It involves the advent of what we may call " mental coherence," an attempt to understand the world as a whole and an acceptance of the view that the world, being comprehensible, must have certain governing principles which can be widely traced through it.

Such religions or systems of religion we encounter in the Empires of the ancient East. Egypt, for instance, provides us with a whole series of *systems* of theology. The later Egyptian religion is a syncretic product. In it the series of earlier systems have become fused and often confused. It is easy, however, to see in the final product the various strata of Egyptian theology which succeeded and, to some extent, replaced each other. The fusion, as in the case of modern theological systems, is always incomplete and the joints " show through." As with nearly all great religions the final result is a patchwork. Yet it is evident that each system in its day was an attempt to explain Man and the World and their relation to each other. These systems deal too with man's origin and his fate. They cover the whole field not only of what we now call religion but also of what we now call science. In other words, religion and science are both present but are so interconnected that they cannot be separated.

A similar system or series of systems is traceable in the beliefs of the Mesopotamian peoples. Best known to us, however, is the kindred religion which arose in Palestine. In the beliefs of the Hebrews, as in those of the Egyptian and Mesopotamian folk, we may detect successive attempts to " cover the phenomena," the actual succession being still traceable in the composite record that has come down to us. It is important for us to note that in the early Hebrew religious system, as in the other religions of the ancient East, there is no trace of a suggestion that natural knowledge, or any conception of the nature of the world, was regarded as an impediment or handicap to religion. Thus the fields of religion and science have not yet been differentiated. It would therefore be idle to seek here evidence of any opposition between the two.

Nevertheless, even in this stage we see man giving reasons for the faith that is in him. Religions on this level seek to justify themselves and to explain their origin and nature in a manner that shall conform with observed phenomena. | There is thus a tendency to develop ritual into a legal system, and attempts are consciously made to fix tradition. It is a stage that clearly corresponds to the present needs of the vast majority of civilised mankind, and is to a large extent expressed to-day by the great religions. These all have sought to provide their followers with an explanation of the world in which they live. Such cosmologies were once the very bases of the appeal that these religions made to the rationalising mind. Historically we now know that on another mental level such cosmologies form an obstacle where they were once an aid.

4. *Earlier Greek Thought*

It was, however, neither in Palestine, nor in Mesopotamia, nor in the valley of the Nile that the scientific element was first differentiated from the religious. That task was the work of the Hellenes.

When we examine the literary monuments of the classical culture—of which we are the heirs and the Greeks the earlier and main intellectual representatives—we cannot fail to be impressed by the vastness of its interests, the enormous mental energy that it displays and the bulk and completeness of its remains. Considering these things the comparative backwardness of the religious development of that culture is a very striking feature. Greek religion—using that word in the restricted sense—never reached the rational standard of the Hebrew religion. Thus no complete and worked-out Greek cosmology, incorporated in a religious atmosphere, has come down to us. The popular Greek religion, in fact, never reached the coherent level of the Hebrew, or reached it only in later times and then in competition with philosophical or other systems which themselves made religious claims, and notably in contact with Christianity.

It has often been remarked that the Greeks had no Canon of sacred literature. Yet even more noteworthy is it that in the whole corpus of pagan classical literature—Greek and Latin— there has survived no work by a priest. Imagine the corpus of medieval and modern literature from which the clergy and almost all ecclesiastical influence had been excluded !

'The absence of a sacred Canon and the relatively low grade of their religion is in contrast to their scientific and philosophical development for which, as some think, way was thus made. At a remarkably early stage in their development the Greeks observed not only that their world was subject to laws, but that by investigation these laws are ever further and further discoverable. A belief in such natural laws plays no part in the more ancient Hebrew scriptures, which, moreover, contain very little of that curiosity which is the parent of science. It was with the Ionian Greeks that the scientific idea was born, and it can be traced back among them with some clearness to the sixth century B.C.

In order to avoid misunderstanding it is necessary to enlarge a little on this statement that the scientific idea begins with the Ionian Greeks of the sixth century B.C. It is not suggested that the careful and accurate observation of nature began with them—in such observation every hunter must be an expert, and we have evidence of its existence far back in palaeolithic times. Nor is it even suggested that the Ionian Greeks were the first to formulate general laws concerning natural phenomena. Thus the Ahmes papyrus of about 1700 B.C., believed to be founded on much older work, shows that the Egyptians were in possession of certain mathematical laws even at that date. The Ionian Thales of Miletus (*c.* 640–*c.* 546 B.C.), the founder of Greek geometry, astronomy, and philosophy, predicted the eclipse that took place on May 28, 585 B.C., but he did this from data derived from Mesopotamian sources. Astronomical observatories were, as we know, to be found in the great cities of the Euphrates valley at least as far back as the eighth century B.C., when professional astronomers were taking regular observations of the heavens. Similarly rational Greek medicine can be shown to have been preceded, in some of its findings, by the Ebers Papyrus of about 1500 B.C., by the Edwin Smith Papyrus of about 1700 B.C., and by the Babylonian records.

It was thus not the *practice* of science which the Greeks invented, but the *scientific idea*, the conception that the world was knowable inasmuch and in so far as it could be investigated. In ancient times this idea led to a special point of view and to some amelioration of man's lot. In modern times it has led to a complete transformation of our mode of life, to a profound modification of the interrelations of peoples, and to an alteration in our attitude to each other and to the world around us. It would be idle to pretend that these changes have been entirely to the good. We believe, however, that an impartial survey of the general effects of the scientific idea upon men's minds and hearts throughout the ages will result in an overwhelming verdict in its favour as a very beneficent and humanising instrument. In helping man to gain a clear idea of the knowable world, science has also helped him to understand his fellow-man.

To give any adequate account of the development of ancient conceptions of the knowable world would involve a description of the whole course of Greek thought. Here we are only concerned with the process by which rational ideas became applied to the known physical universe, and with the bearing of this process on religious thought. The process is precisely that which we nowadays call *science*, a department which in antiquity was, however, by no means always clearly separated from other modes of thought and particularly was linked with philosophy. Among the Greek " philosophers " who worked before the close of the fifth century B.C. we are able to trace how these rational ideas came gradually to be universally applied. Far back in the history of Greek thought we see men feeling their way to a new interpretation of that universal principle which they distinguish as φύσις, " *physis*," a word which survives in our modern terms, *physics, physiology, physical, physician,* etc.

Physis meant at first *growth* or *development*, the essential element of all existence, and it was specially applied to living things. Gradually there dawned on the Greek mind the idea that this growth proceeded according to definite rules which differed in different cases but in which a certain common character might be distinguished. By a simple process of transference *physis* came to be regarded as this rule or manner of development itself, and so it came to mean something very near to what we should now call a *natural law.*

As knowledge grew, these rules or laws were traced more and more widely. Under such circumstances the philosophers tried to discern that which was behind the laws. It was inevitable that some, at least, should see there an individual and personal power. Thus *physis* was given a real existence apart from the individual laws which the philosophers had succeeded in tracing. *Physis,* in fact, was more or less personified. Had the religion of the Greeks advanced along rational lines with their other departments of thought, *Physis* would doubtless have been raised to the rank of a god. Although the greatest among the Greek investigators of nature never took the step of actually personifying *physis*, yet the tendency to do so is distinguishable throughout large departments of Greek thought. This tendency is, in a sense, a combination of the religious, philosophic, and scientific standpoints.

The word *physis* has an interesting later history among the Greeks where we can hardly follow it. There is, however, one incident in the history of the idea represented by the word which had a deep influence on the subsequent development of thought. When the Greek world became absorbed into the Roman Empire, Greek thought gradually assumed a Latin dress. During this process the philosophical term *physis* was mistranslated by the word *natura*. The Latin word contains not so much the idea of *growth* as of *birth*. Emphasis was thus transferred from the idea of *law* to the idea of *origin*. This we can clearly see if we contrast two works in which these words are used. Thus we have a work of about 400 B.C. falsely ascribed to Hippocrates entitled Περὶ φύσεως ἀνθρώπου, *i.e.*, " On the way things happen in man." It is a scientific attempt to explain a limited part of the universe, to wit man's body, by a series of general ideas based on observation. We can compare this with the approach of the Latin philosopher Lucretius, who died about 55 B.C. and wrote a work " *De rerum natura*," *i.e.*, " On the origin of things in general," a philosophical thesis which seeks to explain the entire workings of the universe on a particular hypothesis about its origin.

In glancing at these two works we moderns can perceive that we have before us two entirely different and perhaps incompatible things. On the one hand, we see a work of pure science in which the investigator is interested only in a particular problem and explains it in terms which might obtain universal assent. On the other hand, we see a work which we may describe as pertaining to the nature of philosophy or religion—according to our manner of approach—in which the writer is less interested in the solution of any special problem than in finding a common element at the back of all problems.

The position gives us the key to many of the happenings in the subsequent relations of science on the one hand and religion and philosophy on the other. It is the business of the man of science to investigate only such parts of nature as are in his particular field.

In doing so he traces laws, seeing essential unity behind apparent diversity. There is, however, another class of thinker who is no less occupied in seeking unity in diversity, but who is concerned with a much wider field than is the working man of science. The philosopher or religionist may well adopt the conclusions of the scientific observer. Nevertheless he is occupied in a different task and applies a different method.

One of the reasons why ancient science was not more successful in solving specific problems was precisely that ancient thinkers were less able than ourselves to forsake even temporarily the great general problems or, indeed, to differentiate the one type of investigation from the other. Some there were, however, in antiquity who did succeed in distinguishing between the two categories. The first writer to make clear in practice this separation between science and philosophy is said by tradition to have been the Coan physician, Hippocrates the Great. If, therefore, Greek philosophy —or a department of it—sought to give a rational basis to our knowledge of the world, it was Greek medicine that first put that rational basis to the test.

There is one great monument of the rational spirit in medicine to which we must specially refer. This book was composed a little before 400 B.C. It is the first work that has come down to us in which the scientific is clearly set over against the religious point of view and it deals with what is described as the *Sacred disease*, the condition that we nowadays call epilepsy.

We are here not at all concerned with the hypothesis proposed by the unknown author of this very remarkable work to explain the phenomena that he is describing. He is led to this hypothesis by a general law which he thinks he has discovered behind the diverse phenomena of the disease. What is of importance for our purpose is that the book presents to the reader two opposing views of the nature of disease. One view, which is rejected, is based on that form of religion in which the more striking phenomena at least are ascribed to the action of supernatural powers. The other view, claiming the disease as the result of the inevitable action of a natural law, may be classed as a scientific hypothesis. Incidentally the book contains a hint that such laws are of universal application. The essential part of this most remarkable work we shall proceed to render in a greatly abbreviated and somewhat paraphrased form.

" As regards the disease called *Sacred*, to me it appears to be no more divine than other diseases, but to have a *physis* just like other diseases. Men regard its origin as divine from ignorance and wonder, since it is a peculiar condition and not readily understood. Yet if it be reckoned divine merely because wonderful, then instead of one there would be many sacred diseases.

"To me, then, it appears that they who refer such conditions to the gods are but as certain charlatans who claim to be excessively religious and to know what is hidden from others. These men do but use divinity as cloak to their own ignorance. They give out the disease is sacred and adopt a mode of treatment that shall be safe for themselves whatever happens. They apply purifications and incantations and all manner of charlatanry, but mark! they also enforce abstinence from unwholesome food. All these things they enjoin, they say, with reference to the divinity of the disease. If the patient recover, theirs is the honour; if he do not, it is the god, not they, that is to blame, seeing they have administered nothing unwholesome.

"But consider! Surely if these foods aggravate the disease and it be cured by abstinence, then the god is not the cause of the disease at all, and they who seek thus to cure it are by their very act showing that it is neither sacred nor divine. Nay, more, the very assertion of its sacredness and divinity savours of impiety, as though there were no gods.

"If these fellows professed to bring down the moon, to darken the sun, or to induce storms or fine weather, should we not accuse them of impiety, whether they claimed this power as derived from the sacred mysteries or from any other knowledge? Nay, more, even if they could do these things, I, for my part, should still not believe there was anything divine therein, since the divine would have been overpowered by human knowledge and have become subject thereto.

"Surely then this disease has its *physis* and causes whence it originates, even as have other diseases, and it is curable by means comparable to their cure. It arises like them from things which enter and quit the body, such as cold, the sun, and the winds, things which are ever changing and are never at rest. Such things are divine or no—as you will, for the distinction matters not—nor is there need to make this distinction anywhere in Nature, wherein all things are alike divine and all are alike human, for have not all a *physis* which can be found by those who seek it steadfastly?"

A clear conception of natural law has here emerged. We note that the writer is entirely without opposition to the theory of the existence of a separate and ultimate cause of all things, but he refuses to confuse that cause with natural law. He has distinguished sharply between science on the one hand and religion on the other. How long will his distinction be remembered? The sequel will show.

Towards the end of the fifth century B.C. there were several schools of thought in Greece that claimed to offer an explanation of material phenomena. One of these schools, that of Democritus, was very important for its influence on later thought. Democritus (*c*. 470–*c*. 400) was the founder of the *atomic theory*. He regarded *atoms* and the *void* as the only existence. Everything, even the phenomena of life and thought, was to be explained as the result of the action of these atoms moving or otherwise acting in the void. Atoms he held were eternal, being neither created nor destroyed, though the combinations in which they occur constantly change. He considered that atoms were infinite in number. Motion of atoms had always existed. Democritus held that there must by consequence have been an infinite number of worlds in various stages of growth and decay. Everything, in his system, could be explained on purely mechanical grounds without introducing any idea of a Providence or of an intelligent cause working toward an end.

5. *The Revolution in Greek Thought*

The earlier and simpler phase of Greek thought terminates with the fifth century in a thinker of an entirely different type, Socrates (470–399 B.C.). His name is associated with the advent of a great intellectual revolution, perhaps the greatest that the world has seen. With the general trend of Socratic thought, however, we are not concerned, but only with certain special tendencies to which it gave rise.

The position assumed by Socrates was one of scepticism as to the validity of all human knowledge. The direction of his thought and of those of his followers was thus little determined by physical philosophy, which, in those days, set forth very complete and definite and yet very inadequately based doctrines, such as that of Democritus, as to the general nature of the world. The Greek philosophers before the time of Socrates had largely concentrated on the *physis* of the sensible Universe and had developed a system of *physics*. The overwhelming interest of Socrates, however, was in the direction of *conduct*. In seeking guidance for right conduct he was led to suppose that the soul of man partook of the divine. He reached the conception of an immortal soul which he maintained as an article of faith, but not of knowledge. He thus rejected the whole structure that the physicists had reared. Nor would he have any parley with the conflicting theories of these men, of whom " some conceived existence as a unity, others as a plurality ; some affirmed perpetual motion, others perpetual rest; some declared coming into being and passing away to be universal, others altogether denied such things." He thus regarded as futile all attempts " to pursue knowledge for its own sake." Nevertheless, he recognised the existence of practical wisdom (Φρόνησις), leading to right action. It was *phronēsis* against *physis*. This *phronēsis* bears some relation to the *Wisdom* of the later Jewish " Wisdom Literature." In due course of time it went through a process of development something like that which we have seen with *physis* and tended to personification under various names. The Wisdom Literature exhibits an interesting parallel to this process.

The Socratic revolution depressed for a time the activity of Greek physical philosophy, but did not destroy it. Out of the conflict between the Socratics and the physical philosophers arose the main streams of later Greek thought. One of these streams exhibits a development of the characteristic Socratic interest ; this stream leads on to Plato and to the *doctrine of ideas*. In its ultimate development it expressed itself as a complete indifference to worldly happenings. Its final stage in the pagan world is associated with the Neoplatonists and the name of Plotinus. On the other hand, the physical philosophy, having recovered from its submergence, revived in even more dogmatic form and became associated with the school to which Epicurus gave his name. It is extremely interesting and significant to note that both the Neoplatonic and the Epicurean schools became inimical to science, while neither was conducive to the current practice of religion. The subsequent development both of science and of religion is thus historically associated with other systems of thought which chose a *via media* : for science that of the Peripatetics and their successors in after ages ; for religion that of the great Judaeo-Christian system of thought.

Surrounded by the amenities of our age, there is an aspect of ancient life that we are liable to forget. It is the very incomplete record of the past that was in the hands of a scholar of those days. Written books with them were far less easy to obtain or to read than are printed books with us, and the accumulation of what we would regard as an adequate library was impossible. Thus great progressive lines of study, such as philosophy or science, tended to be represented only by their final development. The purchasers of books naturally selected only the latest presentation. Earlier versions, not being further multiplied, tended always to disappear. So it comes about that in many departments of science, *e.g.*, astronomy, botany, medicine, the most completely represented authors that have come down to us, Ptolemy, Theophrastus, Galen, are the latest rather than the greatest, those who made the final synthesis of knowledge rather than those who created that knowledge. Because of this limitation our view of the development of ancient science must necessarily be incomplete, while its final synthesis can be sketched with confidence and in considerable detail.

In the case of philosophy it happens that two very great figures, Plato and Aristotle, fill the stage of the fourth century. Their work, which has come down to us in considerable bulk, caused the destruction of almost all that went before them. The history of thought until their time has to be pieced together from hints and fragments most of which are derived from their writings. For these two writers, however, we are provided with the fullest documentary material.

The thought of Plato (427–347), like that of his master, Socrates, was dominated by the ethical motive. Convinced like his master that Truth and Good exist and that they are inseparable, he embarked on an inquiry which had as its object to expose, account for, and resolve into one comprehensive theory the discrepancies of ordinary thinking. During this process he developed a doctrine destined to be of great moment for the subsequent relations of religious and scientific thought. It is the so-called *doctrine of ideas*.

The nature of this doctrine and the manner in which Plato reached it has been briefly set forth by his pupil Aristotle. " In his youth," says Aristotle, " Plato became familiar with the doctrines (of certain philosophers) that all things perceived by the senses are ever in a state of flux and there is no knowledge concerning them. To these views he held even in later years. Socrates, however, was busying himself about ethical matters, neglecting

the world of nature as a whole, but seeking the universal in these
ethical matters.   It was he who fixed thought for the first time
on *definitions*.   Plato accepted his teaching but held that the problem
applied not to anything perceived by the senses but to something
of another sort.   His reason was that the common definition could
not be a definition of things perceived by the senses, because they
were always changing.   Things of this other sort he called *Ideas*
and things perceived by the senses, he said, were different from
these (Ideas) and were all called after them."   (Aristotle's
" Metaphysics," i. § 6.)

Thus concepts became for Plato · something very concrete,
while our impressions of the material universe, percepts, became
something very vague.   Such a theory, it is evident, could easily
ally itself with religious teaching which deals with concepts.
Historically the great religions have not been backward in profiting
by the mighty assistance which the greatest of all philosophers
could lend.   It is not, however, our concern here to follow that
development of his influence.   To scientific advance, on the
other hand, his attitude was by no means helpful.

Plato expresses a great admiration for mathematical principles
and he regards mathematics as exhibiting that type of certitude
and exactness to which other studies should conform.   Now
mathematics relies for the material on which it works upon something of the nature of Plato's Ideas.   It therefore might be
expected that mathematics would appeal to him.   Many of Plato's
thoughts assume a mathematical guise and he exhibits at certain
times a view which seems to approach that of Pythagoras (sixth
century B.C.), who had attached a moral and spiritual value to
numbers.

The general attitude of Plato was, however, much less favourable to the physical sciences.   He naturally could not regard with
aught than scorn the material theories of such writers as Democritus.
Nevertheless he speaks with respect of Hippocrates, the very type
of scientific investigator in antiquity.   Plato's respect in this
matter was, however, quite devoid of any inclination to follow in
his footsteps.   Nor is this to be wondered at, for, apart from the
relative unimportance of the place that he assigned to phenomena,
Plato was in fact quite without those qualities which lend themselves
to patient inductive observation.   Nevertheless the great philosopher
could not refrain from producing something in the way of a cosmic

theory. The work in which this cosmic theory appeared, the
"*Timaeus*," gives us a picture of the depth to which natural science
can be degraded by a great mind in its endeavour to give a specific
teleological meaning to all parts of the universe. The trend of
Platonism in general, and of the schools that arose from it, was
always away from observational science, though not unfriendly to
mathematical development.

The physical philosophers of the fourth century, of whom
Aristotle is the greatest and most permanent type, were more
successful than Plato in their efforts at constructing a coherent and
lasting cosmic theory. We may glance at the picture of the material
universe presented by Aristotle. That great thinker was himself
an absolutely first-class naturalist. Thus the cosmic scheme that
he produced, unlike that of Plato, absorbed a vast mass of observational material, notably in the department of biology. Yet the
bases of the scheme were certain preconceived notions which did
not and could not depend upon observation. Into this scheme
observations had to be fitted. The difficulty of fitting them represents a struggle between the observational and theoretical interests
which is a prototype of that so often encountered in later centuries.

We may observe here that the general history of later Greek
physical philosophy presents certain features which are closely
parallel to that of science in the West in modern times. The
philosophical scheme once established becomes part of the religious
or semi-religious systems of thought, and any attempt to disturb
it is resented. An effort, too, is made to confine the activities of
the men of science to the adjustment of the details of the scheme.
An attempt, for instance, such as that of Aristarchus of Samos
(about 250 B.C.) to show that the earth moves round the sun is
denounced by the Stoic Cleanthes as impious, just in the manner
that Galileo was denounced by the theologians in the seventeenth
century.

Let us now turn to the actual Aristotelian system of *physics*.
That system, in a more or less modified form, was absorbed by
the various philosophical schools of antiquity and played a very
important part in the history of Christian thought. It is therefore
necessary to note its fundamental bases. These may be briefly
drawn up thus :

(*a*) Matter is continuous.

(*b*) All matter is somehow made up of the four elements,

Earth, Air, Fire, and Water, which in their turn contain the four
" qualities," hotness, coldness, dryness, and moisture, in binary
combination.

(c) The earth is a sphere. It is fixed as the centre of the
universe, which is itself spherical.

(d) The stars and planets move with uniform velocity in
concentric circles round the earth.

(e) Circular movement is the most perfect conceivable and
represents the changeless, eternal, and perfect order of the Heavens
as contrasted with the mutable, mortal, and imperfect order that
prevails on this our earth.

(f) The universe is finite.

This system lasted unshaken for 2000 years, roughly from
350 B.C. to A.D. 1650. But while universally accepted there were
certain corollaries to it that obtained less wide or more partial
acceptance.

6. *Later Greek Thought*

By the end of the fourth century B.C. science had reached
the zenith of its creative activity in the ancient world. Nevertheless much important work was done during the two centuries
which followed. This was due to the Alexandrian School, with
which names such as those of Euclid, Herophilus, Archimedes,
Eratosthenes, are associated. The members of the School, able
though they were, give the impression of being *epigoni*, heirs or
successors to a great heritage, an inspiring vision. These men were
the successors of the Lyceum and of the Academy in the same
way as their royal masters were successors of the Alexandrian
Empire. Archimedes stands out perhaps as the great and brilliant
exception.

While, then, much was done by these Hellenistic writers to
develop the details of the scientific scheme, we note that already
by the end of the fourth century B.C. a complete and coherent
scheme of the physical universe had been evolved which was not
fundamentally altered by later investigations. That scheme had
been set forth in the Aristotelian writings. Now the corner-stone
of the Aristotelian scheme, as indeed of nearly all Greek physical
philosophy, was the view that substance is not *created* in the older
Hebraic sense. The point is repeatedly raised by Aristotle himself,
and is perhaps inherent in the scientific method of investigating
the universe. It is a working hypothesis without which the

application of the scientific method is perhaps impossible. Matter is for the ancient physical philosophy, as for modern science, uncreatable and indestructible. This is the condition under which alone investigation of the material universe becomes worth while. " That nothing," says Aristotle in his " Metaphysics " (xi. § 6), " comes to be out of that which is not, but everything out of that which is, is a doctrine common to nearly all the natural philosophers." Nor is the position altered by those modern conceptions which would reinterpret matter in terms of physical forces. We may note in passing that among the ancients there were those who did, in fact, reinterpret matter in such terms somewhat in the manner of modern physicists, though, of course, in a much more elementary fashion.

The Greek scientific scheme developed along such lines as these a complete and coherent view of the universe. This conception would doubtless have found itself in violent conflict with the religious system of the day if formal religion among the Greeks had reached the high rational level that it had attained among the Hebrews. We shall see the clash in later Jewish and early Christian thought under Greek influence. Among the pagan Greeks, however, little opposition is encountered, at least until very late times. With Greek popular religion in so relatively primitive a state, there were, in fact, few points of contact between priest and philosopher. The two went on independent of each other. The philosophy of the age carried with it certain religious implications and satisfied the religious aspirations of those who studied it. Thus, though there was no great open conflict between religion and science in the pagan world, yet the popular religion continued to be steadily undermined by the physical philosophy.

There were, however, certain necessary corollaries to the physical philosophy which ultimately brought to an end not only the popular religion but the ancient civilisation itself. In a world in which, to use the phrase of Lucretius (*c.* 60 B.C.), " nothing is ever begotten of nothing by divine will," and in which too " things cannot then ever be turned again to naught," it must needs be that all things act by those rules which are inherent in everlasting matter. What is there then left that is ourselves, our real inner self-conscious selves ? The question was variously answered by various schools of thought. It is a question that is asked to this very day. The Stoic philosophy, which was the most popular and one of the most

" religious " of the later pagan schools, would reply that what is left to the man himself is the will, the power, to play his part like a man, doing his duty in that walk of life to which Providence has called him. We are just parts of Nature. "Thou hast subsisted as part of the whole. Thou shalt vanish into that which begat thee, or rather thou shalt be taken again into its Seminal Reason by a process of change" ("Meditations" iv. § 14), so muses the Stoic Emperor, Marcus Aurelius (121–180 A.D.). Such philosophers would take little interest in this tyrant Nature. Why should they ? In our age men learn the ways of Nature that they may control her, but the time for that was not yet. Epicurus would have us know only so much about her as would remove from us all fear of supernatural interference. Stoic and Epicurean literature show therefore in later antiquity a flagging of scientific curiosity. Men were weary of the world. For what reason should they seek to know Nature more intimately, Nature the compassionless, the tyrannical, the cruel ?

With this fading of interest among philosophers, something had happened also among the more ordinary run of men that turned their eyes and hands from investigating Nature too nearly. Into the welter of philosophic sects, of contending oriental cults, of decaying scientific interest, of rhetorical exercise, that made up the spiritual life of later antiquity there came a new ray of hope. That hope suggested not indeed that man might control his fate but that he might at least come to know it and so prepare himself the better for it. Astrology came to the West and was eagerly absorbed into popular as well as into philosophical thought. This was essentially a task for the " Chaldaean " specialist to whom alone the details themselves were of interest. The future, it was believed, could be read, and once read—who cared then for the wretched rules by which it had been read ? They were at best but means. It was the end that mattered.

The astrological system of antiquity was, after all, only a formal statement of those beliefs concerning the nature and working of our mundane sphere that had been fostered by the ideas of such science as had survived. Faith in astrology became part of the Stoic creed. It gave an inevitable interrelationship of all things. In the presentment of the world thus made, there was no room for those anthropomorphic gods the belief in whom was still urged by the priests and held to by the multitude. The spread of science, or of what passed for science, had led at last to a complete breach between the official faith and the opinions not only of the educated classes but of all intelligent men. The idea of " universal solidarity," of the interdependence on one another of all parts of the universe, produced a new form of religion. The world itself must be divine. " Deity," says Pliny, " only means Nature." From such a view to the monotheism of Virgil, in which the world as a whole is regarded as the artistic product of an external god, might perhaps be no great step, but the pagan world as a whole failed to take interest in that step. God, if God there be, had made the world and in making it had made its laws. It was the laws that were the effectual rulers, and it was by those laws that the pagan world was hypnotised. The position was the opposite of that of those later Deists who "sought through Nature, Nature's God." It was precisely Nature that made God meaningless.

Science, linked with Stoicism, thus assumed a fatalistic and pessimistic mood. " God, if God there be, is outside the world and could not be expected to care for it," says Pliny. The idea of immortality seems to him but the " childish babble" of those who are possessed by the fear of death. After death, so Pliny, like Lucretius, would have us believe, man is as he was before he was born.

Once, and once only, in these later classical scientific writings have we a clear note of real hope. It is very significant that that note is sounded in connection with a statement of a belief in the *progress* of knowledge, an echo of the Greek thought of the fifth and fourth centuries B.C. It is even more significant too that the note is sounded by one who approached, nearer perhaps than any other pagan Latin philosopher, to the idea of the divine immanence. In his " *Quaestiones Naturale:*," Seneca wrote :

" There are many things akin to highest deity that are still obscure. Some may be too subtle for our powers of comprehension, others imperceptible to us because such exalted majesty conceals itself in the holiest part of its sanctuary, *forbidding access to any power save that of the spirit. How many heavenly bodies revolve unseen by human eye ? . . . How many discoveries are reserved for the ages to come when our memory shall be no more, for this world of ours contains matter for investigation for all generations ? . . .* God has not revealed all things to man and has entrusted us with but a fragment of His mighty work. But *He who directs all things, who established and laid the foundation of the world, and who has clothed*

Himself with Creation, He is greater and better than that which He has wrought. Hidden from our eyes, He can only be reached by the spirit. . . . On entering a temple we assume all signs of reverence. How much more reverent then should we be before the heavenly bodies, the stars, the very nature of God ? "

But the science of antiquity as exhibited elsewhere in later pagan writings contains very little of this belief in man's destiny, this hope for human knowledge. The world in which the Imperial Roman lived was a finite world bound by the firmament and limited by a flaming rampart. His fathers had thought that great space peopled by *numina,* " divinities " that needed to be propitiated. The new dispensation—the *lex naturae* of the world that had so many parallels with the *jus gentium* of the Empire— had now taken the place of those awesome beings.

In the inevitableness of the action of that law Lucretius the Epicurean might find comfort from the unknown terror. Yet for the Stoic it must have remained a cruel law. His vision, we must remember, was very different from that given by the spacious claim of modern science which explores into ever wider and wider regions of space and time and thought. It was an iron, nerveless, tyrannical universe which science had raised and in which man felt himself fettered, imprisoned, crushed. The Roman had forsaken his early gods, that crowd of strangely vague yet personal beings whose ceremonial propitiation in every event and circumstance had filled his fathers' lives. He had had before him an alternative of the oriental cults whose gods were but mad magicians—a religion unworthy of a philosopher—and the new religion of science whose god, he now sadly saw, worked by a mechanical rule. He had abandoned the faith of his fathers and had flung himself into the arms of what he believed to be a lovelier goddess, and lo ! he was embracing a machine ! His soul recoiled and he fled into Christianity. Science had induced that essential pessimism which clouds the thought of later antiquity. It was reaction against this pessimism which led to the great spiritual changes in the midst of which antiquity went up in flames and smoke.

7. *Later Jewish and Early Christian Thought. The Influence of Hellenism*

In the earlier books of the Old Testament there is, as we have seen, no conception of natural law. Natural phenomena and especially the more dramatic events, the thunder and the whirlwind, drought, plague and famine are the result of God's immediate action. "The voice of the Lord is upon the waters, the God of Glory thundereth" (Psalm xxix. 3). Even in a less anthropomorphic atmosphere there is still no element intervening between God and natural phenomena. All are the result of His direct action.

"Who hath measured the waters in the hollow of his hand,
And meted out heaven with the span
And comprehended the dust of the earth in a measure,
And weighed the mountains in scales
And the hills in a balance.

    . . . .

It is He that sitteth upon the circle of the earth,
And the inhabitants thereof are as grasshoppers,
That stretched out the heavens as a curtain,
And spreadeth them out as a tent to dwell in.

    . . . .

I am the Lord, and there is none else,
There is no God beside me.

    . . . .

I form the light and create darkness ;
I make peace and create evil ;
I, the Lord, do all these things."
           (Isaiah xl. 12, 22 ; xlv. 5, 7.)

Such a work as Job reveals a new development. Critics would place this book at least as late as 400 B.C. and therefore after "The Sacred Disease." The author of Job has attained to a definite recognition of natural law. The argument of the book is, indeed, based on the wonder and majesty of the laws by which God rules His world. If Job does not comprehend those laws how can he hope to comprehend the purpose that is behind them ? It is with irony that the Almighty demands :

"Dost thou bind the cluster of the Pleiades
Or loose the bands of Orion ?
Dost thou lead forth the Mazzaroth in their season ?
Or canst thou guide the Bear with her train ?
Dost thou make the heavens to know the laws ?
Dost thou establish the dominion thereof in the earth ? "
           (Job xxxviii. 31–33.)

These very laws are used as proof of the power, wisdom and goodness of God, for the same reason that they are invoked in the " Bridgewater Treatises " of more than two thousand years later. The recognition of natural laws in Job is doubtless the result of contact with Greek thought.

In the yet later " Wisdom Literature," the contact with Greek thought is yet closer. The characteristic features of Greek physical philosophy have been largely absorbed, and peep out unmistakably here and there. The relation of God to the natural laws has also become modified. Not only does He not act on the world directly, but He has become further removed therefrom than in Job. There is another existence that governs the laws of Nature and indeed makes them ; it is that elusive *Wisdom*, an entity almost as hard to define as the Greek *physis* which it in some ways resembles. Wisdom has some of the attributes of Deity. She is omniscient, omnipotent, " she reaches from one end of the world to the other and ordereth all things well " (Wisdom viii. 1). So far from God acting directly, it is " by His *word* that He made all things and by His *wisdom* then He formed man " (Wisdom iv. 1).

Moreover, this new Jewish mode of thought has become self-conscious and polemic. It sets itself deliberately over against Greek thought. Among the Greeks various " first principles " had been adopted. Thales had proposed water, Heracleitus fire, Pythagoras the " circling stars," Anaximenes air, yet other philosophers some vague essence that may perhaps be translated " winds," and finally the new astrological science coming in from Babylon had suggested the complex mathematical order of the heavenly bodies as the motive power of all things. The "Wisdom of Solomon," which was written in Alexandria about 100 B.C., inveighs against all these :

> " Surely vain were all men in their natures, and without
> perception of God
> Who could not from the good things that are seen know
> Him that is.
> Neither by giving heed to the works did they recognise Him
> who hath wrought them,
> But either fire, or wind or the swift air,
> Or circling stars, or raging water, or the lights of heaven
> They deemed the gods which govern the world."
>
> (Wisdom xiii. 1–2.).

At this late date there were, however, Jewish writers who still held to the older view with great tenacity. Thus the " Book of Jubilees," which dates from the latter half of the second century B.C., was composed as a defence of Judaism against the Hellenistic spirit. It thus exalts the Divine Law, the Torah, at the expense of the natural law, and all physical phenomena are represented as due to the direct action of God :

" Worship the God of heaven.
Who causeth the rain and the dew to descend on the earth
And doeth everything upon the earth.

.   .   .   .

If He desireth, He withholdeth it,
And all things are in His hand."

(Jubilees xii. 4 and 18.)

The attitude of this work is a crude presentation of the Hebrew revolt against Greek philosophy. In the extremer form this revolt had no rational future, and we need not follow further the movement for which it stands. There are, however, other channels of later Hebrew thought which are more in the direct line of our story. The best representative of this later Jewish movement is the Alexandrian philosopher Philo.

Philo was a thinker who drew on many sources, but his general trend was along Platonic lines and far removed from the study of phenomena. He therefore represents a further separation of religion from science. Religion and science had touched each other in the days of the " Wisdom Literature." It is evident that in Jewish feeling, so far as it is exhibited by Philo, they are again diverging. Philo was conscious of being a " philosopher " in the Greek sense, and he betrays this consciousness in his works in a way that is not exhibited in any earlier Jewish writings.

Just as the Stoics treated Homer allegorically in their search for a justification of their views, so did Philo with the Old Testament. This often leads him to what we should now regard as an extreme straining of the text. The process, though very characteristic of a large amount of subsequent theological writing, is devoid of interest for our purpose. It takes religion ever further from the scientific standpoint.

It is the mechanism of Philo's attempt to deal with the problem of Creation that alone brings him into contact with our subject. On the one hand, he had before him the Hebrew biblical doctrine of Creation with God as a separate existence outside the world which He had produced at a definite date by definite acts and which He continued to guide in every detail. On the other hand, Philo, basing himself on Platonic thought, developed a conception of a God without emotions, without attributes and consequently without name, changeless and imperceptible by man, self-sufficient. This God is simply existent and has no relations to any other being. Such is the God of the Platonic idea. Such a God could not act upon the world nor create nor guide it. The two views were incompatible.

Under these circumstances Philo resorted to a device which we have already seen adopted and which can be traced in one form or another as far back as Heracleitus (535-475 B.C.). He introduced an existence between God and the world. *Physis, phronesis, wisdom* were similar previous attempts. Philo's device was the *logos*. The concentration of attention on these and similar theological complexities was bound to turn men's attention away from phenomenological study.

There was, however, a yet further reason for the " flight from phenomena " in late Jewish and early Christian thought. Ever since the Socratic revolution a section of thinkers had regarded the material universe as containing something essentially without worth or even evil. This had been emphasised by certain interpreters, at least, of the Platonic doctrine of Ideas. The worthlessness and evil charcter of the world fitted in well with the Jewish doctrine of the Fall. Thus the view had no difficulty in entering Jewish thought. Though Philo is at some pains to avoid the conclusion that the world is necessarily evil, it may be doubted whether his efforts are successful. Thus the " sins of the flesh " became a theological commonplace which passed over into Christian thought.

St. Paul's teaching was certainly influenced by this idea of the physical basis of sin. " We know that the Law is spiritual : but I am carnal, sold under sin " (Romans vii. 14). Under these circumstances Christianity for a time turned entirely away from phenomena. St. Paul does not conceal his contempt for the triviality of Greek physical philosophy. It is not so much that it is false as that, for him, it is trivial and irrelevant. " When ye knew not God, ye did service unto them which by *physis* are no gods. But now, after that ye have known God, or rather are known of God, how turn yet again to the weak and

beggarly elements, whereunto ye desire again to be in bondage ? "
(Galatians iv. 8-9).

With this contempt for the study of phenomena was soon,
however, welded another belief which was very widely current in
Judaeo-Christian literature. The end of the world was a constant
preoccupation of that literature and is described over and over
again in lurid colours.

But in much of Greek physical philosophy, as in that of
Democritus, this world is but one of a long series of worlds, and the
end thereof would mean but the beginning of another world like
to it. This ill-fitted Judaeo-Christian idea of eschatology and a
conception of the destruction of the elements themselves was
adopted. " The day of the Lord will come as a thief in the night ;
in the which the heavens shall pass away with a great noise and the
elements shall melt with fervent heat, the earth also and the works
that are therein shall be burned up" (II Peter iii. 10). So long as
that idea was prominent in men's minds there could be no serious
attention paid to phenomena. " The day of the Lord " rang the
death-knell of science. The development of Christian and of Jewish
theology ceases, at this point, to have an interest for our purpose.

8. *An attempted Compromise between the Pagan and the Christian standpoint*

Before we part with the ancient world, we may consider the
work of one pagan writer who, coming near to the Christian standpoint, exercised a vast influence in the centuries which followed.
The physician Galen of Pergamum (150–200 A.D.) was an Asiatic
Greek who practised with great success at Rome and was the
medical attendant of several Emperors, Marcus Aurelius among
them. Galen was an exceedingly voluminous writer and a vast
mass of his works has come down to us. He was an ingenious,
a practical, and an industrious investigator, and the anatomical and
physiological system which he sets forth remained in current use
until the middle of the sixteenth century. For our purpose the
interest of that system is in its philosophical assumptions.

The philosophical standpoint of Galen in relation to his science
comes out most clearly and consistently in his treatise " On the
Uses of the Parts of the Body of Man." In that remarkable work,
vastly influential in the ages which followed, Galen seeks to prove
that the bodily organs are so well constructed, and in such perfect

relation to the functions to which they minister, that it is impossible to imagine anything better. Thus, following the Aristotelian principle that Nature makes nought in vain, Galen seeks to justify the form and structure of all the organs—nay, of every part of every organ—with reference to the functions for which he believes they are destined. We are thus in the presence of a work that is not, strictly speaking, a treatise either of Anatomy or of Physiology, but in which Anatomy and Physiology are subservient to a particular doctrine and are used to justify the ways of God to man. We have, in fact, the thesis of final causes applied to the study of the animal organism.

The problem of final causes is developed by Galen along definite lines. He considers that it is possible to discover the end served by every part of the animal, and, moreover, to show that such a part, being perfectly adapted to its end, could not be constructed other than as it is. To say this is to go even further than the " Bridgewater Treatises " which undertook to demonstrate the " Power, Wisdom, and Goodness of God, as manifested in the Creation." It is to claim that in every work of Creation, and in every detail of such work, we can demonstrate these attributes along the lines of known principles. It is to claim, in fact, a complete knowledge of the laws of Nature. No flamboyant modern man of science, however inflated with confidence drawn from the most sweeping presentations of scientific determinism, however intoxicated with his own scientific achievements, has as yet arrogated such powers to himself. To conceive that such claims should be made by a pious theistically minded author, the reader must think himself back into a very different philosophical environment from that to which we are nowadays accustomed.

The prevailing philosophy of Galen's world was the Stoic scheme, so admirable and beautifully expounded by his royal master, Marcus Aurelius. There were, of course, other systems of philosophy in vogue—Epicurean, Gnostic, Neoplatonic, and the rest, to say nothing of the various Oriental cults, such as that of Persian Mithra, of Egyptian Isis, of Phrygian Cybele, that were permeating the Empire. None of these systems, however, interested their followers in phenomena, nor was there any system but that of the Stoics which could make an appeal at once to men of action and to men of scientific knowledge.

Now, in the world of the Stoic philosopher all things were

determinate, and they were determined by forces acting wholly outside man. The type and origin of that determination the Stoic sought in the heavens, in the majestic and overwhelming procession of the stars. The recurring phenomena of the spheres typified, foreshadowed, nay, exhibited and controlled, the cycle of man's life. Man dwelt in a finite world bounded by the firmament and limited by a flaming rampart. Within that rampart all worked by rule—and that rule was the rule of the heavenly bodies. Astrology had become one of the dogmas of the Stoic creed.

To such a world Galen's determinism was in itself no strange thought. Remember that Galen had, in his youth, been well trained in the Stoic philosophy. Yet Galen's view was far from being in accord with Stoicism. Though a determinism, it was a determinism of perfection in which all was fixed by a wise and far-seeing God, and was a reflection of His own perfection. That perfection can be traced in the body of man, and Galen exclaims outright that a knowledge of the uses of the organs reveals Deity more clearly than any sacred mysteries. Galen repeatedly adopts the argument from design for the existence of God ; indeed, it is his sole argument. Now such a scheme did not ill fit the new creed which was just beginning to raise its head and was destined to replace Stoicism and all the other pagan schemes. Galen's thought, in fact, made a special appeal to the Christian point of view, and this is doubtless the reason that a larger bulk has been preserved of his works than of those of any other pagan writer.

In several places Galen mentions both Judaism and Christianity, though without much respect. In the great anatomical work under discussion he explains that in his belief God always works by law, and that it is just for this reason that Natural Law reveals Him, and he adds that " in this matter our view . . . differs from that of Moses." It seems very probable that he had read some books of the Bible. His position can thus be summed up as intermediate between Stoicism and Christianity. On the one hand he accepted the Natural Law of the Stoic philosophy, but rejected its astrological corollary. On the other hand he accepted the Divine Guide and Architect of the Universe which corresponded to the Christian scheme, but rejected all idea of miracle.

Let us, however, consider the results of Galen's doctrine of the uses of all the parts. Treated, as it must be, on the *a priori* basis, the doctrine inevitably turned men away from the observation of Nature and made them content with arbitrary solutions of the many problems which his principle raised. In the case of Galen himself, who came as a pioneer, this belief offered a novel presentation of the world which was thus still worth exploring. Galen explored it, and his Anatomy—within certain limits—was exact. His teleological theory, however, removed the motive for further exploration on the part of his successors, and with Galen's death, science too fell dead, and was not reborn for a thousand years.

9. *The Middle Ages*

Despite the spread of philosophy based on science, the observational activity of antiquity was slowly dying from about 100 B.C. In A.D. 200 it expired with Galen. The decay of observation, as we have seen, was the result of internally acting causes. In origin it had nothing to do with Christianity, which was not yet in a position to have its full effect on pagan thought.

But Christianity did come as a protest and a revulsion against the prevailing and extremely pessimistic outlook. Men had lost interest in the world and Christianity brought them something to live for, it brought a *cause*. It was natural under these circumstances that Christian thought should oppose the philosophical basis of pagan thought. In this sense early Christian thought was certainly anti-scientific and exhibits an aversion to the view which places the whole of man's fate under the dominion, the inescapable tyranny, of natural law. It is, however, essential to remember that the Early Church in developing this opposition was not dealing with living observational science. The conflict was simply with a philosophical tradition which contained dead, non-progressive, and misunderstood scientific elements. The conflict in the Early Church, therefore, though exceedingly interesting in itself, is of little importance for our subject and we can afford to pass it by.

As the centuries wear on and as Christianity becomes more firmly established as the state religion, the need for a coherent philosophical system becomes more pressing. During the earlier Middle Ages this need is met on the scientific side largely by that bizarre work of Plato, the "*Timaeus*." As time goes on Aristotelian elements become more and more prominent, and by the thirteenth century these Aristotelian elements occupy the main field. The great system of Catholic philosophy, of which St. Thomas Aquinas was the leading architect, was built upon the recovered writings of Aristotle. The work of Aquinas is merely the greatest and most lucid effort of a process that had been going on for centuries. His "*Summa Theologica,*" regarded as a sustained intellectual effort, must be considered one of the most remarkable and fatiguing performances that the human race has yet achieved. As an investigation of evidence for the views that it sets forth, the modern working scientist will pass it by.

But although the Church accepted or professed to accept the Aristotelian philosophy, there were certain points in that philosophy which could not be effectively incorporated into a Christian system. Many elements of the Aristotelian philosophy were, of course, incompatible with the biblical account. Such, for instance, was the spherical earth. Details of this type were glossed over without grave difficulty. The incompatibility was ignored, or the biblical account was held to be allegorical or to have some mystical or moral meaning, or, again, it was pointed out that the Bible was not written for the purpose of teaching science and that such matters were without profound significance. Discussion of these questions was endless and gave rise to a vast literature, which is, however, neither interesting nor important for our theme. On the whole Christianity plus Aristotelianism explained more than either system by itself, and there was therefore no reason why men should abandon either, still less both. Nevertheless, in the Aristotelian philosophy there certainly were very disturbing elements which might have led to profounder conflict. Such, for instance, was the basic Aristotelian view of the indestructibility and uncreatability of matter, with the corollary that the Universe itself is uncreated and timeless.

If the actual words of Aristotle had been confronted with the biblical phrases the result would have been a very serious clash. But in fact this contrast could hardly be directly made. The access of the medieval scholastics to the Aristotelian writings was very imperfect. To begin with, the writings themselves are obscure and the language in which they are written is very difficult. Further, although attempts were made by Aquinas and others to have translations made direct from the Greek, these translations were most imperfect and were, moreover, very rare. It is not certain that even Aquinas was able to employ them to any large extent. The overwhelming majority of medieval Aristotelian translations and commentaries were made not directly from the Greek but through the intervention of Arabic or Hebrew commentators.

During the Middle Ages the tradition of Greek learning was mainly in the keeping of people of Arabic speech, and largely resided with the Jews so far as Europe was concerned. Among these " Arabians " and " Arabists " there was a difference of opinion as to the interpretation of the Aristotelian philosophy. One great group, followers of the Mohammedan philosopher Averroes, held that the world was eternal. That view was shared in a more or less veiled manner by a number of Christian writers, but was clearly heretical and could never be formally accepted by the Catholic Church. The other interpretation of the Aristotelian record represented the world as created. This view was presented by the Jewish writer Maimonides, whose account was generally current. Thus Maimonides came to exercise an immense influence on Christian scholasticism. Aquinas, who depended largely on Maimonides and similar writers, became represented as the protagonist against the " atheistical " Averroes. Opposition to the great Moslem thinker was, moreover, intensified by his denial of the persistence of the individual soul. Aquinas held, however, that the temporal character of the world could not be proved but must be accepted as an act of faith.

On this matter of the eternal or non-eternal character of the world there arose a prodigious literature, the examination of which would be of little profit for our purpose. We may note, however, that with our improved understanding of the Aristotelian writings we can now say that the Maimonidean party was mainly wrong in its interpretation and the Averroan party mainly right. Such was the prestige of Aristotle's name that any view had to claim that it was based on, or at least consistent with, Aristotle in order to have the least chance of a hearing. The Middle Ages were on somewhat surer ground in their account of the Aristotelian physics. They at least came fairly near to understanding Aristotle in this department. But the medieval Aristotelian view, however interpreted, cannot be regarded as partaking of the nature of a scientific hypothesis. It was an accepted doctrine, part of the tradition of antiquity. No attempt was made, nor could be made, to put it to the test of experience, nor was it in any sense an organically growing body of knowledge. The great and important contest that arose concerning the interpretation of Aristotelian doctrine exhibits at times the appearance of a conflict between the religious and the scientific standpoint. That appearance is illusory. The conflict was not of faith *versus* observation, but of opinion *versus* opinion.

But it may be asked, was there then no science in the Middle Ages ? Were none of the heresies, for instance, with which the Church had to deal of the nature of scientific hypotheses ?

To answer this question is difficult, and yet we must attempt it. To answer it with completeness we should have to define what we mean by science and this would lead us far afield. We may note, however, that science in its most developed form exhibits certain characteristic features.

(*a*) It deals with judgements to which universal assent is obtainable.

(*b*) It is a consciously progressively increasing body of knowledge and doctrine.

(*c*) The only tests of validity that it can accept are the tests of experience, and these tests it must always demand.

(*d*) An essential process of science is the drawing up of general laws from the results of observation.

(*e*) It is necessary for the growth of science and is perhaps a corollary of the other features that the conclusions, being based on the evidence, should not be prejudged.

Now a fixed and definite scheme of the Universe was accepted as a postulate by all thinkers of the Middle Ages. That scheme was derived from Aristotle but modified to fit the specific Christian doctrine of creation. With these things always before the mind, scientific investigation in our sense of the word was almost impossible to the medieval man. He could never embark on that great voyage of exploration with the sense of infinite possibilities which is the birthright of every young researcher nowadays.

Moreover, the scholastic's universe, it must be remembered, so far as it was material, was limited. The outer limit was the *primum mobile*, the outermost of the concentric spheres of which the Aristotelian world was composed. Of the structure and nature of all within the sphere of the *primum mobile* Aristotle and Ptolemy had equipped him with a definite scheme. The self-appointed task of medieval science was to elaborate that scheme in connection with the moral world. This was especially undertaken by mystical writers, often working more or less consciously under the stimulus of Arabian learning. The schemes thus produced took into account the form of the world and of man as derived from Arabian sources, and read into each relationship a spiritual meaning. For such an attitude of mind there could be no ultimate distinction between physical events, moral truths, and spiritual experiences. In their fusion of the internal and external universe these mystics have much in common with the mystics of all ages. The culmination of the process is reached with Dante (1265–1321).

The medieval world thus knew nothing of that infinite sea of experience on which the man of science nowadays launches his bark in adventurous exploration. The task of these writers of scholastic " science " was rather to give a general outline of know-ledge, to set forth such a survey of the universe as would be in accord with spiritual truth. The framework on which this encyclopaedic scheme was built was Aristotle, largely as conveyed by his Arabic commentators.

Yet despite all these drawbacks, it is a fact that man is an inquisitive, an observing, a classifying animal. Scholasticism could not and did not alter his nature ; it could only mask it and overlay it. Precisely in the period when the respect for ratiocination and the indifference to direct access to nature had reached their zenith among the learned, the craftsman asserted his humanity. The great theological movement of the thirteenth century reared vast cathedrals that stand as monuments of what the faith meant in those days. This faith adorned them with images, beautiful if you will, but such as never were on land or sea. Those dislocated joints, those impossibly attenuated bodies, those fantastic anatomies, however noble as an artistic expression, tell their own tale of the ignorance on the part of their makers of the world without. But look at the capitals of the columns or the stone frames of these anatomical monstrosities and you will see something different. You will see ivy and vine, buttercup and columbine, growing, twining, shooting as they do in the craftsman's own garden. The mason is, a better naturalist than the saint, the professor, or the architect. Natural curiosity, the mother of science, is beginning to awake from her millennial slumber.

There are other minor arts, *e.g.*, that of miniature, in which the love of nature early asserts itself. The complete story of the birth of naturalism in medieval art has yet to be written. When we have such a work in our hands it will provide us with the introductory and perhaps the most fascinating chapter in a great History of Modern Science. Nor was there long delay before the affection for the outer visible world spread to other and higher walks of life. It had early expressed itself in the career of St. Francis, and it was not long in entering the schools themselves. The literature of the later scholastic centuries is inconceivably tedious to those who are not by temper in sympathy with its special themes. Yet even that literature is relieved by an occasional rare and precious ray of nature study.

It is an amusing reflection on the incompleteness of all philosophical systems to recall that Albertus Magnus (1206-1280), the teacher of Aquinas, who perhaps more than any man was responsible for the scholastic world-system, was among those few medieval writers who were real observers of nature. To love the world around and to watch its creatures is, after all, of the very essence of the human animal. *Naturam expellas furca tamen usque recurret.* Albert, scholastic of the scholastics, drowned in erudition, the most learned man of his time, reviver of the Aristotelian cosmology, the typical medieval philosopher, has left us evidence in his great works on natural history that the scientific spirit was again astir. As an independent observer he is not altogether contemptible, and this element in him marks the beginning of the modern scientific movement. It was, however, centuries before observational activity obtained sufficient momentum or coherence to affect the religious standpoint with any gravity.

But Albert was not quite alone in his observations. Other observers were about, and some of them made discoveries of no mean importance. During the thirteenth century there was much interest in optics ; the attention devoted to the subject led in about the year 1300 to the application of lenses—which had been known to the Arabian writers—as spectacles. A similar process had led at an even earlier date to the adaptation of the magnet to the mariner's compass. These are discoveries of first-rate importance and we cannot pass them by in silence. But—and this is where we sense the characteristic medieval atmosphere—*these discoveries led to the production of no general laws.* The lens led to no advance in the doctrine of refraction or in the theory of light. The compass revealed nothing of the nature of terrestrial magnetism to the medieval thinker. They were on the level of *inventions* rather than definite steps in scientific progress. The actual application of these discoveries was far more important to the men of the time than were the principles involved. If we seek for interest in the eliciting of new general laws of nature we shall have a long and fruitless hunt in the vast wilderness of time that we call the Middle Ages.

10. *The Close of the Middle Ages*

We have seen that while the Middle Ages present to us instances of discoveries and inventions and are not without traces of real scientific advance, they are singularly devoid of any activity in the discovery of new natural laws. It is such general ideas that alone bring science into relation with religion or philosophy. The existence of observational activity devoid of scientific elements is particularly evident in the last phase of medieval science.[1] The point may be further brought out by adducing special instances.

Thus, consider the three great departments of Anatomy, Astronomy, Botany. Dissection of the human body was practised systematically from the thirteenth century onward and important additions to the knowledge of the time were made by several investigators. Despite the results that these men obtained, the physiological theories of Galen prevailed without question in the textbooks of the time. Again, Astronomy was the main scientific interest of the Middle Ages and important new observations were recorded in the Alphonsine Tables by Levi ben Gerson (1288–1344), and by Regiomontanus (1436–1476), and others. Yet none of these left the least impress on astronomical *theory*. Botany, again, was the chosen study of the physicians whose remedies were chiefly of vegetable origin and who professed to be interested in the properties and characters of herbs. Manuscripts of the fourteenth and fifteenth centuries contain many accurate and beautiful figures of plants. The magnificently illustrated works of the so-called " German fathers of Botany " in the first half of the sixteenth century, with Leonard Fuchs as their leader, contain illustrations of herbs which in accuracy and beauty are unsurpassed to this day. Yet these men threw not the least light on

---

[1] For the purposes of science the Middle Ages must be prolonged beyond the period usually recognised by historians. I have discussed this point in articles contributed to F. J. C. Hearnshaw's *Medieval Contributions to Modern Civilisation*, and to F. S. Marvin's *Science and Civilisation*, and need not enlarge on it here.

the general laws of the nature, growth, and distribution of plants. Nay, they are even devoid of theories on these great biological topics. They can but go to the ancients.[1]

During the period between the beginning of the thirteenth and the beginning of the sixteenth century there was a series of movements of vast importance for the history of culture but which we shall fortunately be able to pass over in almost complete silence. These movements were (*a*) the firm establishment of the Inquisition, (*b*) the religious upheaval known as the Reformation, and (*c*) the Revival or Renaissance of Learning. We may very briefly consider them in this order.

The Inquisition as a separate, regular, and legally established method of establishing faith and uprooting error makes its appearance in the thirteenth century. Our horror at its methods, our indignation at its injustice, our detestation of its blood-stained and infamous history, must not mislead us into regarding it as an attack on the experimental method, or as a means of suppressing at its birth a monster which if allowed to live and grow would one day strangle religion. There can be no reasonable doubt that in the sixteenth, seventeenth, and eighteenth centuries the activities of the officers of the Inquisition were directed to the suppression of scientific views that were held to be dangerous to the faith. In the centuries that preceded, however, no such tendency can be distinguished. The reasons for this are simple. During those earlier centuries, on the one hand experimental methods produced no conclusions that were dangerous to current theology, and on the other it is extremely unlikely that any officer of the Inquisition ever grasped the nature of the scientific method. So far as the Middle Ages are concerned we can therefore put aside the Inquisition as irrelevant to our discussion.

We may turn now to the great religious movement, the Reformation, which has determined the main religious configuration of Europe. Those who profess the reformed faith will naturally, and from their point of view quite rightly, regard their faith as truer and more reasonable than the faith which it displaced. But Truth and Reason are not in themselves science, and search

---

[1] It must be admitted that some slight theoretical advances were made in alchemy. It is, however, very doubtful if these were the work of Europeans until the sixteenth century. The science was essentially Arabian, and Paracelsus was perhaps the first effective European investigator.

how we may we shall fail to find any special influence of the experimental philosophy in the establishment of the Reformed Religion. The reforming leaders were, if anything, less sympathetic to scientific investigation than were the Catholic leaders. The most that can be urged is that the unsettling discoveries of the new-born experimental method helped the ferment of discontent which expressed itself in religious matters as the Reformation. Even that interpretation, however, somewhat strains the facts, and it is an argument, moreover, which may be used both ways. For one sixteenth-century man of science of the reformed faith, such as Paracelsus, a dozen Catholics might be named. In truth the reforming leaders from Wycliff to Calvin showed no more sympathy with the experimental method than did their opponents. Thus Calvin was responsible for the burning of Servetus, the discoverer of the lesser circulation of the blood, and Servetus is sometimes described as a martyr of science. The guilt lies with Calvin, but only after Servetus had escaped from a Catholic prison. Nor did Calvin show any interest whatever in the discovery of Servetus, nor did it make any part in the indictment. Indeed, Servetus himself esteemed his discovery lightly or not at all. The conflict between Catholic and Protestant assuredly does not concern us here.

It may be a cause of surprise that we propose to omit discussion of the Revival of Learning as irrelevant to our subject. Yet so far as the Renaissance meant anything for science it meant a rebirth or resurrection of *ancient* science. The earlier humanists were as little sympathetic to, or understanding of, the experimental method as were the great religious leaders. The backward-looking habit, strong in man from his nature, was further enforced, not weakened, by these humanists. From Petrarch onward they were ever brooding on the past that had been Greece and Rome. Their attitude was often not without opposition to the current religion, but again that conflict has nothing to do with the relation of religion and science. Improved access to Greek works of observational science gradually became possible through the agency of Humanism. On the renewed acquaintance with Greek science the modern application of the experimental method was based, but Humanism as such hardly comes into our story. After all, the scientific views of the Middle Ages were substantially those of the classical decline, and it was long before any great change was made in them by the revival of antiquity. For the purpose of our theme the Revival of Learning is therefore most reasonably considered as an incident of the later Middle Ages.

Looking back on the Middle Ages we can discern only one figure of first-class importance in whom interest in the discovery of new laws is prominent. In our search it would be easy to be misled by words. The interest of the scholastic period was in classification, and we encounter much discussion on the classification of the sciences, as, for instance, in the pages of Vincent of Beauvais (1190–1264). But if you seek science as we understand it, even in its most elementary form, in these vast encyclopaedias you will seek in vain. Albert, as we have seen, and a few other scholastic writers took a real interest in Nature, but the character of that interest almost expressly excluded the drawing up of general laws. " It is not enough," says Albert, " to know in terms of Universals, *but we seek to know each object's own peculiar characteristics, for this is the best and most perfect kind of science."* Albert was in practice content enough to take his Universals from Aristotle. It is in the writings of Roger Bacon alone that we encounter a clear and unmistakable demand for the search for natural laws.

The works of Roger Bacon (1214–1294) are open to much criticism, which they have not failed to receive. It is pointed out that personally he was jealous and censorious, that he demands of others criteria which he does not apply to himself, that despite his own constant demand for an investigation of Nature and despite the legends and his own claims as an investigator, when we look for evidence of his actual scientific achievements we are met with something very like a blank. But the claim that he realised in advance of his age the nature and application of the experimental method is, I think, clearly established. He frequently uses the phrase *experimental science,* which is for him the sole means of obtaining knowledge. " All sciences except this," he writes, " either merely employ arguments to prove conclusions, like the purely speculative sciences, or have universal and imperfect conclusions. Experimental science alone can ascertain to perfection what can be effected by Nature, what by art, what by fraud. It alone teaches how to judge all the follies of the magicians just as logic tests argument."

Now, it is very important for us to note that there is no trace in Roger Bacon's writings of any consciousness of opposition to religion. He thinks he is writing in support of the faith. We to-day are well aware that, in some at least, religious faith has been shaken by the course of science of which Bacon may be regarded as one of the prophets. To Bacon, however, it is not at all evident that this would or could be so, and there is nothing in any of the works by him that would lead us to consider that by his contemporaries he was regarded as heretical or unorthodox in matters of religion. Since his day many legends have arisen around his name, butt here is not the least historical evidence that his views were held to be subversive of religion.

The truth is that, even with many of his works printed and with the whole apparatus of modern research in our hands, it is by no means easy to get at the real principles underlying Bacon's philosophical position. In his own time and without the aid of printed books it was perhaps not greatly easier. We know little of Bacon's life and are in the dark at many critical points. It seems probable, however, that the opposition to him was neither an opposition to his actual scientific achievements nor to the effects of those achievements on religion. The opposition was based on a misunderstanding of his method of interrogating Nature. It may reasonably be doubted if in the thirteenth century there were enough men who understood what he meant by *Experimental Science* to constitute a serious opposition to that. But clear thinkers in those days, as in these, were rare. Bacon was a quarrelsome and irritable man, and despite endless discussion nobody was then, or is now, quite in a position to tell us exactly what he means by "magic." There is an opposition to science that comes from those who know what it is and where it leads. There is another opposition to science which arises from sheer misunderstanding. It was from that that Roger Bacon suffered. The generations that came after him set the seal on that misunderstanding by dubbing him "magician," but of Bacon as a heretic or as a protagonist of any war against religious belief we hear never a word. Thus the very interesting incidents of his life and work, important for the history alike of philosophy, of theology and of science, have little significance for the relation of these departments to each other.

In the next generation and even more clearly than Roger, a herald of the dawn was the Cardinal usually known as Nicholas of Cusa (1401–1646). This interesting and many-sided thinker is important for us for more than one reason. We may glance first at his scientific standpoint and achievements. He ranks as a real

experimental scientist, for he clearly perceived the nature and some
of the possibilities of the experimental method and did not hesitate
to draw general laws from his conclusions. Nicholas was a trained
mathematician and took much interest in astronomical and calen-
darial matters. He proposed a reform of the calendar similar to
that which was adopted by Pope Gregory. Among the most
arresting of the passages in his works is a statement in the course of
a philosophical treatise that " I have long considered that this earth
is not fixed but moves, even as do other stars . . . To my mind the
earth turns upon its axis once in a day and a night." Apart from this
matter he has left us a short experimental sketch " On experiments
with the balance." This is the outline of a really scientific treatise
and shows a fair grasp of the experimental method. The basis of
the work is that whenever weight is lost or gained the loss or gain
can be accounted for by further investigation. This is little else
than the older Greek scientific view which formed the basis of the
Epicurean philosophy. The working out of the details is most
interesting. For example, he shows that earth in a confined
vessel in which plants are growing loses weight. He infers that
this weight is gained by the plants. He seems, too, to suggest that
the plants gain in weight from something that they take from the air,
and he affirms that the air itself has weight. The book is written
in what, for the time, is a revolutionary spirit. To find a parallel
to it one would have to go back to Greek science, a subject in
which, by the way, Nicholas was deeply interested. Nicholas had
evidently the germs of the idea of the Reign of Law, and on this
account his theological and philosophical position is of special
interest to us.

The theological standpoint of Nicholas is set forth in his work
" *De Docta Ignorantia*," which has nothing to do with the
absurdity of erudition, as its name might be thought to imply, but
concerns itself with man's essential incapacity to attain to absolute
truth. It was followed by the " *De Conjecturis*," in which he
comes to the conclusion that all knowledge is but conjecture and
that man's wisdom is to recognise that he can know nothing.
From this attitude of apparently pure scepticism he escapes by the
mystic way. God, about whom we can know nothing by experience or reasoning, can be apprehended by a special process
(*intuition*), a state in which all intellectual limitations disappear.
We need follow Nicholas no further on his theological path, but

we may remark that he seems dimly to have foreseen the approaching clash between the scientific and the religious standpoints, and
that he solved the difficulty in the way chosen by many other
scientific men since his day. He accepted the existence of two
forms of experience : an outer, subject to natural law, about which
we may reason, and an inner which has no relation to such law and
is above and beyond reason. The position, if rigidly maintained,
is quite impregnable from the scientific side. Between it and
science there could never be any real conflict.

11. *The Dawn of Modern Science*

The period that represents the growth of the modern attitude
to science—say from about 1500 to about 1700—may be roughly
divided into two sections. During the earlier of these periods
the experimental method, though gradually more and more
recognised in practice, is still regarded as an uncertain instrument.
It is still largely a subject the nature of which it is for the philosophers to discuss. Those who occupy themselves with the actual
business of observation, men of science as we call them to-day, are
few and their work is as yet inconspicuous.

Pietro Pomponazzi (1462–1525), Antonio Telesio (1482–
1534), Bernardino Telesio (1509–1588), Francesco Patrizzi
(1529–1597), Giordano Bruno (1548–1600), Francis Bacon
(1561–1639), Tommaso Campanella (1568–1639), Marin
Mersenne (1588–1648), Pierre Gassendi (1592–1655), culminating with René Descartes (1595–1650), represent a long line of
thinkers, all of whom had some share in forging the great instrument of scientific thought, yet none of whom, save the last, have
left any deep impression on the actual body of scientific knowledge.
Associated with this army of philosophers is a small body of actual
scientific workers, of whom the most prominent are Johannes
Müller of Königsberg (Regiomontanus, 1436–1478), Nicholas
Copernicus (1473–1543), Andreas Vesalius (1514–1564), and
Tycho Brahe (1546–1601). We observe that the danger to the
prevalent religious systems of the day is now becoming apparent.
Pomponazzi dies without the consolations of the Church ;
Bernardino Telesio arouses the anger of the Church on behalf of
its cherished Aristotelianism, and a short time after his death his
books are placed on the Index ; Bruno, the exponent of the
philosophical implications of Copernicus, is burnt for his pains ;

Campanella, after twenty-seven years in prison, is detained for three more in the chambers of the Inquisition ; Mersenne escapes criticism by professing the narrowest theological orthodoxy ; Descartes, despite his claim to be regarded as a faithful follower of the Church in which he had been born, consistently finds discretion the better part of valour on all questions which involve theological judgements.

In great contrast to such men as these are the character and fate of the small band of practical investigators. Regiomontanus completes his work under the patronage of a Cardinal but unnoticed by the theologians ; Copernicus and Vesalius lay their axes to the tree of Aristotelian science and go their ways in peace ; Tycho, in a Lutheran country, prepares the path for Galileo without suffering hindrance.

Among the practical exponents of the new experimental method we will select for special discussion two brilliant practitioners, Copernicus and Vesalius. By a curious coincidence these two—both men of one book—published the great works with which their names are associated in the same year, 1543, which perhaps better than any other may be regarded as the birth-year of modern science.

Copernicus, much the older, much the less striking, much the less of an " observer " in the modern sense of the word, was also much the more conservative of the two. Despite the vast change introduced in his name, he was himself more in line with such comparatively conservative scholars as Nicholas of Cusa and Regiomontanus than with the more revolutionary thinkers such as Pomponazzi and Telesio, who were perhaps more typical of the thought of his time. No man was ever more " academic " than Copernicus, and he inherited the learning of the Italian Universities, at almost all of which he studied. Despite—or perhaps because of—his learning, he was not to any large extent a first-hand observer. He had, it is true, taken a small number of observations of eclipses and planets, but for the most part his results were obtained in the study. In his dedication to the Pope he recounts that he was induced to seek a new theory of the heavenly bodies by finding that mathematicians differed among themselves on this subject. It is evident, both from his long delay in publication and also from certain notes in the preface to his work " On the Revolutions of the Celestial Orbs," that he had anticipated opposition on religious grounds, which indeed the book immediately encountered.   Yet, in fact, when we come to examine the work, the actual changes that he introduces are not as great as we might expect.   It is true that he makes the earth move round the sun.   He retains, however, the ancient theory of the uniform circular motion of the heavenly bodies, nor does he make any attempt to treat the fixed stars as other than placed at a uniform distance from the centre of the universe, which thus remains spherical and finite.   It is only in the bold speculations of Giordano Bruno, suggested, it is true, by the work of Copernicus, that we meet with a limitless universe. The Copernican hypothesis is intimately bound up with the relations of religion and science in the century which followed.

Vesalius was in almost every respect a contrast to Copernicus. Young, ardent, and combative, his life's work was well-nigh complete at twenty-eight, and its effective and creative part was packed into the four years that preceded the publication of his " Fabric of the Human Body" in 1543.   The contents of that great work were delivered in the form of lecture-demonstrations to crowded audiences.   It contains an enormous number of first-hand observations, accumulated while working under the most extreme pressure. The work at one stroke placed the investigation of the structure of the human body in the position of a science in the modern acceptance of that term.   But vigorous and fearless in the demonstration of observed fact, Vesalius becomes timid and ineffective in the discussion of theory.   Vesalius did not hesitate to attack the accuracy of the anatomical observations of Galen.   The physiology of Galen, however, occupied in the mind of the age somewhat the same position as the physics of Aristotle, and Vesalius left the physiology of Galen even more intact than Copernicus left the physics of Aristotle.

A word must be said of the background of Vesalius, which presents a great contrast to that of Copernicus.   If Copernicus represents the learned side of Renaissance activity, Vesalius represents its artistic side, and in this relation his work is of peculiar interest.   Labouring as an anatomist and as an artist in that age, he could not help thinking always of the *end* to which man was made. Despite his occasional revolt from Galen as an observer, he was yet steeped in the Galenic teleology.   But, with an artist's mind and eye, Vesalius transmuted that age-old, moss-grown scheme into something higher and nobler.   For him man is a work of art,

God an artist. Vesalius was no philosopher, nor must we seek in his pages for any formal justification of this view. But so much he says and says well, over and over again. Men and women he saw, as it were, as " studies " for God's great design. Imperfect studies indeed. Vesalius did not, like Galen, harp constantly on the perfection of man's form. He had only the bodies of criminals and worn-out paupers on which to practise his arts. Yet even these were worthy of attention as setting forth, however distantly, the design in the mind of the Godhead. To reach closer than these poor corpses to that design was the real aim of Vesalius. We think of biological investigations in terms of evolution and our questions are whence ? and how ? Our evolutionary doctrine has perforce answered these questions in a way far different from that conveyed to us by the religious tradition. But to Vesalius no such dis-crepancy was present. He thought of anatomy in terms not of evolution but of design, and his questions, had he been philosophically articulate, would have been whither ? and why ? To these questions he and his followers, for generations to come, had no answer other than that provided by the religious systems of their day. Thus, though Vesalius profoundly altered the attitude towards biological phenomena, he yet prosecuted his researches undisturbed by the ecclesiastical authorities.

To us who live only a generation or two after the disturbances of the spirit caused by the Evolution controversy, it may seem that biological rather than physical science is the department likely to clash with the claims of traditional religion. Yet historically this is not the case. The successors of Vesalius continued to prosecute their studies until the nineteenth century unnoticed or even directly aided by the Churches. It was the cosmical speculations of the astronomers and physicists, not the investigations of the biologists, that attracted unwelcome ecclesiastical attention.

Before we leave Vesalius and Copernicus we would draw attention to one direction in which their work was an actual aid to the current religious attitude. The beliefs of mankind con-cerning the physical constitution of the world had been based on the idea of a parallel between the Macrocosm and Microcosm. This doctrine had developed as the characteristic astrology of the Middle Ages. The Church at first had been at war with the doctrine, but later she had compromised and finally accepted it. The acceptance was, however, with an ill grace, for extreme astrological teaching always tended to limit the freedom of the human will and the omnipotence of the Creator. It had been thus used by the heretic Pomponazzi. Now the detailed display of the structure of the human body by Vesalius and his followers, and the detailed study of the structure of the universe by such astronomers as Copernicus, made the astrological point of view less tenable. Thus it was that the two great publications of 1543 laid the axe to medieval science from both sides. While, therefore, the Church thrust from her the new interpretation of the world, she was by no means reluctant to be quit of her old enemy. That enemy died in giving birth to a new foe.

This early modern period of conflict between religion and science closes naturally with the year 1600. The manifestations of the human spirit are not accustomed to confine themselves naturally to exact secular limits. Yet it happens, in this case, that the year 1600 really does mark a turning-point. Giordano Bruno (1548–1600), who was no practical scientist, had eagerly incorporated into his often fantastic philosophy the ill-worked-out conclusions of Copernicus. Despite the allegorical presentation of his thoughts, his works leave us in no doubt of the vehemence of his attack on established religion. His denial of particular providence leads him to a rejection of miracle, to the identification of liberty and necessity, and to the doctrine of the uselessness of prayer. Bruno in his search for unity regards God as the universal substance. Nominally adopting the Copernican theory, he modified it fundamentally. Praising the genius of Copernicus for its freedom from prejudice, he regrets that the astronomer was more a student of mathematics than of Nature, and was therefore unable to free himself from untenable principles. The limitation of the sphere of the fixed stars was obnoxious to Giordano, and he removed the boundaries of the world to an infinite distance in accordance with the principles of his philosophy.

Giordano was burned at the stake at Rome, after seven years' imprisonment, on February 17, 1600. In the same year the experimental era was ushered in with the work of William Gilbert, " On the Magnet," in which he not only demonstrates experimentally the properties of magnets but also shows that the earth . itself is a magnet. In the same year Tycho Brahe handed over the torch to Johannes Kepler. Tycho was the last of the older astronomers who worked on the Aristotelian view of circular and uniform movements of heavenly bodies. Kepler was the real founder of the modern astronomical system. The period from 1600 onward lies with new men, Galileo and Kepler among astronomers and physicists, Harvey among biologists, Descartes among philosophers. The year 1600 thus represents as real a division as any that we can expect in the history of thought.

12. *The Reign of Law*

The seventeenth century opened with an extraordinary wealth of scientific discovery. As we glance at the mass of fundamental work produced during that period, we perceive the major departments of science as we know them· to-day becoming clearly differentiated. The acceptance of observation and experiment as the only method of eliciting the laws of nature reaches an ever-widening circle. Even to enumerate the names of the seventeenth-century scientific pioneers would be a formidable task. The sciences penetrated to the universities and influenced the curricula. The number of scientific men became so large and so influential that separate organisations were formed by them in the interests of their studies. It is the age of the foundations of the Academies.

In the realm of experimental physics, Galileo's invention of the thermometer, with his discovery of the isochronism of the pendulum and of the law of acceleration of falling bodies, had a little preceded the publication of Gilbert's epoch-making work on the magnet. Soon there followed the construction of the telescope and microscope by Galileo, and the elucidation of the optical principles of these instruments by Johannes Kepler. Biology, still apart from the main development of scientific thought, had made great advances before a third of the century was out. The first scientific attempts at a classification of plants had been made by Cesalpino (1579–1603). The Paduan school had launched human anatomy on to the final stage of its development and had laid sound foundations to the study of the comparative structure of animals. Nor had the advance in experimental physics been without its influence on biological development, for the first application of instrumental methods had been made to bodily processes. Above all, a firm foundation had been provided for the mechanical explanation of these processes by the demonstration of the circulation of the blood by William Harvey (1578–1657), a disciple of the Paduan school. Thereby was the Galenic physiological system finally sent to limbo. We hear of it no more.

It is remarkable that all these biological advances, and even the introduction and revelations of the microscope, left the theological world almost unmoved. Even the idea of the automatism of animal movements and reactions developed by Descartes, and further extended later in the century by Borelli and his school, had little or no effect on the position. It was much the same with the work of the chemists. Far otherwise was it with the physical and astronomical discoveries. From the first these attracted theological attention, and throughout the. century there was great activity in these departments.

From the multitude of workers on these subjects we can but select types. Those we choose are men whose investigations most directly influenced the relation of scientific to religious thought. In the first half of the century Galileo and Kepler are the main exponents of natural law. Descartes takes his place here as the first since antiquity who sought to explain the phenomenal universe on a unitary basis. In the second half of the period comes the mighty figure of Newton, whose researches ushered in that phase in our story in which we live to-day.

Galileo Galilei (1564–1642) lived a long life of almost unparalleled intellectual activity. Many of the products of his genius were of immediate practical application, many more involved profound modification of the current scientific opinions, yet others struck at the very basis of the general beliefs of the day. It is with the last class alone that we are here concerned.

The early training of Galileo had been along strictly scholastic and Aristotelian lines, as is shown by his lecture note-books written in or before 1584. Soon after this date he seems to have begun a systematic experimental investigation of the mechanical doctrines of Aristotle. There resulted the " *Sermones de Motu Gravium,*" which was circulating in manuscript in 1590 though it did not appear in print until 250 years later. The work contains a number of objections to Aristotelian teaching, together with a record of experiments on the rate of acceleration of falling bodies. These doctrines were announced from his professorial chair and in the following year were demonstrated from the leaning tower of Pisa. By that famous experiment he showed in the most public manner the error of the Aristotelian view that treated the rate of fall as a function not of the period of fall but of the weight of the object. Galileo's critical attitude to Aristotle, the bulwark of the scholastic system, earned him the virulent enmity of the academic classes. Immediately it cost him his chair. He had, however, made the first definitive breach in the Aristotelian armour.

The next twelve years, though fruitful in scientific discovery, are not important for our theme. Galileo's work of 1604 was more revolutionary. In that year a new star appeared in the constellation *Serpentarius*. He demonstrated that this star was without parallax and must inferentially be situated beyond the planets and among the remote heavenly bodies. Now this remote region was regarded in the Aristotelian scheme as absolutely changeless. Although new stars had been previously noticed, they had been considered to belong to the lower and less perfect regions nearer to earth. To the same lower region, according to the then current theory, belonged such temporary and rapidly changing bodies as meteors and comets. Galileo had thus attacked the incorruptible and unchangeable heavens.

In 1609 Galileo made accessible two instruments that were to have a deep influence on the subsequent development of science, the telescope and microscope. The latter instrument he seldom used. For long it was employed almost exclusively by biologists, and Galileo was no biologist. It is with the former instrument that his name is most frequently associated. His first discoveries made by means of the telescope were issued in 1610. That year was crowded with important observations which we may consider briefly.

The first yield of the telescope was an immense number of hitherto unobserved fixed stars. It was soon found that these were at least ten times as numerous as those that had been catalogued. The more conspicuous star clusters were found to contain many stars too faint for recognition by the naked eye. Parts of the milky way and some of the nebulous patches were resolved into congeries of stars of various magnitudes. The surface of the moon, so far from being smooth and polished, was " very similar to the earth," rough with depressions and high mountains. The height of the lunar mountains was even measured by means of the shadows that they cast. The four satellites of Jupiter were discovered. The comparison of their movements to that of our moon suggested resemblances of our earth to the planet Jupiter. The outermost of the known planets, Saturn, was investigated. Peculiar appearances in him were noted by Galileo, though their interpretation as rings was the work of Christian Huygens (1629–1695) at a later date.

Among the most important of all the observations of the year 1610 were those on the inner planets and notably on Venus. It had been a real objection to the Copernican hypothesis that if the planets resemble the earth in revolving round a central sun, they might be expected to be luminous only when exposed to the sun's rays. In other words, they should exhibit phases like the moon. Such phases in Venus were now actually observed and described by Galileo.

At this time, though Galileo had earned the enmity of the Aristotelians, he was not yet in bad grace with the heads of the Church. In the year 1611 he repaired to Rome to exhibit his " celestial novelties " and was well received by Pope Paul V. It was about this time that he first observed dark spots on the surface of the sun. These, he noted, narrowed continuously as they approached the edges of the sun's disc. He rightly regarded this process as foreshortening and as indicating that they were on the surface of the sun's orb. The date and circumstance of the announcement were unfortunate, since they involved him in a controversy with a powerful Jesuit rival who not only claimed priority of observation but also put another interpretation on the spots. The controversy spread far beyond its original focus. We shall not follow it. An aspect of the dispute, however, was the question of the habitability of the moon and planets. His critics believed that this was a natural corollary of Galileo's development of the Copernican hypothesis which he had now openly espoused. The habitability of the moon was contrary to what was regarded as Aristotelian and Christian doctrine.

Thus became united against Galileo a variety of interests. The band of Academic Aristotelians had long been fuming against him, the Jesuits and some political churchmen now joined them, and with them were united many of that intellectually timid and novelty-hating class that forms the mass of every population in every age. From at least 1614 onward sermons were preached against him. The opposition was gaining force. The matter came before the Inquisition early in 1616 and Cardinal Bellarmine was directed " to admonish Galileo to abandon these opinions and, in the event of a refusal, to command him to abstain altogether from teaching or defending or even discussing these opinions. If he do not acquiesce he is to be imprisoned." A few days later a decree was issued ordering the work of Copernicus to be " suspended until corrected."

During the following years the agitation against Galileo gathered further strength. In 1623, however, something was hoped by him and his supporters from the accession to the Papal throne of Urban VIII, who as Cardinal had appeared not unfriendly to scientific research in general and to Galileo in particular. In 1624 Galileo visited him but failed to obtain promise of any toleration, even in a passive form, for the new doctrines. For the next six years little was heard publicly from Galileo on the subject. Then in 1630 he broke silence and between that date and 1633 was played the final scene in the great drama of his contest with the Church.

By the beginning of 1630 Galileo had after many years' work completed the composition which was finally published as the " Dialogue on the Two Chief Systems of the World " (*i.e.*, the Ptolemaic and Copernican). Galileo obtained an interview with the Pope, who gave him to understand that no objection would be raised to publication if certain conditions were accepted. The more important of these may be thus set forth :

(*a*) The title must clearly indicate the character of the book.

(*b*) The subject must be treated from the theoretical standpoint and this must be clearly set forth in the preface.

(*c*) The book, being largely concerned with the tides, must be made to terminate with the following argument : " God is all-powerful. All things are thus possible to Him. Therefore the tides cannot be adduced as a necessary proof of the double motion of the earth without limiting His omnipotence."

The suggestions were accepted, as were some other minor revisions and alterations made by an official, and this great work was issued at the beginning of 1632. It is full of prophecies of the development of cosmic theory. Thus, it foreshadows the conception of universal gravitation and of the first law of motion. We turn, however, to those elements in the work which had a more immediate effect on the attitude of the theologians.

The dialogue is represented as between three persons, an open advocate of the Copernican doctrine, an obtuse and obstinate follower of Aristotle and Ptolemy, and an impartial participator who is open to conviction. The demand that the Copernican view be treated as a mere hypothesis is but superficially complied with, and the terminal argument, though included as agreed, is treated with scant respect. The tone of the work, witty and biting, leaves no doubt as to Galileo's real opinions. The Aristotelian is represented as hopelessly stupid. The book claims acceptance of the Copernican view. In fact, however, it passes far beyond Copernicus, notably in the total rejection of the idea of the stars as fixed in a crystal sphere. The stars are held to be at inconceivable but varying distance from our earth, and the absence of visible stellar parallax is considered as due to the vastness of this interval. The actual measurement of the parallax of a fixed star was, in fact, not achieved until 1838, by Friedrich Wilhelm Bessel (1784–1846).

The Dialogue brought matters to a head. The Jesuits being specially occupied with teaching were specially enraged. In August 1632 the sale of the book was prohibited and its contents submitted for examination to a special commission that reported as follows :

(*a*) " Galileo has transgressed orders in deviating from the hypothetical standpoint, by maintaining *decidedly* that the earth moves and that the sun is stationary."

(*b*) " He has erroneously ascribed the phenomena of the tides to the stability of the sun and the motion of the earth, which is not true."

(*c*) " He has been deceitfully silent about the command laid upon him in 1616, viz., to relinquish altogether the opinion that the sun is the centre of the world and immovable and that the earth moves, nor henceforth to hold, teach, or defend it in any way whatsoever, verbally or in writing."

There rapidly followed perhaps the most dramatic event in the entire history of science, the trial, condemnation, and abjuration of Galileo (1633). The moving story has been often told. In passing judgement on that great man, an eminent historian of science has compared him disadvantageously to the Christian martyrs. " Had Galileo," Sir David Brewster assures us, " but added the courage of the martyr to the wisdom of the sage ; had he carried the glance of his indignant eye round the circle of his judges ; had he lifted his hands to Heaven and called on the living God to witness the truth and immutability of his opinions, the bigotry of his enemies would have been disarmed, and Science would have enjoyed a memorable triumph." It is a comfortable and bracing assurance, but there is an alternative hypothesis. It may also be that instead of his judges being thus awed they would have sent him to the stake as they did Giordano Bruno. The blood of the martyrs is perhaps the seed of the Church, but scientific truth is not thus established, and it is quite certain that more men have suffered for opinions that are demonstrably false than for opinions that are demonstrably true. It may be convenient to have here the actual sentence of the Inquisition. It runs as follows :

" Having seen and maturely considered the merits of your case with your confessions and excuses, and everything else which ought to be seen and considered, we pronounce, judge and declare that you have rendered yourself vehemently suspected by this Holy Office of heresy, in that (*a*) you have believed and held the doctrine (which is false and contrary to the Holy and Divine Scriptures) that the sun is the centre of the world and that it does not move from east to west, and that the earth does move and is not the centre of the world ; and (*b*) that an opinion can be held and defended as probable after it has been decreed contrary to the Holy Scriptures, and, consequently, that you have incurred all the censures and penalties enjoined in the sacred canons and other general and particular codes against delinquents of this description. From this it is Our pleasure that you be absolved provided that, with a sincere heart and unfeigned faith, in Our presence you abjure, curse and detest the said errors and heresies, and every other error and heresy contrary to the Catholic and Apostolic Church of Rome, and in the form that shall be prescribed to you. But that your grievous and pernicious error may not go altogether unpunished, and that you may be more cautious in future, and as a warning to others to abstain from delinquencies of this sort, We decree that the book, ' Dialogue of Galileo Galilei,' be prohibited by public edict, and We condemn you to the prison of this Holy Office for a period determinable at Our pleasure, and by way of salutary penance We order you during the next three years to recite, once a week, the seven penitential psalms, reserving to Ourselves the power of moderating, commuting, or taking off the whole or part of the said punishment or penance."

In response to this sentence Galileo had to kneel and make a declaration of which the following is the terminal passage :

" I abjure, curse and detest the said errors and heresies, and

generally every other error and heresy contrary to the said Holy
Church, and I swear that I will never more in future say, or assert
anything, verbally or in writing, which may give rise to a similar
suspicion of me ; and that if I shall know any heretic or any one
suspected of heresy, I will denounce him to this Holy Office, or to
the Inquisitor and Ordinary of the place in which I may be. I
swear, moreover, and promise that I will fulfil and observe fully all
the penances which have been or shall be laid on me by this Holy
Office. But if it shall happen that I violate any of my said
promises, oaths, and protestations (which God avert), I subject
myself to all the pains and punishments which have been decreed
and promulgated by the sacred canons and other general and particular constitutions against delinquents of this description. So,
may God help me, and these His Holy Gospels which I touch with
my own hands."

In character and temper Johannes Kepler (1571–1630) was
almost as much a contrast to Galileo as was Copernicus to Vesalius
in the previous century. Kepler, a German, a mystic and dreamer,
essentially a mathematician rather than an experimenter, produced
voluminous works that are now almost unreadable. He stands over
against Galileo, the Italian, with his clear cold intellect, his un-
rivalled experimental skill, his wit and his great artistic and literary
prowess. In sheer genius, however, the two men were not rivals
but peers and comrades. On them in equal measure rest the
foundations of the great physical synthesis.

Kepler's idea of the universe was from the first essentially
Platonic, or perhaps we should say Pythagorean. He was convinced that the arrangement of the world and its parts must correspond with certain abstract conceptions of the beautiful and the
harmonious. It was this faith that sustained him in his vast and
almost incredible labours. In estimating those labours the reader
may be reminded that he spent years of his life chained to the mere
drudgery of computation, without any outside assistance and without any of the devices such as mechanical computers or the use of
logarithms that lighten the task of the modern worker. Nothing
but a burning faith could have made such drudgery possible.

We gain an insight into the transition state between the old
and the new in which Kepler worked when we recall that his professed occupation was largely astrological calculation. Nor was
he cynically sceptical as to the claims of astrology as were some of

his contemporaries. Kepler sought in the events of his life a verification of the theory of the influence of the heavenly bodies. For this purpose he kept all his life what is nothing more nor less than an astrological diary.

Kepler adopted the Copernican view from an early date, and before 1595 he had turned his mind to the question of the number, size, and relation of the orbits of the planets. He was ever seeking a law binding the members of the solar system together. After trying various simple numerical relations, after attempting to fill the gaps by hypothetical planets, and after discarding various other suggestions, he finally lighted on a device which satisfied him. There are only five possible regular solid figures (*i.e.*, figures with equal sides and equal angles) and there are only five intervals between the six planets that he recognised. As far as the calculations of Kepler extended at that time, the five regular solids could be fitted between the spheres of the planets thus :

Sphere of Saturn
Cube
Sphere of Jupiter
Tetrahedron
Sphere of Mars
Dodecahedron
Sphere of Earth
Icosahedron
Sphere of Venus
Octahedron
Sphere of Mercury.

For the first time a unitary system had been introduced in explanation of the structure of the universe. We may join the firm believer in revealed religion in smiling at this instance of human fallibility and presumption. The basis of this unitary system was miscalculation ! It endured but a day. We can smile too with those who reject revealed religion at the manner in which Kepler himself treated this discovery. The regular solids, he observed, were of two classes, primary (cube, tetrahedron, dodecahedron) and secondary (icosahedron and octahedron) differing in various ways. What more fitting than that the earth, the residence of man created in God's image, be placed between the two kinds of solids ! The scheme, he held, was wholly consistent with—nay, was confirmatory of—many of the tenets of his religious belief.

He still pursued the main object of his life, the foundation of an astronomy in which demonstrable causes should replace arbitrary hypothesis. The next subject that Kepler set himself to investigate was the relation of the distances of the planets to their time of revolution round the central sun. It was clear that the time of revolution was not proportional to the distance. For that the outer planets were too slow. Why was this ? " Either," he said, " the moving intelligence of the planets is weakest in these that are furthest, or there is one moving intelligence in the sun that forces all round but most the nearest, languishing and weakening in the most distant by attenuation of its virtue by remoteness."

As the sixteenth century turned into the seventeenth century Kepler received a great incentive to work by joining Tycho Brahe as assistant. By the death of Tycho in 1601 Kepler became effectively his literary legatee. The next nine years saw him largely occupied with the papers of Tycho and with work on optics, in the course of which he developed an approximation to the law of the refraction of light. In 1609 was issued his greatest work, the " New Astronomy, with Commentaries on the Motions of Mars." It is full of important discoveries and suggestions. Among them we may enumerate the following :

(*a*) Important truths relating to gravity are enunciated, *e.g.*, that the earth attracts a stone rather than the stone seeks the earth, and that two bodies near each other will always attract each other if adequately beyond influence of a third body.

(*b*) A theory of the tides is developed in relation to attraction by the moon.

(*c*) An attempt to explain planetary revolutions results in a theory of vortices not unlike that elaborated later by Descartes.

Above and beyond all, the work sets forth the cardinal principles of modern astronomy, the so-called first two planetary laws of Kepler by which

(i) Planets move round the sun not in circles but in ellipses.

(ii) Planets move not uniformly but in such a way as to sweep out equal areas about their centres in equal times.

It was another nine years before Kepler enunciated his third law to the effect that

(iii) The squares of the period of revolution round the sun are proportional to the cubes of their distance (1618).

The Aristotelian physics and cosmology now lay derelict and

could only be defended by such men as Galileo's accusers, who were unable or unwilling to investigate the matter for themselves. Every one of the foundations of the Aristotelian system (see pp. 101–102) had been undermined by Galileo or by Kepler and their place taken by an intelligible mathematical relationship. From now on the scholastic Aristotelianism was as much an embarrassment to official religion as the narratives of miracle became at a later date. It was, however, as hard for one section of the Church to rid itself of its scholastic heritage as it was for another at a later date to disembarrass itself of the dead-weight of miracle. There may have been truth in the words of Bruno : " Perchance your fear in passing judgement is greater than mine in receiving it."

Kepler, despite the mystical and doubtless heretical tendencies of many of his religious views, retained a perfectly simple religious faith, and regarded scientific discovery as a process of the revelation of the greatness of the Creator. It will be seen that he died a few years before the appearance of the first publication by Descartes. It may not be inappropriate to quote here a prayer by Kepler with which he concludes one of his astronomical works. It is a revealing document, exhibiting at once the strength of his simple faith and the absence from it of any clear philosophical element.

" It remains only that I should lift up to heaven my eyes and hands from the table of my pursuits, and humbly and devoutly supplicate the Father of lights. O thou, who by the light of nature dost enkindle in us a desire after the light of grace, that by this thou mayst translate us into the light of glory ; I give thee thanks, O Lord and Creator, that thou hast gladdened me by thy creation, when I was enraptured by the work of thy hands. Behold, I have here completed a work of my calling, with as much of intellectual strength as thou hast granted me. I have declared the praise of thy works to the men who will read the evidences of it, so far as my finite spirit could comprehend them in their infinity. My mind endeavoured to its utmost to reach the truth by philosophy ; but if any thing unworthy of thee has been taught by me—a worm born and nourished in sin—do thou teach me that I may correct it. Have I been seduced into presumption by the admirable beauty of thy works, or have I sought my own glory among men, in the construction of a work designed for thine honour ? O then graciously and mercifully forgive me ; and finally grant me this favour, that this work may never be injurious, but may conduce to thy glory and the good of souls."

René Descartes (1596-1650) was the first in modern times to propound a unitary and effective theory of the universe that became widely current. In the course of his life he made striking contributions both to scientific theory and practice, but these are less important for our purpose than his attitude toward religion and the cosmic theory that he developed.

In the year 1633 Descartes was about to publish his work which he termed " The World," when he heard of the condemnation of Galileo. He withdrew the book and in the event his first publication was the " Discourse on Method," in 1637.

From an early date Descartes felt great dissatisfaction with the results of the usual studies of his time. It seemed to him that there was no clear distinction between facts, theories, and tradition. Want of clarity was always abhorrent to him. He attempted to divest himself of every preconceived notion and then to build up his knowledge. With this end in view he tells us in his Discourse that he made certain resolutions :

(*a*) " Never to accept anything for true which he did not clearly know to be such, avoiding precipitancy and prejudice and comprising nothing more in his judgement than was absolutely clear and distinct in his mind."

(*b*) " To divide each of the difficulties under examination into as many parts as possible."

(*c*) " To proceed in his thoughts always from the simplest and easiest to the more complex, assigning in thought a certain order even to those objects which in their own nature do not stand in a relation of antecedence and sequence," *i.e.*, to seek relation everywhere.

(*d*) " To make enumerations so complete and reviews so general that he might be assured that nothing was omitted."

He believed that all truth that is ascertainable is so only by the application of these principles and thus applies as much in the sphere of religion as in mathematical or physical matters. In essence, therefore, revealed religion in the ordinary sense is superfluous. For him the fundamental test of truth is the clearness with which we can apprehend it. *I think, therefore I am*, is the most clearly apprehended of all truths, and therefore personality cannot be an illusion. Similarly, to him the conception of the soul as separate from the body was clear and even obvious ; therefore, he maintained, it must be true. Moreover, he considered that the mind could not create something greater than itself. Therefore the conception of infinite perfection transcending humanity must have been put into our minds by infinite perfection itself ; that is, by God.

We may now turn to his conceptions of the material universe. The form of the world is inevitable, in the sense that, if God had created more worlds, " provided only God had established certain laws of nature and had lent them his concurrence to act as is their wont, the physical features of these worlds would inevitably form as they have done on our earth." He accepted the probability of creation of matter as a momentary act, but held that this act of creation was the same as that by which creation is now sustained.

Descartes regards the universe as infinite and devoid of any empty space. The primary quality of matter is extension, but there are also the secondary and derived qualities of divisibility and mobility, which are created by God. We may connect the assertion of Descartes that divisibility and mobility are secondary qualities with the formulation of the law that matter, in so far as it is unaffected by extraneous forces, remains in motion or at rest.

He regarded matter as uniform, *i.e.*, made of the same basic stuff, though divided and figured in endless variety. Matter is closely packed, without any vacuum. Therefore the movement of any part of matter produces the movement of all matter. It thus follows that throughout the universe there are circular vortices of material particles that vary in size and in velocity. If one considers any limited part of the universe, as the particles in it whirl round in their vortices they get their corners rubbed off. These being rubbed finer and finer become a minutely divided dust which tends to centripetal action. This fine dust is the *first matter* and forms the sun and stars. The spherical globules whose corners have thus been rubbed off to form the first matter will have on the contrary a centrifugal action, and will form the *second matter*, which constitutes the atmosphere or firmament enveloping the *first matter*. The centrifugal tendency of the *second matter* produces rays of light which come in waves from the sun or the stars to our eyes. There remains the *third matter*, formed from those parts of the fine dust which get detained and twisted on their way to the centre of the vortex and therefore settle round the edge of the sun or star, like froth or foam. This *third matter* can be recognised as the sun-spots. Sometimes this *third matter* melts in the surrounding firmament, sometimes it forms a crust for the sun or star.

The vortices impinge on one another. As a star decays and its expansive force becomes encrusted by the *third matter* another vortex will join with it. But if the central star be of greater velocity than the new vortex, it will dash through the new vortex and be seen as a comet. Sometimes the encrusted star will settle in that part of the new vortex whose velocity equals its own, and is then seen as a planet. The planets of our solar system have all been caught up in the sun vortex.

For the completion of the system of Descartes, it was necessary for him to include the phenomena presented by living things. Here his descriptions illustrate how much in the dark his age was concerning the actual workings of the animal body.

" I remained satisfied with the supposition that God formed the body of man wholly like to one of ours, as well in the external shape of the members as in the internal conformation of the organs, of the same matter with that I had described, and at first placed in it no rational soul, nor any other principle, in room of the vegetative or sensitive soul, beyond kindling in the heart one of those fires without light, such as I had already described, and which I thought was not different from the heat in hay that had been heaped together before it is dry, or that which causes fermentation in new wines before they are run clear of the fruit. For, when I examined the kind of functions which might, as consequences of this supposition, exist in this body, I found precisely all those which may exist in us independently of all power of thinking, and consequently without being in any measure owing to the soul ; in other words, to that part of us which is distinct from the body, and of which it has been said above that the nature distinctively consists in thinking—functions in which the animals void of reason may be said wholly to resemble us ; but among which I could not discover any of those that, as dependent on thought alone, belong to us as men, while, on the other hand, I did afterwards discover these as soon as I supposed God to have created a rational soul, and to have annexed it to this body in a particular manner which I described."

Thus he regarded animals as automata. He knew, for instance, of the circulation of the blood, and, working from it, he developed a most elaborate and carefully worked out theory of the action of the animal body. Man, however, differed from animals, at least in his present state, in the possession of a soul. This he believed to be especially associated with a particular part of the body, the pineal gland, a structure within the brain which, in his erroneous opinion, was not found in animals. In the pineal gland two clear and distinct ideas produce an absolute mystery. It is there that the mystery of creation is concentrated.

The Cartesian philosophy was the first complete and coherent system of modern times. It rapidly found adherents and spread in every country and was popular for several generations. In Descartes' native land it won its way even among churchmen. Gradually, however, the numerous physical errors on which it was based were exposed. Towards the end of the century the theory of vortices became quite untenable. It was in fact shown to be inconsistent with astronomical observation, and it did not fit in with either the cosmical system of Newton or the atomic theory which showed signs of revival. As an explanation of cosmic phenomena it could no longer be held. Moreover, the advance of physiological knowledge exposed the errors of Descartes in the interpretation of the workings of the animal body. Descartes, however, had laid the basis of modern philosophy, and from his time on there has been a continuous chain of thinkers who have claimed to interpret the world by the unaided powers of their own minds.

The crown of the scientific movement of the seventeenth century is the work of Newton (1642–1727). It happens that, while there is great difficulty in describing or discussing in non-technical language the cosmic theories of Copernicus, Galileo, Kepler, and Descartes, the work of Newton, though no less technical and difficult, can be treated for our particular purpose in very brief fashion. Newton had before him the planetary laws of Kepler. He knew that for every planet the cube of the distance is proportional to the square of the time of its revolution, and he sought for some material cause for this. Such a cause he found.

Law had been traced in the heavens from an early age. The actual laws of planetary and stellar motion had been gradually developed from the simple astronomical theories of the ancients. New laws and new mathematical relationships of the heavenly bodies had been discovered. It had not yet, however, been shown that the natural laws that governed the heavenly bodies were in relation to the laws that govern earthly phenomena. To prove that that relation amounted to identity, to show that the force that causes the stone to fall is the same as that which keeps the planets in their path, was the achievement of Newton. Into the details of that achievement it is not necessary to enter here.   But thereby Newton placed in men's hands a law whose writ was universal. The law of the heavens was now the law of earth.

During the century and a half that has elapsed since the publication of the law of universal gravitation, science has developed prodigiously along the same lines.   In reliance on the universality of natural law the stars have been measured, weighed, and analysed. The same scientific process directed to our own planet has traced its history, determined its composition, demonstrated its relation to other bodies.   The investigations of the physicist and chemist have suggested a structure in terrestrial matter similar to that of the stars and suns.   The whole has been reduced to a unitary system.   Living things have been examined with greater and greater powers of analysis and magnification.   Among them, too, Law has been found to rule.   The wild creature is a subject of law ; the migration of the bird that is as " free as air " can be predicted as well as the process of digestion, as well as a chemical reaction.

In this century and a half of vast experimental activity, wherever men have looked they have found law.   It has always been a question of looking skilfully enough and patiently enough, for law to emerge.   Yet it is true that there are certain important gaps which must be recognised.   Thus, no real link has been shown to exist between the living and the not-living.   Despite the extension of our knowledge of the physics and chemistry of the animal body, it yet remains that, as far as we can see, Aristotle was right in the sharp distinction that he made between life and not-life.   But the acceptance of vitalistic theory does not imply the absence of natural law governing living things, and all seems as determinate within living things as outside them.   There are laws of heredity as much as there are laws of chemical combination.

In the second half of the nineteenth century the view gained currency that species were impermanent and that man himself was descended from lower forms.   Despite the commotion that this doctrine evoked it introduced no fundamentally new factor.   That human bodies may be investigated as though they were mechanisms, the laws of whose working are progressively discoverable, had been known in antiquity and had been amply demonstrated by such later workers as Harvey, Stephen, Hales, and Claude Bernard.   That the structure of man was comparable to that of the lower animals had been recognised since the days of Galen, and earlier ; it was the constant theme of Cuvier, Owen, and others. The introduction of a general law to correlate these conclusions in a mere incident in the extension of the Reign of Law. The problem remained as before. After Darwin it was neither easier nor harder to explain how man could escape from the tyranny of natural law. Darwin doubtless brought the problem home to the ordinary man ; he did not create it for the thinker.

It is said, and rightly said, that natural law is not absolute, that it exists in our minds and not in things, and that even in our minds it is subject to change. Philosophically this point is of very great importance, but it is irrelevant in connection with our conceptions of natural law over against revealed religion. The external habiliments of religion, revelation and all that proceeds therefrom, are as much phenomena as are chemical reactions, or the migrations of birds. These things, as being detectable by the senses, are subject to examination by the senses and analysis by scientific method. They, like natural laws, exist in our minds and even in our minds are subject to change.

The rapid introduction of new general laws covering an ever wider field have induced a feeling of insecurity as regards scientific conclusions. This feeling has been specially fostered by certain recent developments, which are sometimes presented as though undermining the Reign of Law. This doubt or hope is unfounded. It has always been recognised that Science is but a conceptual scheme which bears an uncertain relation to the percepts that it correlates. The relation of percepts to each other is, however, fixed and unaltering. When, for example, the substance with all the perceptual qualities summed up by the phrase *Hydrochloric Acid* is poured on the substance with the perceptual qualities of a *Carbonate* there follow perceptual qualities conveniently classed together under the term *Carbonic Acid Gas*. This is the sequence whatever our conceptual view of the event. It is unaltered by any atomic, ionic, electronic, or other concept. The sequence is a Natural Law and so far as the perpetual Universe is concerned such sequences appear to cover the whole field investigated. There is no area that has been exactly investigated that does not seem fully occupied by such sequences. But do there remain fields in which there is a reasonable presumption that such sequences are not universal ? What in fact are the *exact* frontiers of the Kingdom of Law ? If we could define these frontiers, it seems to me, then and then only could we delimit the secular battle-front between Religion and Science.

Historically men of science have found various modes of escape from the tyranny of determinism. The majority of men of science, like the majority of other men, have small philosophical powers. They, like most other men, have accepted their religion as they have found it. They have made their science their daily occupation without clear relation to their religious convictions. A proportion of scientific men, incensed by the mere discrepancy between the biblical and the scientific record, have abandoned more or less completely their relation to religion. A considerable section of these have ranged themselves as " agnostic." Yet there remain two religious points of view that can never be affected by any extension of the scientific realm. The one would completely separate internal experience from external experience. The man who does that is safe ; he has fled, as have many before him, to a haven of peace down the mystic way. The second would regard man's soul not altogether as his own possession, but as part of a great world-soul. This combination of determinism and pantheism is a refuge, not infrequently sought in antiquity, to which many a student of science has turned in modern times, from the days of Spinoza onward.

SCIENCE AND RELIGION IN THE NINETEENTH CENTURY

BY ANTONIO ALIOTTA

Professor of Philosophy in the University of Naples

Translated out of the Italian by

FRED BRITTAIN

Jesus College, Cambridge

CONTENTS

1. INTELLECTUALISM AND THE KANTIAN CRITICISM

FROM the Renaissance until the eighteenth century there was an attempt to solve the conflict of science and religion by rationalising faith and reducing it to the eternal elements which are included in what is wont to be called Deism: that is to say, to the consideration of God as the first cause of the order of the Universe and to the immortality of the soul. In this, rationalists and empiricists—Leibniz and Locke—were in agreement. But this way of solving the conflict, which prevailed during the period of Illuminism, could not satisfy, because at bottom it did not save the concrete reality of positive religion, but only its abstract intellectual content, which, properly speaking, is not religion, but philosophy; and further, because the possibility of demonstrating the existence of God and immortality *a priori* or *a posteriori* was not admitted by everyone. The medieval mystics and Pascal later had already reacted against this cold and abstract intellectualism. Jean Jacques Rousseau, although he too moved in the circle of Deism, did not seek its foundations in an arid rationalism, but in ingenuousness of feeling. "I do not want," says the Savoyard priest when expounding his profession of faith, "to argue with you, or to try to convince you. All I want to do is to expound what I think in the simplicity of my heart. Examine your own heart during my discourse; that is all I ask you to do."

Emanuel Kant gave the *coup de grâce* to religious rationalism by throwing into relief the uselessness of trying to prove theoretically the existence of God and the immortality of the soul. He distinguishes sharply between pure reason and practical reason, although he tries afterwards to bring them into harmony with his doctrine of the primacy of practical reason. Religion, he says, finds its place in the ordering of the moral conscience. Yet this attempt at conciliation could not satisfy either, because, like the old Deism, it did not preserve the positive historical form of religion but only the universality of those principles which are necessary for moral life. Intellectualism persisted at the bottom. In fact, only scientific certainty was truly objective for Kant.

Moral certainty, based on subjective feeling, presented itself as a substitute with which one was to be contented for want of a better. Notwithstanding the doctrine of the primacy of practical reason which permitted one to pass the confines of experience, science really preserved its authority in the Kantian system. But the radical defect of this pretended conciliation was the dualism of pure reason and of practical reason, of phenomenon and *noumenon*, of necessity and liberty, because it is exactly in the world of phenomena that man must act, and because his liberty, relegated from the *noumenon*, does not permit him to break through the necessarily rigid bond of the laws of experience. It was the task of subsequent philosophers to overcome this dualism, and to show that reason is a myth and that liberty lies at the root of necessity, because the ordering of natural laws is freely created by the spirit. The credit of initiating this task, which was afterwards completed by Pragmatism, lies with Fichte.

2. THE ROMANTIC CONCEPTION OF RELIGION

The equilibrium of pure reason and of practical reason was somewhat unstable and destined to be shattered, now leaning towards the subjective feeling of romanticism, and now towards the objective world of science as portrayed by Positivism. In the first instance there was a rebellion against the intellectualism of the eighteenth century and a turning towards the romantic liberty of feeling which breaks the iron bond of natural necessity, together with a disregard for positive science. According to Schleiermacher, neither the intellect nor the will introduces one into the religious sphere. Religion is not knowledge, nor is it a precept ; it is a life, an individual experience, and this life has its origin in the most profound part of our being, in the feelings. The man, however, who experiences religious emotion feels the need of explaining intelligently the nature and the reason of his state of mind, and he interprets it as a feeling of the dependence of our being on the infinite cause of the Universe. This feeling, however, cannot be adequately translated into ideas : representations and concepts are merely symbols which serve for the communication of that feeling. All the ways of representing or of conceiving the Divinity and its relationships with the world and with man, the whole complex of dogmas, are merely symbolical expressions of that direct experience. Even if it is shown that they do not correspond to anything objective, they preserve their value as means of expression, and as symbols which serve for the communication of the direct feeling of the Divine. The proof of dogmatic principles does not lie in logical demonstration, but in the possibility of rekindling in oneself the immediate experiences of which those dogmas are the expression. The personality of God, for example, is nothing but a symbolical transcription in representative terms of that Infinite Spirit which we feel immediately within us. The immortality of the soul is but an expression of the fact that, although we live in time, we participate in the eternal, we are in the Infinite and for the Infinite. The redeeming work of Christ is a symbol of the experience of liberation from perceptible sorrows, and from the impediments which our finite nature places to the sentiment of beatific union with the Infinite. Science, again, can place no obstacle to the individual creation of a religious symbol or to the adoption of those which the positive religions have handed down to us, because science itself is at bottom only a method of symbolic representation, expressing by means of signs the effort of the spirit to understand things—that is, to perceive the identity of existence and of thought, which is an ideal that we can never realise.

Thus romanticism seeks to put an end to the conflict by under-estimating the importance of science. None the less, although its assertions may appear excessive, romanticism has the credit of having brought into relief the fact that faith, feeling, and practical activity lie at the sources of all scientific construction. It deserves also the credit of having regarded religion no longer as an abstract form of Deism, but as a positive concrete whole, and as an historical reality seeking to justify dogma as a symbolical garb of the feelings.

3. Positivism and Social Philosophy

The speculative caprices of the romantic spirit led to a re-action against metaphysics and to an over-valuation of objective science with its positive social advances as against the subjectivism of the individual who sought freedom to create a world for himself. It is not merely by chance that the Positivism of Auguste Comte bears a sociological imprint, because the world of human society is the same as the world of science, with its objective laws which can be controlled by all, and which reasserts itself against the romantic individualism of sentiment which recognises no law outside itself. Auguste Comte, however, did not wish to banish the feelings, but merely to deprive them of all arbitrary character and therefore to make them emerge from the close and uncontrollable intimacy of the subject in order to consider them in their social aspects, which could be observed objectively.   From such a point of view religion could be, and had to be, preserved.   Positive philosophy, by systematising science, aims at realising the intellectual unity of human knowledge.   Yet the intellect is powerless to create or to preserve the social bond.   The feelings alone can really unite men.   Religion which, in the past, had, above all egoistic theories, strengthened the social bond, could and must still fulfil that duty.   It was necessary, however, to purify the traditional religions from their negative and decaying elements, in order to leave in them only the positive, human, and indestructible element.   God and immortality were to be the two dogmas in which the fundamental content of all religions was to be summed up.   It remained to seek their positive significance.   The idea of God was at bottom that of a universal, immense, and eternal Being, with whom human souls communicate, and who fills them with the power to conquer their selfish tendencies in order to harmonise and reunite them in Himself.   The positive significance of immortality is to be found in the fact that it allows a participation in the eternal life of the Divine Being to the just who have truly loved God and their neighbour in this life.   Now the idea of Humanity is the positive notion which corresponds to both these demands.   The traditional religions, purified of their metaphysical elements, are thus transformed into the religion of Humanity, which takes the place of God.

4. Causes which Favoured the Prevalence of Positivism

Positivism held sway in the world of culture for about fifty years down to the year 1870, by reason of the favourable atmosphere for its development which was created by the advances of science.   Let us deal with the most important of these.

1. The atomic theory, with its principle of the conservation of matter and of the equivalence of the weight of the compound with that of its elements in all chemical changes, built itself up on solid experimental foundations and reasserted the ancient aphorism of materialism : " nothing is created and nothing is destroyed."

2. The discovery of the law of the conservation of energy, according to which all forms of energies, such as heat, electric

energy, and chemical energy, can be transformed into motion and vice versa, and according to which the same quality of mechanical power is always equal to a certain quantity of those forms of energies, brought forward a new argument in favour of materialism and the mechanical conception of the world which explains all phenomena by the laws of motion.

3. The progress of physiology showed that the chemical changes of organisms, the exchanges between these and their surroundings, and the relations between animal heat and muscular labour, enter also into the great law of the conservation of energy.

4. The theory of evolution gave rise to the hope that it would be possible to explain on mechanical lines not merely the origin and transformation of living species, but also the genesis of psychic life and human society, eliminating the intervention of supernatural causes.

5. Psychology, by becoming an experimental science, brought out the connection between psychic phenomena and the functioning of the nervous system, and led to the hope that it would be possible to formulate mathematically with necessitatory laws even the life of consciousness, which until then had been the impregnable rock of spiritual theories.

6. Pathological psychology, by experimenting on hypnotic phenomena, on the subconscious mind and on changes in personality, and by establishing their affinity with mystic phenomena, seemed to take from the latter their character of supernatural revelations.

7. Historical, ethnological, and sociological studies of primitive religions explained such phenomena as being due to the same natural, biological, and psychological causes as explained other social facts. Of special note was the school of Durkheim, which, overturning the social philosophy of Comte, regarded religion as a deification of society, brought into existence through the individual consciousness at solemn moments in the collective life.

8. The historical criticism of the Gospels, carried out on scientific lines, and the study of the historical formation of dogmas, helped to shake the belief in supernatural revelation.

5. Beginnings of the Reaction against Naturalism

While science was thus following its ascending curve, the germs of reaction against naturalism were coming to maturity in its own bosom.

1. The theory of evolution called attention to the new qualities which arise in the process of time. How can mechanics, which are the science of eternal laws, and which deal only with facts in their changeless aspect which is repeated time after time in the same manner, how can they deal with those novelties through which the evolution of the world is being accomplished ? Auguste Comte, in his classification of the sciences, had already laid down the impossibility of reducing the more complex phenomena with which the more concrete sciences deal to the level of the more simple phenomena of the more abstract sciences. Boutroux, with his theory of probability, was to insist later on this impossibility of deducing new qualitative forms from the inferior grades of fact, such as physical and chemical properties from geometrical properties, life from physico-chemical phenomena, or biological products from physical facts. Every new quality which is added to existence is a new creation which is outside the determination of laws.

The theory of evolution, in short, by enforcing the consideration of the world from the aspect of concrete historical development, showed the insufficiency of abstract mechanical conceptions and, in general, of all abstract rationalism, through which reality is to be found in a system of types, of immutable beings, and of eternal relationships outside the bounds of time, progress, and development. Reality no longer appeared as a closed system, but as a perennial action, and as an irreversible process in its real duration, which possesses creative efficacy (Bergson).

2. The conception of science also was transfigured by the theory of evolution. The intellect, like all the other organs of life, was considered as a means of adaptation to surroundings, as a weapon in the struggle for existence, as a useful instrument for the preservation and development of life. Like all other organs, it is not something fixed or immutable, but subject to modifications in connection with new conditions of life. The intellectual categories are not for that reason stereotyped forms *a priori*, having a value of necessary universality, but mutable and relative forms.

From this application of the theory of evolution to consciousness arose the empirio-criticism of Avenarius and Mach and the Pragmatism of Dewey, James, and Schiller.

3. Researches into physiological psychology led to the analysis of our notions of space and time, asserting their empirical origin and

their relativity as against rationalistic *a priori* reasoning. Thus was shown the subjective character of those sensorial elements which the mechanical theory had raised to the position of ultimate reality. Were not resistance, space, and time perhaps representations which, no less than sound, colour, scent, and taste, depended on the particular physiological structure of the organisms ? What right have we to consider the former as objective and primary qualities, and the latter as subjective and secondary qualities ? According to Helmholtz, the only legitimate distinction between these elements is of a practical character, in that some of them serve better than the others to make us turn towards facts, by arousing in us expectations which habitually come true. The possibility of discovering the psychological origin of these complexities and of breaking them up into their component parts seemed, in the first enthusiasm aroused by research, a clear proof of the empirical nature of geometrical truths, and, with them, of mechanics.

4. A further contribution was made in the same direction by the new non-Euclidian geometry, which aroused a belief in the incontrovertible certainty of mathematical truths and led to a logical re-elaboration of them. The principles on which they were founded showed themselves to be freely created by the mind, and, losing the character of intuitive evidence which rationalism attributed to them, were reduced merely to " useful fictions " (Poincaré). Mathematical theories assumed the structure of " hypothetical deductive systems " (Pieri), based on a certain number of indefinable factors and undemonstrable propositions freely chosen by convention. Mathematical truths have therefore no character of objective necessity, but are dependent upon those initial conventions. Euclid's postulate, " If two straight lines on the same plane are intersected by a third they will be intersected by that part in which the sum of the two interior angles is less than two right angles," is, in fact, one of these conventions ; while the theorem that " The sum of the interior angles of a triangle is equal to two right angles " is only true if that postulate is admitted.

5. The most serious blow to the mechanical theory came from Carnot's principle. Mechanics, as ordinarily understood, is the study of reversible phenomena. If the parameter, which represents time, and which has taken increasing values during the

development of the phenomenon, is given instead decreasing values to make it turn backwards, the whole system must re-traverse exactly the steps which it has passed. Now Carnot, and, more clearly still, Clausius, have shown that that does not happen at all in the passage from thermal energy to kinetic energy. If we use a given amount of work to raise the temperature of a body, we cannot then return exactly to the initial stage of the process by inverting the cycle. However perfect the machine may be, we shall never obtain, by lowering the thermal level, the same quantity of work with which we began. There will always remain a part of the thermal energy which is not transformed into work, and which is rendered unpotential. This irrevocability, this evolution of Nature in a determined direction, is not explained by the mechanical theory. If physical phenomena were due exclusively to the movements of atoms, the mutual attractions of which depended only on distance, they would have to be reversible. By inverting all the initial velocities, the atoms, always subjected to the same forces, ought to follow their trajectories in a contrary direction, in the same way that the earth would describe in a retrograde direction the same elliptical orbit that it describes in a forward direction, if the original conditions of its movement were inverted.

Carnot's principle shows, then, the impossibility of reducing all the varied forms of energy to kinetic alone. Ostwald therefore substituted for the atomic theory his own theory of energy, and Duhem formulated a theory in which the various energies are preserved as irreducible qualities.

6. In the field of chemistry also new discoveries led scientists to abandon the old idea of the indestructible atom and to substitute for the atomic theory a theory of energy. The analyses made by Crookes of the spectra of certain metals of the series of rare earths, such as yttrium, samarium, and thorium, the discovery of cathode rays, of X-rays, and of radio-active bodies, together with the experimental demonstration that radio-activity does not belong to certain bodies but constitutes a general property of matter, led scientists to believe in an evolutionary genesis of the chemical elements, according to which chemical species must be considered as subject to a process of formation and of dissolution.

Thus the historico-dynamic conception of reality received fresh confirmation, and the possibility of different theories of physical and chemical phenomena drew attention to the subject of their mutability. The physical theory, like the mathematical one, appeared to be not something provided with a necessity *a priori*, but as a free construction of the mind. Several of these constructions can be made. The choice is settled by considerations of practical convenience. Hertz says that several representations are possible, several models of one and the same group of phenomena, and that their value lies in their capacity for pre-vision, that one being chosen which is most convenient. Our theories, therefore, are merely images or useful symbols.

7. Neo-vitalism, which, especially as a result of the labours of Driesch, descended from the metaphysical field to the dominion of experimental biology, shewed the impossibility of explaining certain facts, such as the phenomena of regeneration, by means of physical and chemical laws. The property which fragments of certain organisms have of regenerating the whole does not permit one to compare the organism to a machine, however complicated. ⸮

8. When the first enthusiasm aroused by mathematical formulations of psychic phenomena had disappeared, the discussions concerning the value of the law of Weber and Fechner, and concerning the methods of measuring in experimental psychology, clearly revealed the fact that the conception of measure could not have the same value in this field as in the physical field. Psychic facts are qualitatively different, and therefore cannot be directly measured with regard to each other. The law of the conservation of quantity has no significance in the spiritual life, but is rather a perennial creation of new qualities. Every moment of our interior life has, in its concreteness, its own original physiognomy, which evades all generic schemes of quantitative formulae. (Bergson.)

6. The Crisis of Scientific Intellectualism : Agnosticism

Some of the foregoing observations have shown us that there was a profound contradiction in the very bosom of the theory of evolution, which was the pet idea of Positivism. That is to say, they have shown the contrast between the mechanical conception of the world, according to which everything is settled *ab aeterno* in a changeless system of mathematical relations outside of time, and the historic vision of reality in its concrete development, according to which time has a living efficacy and new forms of existence continually arise which were not contained in the preceding phases. The one is the world of the foreseeable, the other of the unforeseeable. The one is the world of homogeneous quantity, the other is the world of heterogeneous qualities, because evolution has no sense of the purely quantitative point of view, in which nothing new ever arises, but implies stages of development which are qualitatively different. The one is the world considered in its objectivity, where all facts are on the same level as terms of fixed relations and of the same laws which explain equally the fall of a stone and the birth of a man. The other is the world of a hierarchy of beings ascending higher, which presupposes a criterion of subjective valuation, a term of comparison which is considered as the highest step in the evolutionary scale, and in relation to which the lower steps are arranged. This difference was to finish towards the close of the nineteenth century with the triumph of the world of heterogeneous quality and subjective valuation over that of quantity, of the historic vision over the mechanical conception. In the system of Spencer we find the welding of the two worlds and the attempt to make the historical process of development fit into the Procrustean bed of the formulae of universal mechanics. In this welding of two opposite conceptions which are ill-fitted for lying together, lies the crisis of scientific intellectualism, which finds its expression in agnosticism. At bottom it is a confession of the impossibility of enclosing within mechanical schemes the life of the experience in its richness, and of comprehending and exhausting in one finite concept the inexhaustible dynamic infinity of the spirit and of the universe. This is fatal to every kind of intellectualism. Let us try to consider it.

How does intellectualism advance ? Its method is conceptual abstraction. To explain, says Spencer, means to collect similarities of fact, to include them in more and more general classes, until we obtain a law, a principle common to all. This law is for Spencer the law of the conservation of energy. Now, in such a way, by abstracting from the experience of concrete facts the common and persistent elements, we eliminate the variable aspects, the singular physiognomy of events. That which is enclosed in our formulae is not the whole reality, but only some fragments of it. The living continuity of experience is broken when we engrave upon it, with precise limits, stable things exactly determined, which can be fixed by means of equal concepts for all. This purpose is served quite well by the quantitative consideration, which cancels the differences and reduces everything to a texture homogeneous with the schemes of space and time, conceived as abstractions, as an alignment of uniform points and moments.

Not only is the reality of its variable concrete aspects impoverished, but it is deprived of that subjective colouring which is an integral part of all experience. That which is given us—in short, that which is effectively lived by us—is not the things or the facts divorced from the soul, but the world in an indivisible union with our spirit, with our sentiments, and with our acts of will. One should not be surprised therefore if, when these abstractions have been constructed, they are found to be insufficient to exhaust that living experience of which they are only fragments ; or that the attempt to erect these fragments into an hypostasis brings us face to face with those difficulties or with those insoluble antinomies which are the arguments of agnosticism.

Thus space and time, abstractly projected in pretended reality from themselves, give place to contradictions of the actual infinite. Movement, in the attempt to make something absolute from them, leads us also into an infinite process. The dynamic continuity of experience, breaking upon things which ought to act the one upon the other from outside, places us face to face with the difficulty of action from a distance, and so on. It is not difficult to show how all the antinomies on which Spencer bases his agnosticism spring from his abstract intellectualism.

Analogically, the eternal difficulties which have always troubled thought in its effort to conceive God and His relations with the world, and which Spencer repeats after the example of Mansel, spring from an abstract conception of the Deity as a thing in itself, as a system enclosed in the mass of its eternity. Hence spring, for example, the contradictions of a divine prescience in which everything is already given and time exhausted, and of human liberty, which presupposes an unforeseeable and inexhaustible future ; or of an Absolute which is the totality of Being and therefore includes everything in itself, and to which, meanwhile, the creative act ought to be linked as a contingent fact.

Mansel did not stop before these contradictions, just as no agnostic really stops before the supposed limits of thought ; but he had thrown himself beyond them with faith. We must believe in revealed truths, because their incomprehensibility is not greater than that which could be found in any other scientific conception, and depends not on those truths, but on a defect of our intelligence. It is our duty to believe in the personality of God, even though it appears contradictory to think of a personal Absolute, because the character of personality presupposes always the distinction from other persons. We must believe in the dogma of the Redemption and in eternal punishment, even if they are opposed to our conceptions of love and justice, because these ideas, like all the others, are relative to the weakness of the human understanding. Forgiveness, for example, could be a duty only of man, who has need to bridle his selfish tendencies, and not for the Divine conscience. Against the agnosticism of Mansel one could remark that it is not possible to believe in an object except in so far as it is conceived in some way. Faith is, in fact, nothing but the free adhesion of the consciousness to the reality of some thing ; it presupposes therefore the possibility of thinking of that thing as existent. Hamilton and Mansel say, on the contrary, that the Unconditioned is not only unknowable, but is frankly inconceivable. Now if it is incapable of being thought of in any way, what meaning can faith in it have ? Faith in what ? In nothing ? If there is no conception of the Absolute, if religious truths are contradictory and therefore cannot be thought of, they will remain nothing but words. Will people then believe in words which have no meaning ? To believe without knowing in what one believes is a phrase devoid of all meaning.

Spencer tries hard to overcome this difficulty with which agnosticism is faced. The Absolute, although it escapes every attempt to enclose it in a precise thought, is not a mere negation of consciousness, as Hamilton and Mansel considered it. It would be impossible to talk of the relative if there were not the opposite term—the Absolute. If this term were eliminated, the relative would itself become the absolute reality. The unconditioned, the unlimited, and the absolute must therefore be present in consciousness in some way. Mansel and Hamilton speak of the marvellous revelation which faith gives us of the Absolute. They too, then, end by recognising the possibility of learning it in a certain way. Spencer is perfectly right in this. The Absolute escapes from conceptual thought, but not from consciousness in general. In addition to that definite logical consciousness which functions by laying down limits, there is an undefined, indeterminate consciousness which constitutes as it were the common foundation, the raw material from which the various conceptual forms are moulded.

By taking the limits away little by little the whole consciousness is not destroyed, but only that part of it which is definite, limited, and determined. There remains an undefined, unlimited, indeterminate consciousness, a kind of nebula, in which there is a vague comprehension of the Absolute. This is the only way in which we can grasp that inscrutable power. We must not seek farther. It cannot be our duty, as Mansel believed, to imagine God as a Personal Conscience, and as Infinite, if personality and immensity are mutually exclusive ; it cannot be our duty to believe in the absurd. It can only be our duty to subject ourselves to the limits of our thought and to recognise a mystery which really exists. It is derogatory to the Divinity to wish to enclose it in our own concepts, in our own inadequate symbols. Until religion abandons the attempt to conceive the Inscrutable Being in a definite manner, the conflict will continue with science, which will be right to criticise these false concepts. But scientific necessity in its turn will not have to be driven to such a point as to deny that imperishable truth which lies at the foundation of religion—the existence of an Unknowable Power which surpasses all thought and all human symbol.

Spencer, by trying to ascend beyond logical thought to a form of indefinite consciousness in which the precise limits of our concepts are not yet clearly laid down, marks the prelude to the Intuitionism of Bergson. In what he says of the indistinct consciousness, of that kind of nebulous psychic life, in which the solid nucleus of the intelligence is formed afterwards, he seems to read within the lines of Bergson's words : " Autour de la pensée conceptuelle subsiste une frange indistincte qui en rappelle l'origine." In Spencer, however, who is still imprisoned in the old intellectualist conception of consciousness, this way of learning realities does not seem a true and proper consciousness. Science with its determined concepts is for him the true knowledge. The undefined consciousness, although he tries to transform it into a positive notion, remains for him a purely negative abstraction. In this night, the darkness of which is complete, and which not even the light of a symbol can illumine, all possible determination vanishes, and with it all concrete form of religious life. Spencer's pretended conciliation succeeds only in appearance. The Unknowable is, like the Absolute of Schelling, the night in which all the cows are black, and in which everything disappears. Science and religion are brought into agreement only in so far as both are condemned to eternal silence. But the human consciousness could not resign itself to this absolute silence ; and the effort to penetrate the mystery, to issue forth from the narrow barriers of intellectualism, to assert life in all its concrete fullness—ideas which are ill-fitted to the fragmentary schemes of scientific concepts—was bound to lead to the rebirth of romanticism.

7. THE RADICAL DUALISM OF RITSCHL

The undefined consciousness of which Spencer speaks is too vague and indeterminable to be able to contain the religious life. If religion is to persist side by side with science in its own dominion, it must, while abandoning every intellectual notion, have a content of its own. This is the point which the school of Ritschl tries to determine.

Religion, he says, as it is commonly professed, is mixed with extraneous elements which corrupt it. The first of these elements is philosophy ; natural theology. There must be first of all a definite break with intellectualism and with scholasticism, which, expelled from the religious consciousness by Luther, has insinuated itself there afresh. The philosophy which works only on the abstract and disposes only of natural phenomena cannot, by definition, attain the religious element which is life, being, and supernatural activity. The faculty of knowledge which exists in man is limited to the understanding of the laws of matter, while religion deals with purely spiritual things. The second parasitic element of which religion must be disembarrassed is the human authority which enslaves it in Christianity. The Christian must recognise no other master than Jesus Christ.

Ritschl tries to realise in its true life a religion thus purified of its extraneous elements. With Schleiermacher he sees in sentiment the organ of piety. But it seems to him that this is an insufficient basis for that systematic theology without which religion dissolves into individual opinions. Sentiment must be nourished with universal religious truths. Sentiment finds and recognises in the Bible and in general history the concrete content which it cannot do without and which it cannot produce unaided. For example, the heart experiences the feeling of sin and the desire for beatitude   Now in Revelation there are, corresponding to these sentiments, on the one hand a just and irritated God and on the other a merciful God. The religious conscience thus finds the cause of impressions which natural objects do not explain to it. In this way the religious sentiment, seeking its significance and its foundation in the sacred books, becomes more and more clear, rich, and steady. It passes the individual " ego " and can communicate with the sentiment of other people in a Church.

The essential office of internal disposition is therefore diminished, because it is, after all, in sentiment and in immediate experience that religion is realised. If the Gospel is true, it is not because the intellect recognises it as such, but because the conscience judges it worthy of being true. This is judgement of its value and not of its existence.

One could object (and this has been observed by a pupil of Ritschl, Wilhelm Hermann) that the theological formulae which are found, for example, in St. Paul, represent religious experiences belonging to him, but which we probably have not undergone. How can we adopt them ? Hermann solves the difficulty by distinguishing the foundation of faith from its contents. The foundation is absolutely necessary, and is identical in all individual consciousnesses. It is sufficient to expound faithfully this part of Revelation alone, because it is directly experienced by every sincere soul. But the special content of faith, the definite form of dogma, represents a more determinative experience, which may vary with individuals and may be expressed in different ways. For example, the consideration of the inner life of Christ produces in the human soul such an impression that it believes in Him out of moral necessity; but the special idea of a vicarious expiation realised by the death of Christ is merely a contingent expression, which may vary or be lacking in different individuals. There is no longer, therefore, dogma or Church in the traditional sense of the word. The individual cannot come out of himself. He sees in dogmas metaphors which he interprets according to his own experience. A Church is for him a group of men united with the idea of rejecting every compulsory creed.

Thus we see in Hermann very clearly that subjectivism which Ritschl in vain tried to overcome by having recourse to the universal element of revealed truth. When, in fact, the criterion of the validity of Revelation has been brought into agreement with sentiment and into the possibility of vivifying it with our immediate experience, the acceptance of dogma is seen to depend entirely on the individual conscience.

But there is a still graver defect in the radical dualism of Ritschl. This is the supposedly sharp division between the two dominions, according to which science ought to confine itself solely to physical phenomena, leaving spiritual facts to religion. The scientist will not easily adapt himself to remaining shut up in the world of nature, and no one can deny him the right of submitting even religious feelings to the method of scientific research. It is of no use to put up a notice " No admission." It is more useful to examine its procedure in order the better to sound its value. This is just what Pragmatism has done.

8. Pragmatism, Modernism, and the Philosophy of Action

The confession of impotence by agnostic naturalism led, towards the end of the century, to a return to the romantic spirit of the beginning of the century. Science, of which Positivism had been the first to proclaim the apotheosis, was submitted to criticism, and revealed the abstraction of its concepts and of its theories, which do not make us gather the reality of its living richness, but only the skeleton of it. It was found that those theories are also at bottom a human construction, variable and relative, and that they suppose an act of faith at their roots. In this way the distinction between pure reason and practical reason which Kant had made was shown to be artificial, because the activity of the scientists is itself directed to a practical end ; that is, to that of dominating nature, of finding suitable schemes which may serve to guide us through the complexity of the phenomena of experience. Thus religion and science were reconciled in their common origin, which is always an act of free will, a free adhesion of the spirit ; and dualism was superseded.

According to Pragmatism, of which William James and F. C. S. Schiller are the most illustrious representatives, the sole function of science is to serve for action, to provide us with methods to follow in order that we may see this or that phenomenon appear, or in order that we may obtain this or that result. A proposition which does not generate practical results has no meaning. Two propositions which bring no result in their manner of acting differ only verbally. According to the Pragmatist, there is no truth which must be reflected from without, or to which the thought must correspond to be called true. Truth and reality are constructed actively by ourselves. There exists no perfect system laid down *ab aeterno*, with immutable laws ; but reality is always on the road towards being made, a ceaseless creation, in which we collaborate with our energetic forces.

Religious truth too, like all truths, has the same practical value. It is of no use to ask ourselves whether our religious conceptions reflect an objective reality, but only whether religious vision brings better practical results than naturalism.

Pragmatism received a great repercussion in the religious field because it really constitutes the philosophical basis of that tendency which goes under the name of Modernism and which is characterised by its decisive opposition to traditional intellectualism, which considered religious truths as knowable and partly even demonstrable by means of reason ; and, where reason could not reach with its own forces alone, recourse was had to external revelation and to the authority of tradition. Modernism denies to the intellect the capacity of demonstrating and understanding the Absolute, which is the object of religious faith ; and it admits a special organ of experience, an experience directed by the Divine, which really reduces itself to moral activity, to the ethical conscience. In this intimate experience, in which we immediately grasp God in his concrete life, lies the essence of piety. God is not an object external to ourselves, an immutable Being, endowed with certain eternal attributes, and who must be respected from without and known in his objective properties, but a living spirit who works eternally through the human spirit and is eternally revealed in it in his profound intimacy. From the philosophical point of view the Modernists arrive at a kind of dynamic Pantheism, which has much affinity with the Idealism of Fichte. Divinity is immanent in our consciousness ; but, as our finite activity never finally succeeds in exhausting the infinity of the Divine, there is always in it something which escapes us and surpasses us ; in this sense therefore it can be called transcendent. Its revelation did not happen once and for all at a fixed moment of time, but is eternally taking place in the consciousness of humanity and in its development. There is therefore no fixed body of unchangeable religious dogmas, but a truth which is developed and revealed progressively through the moral experiences of the human spirit. The intellectual formula of dogma is only a symbol of these experiences which has a value only in so far as it is translated into a rule of practical conduct.

The first germ of the modernist doctrines is found in Newman, who, while constraining himself to remain in the ranks of Catholic orthodoxy, fought against traditional intellectualism. According to him, the adhesion which our spirit makes to religious truths is not brought about by reasons of logical order, although it has its starting-point in the moral conscience. The profound feeling of obligation and responsibility which we find within us leads us to the belief in a Divine Judge, not by a logical reasoning, but by a kind of instinct which makes us divine the true path, and which resembles the divination of genius. Upon this, which Newman calls the illative sense, assent to the truths of faith is based. By a kind of instinct, he says, analogous to that by which the dog knows his master and the sheep its lambs, the image of God is revealed to the soul of the child without any reasoning, not as an abstract notion, but in a form of concrete and living reality. Reason with its syllogisms does not bring us to certainty, because it is based on undemonstrable premises, and because, with its abstractions, it can never be equal to concrete reality. Something always escapes us, the proofs are never complete. Probability alone, therefore, can be produced from logical inference. In order to transform it into certainty there is need of the illative sense, the procedure of which has its roots in the non-conscious depths of our personality. The illative sense does not pass, like logical inference, from one abstract proposition, but from one concrete thing to another concrete thing. And even when we apparently assent to the conclusions of a certain abstract reasoning, we are not certain of these by virtue of that syllogism, but because the illative sense carries us to the same conclusion ; and we can in fact eliminate logical proofs without taking anything from certainty, just as the scaffolding is taken away from a building after it has been constructed. Abstract logic stands in the same relation to the illative sense as the rules of rhetoric do to poetic creation.

It might be objected that in this manner assent to truth is left to the personal judgement of the individual ; but Newman replies that the illative sense is based, for religious truths, on the moral conscience, which is the same in all men ; and he who trusts to the voice of this conscience and to all that the illative sense draws from it cannot go wrong, because it is as infallible as the instinct. It is certain that deviations are possible, but only in the same sense and in the same manner as it is possible to deviate from the moral conscience. The man who follows faithfully the voice of moral conscience, and who finds himself face to face with a church like the Christian Church, feels that it is the voice of God Himself ordering him to accept its truths. The Nicene Creed appears to him as the portrait of which the moral conscience was but a rough sketch.

The dogmatic proposition is but the translation in explicit terms, through the medium of reflection, of truths in which we implicitly believed by unconscious instinctive intuition. Centuries have been able to pass without the formal expression of truth which has been for a long time the secret life of many millions of faithful souls. Theology is the elaboration of internal truths, known by instinct ; an elaboration which needs the labour of many centuries and is carried out tentatively. Formulae never exhaust by their abstractness the intuitions of the divine which are felt in the intimate conscience. Christian dogmas are really nothing but symbols of a divine experience which has never been attained by them and never can be, even if millions of other dogmatic propositions were added. Dogmas, therefore, are subject to a process of development through age-long attempts to translate intimate and concrete religious experiences into intellectual formulae which become more and more adequate.

Still more than Newman, Blondel has exercised influence on the Modernists by his book " l'Action," dedicated to his master, Ollé-Laprune. The latter, in his book " De la Certitude Morale," had maintained, after the example of Renouvier, that the distinction drawn by Kant between pure reason and practical reason, between scientific certainty and moral certainty, does not exist. Reason, he says, is always practical, certainty has always a moral foundation and depends on a predecision of our will. Not only metaphysical and religious truths, but also scientific truths are based on acts of faith. The sciences in fact all start from certain undemonstrable principles, which we accept freely, because only by accepting them is practical life possible, or even agreement with other men ; but we can also doubt even these principles. For example, the postulate of the uniformity of the laws of nature, which lies at the foundation of scientific induction—it would not

indeed be possible to arrive at a universal law from a certain number
of cases under observation, unless it were postulated that Nature
will remain always coherent in itself—is an undemonstrable
principle which has been doubted by certain philosophers, by
Hume for example.   Yet, generally speaking, all men believe in it,
because if that principle is not admitted, practical life is impossible.
How could we live, in fact, if we were not sure of the constancy of
the properties of such bodies as food-stuffs ?   Further, the very
affirmation that an objective world exists independently of our
own individual experience is an act of faith, because we shall never
be able to verify the existence of things beyond the limits of our
own senses.   If we admit the reality of external things it is solely
because in that way we make social and moral life possible, and
because we feel the duty of believing.   It is not by a necessity
which exercises an insuperable force from without, but by a free
exercise of our will, which feels itself morally obliged to believe.
Scientific truths are admitted by us in that we may recognise that
they are necessary means for the attainment of our ethical ideals.
From this it follows as a consequence that when we find ourselves
faced with two equally possible hypotheses, we shall always have
to choose that one which fits in better with our moral needs.
Between liberty and absolute determinism, for example, we shall
choose the first.   Now, according to Ollé-Laprune, even religious
truths are necessary for the moral life, and we shall therefore have
to decide to accept them, just as we accept scientific truths, and the
certainty which we shall have will be always of the same order
—a moral faith.   If we *will* to be moral, we must also *will*
everything which is a means to it, a necessary presupposition
of ethical life ; and therefore we must accept also religious
truths.

Blondel's " Philosophy of Action " takes as the principle of all
spiritual development a will which seeks to actuate itself completely,
but which never entirely succeeds, and, unsatisfied by the position
it has attained, strives always to pass beyond it.   There is at the
bottom of us all an unconscious tendency to attain full development
and to complete our being more and more—a tendency which is
never satisfied and which is inexhaustible.   This is the *voluntas
volens* (which corresponds to the Infinite Ego of Fichte).   There
is also the *voluntas voluta*—that is to say, that part of it which is
effected little by little in our consciousness during its development

(the Finite Ego of Fichte). Action consists in the passage from the *voluntas volens* to the *voluntas voluta*, in the movement of man towards everything the possession of which helps to increase the dominion of his own will, towards everything which he needs to translate into action his infinite potentiality.

The *voluntas voluta*, which is realised in consciousness, never succeeds in exhausting the *voluntas volens*, so long as we remain in the sphere of phenomena, and it is this inadequacy which drives the Ego continually to fresh actions. Now Blondel's method exists in demonstrating that the will, if it wishes to arrive at its full possession and to exhaust its infinite potentiality, must accept the revelation of the supernatural. Only thus can the *voluntas voluta* be adequate for the *voluntas volens* ; and Blondel makes us pass, in fact, through the various phases of action in the world of phenomena, and makes us see from each how the *voluntas volens* cannot be satisfied and how there is therefore a need to go further. One of these stages is, for example, science, which makes the forces of the physical world enter into the plane of our conscious will, and makes them co-operate with us ; but it is not sufficient, because outside each individual there are other men who limit its truth. In order to bring about co-operation in the development of their own existence, the various forms of human society have been constituted. But the Ego does not find complete satisfaction even in society, and from this follows the construction of the ethical ideal which transcends phenomena. Even this does not satisfy the *voluntas volens*, which needs something actual and real. Man therefore makes a supreme effort to fill with his own energies alone the abyss which separates the will from that which he wishes to be, and he makes in his own image and likeness a God in whom his supreme ideal may be concentrated. We thus have natural or superstitious religion. Even this does not satisfy the will, because the inexhaustible and infinite ideal cannot be adequately met by representations and limited concepts. There always remains therefore the need for a completion, which man cannot realise by his own efforts alone. The *voluntas volens* is not yet entirely exhausted by the *voluntas voluta*. Evil, suffering, and death present themselves to us as a yoke which we carry and which we must endure, while our profound ambition was to make everything enter into the sphere of our dominion and to include the entire universe in our Ego. So long as we have an external limit, so long as there is compulsion—that is to say, something which is not freely willed by us—the process of action cannot therefore be considered complete.

In order to be all that we wished to be, we must take a last step—accept the Christian revelation. One cannot, in fact, object to this that it presents itself as a complexity of truths superior to reason, because reason has shown itself insufficient to satisfy our Ego. What we still desire must lie beyond that.

Man must, then, accept as a provisional hypothesis the dogmas which the Christian religion sets before him, and act in conformity with them, in order to test whether he finds in them that satisfaction of his profound desires which he had sought in vain in the sphere of phenomena. Faith does not pass from the thought to the heart, says Blondel, but draws a divine light from experience through the mind. In that lies the importance of ritual acts, which are not symbols, but the vehicle and the very body of the transcendental. In them man finds God, who thus comes to be realised through the very conscience. In religious experience he is indeed identified with God, and fuses his will with the Divine Will. The *voluntas voluta*, being made conscious, is thus entirely equalised with the *voluntas volens*, which was really God himself, the agent of the unknown profundity of our spirit.

Le Roy, drawing his inspiration from the doctrines of Bergson and Blondel, has given an interpretation of religious dogmas which has since been accepted by the Modernists. A dogma is not a knowledge of an objective truth, but is above all a rule of conduct and enunciates a prescription of a practical character. For example, to assert that God is personal would only mean, " Act in your relations with him as you would with a human person " ; while the resurrection of Christ would mean that one must act with regard to Him as one would have done before His death, or as one would do towards a contemporary. The Christian, by accepting dogmas in this sense, is left perfectly free to make for himself whatever theory or representation he wishes of corresponding objects, such as the personality of God, the Resurrection of Christ, or His Real Presence in the Sacrament. A single condition is imposed upon him, that his theory will have to justify the practical rules enunciated by the dogma, and that its intellectual representation will have to take those prescriptions into account. From that springs the possibility of the evolution of dogmas. Their formulae can be transformed, although their rule of conduct and their practical application remain the same.

9. CRITICAL DISCUSSION OF THE ABOVE THEORIES AND CONCLUSION

To Pragmatism belongs the great credit of having eliminated many of those insoluble problems which sprang from the hypostases of abstractions. Traditional intellectualism conceived of reality as being completely outside ourselves, so that we ought to confine ourselves to reflecting passively upon it. On one side stood the soul, on the other the world, both existing in their immutable substances. The question was how they could communicate with each other ; and the thought laboured with the endeavour to understand how the two could be united, or how the spirit could be brought into relation with nature in order to know it and to act. Intellectualism created similar difficulties by making God a perfect reality outside our spirit, an ever-present infinity which one never succeeds in understanding. The determination of His attributes led to insuperable contradictions, in which the thought vainly oscillated between divine predestination and human liberty, in a desperate effort to conciliate them. The preordained plan of the world took all significance from the spontaneity of the will. When faced with a perfect reality, there is nothing more to be done : there is nothing more to be added to existence in its infinite fullness. Everything is exhausted in eternity, and time is only the illusory projection of its shadow. But one could not understand how those shadows could be generated outside the infinite, how the perfect could decline into the imperfect, or the light of the spirit into the darkness of matter. Theological disputes, syllogistic developments, and sceptical and agnostic conclusions were the consequences of those intellectualistic postulates. Tired of such vain subtleties, a few souls fled to the simple ingenuousness of love, and intoned the Canticle of Creation, like St. Francis of Assisi. They felt, as if by a miracle, the ice of enigmas melt in the fraternal light of the sun. They felt that there are no precise limits where God ends and the world begins, where the eternal passes by in the natural rhythm of the song of birds, the rustle of leaves, the breath of men.

" Let us draw near, then, to reality with love, let us return to the fresh springs of life," says William James. We shall see God and nature issue forth from the enclosed mass of their infinity which weighed upon us from without. We shall see them draw near to us to give warmth to our souls. Let us put arbitrary constructions on one side. It is of no use to talk of a thing within us or of a spirit within us. Reality exists in our integral experience, of which God, the soul, and the world are indivisible aspects. God and the world are complete *ab aeterno* outside ourselves, but live and are transformed with us, and with us rise to higher levels of truth and harmony. Our thought is not the passive reflection of reality in its stereotyped nature, but an active elevation of it to a higher form ; for the world is not, as intellectualism thought, already pruned into a definite shape, already arranged in a changeless design with perfect harmony, but is always on the road to completion and to harmony along the conflicts and active experiences of the difficult and ever-open road of history. James calls us back from intellectualism to the experience which we have lived, and which is not constituted entirely of clearly distinguished parts which we can distinguish by means of representations and concepts from those parts which, isolated from the remainder, go to make up the common world of science. It is a dynamic continuity in which these clearer phenomena are immersed as in a stream, of which the beginning and the end fall away into the darkness of the sub-consciousness. There is no separation between the one state and the other, but merely an imperceptible passage. Thus our personality which can be clearly grasped lives in continuity with a more vast, obscure life of which it has direct experience. This feeling of living contact by which the spirit attains peace and energy, this communion with a more extensive Ego from which we feel that salvation and liberation come to us, is, according to James, the essence of religion. The rest—rites, dogmas, intellectual representations—are an accessory superstructure.

The mysticism of James, although distinguished from traditional mysticism by its dynamic character, according to which participation in the more vast subconscious life is not static union but energetic activity, does not escape the defect of subjectivism. It might be remarked against the old mysticism that the soul of the mystic experienced what he described, and it could also be admitted. But it is one thing to say " I have had these subjective experiences," and another to assert that they are brought about by a real object, by a Divine Being, existing outside the mystic's consciousness. In order to be able to say that, it is necessary to make a decision, to pass beyond the moment lived, and to give an interpretation of it in intellectual terms. It is not the state of ecstasy alone, therefore, which constitutes the certain revelation of the reality of God, but the intellectual interpretation which the mystic, restored to himself, makes of what he has experienced. Without the function of the intelligence as judge, therefore, the ecstasy would have no discernible significance.

Further, can we accept with closed eyes the idea that the interpretation given by the mystic of his subjective experiences is correct ? Can we bluntly exclude *a priori* the possibility of errors and illusions ?

The content of the revelations which the mystics say they have had, the truths which they say they have gathered by direct intuition in the state of ecstasy, vary according to the different religions. Which of them is to be held as true ? If the attestations are contradictory, it is clear that some of them at least must have exchanged subjective phenomena of their consciences for objective revelations.

James sees this clearly, and does not hesitate to regard the incidents described by the mystics as hallucinations, from which it is necessary to purify religious experience, which consists essentially of that feeling of the presence of, and of contact with, a vaster life which has no representation. But how can this feeling, we insist, guarantee to us the reality of its object ? And can it alone exhaust the religious life ?

Feeling cannot reveal to us the fullness or the completeness of reality. It is merely a moment of consciousness, which does not include in itself the whole of our personality, and still less can it include the life of other souls or of the whole universe. Any particular emotion reveals no more than itself—a fugitive moment of one's life, and nothing more which differs from itself. Pain, for instance, as a pure feeling, tells us nothing concerning the causes which have produced it, unless there is added to it a representation, a concept, or an opinion. "I experience fear or veneration" —this is a sentimental experience. But the sentiment, as such, does not tell me whether this fear or this veneration comes from any other man whatsoever or from a Supreme Being. In order, therefore, to distinguish the emotion which one feels towards another man, animal, or inanimate thing from the emotion which one feels towards God, it is necessary for the sentiment to be accompanied by a representation and a concept. While admitting that religious emotion has a different tone and character from the others, something special to itself, we are not thereby authorised to say that (as a pure sentiment without representation or concept) it has, as Schleiermacher maintained, an immediate consciousness of an *absolute dependence.*

Dependence implies a relationship between two terms, and cannot be present to consciousness unless these two terms are conceived in some way : that is to say, my person, which is dependent, and the spirit, on which it depends. The feeling taken by itself is a modification of my subjective consciousness, which gives me only the experience of itself, and does not tell me anything either of my personality as a whole (which is not indeed exhausted by that particular feeling) or of the Infinite Reality on which it depends. The feeling alone is not sufficient in order to be conscious of this dependence. At least three concepts are necessary—that of the finite, that of the infinite, and that of the relation between them. There must also be added the idea that the dependence is not relative (that is, such that we can withdraw from it), but absolute, and for this idea other concepts are necessary.

Feeling alone is impotent to bring us out of subjectivity, as it easily degenerates into individual choice. Every individual, in fact, will be able to create for himself his own religion, and there are innumerable varieties of religious experience, as the very title of James's book tells us.

In order to overcome subjectivism, the Pragmatists, the Modernists, and the philosophers of action turn to the criterion of social utility and to the necessity of moral demands, which have a character of universality. But it will be easy to show that that does not serve for the purpose, and if it succeeds, it is because they imply an intellectualist criterion without appearing to do so. It is certainly of no use to bring out of subjectivism the illative sense of Newman, which, as a source of certainty, cannot be considered superior to logical reasoning, since it is even more subject to errors. The instinct is not as infallible as Newman thinks. Inspiration and divination often give fantastic products which correspond to nothing real. The passage from one concrete image to another can be determined by relationships of accidental association. How shall we distinguish the legitimate passages from those which are arbitrary ? It is very dangerous to trust to inspiration, because all subjective imaginations can be justified in that way.

If the illative sense is infallible, as Newman asserts, why do not men furnished with one and the same moral conscience all arrive equally at the same religion ? How can we explain the existence of so many different religious professions, even in men who agree among themselves in moral feelings ? Ought not the illative sense, beginning with these, to arrive always at the same conclusion if it is really infallible ? We cannot maintain that Christians alone have the privilege of morality, others too could assert that their particular religious creed is a development of that which was contained potentially in the moral conscience by virtue of the illative sense.

In this way we are sure to fall into subjectivity. We shall never have the right to say that one inspiration is true in preference to another while we lack some objective criterion of judgement. Nor does Blondel's method of action succeed any better in making us overcome subjectivism. First of all from the fact that our will never succeeds in satisfying itself in the world of phenomena, it is not right to argue that there must be an object such as to satisfy it fully. Who authorises us to exclude the idea that our individual life must not instead develop without ever reaching the desired goal ? It must not of necessity exist because there is need of it. Could not the ideal at which the will aims be inexhaustible and therefore unable to effect itself completely ? Everything which is willed need not of necessity exist; nor, on the other hand, do things exist solely in so far as they are willed. Blondel founds all his philosophy on an entirely arbitrary equation, that " to exist " equals " to be willed."

On the other hand, not only do other beings exist, but we ourselves exist, even in despite of our will. Perhaps that which we must endure passively is not real because we have never succeeded in dominating it ? It is exactly the contrary ; at the very point where we feel external compulsion most strongly there is a more evident sign of objective, independent reality.

The assertion of existence from the desire of something cannot and must not be confused with the desire for that same thing. We do not recognise the existence of our Ego, of our ideas, or of our feelings, by being convinced that all this does not depend on our free will at all ; and we never reach a stage of development when we can say that our consciousness is willed by us. The formula " I am that which I will," which Blondel takes from Secrétan, is an expression without meaning ; the will supposes a determinate psychological structure which, just because it is presupposed by the will, cannot be considered as created by it.

Further, even by adopting the point of view of Blondel and conceding to him that the final completion which the Ego needs exists, why shall we have to limit ourselves to making the experiment of the practice of the Christian religion and not that of the other religions ? In order to decide which satisfies best, we should have to put them all to the test. The Buddhist believer is not less satisfied than the Christian believer. Who will assure us that this state of satisfaction is not a purely subjective phenomenon depending on certain habits already contracted ? The satisfaction is relative to the needs of the particular individual, and the needs in their turn depend on education, habits, etc. How can it be assumed outright from the index of a supernatural intervention ? Very many individuals, moreover, are equally satisfied, or at least believe themselves to be so, without any practical religion. Who tells us that our satisfaction is superior to theirs ? The method of immanence adopted by Blondel will enable us to assert that there exists in the soul a state of satisfaction ; but whether this satisfaction is brought about by natural causes, or whether it depends on supernatural intervention, cannot be decided. In order to distinguish God from my subjective feelings, in order to consider Him as transcendent—that is, as real even outside my subjective experience (and Blondel says that he wishes to recognise Him as such)— I cannot do less than turn to an opinion of intellectual character in which existence is placed independently of the two terms ; that is to say, of my state of satisfaction and of the supernatural which gives it to me. Logical reflection alone will be able to decide whether the satisfaction is due to natural causes or to the action of a supernatural principle.

It might be remarked to Le Roy that dogma could not serve as a rule of practical conduct unless it has a theoretical content ; and even the manner of acting varies in relation to this content. Thus, in order to act towards God as towards a person one must have a concept, however vague, of this personality, and just as the manner of acting varies according to the persons with whom one deals, in order that the rule of conduct may be precise, one must have a more determinate idea of the specific character of that person. Will it be necessary to act towards the personality of God as towards any mortal person ? Or is it necessary to distinguish this special form of conduct ? And how will it be possible to distinguish if the character proper to the Divine Reality is not determined ?

Practical action always supposes an opinion, although it is only implicit, and not expressed. When I act in a certain manner with regard to a thing, I tacitly recognise that it possesses those characteristics which make my action possible and which give it a meaning. If I treat an object as a person, I implicitly consider it such. Dogma therefore, if it gives the rules of action towards God, must contain within itself a totality of knowledge with regard to the Divine Being and to His relationships with our consciousness and with the world. This discernible content can even be indeterminate in all its particulars, but must at least be such as to distinguish religious action from any other form of conduct. And if I act in a certain way, it means that I accept that knowledge upon which my conduct is based. He who finds difficulties in accepting dogmas theoretically will certainly not persuade himself to act in conformity with them. For instance, he who considers the attribution of personality to God as absurd will certainly not come to treat God as a person. In short, the practical significance of dogmas is not separable from their theoretical content. He who accepts the one must accept also the other ; he who refuses the one must refuse also the other.

Let it be remarked further that, in order to believe, it is not sufficient to will. The will does not create, nor does it destroy belief. Faith in its instinctive phase previous to the period of logical reflection (as we see in ignorant people) is based on impulses of an emotional character, upon which the will has no power. The feelings can neither generate nor destroy themselves within us by an act of will. Just as one does not love because *one wishes to love,* so one does not believe because *one wishes to believe.* When the period of logical reflection arrives, instinctive faith either persists and is reinforced by rational motives, or it gives place in the individual consciousness to the criticism of reason.

In this last case no effort of the will will be able to resurrect it from its ruins ; because, if the emotional motives upon which ingenuous faith is based no longer exist, the will, in order to make itself believe, must be brought to it by logical reflection ; and if no logical reflection finds arguments to decide it, it is clear, in a contrary sense, that it will not lead itself to accept that belief. Religious intuitionism parts from the false concepts of a liberated will above the sentiment and the reason and capable of dominating them at will, while the will in reality does not subsist except in so far as there are certain motives, either sentimental or logical, which determine it : a will without motives is a psychological absurdity. But, it could be objected, there are cases in which, from the point of view of theoretical reasons, we find ourselves faced with two equally probable hypotheses. The will will then, say Renouvier, Ollé-Laprune, and James, be able to weigh the scales down on the side which corresponds to the exigencies of moral life. We reply that a philosophical hypothesis, in order to be acceptable from the rational point of view, must take into account all the facts, and therefore the moral feelings and the law of beauty also as it is experimented with in consciousness. Of two hypotheses, therefore, one of which takes count of the moral life and the other does not, we must choose the first by that same methodical principle by which we put on one side a physical theory if there is even one fact which is contrary to it. But it is clear that the hypothesis harmonising with moral facts is not here chosen by an arbitrary exercise of the will, but because it is the most satisfactory from the rational point of view. If the religious hypothesis, therefore, presents itself *as the only one* which explains all the facts of experience, including the moral life, it will be justified from the logical point of view, and we shall have not only a moral certainty of it, but also a theoretical and rational one ; and we shall not be authorised thereby, with irrationalism, to place above the intellect a higher source of inspiration and of certainty.

The foregoing discussion has brought out the fact that the intellectual element is an integral part of religion. If we try to eliminate it, there remains only the nebula of emotion, in which we are able to recognise not only no positive, determinate religion, but not even any religion in its more generic form. Further, the moral conscience which the Pragmatists wish to make the organ of piety has a universal character and overflows the circle of individual subjectivity in so far as it contains within itself rational elements. It is a false way of understanding the spiritual life, to claim to divide the soul into various compartments, in one of which, for example, would stand philosophy, in another religion, in another art, and so on. The spirit is entire in all its functions, and their variety comes solely from the dynamic accentuation of one of its aspects.

How then can the relationship between science and religion be understood ? Let me be permitted to outline here what seems to me the right way of understanding this relationship, all the more because my ideas on the subject are no longer exactly those put forward in my book " The Idealistic Reaction against Science." It is necessary first of all to put on one side the old intellectualistic conception of reality as a thing in itself, and of truth as the correspondence of our ideas with this existence in itself. To compare our ideas with these things in themselves would be a desperate undertaking ; and, moreover, it is not even possible to think of an object without putting it in relationship with our consciousness. Reality is the very life of our experience in its most concrete form, and of which the Ego and the world are indivisible aspects. I have experiences of myself only in relation to all the other beings and to all the other activities of the world of experience, and I know all the others only in relation to myself. It is absurd to wish to transcend this living relation, this concrete Unity of experience. In them the Divine and the Human are not two realities which stand face to face with each other. There is not on the one side the infinite, and on the other the finite, drawn up with the sharp figures of intellectualism, but they are fused and yet distinguished in such a way that any logical transcription would misrepresent them. Love and thou shalt understand. The Divine Life is not the simple sum of our individual experiences, as if they were placed the one beside the other, but it is a superior integration of them in one dynamic whole. God is not exhausted within us, but He does not live without us. His work is not without our work. His Creation is not without our creation. Grace and providence are not gifts which we receive passively, they are not preordained designs which annul our spontaneous will, but aids for our activity. We cooperate with God for the redemption of the world. He is not suspended on high in a changeless Olympus, but lives, suffers, and hopes with us. In this lies the profound truth of Christianity which made God descend in sacrifice for Man. Is this Pantheism or Theism, Immanence or Transcendence ? Let us leave to intellectualism these sharp contrasts, which are the product of conceptual abstractions. We shall try in vain to define by a formula the relation of the human with the divine, just as one would try in vain to conceive abstractly the relation between two enamoured souls.

The concrete unity of experience must not be statically conceived as the totality of a system which encloses the infinity of being and exhausts time. From this intellectualistic conception, which still persists in English neo-Hegelianism ; in Royce, for example, spring the paradoxes of the real infinite, and the thought struggles vainly with the effort to understand how, where everything is made from eternity, there is still something to accomplish. These difficulties disappear if for the absurd " Real infinity " we substitute the idea of dynamic infinity and of an inexhaustible creation, and if for the concept of an eternity which includes all time we substitute that of an eternal production of time.

Thus the problems of evil and of liberty are resolved into a dynamic view. There is no longer, in fact, a preordained design, there is no pre-established harmony. The concrete unity of the universe, as I understand it, is not a static unity in which all harmony is arranged from the beginning once and for all ; but it is a unity which is realised progressively with the collaboration of the individual activities which make up the world of experience. It is not a gift from the beginning, but a laborious conquest which is achieved little by little through the evolution of organisms and of human societies.

In this progressive realisation of superior harmonies the religious life, with its age-long development, has a function which cannot be replaced. Science and philosophy strive to order the world of our symbols and concepts into the unity of an idea. But the idea does not exhaust the reality ; the articulation of concepts will never bring about the attainment of the fullness of life, in which, therefore, our spirit does not find itself understood. Harmony of thought is not sufficient ; we wish to feel ourselves to be truly living souls. We do not wish merely to conceive, we wish also to realise in sentiment and action the concrete unity of life. That is exactly the meaning of religion. The love of our neighbour and the love of God are at the bottom the same aspiration towards this harmony of the lived experiences. Harmony and love must not be understood statically, as a definite harmony in which existence is filled, but as a concord which makes us hope for other and more perfect concords, as the love which opens our soul to a belief in a still higher love. Experience of the divine is not contact and absorption in an infinite immobility, but the dynamic apprehension of an inexhaustible activity which makes us participators in a creative power which has no end.

It would appear that thought must be condemned by these premises, and that religion, which seeks the harmony of life in its fullness, must place itself above philosophy, which aims at harmony of thought. But religious experience would remain shut up in the intimacy of the fugitive moment and would spend the treasure of its riches unless it sought, by making itself known to itself, to preserve itself in the life of the individual and of human society. The agreement of our experiences among themselves and with those of other individuals cannot be obtained if each remains in the immediacy of the life which it has lived, in its incommunicable subjective intuition. It is the conceptual schemes constructed by reflection, and which transcribe those experiences into the universal language of thought, that make it possible to render them clear to the individual and to communicate those intuitions to others. Only by means of these objective expressions can concord be realised. Religion, if it wishes to become a universal possession, flows necessarily into philosophy. Intuition, if it wishes to become eternal, must rise to the level of thought. The mystic cannot hold aloof from this law. Otherwise, he encloses himself in the ineffable, and his religion flashes and dies out in the spark of genius. The moment of experience is lost, if it is not preserved in order to be enriched and integrated in the life of other experiences. The work of reflection is therefore not useless ; and its office is illegitimate only if it tries to substitute itself for life, and to absorb in itself the immediateness of religious intuition, which remains the necessary starting-point and the point to which we must return, because the unity of the idea is realised in the concrete harmony of experience. Yet the travail of the thought will never have been in vain. Plunging again into the ways of life, we shall never return there as before, but shall be capable of more profound and complex experiences and of more vast concords. The richest and fullest faith is not the ingenuous simplicity which lies on this side of the anguish of thought, but that which is recomposed beyond it and includes within itself the torment of a doubt which has been overcome.

Dogmas, rites, and the Church, can appear accessory elements of religion only to him who erroneously claims to enclose the religious life within the incommunicable individual sentiment, whereas it is realised only in human society. Even when the solitary anchorite seems alone in the face of God, the voice of the whole of humanity is in his prayer and in the pain which is offered, together with the torment of all creatures, as in the sacrifice of Christ. The Church of the faithful is always vivid and present to his inward consciousness. Even when the heretic rebels against a religious community there vibrates in his spirit the aspiration for a renovated Church of which he feels himself to be the apostle. In other terms religion is, and cannot be other than, a determinate positive religion with its beliefs and its ceremonies—that is, with all its concrete intellectual and aesthetic expressions, through which the Divine Unity of experience is realised in a form drawn from life. If we try to eliminate every concept and every symbol, there is left only the dark night of emotion in which religion vanishes.

Religious intuitionism has had the merit of vindicating against abstract intellectualism the reality of experience lived in the richness of mobile individual aspects. Every moment of life, every subjective vibration of the feelings, every fleeting vision, is a real moment in the history of the world. The objective does not subsist if severed from these particular subjective impressions ; and the attempt to separate it leads to the hypostasis of abstractions. Reality does not exist in things absurd in themselves, but in things which have been loved or suffered, and which are radiated by our smile or veiled by our sadness.

Intuitionism has done wrong to deny all theoretical value to the conception, because the latter, when it does not try to take the place of intuition, is the only means which permits us to integrate the fugitive moment of life, which is an aspect of reality, with all the other concrete moments which constitute the life of the universe ; or to co-ordinate the experience of the instant with all the other experiences of different moments and of other individuals. In this way our life is enriched and rises to a fuller vitality, ascending to a superior level of reality.

We must in fact distinguish different degrees of reality and thought according as more integral, more comprehensive, and more harmonious forms of experience, individual and social, are attained through the medium of science and philosophy. Yet scientific and philosophic concepts, if they are able to complete the lived experience, do not take its place. When we have risen to a higher idea of reality, we feel the need of making it concrete in an intuition, and of realising it in the life which we live. In this the work of reflection is not cancelled, but is assimilated, becoming blood of our blood, just as mathematical reflection is incorporated in physical action and fills it with itself, even when there is no longer any explicit calculation, but it has become a habit.

Scientific and philosophic criticism may disintegrate the intellectual content of ancient beliefs, but it can never destroy religion, because the concept will never take the place of lived experience. By elaborating a more comprehensive and more integral idea of reality, it can only prepare a new form of religious life if that idea succeeds in becoming concrete in a form of life. From science and philosophy to religion, from religion to science and philosophy —that is the eternal rhythm of the process of the spirit, which rises from life to thought and returns from thought to life in a progressive enrichment which is the attainment of ever higher levels of reality and truth. The mystic intuition of genius is enkindled with the light of thought and, by its divination, makes possible the attainment of a higher idea. This, in its turn, elaborated by reflection, permits us to attain a more profound intuition. Religion and philosophy are only abstractly separable ; the one always calls us back to the other. There is a flash of mystic intuition at the roots of all philosophy ; there is a philosophic exigency at the foundation of all religious rapture. Religion, therefore, exercises a function which cannot be replaced in the progressive attainment of ever higher levels of reality, of an ever fuller and more complete unity between our spirits and the world. The individual choice of the feelings does not decide the truth of religion or the truth of philosophy, just as the choice of *a priori* dialectics does not decide it. No individual whatever can constitute himself outright a judge of that truth, or of the value of its intuitions. As with scientific hypotheses, so with religious intuitions, it is the social experiment which decides—the experiment understood, not in its restricted physical sense, but in a broader historical sense. We have already said that we must put on one side the old conception of truth as corresponding to the idea of an external object. It is not a criterion which can be of service, but really has no meaning. The scientist does not compare his theories with things in themselves, but acts in conformity·with them in the world of his experience, and calls them true if by means of them he succeeds in realising a concrete agreement between his activity and the other energies. Philosophical theories and religious intuitions must be verified in the same way. We must submit to experiments, we must act with them. Who can deny, indeed, that they are energies operating in the world of history ? One religion will be more true than another, not because our subjective intuition proclaims it such, but because it succeeds in realising a higher level of the harmony of spirits, a more integral concord of the experiences through which we live. Further, our positive religion gives place to another when the latter shows itself by experiment to be better able to fulfil the same mission in life. It is of no use to ask, for example, whether the dogmas of Christianity correspond to objective entities ; its truth must be measured by its historic efficacy, and by the organisation of souls into a concrete harmony which it has been able to realise for so many centuries through the medium of its dogmatic and ritual structure. Neither is it of any use to examine abstractly, by logic or by emotion, whether the structure of Protestantism makes it superior to Catholicism. Historical experiment alone can decide the value of the Reformation.

Can we never attain in this way absolute and definite truth ? Let it be so. But this is the only truth and the only reality of which we can humanly speak and which has a meaning for us.[1]

---

[1] In addition to my book *The Idealistic Reaction against Science* (London, Macmillan), see also my more recent works : *La Guerra Eterna e il Dramma dell' Esistenza* (Naples, Perrella), translated into French under the title *L'Eternité des Esprits* (Paris, Alcan); *La Teoria di Einstein e le mutevoli prospettive del Mondo* (Palermo, Sandron); *Relativismo e Idealismo* (Naples, Perrella) ; *Il Problema di Dio e il nuovo Pluralismo* (Città di Castello, Casa Editrice *Il Seclo*).

THE DOMAIN OF PHYSICAL SCIENCE

BY ARTHUR S. EDDINGTON

Fellow of Trinity College, Professor of Astronomy,
University of Cambridge

CONTENTS

1. The Nature of the Scientific Method

THE learned physicist and the man in the street were standing together on the threshold about to enter a room.

The man in the street moved forward without trouble, planted his foot on a solid unyielding plank at rest before him, and entered.

The physicist was faced with an intricate problem. To make any movement he must shove against the atmosphere, which presses with a force of fourteen pounds on every square inch of his body. He must land on a plank travelling at twenty miles a second round the sun—a fraction of a second earlier or later the plank would be miles away from the chosen spot. He must do this whilst hanging from a round planet head outward into space, and with a wind of ether blowing at no one knows how many miles a second through every interstice of his body. He reflects too that the plank is not what it appears to be—a continuous support for his weight. The plank is mostly emptiness; very sparsely scattered in that emptiness are myriads of electric charges dashing about at great speeds but occupying at any moment less than a billionth part of the volume which the plank seems to fill continuously. It is like stepping on a swarm of flies. Will he not slip through ? No, if he makes the venture, he falls for an instant till an electron hits him and gives a boost up again ; he falls again, and is knocked upwards by another electron ; and so on. The net result is that he neither slips through the swarm nor is bombarded up to the ceiling, but is kept about steady in this shuttlecock fashion. Or rather, it is not certain but highly probable that he remains steady ; and if, unfortunately, he should sink through the floor or hit the ceiling, the occurrence would not be a violation of the laws of nature but a rare coincidence.

By careful calculation of these and other conditions the physicist may reach a solution of the problem of entering a room ; and, if he is fortunate enough to avoid mathematical blunders, he will prove satisfactorily that the feat can be accomplished in the manner already adopted by his ignorant companion. Happily even a learned physicist has usually some sense of proportion ; and it is probable that for this occasion he put out of mind scientific truths about astronomical motions, the constitution of planks and the laws of probability, and was content to follow the same crude conception of his task that presented itself to the mind of his unscientific colleague.

What is the purpose and status of the strange conception of our environment here alluded to, which we docket as scientific truth—to be kept, as it were, pigeon-holed and not employed indiscriminately in practical affairs? The question is not to be dismissed by a dogmatic classification of scientific truth as superior and commonplace truth as inferior, or of commonplace truth as practical and scientific truth as pedantic. Each has its legitimate sphere distinguished not by hard and fast boundaries but by that more elusive criterion "a sense of proportion." Usually the limits are reasonably well observed in matters of daily life ; perhaps they have not been so well recognised (by either side) in regard to religion, which is after all a very commonplace matter of daily life. At least it should be realised that just as there is one conception of our physical environment appropriate to scientific inquiry and another conception appropriate to the ordinary daily contact, so there will be one conception of our spiritual environment appropriate to philosophical theology and another conception appropriate to daily needs. In applying scientific conceptions to religion we must guard not only against errors but against pedantry. It is said that a steam-hammer can be adjusted to crack a nut, but notwithstanding this triumph it is still expedient to employ nut-crackers.

It would not be fair to conclude from a special illustration that scientific truth has no concern with the practical affairs of life. If instead of stepping into a room our two friends were, for the first time in their lives, about to step off an escalator, the physicist (if he did not in the excitement of the occasion forget the principles of mechanics) would presumably be the more successful. Everyone knows that science has profound application in practical affairs, and there is great need for wider dissemination of scientific truth. But the point of the illustration is that we shall not advance the cause of science in practical affairs by insisting on scientific conceptions for all occasions, with no sense of proportion. Perhaps the stern moralist will say reprovingly, " How can you be content with less than the highest truth as known to you ? Whatever practical expediency may suggest, do not continue to surround yourself with false conceptions of things—an atmosphere of lies. More particularly in religion anything but the highest truth is a lie." But surely there must be something wrong if reverence for the highest truth demands that we should make the ludicrous exhibition of it described in our opening paragraphs. Nay, stern moralist ! You are begging the question with your higher truths and lower truths. Truth is a diamond of many facets, darting now one ray, now another, into our lives. The scientist may find the pure element within and express its essence by the precise formula of a cubic lattice—it is his business to make such analyses. But is the dull carbon to be prized higher than the radiant lustre ?

We ask the method and purpose of the scientist in seeking out a conception of the things around us so much at variance with our usual conception of them. To a certain extent the answer is simple ; the scientist looks at the world through a magnifying glass. Under magnification the plank dissolves into atoms ; these in turn under higher power of scrutiny dissolve into still smaller electric charges. The original plank is lost ; as the saying is, we cannot see the wood for the trees. Magnification gives us the world as we might suppose it to appear to creatures built on a smaller scale than ourselves, capable of appreciating smaller distances, shorter moments of time. Do we really get nearer to the truth of things by changing from the point of view of a man to that of a microbe ? Attention has often been called to the insignificance of the human creature in the great universe ; he strives for knowledge as an atom battling with immensity. It would be strange indeed if the efforts of science were solely to secure the vantage-point of greater insignificance.

Before we can state the truth about the external world, before we can quarrel as to whether it is like *this* or like *that*, we must agree on some kind of definition of what is to be understood by the phrase " external world." I do not think there ought to be much difficulty in coming to an understanding. The reader should perhaps first be warned against such definitions as " the external world consists of those things which really exist," a statement which merely provokes the much more difficult question of whether you or I have the faintest notion of how the process of " existing " is performed. The idea of an external world suggests something that can be looked at from a point of view other than our own ; unless we discover or imagine beings looking at it from another point of view, we cannot differentiate between the external world and the apprehension of it in our own consciousness. If I were the only conscious being in the universe the only data presented for investigation would consist in the content of my consciousness, and there would be no reason to suspect that the data had reference to anything external to my consciousness. It is true that I might make the hypothesis that there was an external world responsible for what was going on in my consciousness ; but it would be an idle hypothesis, since the knowledge that could be asserted of this supposed external world would be a mere duplication of the knowledge that could be much more confidently asserted of the world of my consciousness. The motive for the conception of an external world—a world which will remain significant when my consciousness ceases to be—lies in the existence of other conscious beings. We compare notes and we find that our experiences are not independent of one another. Much that is in my consciousness is individual, but there is an element common to other conscious beings. That common element we desire to study, to describe as fully and accurately as possible, and to discover the laws by which it is modified as it appears now in one consciousness, now in another. That common element cannot be placed in one man's consciousness rather than another's ; it must be placed in neutral ground—an *external* world. It is the essence of such an external world that we are all partners in it on the same footing. The external world is not a mere duplication of the presentation of it in any one man's mind ; it is a symposium of the presentations to individuals in all sorts of circumstances.

Individuals may differ in physical circumstances (position, motion, size) and also in more subtle mental characters. We do not usually attempt to extend the symposium to differences of the latter kind. We have a fairly definite idea of a normally equipped human being, and it is to his standard of appreciation that the conception of the external world of physics particularly relates. But as regards physical circumstances it would be illogical to attach greater weight to one position, motion, and size rather than another. We are beings who happen to be situated in a particular part of the stellar universe, compelled to journey with the motion of a rather small globe ; our size is presumably regulated by the value of gravity and other physical conditions peculiar to that globe. We renounce the idea that these are privileged circumstances ; the purpose of conceiving an external world is to obtain a conception which could be shared by beings in any other physical circumstances whatever.

The external world is accordingly a synthesis of appearances from all possible points of view. In the main, modern science accepts this principle and arrives at its adopted conception of our environment by following it. The man and the microbe afford only one example of the possible variety of points of view. Recently physicists have been much occupied in comparing the points of view of observers travelling with different motions, *e.g.*, attached to different stars. The result has been entirely to revolutionise the conception of space and time in the external world. The detailed frame of space and time in which we are accustomed to locate the events happening around us belongs not to the external world but to a particular presentation of it—namely, to those observers who are travelling with the same velocity as the earth. A being on a star with different velocity would, if he followed our methods and assumptions, obtain a different reckoning of space and time, and his location of external events would be a distorted version of our own. In the external world, which is a synthesis of all points of view, we cannot give preference to one version rather than the other ; space and time, in the form in which we commonly represent them, cannot belong to the external world. The work of Einstein and Minkowski has shown how the synthesis is to be made ; it leads to the conception of a four-dimensional space-time (*i.e.*, a fourfold order of events) in which there is no straight-cut separation into space and time, although there is a definite structural arrangement on a rather simple plan which is the genesis of the separation by the various possible observers. Following up this success, Einstein began to synthesise the points of view of observers differing not merely in uniform velocity but in accelera-tion of velocity, *e.g.*, a man on terra firma and a man falling from a precipice. Strange as it may seem, this bold extension of the principle of synthesis—this refusal to reject any natural point of view as a " wrong " one—led to a striking success. It was found that gravitation, previously a *deus ex machina* in physical science, became incorporated in the results of the synthesis ; that is to say, the conception of the external world as modified so as to include the additional points of view, predicted without further hypothesis those phenomena of experience which had hitherto been attributed to an entirely mysterious agency called gravitation. Not only so, but the test of observation has shown that the prediction is more accurate than the predictions from the old Newtonian law of gravitation in the three cases in which the difference is sufficiently great to be observed.

Change of position of the observer gives him another point of view ; but man is so used to changing his position that he very early acquired the habit of synthesis for this kind of change. He would be badly handicapped in the struggle for existence if he were unable to conceive an external world which remained unchanged whatever position he himself happened to occupy. But he is not in the habit of taking trips on other stars or of falling over precipices, so that the corresponding syntheses have been left to scientific research, and the conceptions of the external world which result from them are outside anything which he has hitherto imagined.

I hope the reader will not attempt to judge the great theory of relativity by the brief reference to it above. These remarks may possibly put a right idea in his head, but they will almost certainly also put in some wrong ideas unless he refers to a fuller account of the subject. Its relevance here is that it shows us modern physics in the act of synthesizing the conception of observers with different points of view and declaring (rightly or wrongly) the result of the synthesis to be the real external world. Most of this essay will be dominated by the modern conceptions of the external world of physics which have arisen from Einstein's theory of relativity. We think that the reader may take it that the theory has come to stay, and that it marks a firmly established stage in the development of science. No doubt it may in the future have to give place to a fuller conception embodying a still larger measure of truth ; but that anticipation does not affect our conviction that in the present relativity theory we have the truth in a purer form than in the Newtonian theory that preceded it, even as the Newtonian theory was a great advance on the conceptions that preceded it. Some of the scientific assertions that will be made here refer to rather advanced deductions from the theory which may not have secured the same wide acceptance among scientific men as the better-known portions of the theory ; and naturally we must not claim the great authority of the scientific theory for the philosophical speculation which we propose to base on it. But granting that the reader may

fairly entertain some doubt as to these assertions which he is unable
to check, it may not be without interest to him to learn something
of the general direction in which scientific thought appears to be
tending (rightly or wrongly) now that it is confronted with a
conception of the material world widely different from that which
was the basis of disputes between science and religion in the last
century.

Notwithstanding its professed principle of treating all points of
view impartially, physics does in practice give a preference to the
the view of the microbe over that of the man.   If you ask a scientist
what is the ultimate truth about the nature of the world so far as
he knows it, he will begin to describe it as it appears under his most
powerful magnifying glass : he will tell you about the trees, not
about the forest—about electrons, not planks.   It would be
incorrect to say that he ignores the large-scale truths.   Whole
branches of his work are devoted to ascertaining how the little
things conspire to give the great things, how new properties arise
in a crowd which are not properties of the individuals of that
crowd.   Care is taken to provide " macroscopic " equations for
the human scale of appreciation of phenomena as well as " microscopic " equations for the microbe.   But there is a difference in
the attitude of the physicist towards these results ; for him the
macroscopic equations—the large-scale results—are just useful
tools for scientific and practical progress ; the microscopic view
contains the real truth as to what is actually occurring.   The
reason for this preference is that our theoretical reasoning is of such
a kind as to pass much more readily from small-scale to large-scale
results than vice versa.   It is, therefore, usually considered that the
large-scale truths are implied by the small-scale truths, and are
therefore not required to be mentioned separately in stating our
conception of the external world.   All the properties of impene-
trability, extension, elasticity, colour, etc., of the plank are (in
their physical aspects) supposed to be deducible from the small-
scale specification of it as a swarm of electric charges ; so that a
sufficiently educated intelligence ought to discern in the conception
of the plank as a swarm of particles all that goes to make up the
appearance of the plank to the human point of view.   On the
other hand, it is not considered that the electronic constitution of
the plank is implied in a description of its large-scale appearance.
There are already signs that this undue insistence on microscopic

analysis may be a passing phase in the physical conception of the external world. It has happened that up to now we have chiefly studied phenomena which are best unravelled by starting with their minutest elements. But in recent years there has come into prominence a large class of phenomena (quantum phenomena) which defy analysis of this kind ; and somewhat painfully, physics is accustoming itself to the idea that its microscopic picture of nature is not capable of containing the conceptions which these latest phenomena require.

It is often said that the purpose of scientific theories is to provide a conception of the world which " economises thought," and that they do not profess to represent the reality which actually exists—the latter aim being considered unattainable. We disagree with the first part of this dictum at any rate. In our view the external world about which the scientific theory attempts to assert something, is capable of precise definition along the lines already indicated—namely, that it is the common element abstracted from the experiences of individuals in all variety of physical circumstances ; and any assertion about it (if it is unambiguous) must be right or wrong—not merely economical or wasteful. Whilst a direct statement about this external world is naturally preferable to a circumlocutory statement, the test of truth of the statement has nothing to do with economy of thought. Science is not describing a world invented to save trouble ; it is following up a problem which took definite shape the first time two human beings compared notes of their experiences ; and it follows it up according to the original rules—namely, to obtain the element common to all human experience separated from the merely individual elements in that experience. If we say of anything in this external world that it is real or that it exists, we are merely expressing our belief that the rules have been properly followed—that it is not an hallucination belonging only to one individual experience, or a mistaken concept due to an error in the process of synthesis. Many philosophers seem to consider that the statement that the external world is real, adds some property to it not comprised in the statement that it is the part of our experience held in common, but I am not aware that anyone has made a suggestion as to what this property could be. I simply do not contemplate the awful contingency that the external world of physics, after all our care in arriving at it, might be disqualified by failing to " exist," because no one seems to know what the supposed qualification is, nor is it explained in what way the prestige of the external world would be enhanced if it passed the test. It is sufficient that it is the world which confronts our common experience and that therefore we are interested in knowing all we can about it. Scientific theories of it are continually changing, and no one would maintain that the present conception is undiluted ultimate truth ; we can, if we like, take comfort in the reflection that, true or not, it " economises thought." But it would be difficult to justify the vehemence of the scientific attack on superstition if the sole objection were that it is wasteful of thought. We are roused because we believe that the victims of superstition are embodying in the external world— the common element of experience—conceptions which have no right to be there, and that our conception though not free from error contains more of the truth than theirs.

We have now discussed to some extent the method employed by physics in reaching its conception of the external world ; we have seen that this world has a claim on our attention not on account of some metaphysical function of " existing," but because it is the world confronting us ; and we have seen why the commonplace view of the world is almost unrecognisable in the scientific view. We have hinted that the scientific view has certain limitations (beyond the ordinary limitations of human fallibility) ; it lays undue stress on the microscopic point of view, and it does not attempt to include a point of view other than that of an intelligence like our own which has presumably developed in rather specialised directions through the operation of natural selection. Those limitations are justified when the scientific conception is used for the purposes of science, but must be borne in mind when the conception is studied from the point of view of philosophy or religion. It is now time to consider what is the general nature of the world of physics reached by these methods.

2. The Scientific Conception of the Universe

A distinguishing characteristic of physics is that it is an " exact science " and the phrase *domain of physics* is often used synonymously with *domain of exact science*. The vision that with the advance of knowledge it may be found that physical laws are sufficient to explain completely the phenomena of life and heredity

would be more accurately described as a forecast that these biological studies may ultimately be reduced to an exact science ; for
it is not so much a question whether the physical entities recognised
as such to-day suffice to account for everything observed, as
whether in supplementing them we can keep exclusively to entities
of *the same category*—the category to which exact science applies.
The accomplishment of this vision now appears very unlikely,
because we have recently realised that the claim of physics to be an
exact science is only allowable because its subject-matter is much
more restricted than is commonly supposed.   To show the kind
of knowledge which physics can handle in an exact manner, let us
examine critically a problem in physics such as might be set in an
examination paper.

The examiner, exercising his ingenuity, begins (let us say) as
follows : " An elephant slides down a grassy hillside . . ." The
experienced examinee knows that he need not pay heed to this ;
it is only a picturesque adornment to give an air of verisimilitude
to the bald essentials of the problem.   He reads on : " The weight
of the elephant is two tons."   Now we are getting to business ;
henceforth the elephant can be dropped ; it is " two tons " that
the examinee will really have to grapple with.   What exactly is
this two tons—the real subject-matter of the physical problem ?
It connotes according to some code a property, which we can only
vaguely describe as *ponderosity*, occurring in a certain region of the
external world.   But never mind what it connotes ; what *is* it ?
Two tons *is* the reading which the pointer indicated when the
elephant was placed on a weighing-machine ; it is just a pointer-
reading.   Similarly with the other data of our problem.   The
mountain flank is replaced by an angle of 60°—the reading of a
plumb-line against the divisions of a protector ; and its verdant
covering is replaced by a coefficient of friction, which though
perhaps not directly a pointer-reading is of kindred nature.   No
doubt there are more roundabout ways used in practice for determining the weights of elephants and the slopes of hills, but they
are justified because they are known to give the same results
as would be obtained by direct pointer-readings.   If then only
pointer-readings (or their equivalents) are put into the machine of
scientific calculation, how can we grind out of it anything but
pointer-readings ?   But that is just what we do grind out of it.
The question was, say, to find the time of descent of the elephant,

and the answer 16·5 seconds—that is to say, the difference of two pointer-readings on the seconds'-dial of our watch.

Leaving out all aesthetic, ethical, or spiritual aspects of our environment, we are faced with qualities such as massiveness, substantiality, extension, duration, which are supposed to belong to the domain of physics. In a sense they do belong ; but physics is not in a position to handle them directly. The essence of their nature is inscrutable ; we may use mental pictures to aid calculations, but no image in the mind can be a replica of that which is not in the mind. And so in its actual procedure physics studies not these inscrutable qualities, but pointer-readings which we can observe. The readings, it is true, reflect the fluctuations of the world-qualities ; but our exact knowledge is of the readings, not of the qualities. The former have as much resemblance to the latter as a telephone-number has to a subscriber. The triumph of exact science in the problem just quoted consisted in establishing a numerical connection between the pointer-reading of the weighing machine in one experiment on the elephant and the pointer-reading of the watch in another experiment. The elephant itself as an object in the external world was only an intermediary, and no knowledge of the kind called exact could be asserted about it.

Perhaps it will seem that a great deal of knowledge about the elephant itself is implicitly contained in a knowledge of these readings occurring in the various kinds of experiments that can be made on it ; that indeed a knowledge of the response of the various objects of the world—weighing-machines and other indicators— to the presence of the elephant is the most complete knowledge of the elephant we could desire. As a relativist I accept this theory of knowledge ; but it should be realised that it transforms our view of the nature and status of physical knowledge in a fundamental way. Until recently physicists took it for granted that they had knowledge of the entities dealt with, which was of a more intimate character ; and the difficulty which many find even now in accepting the theory of relativity arises from an unwillingness to give up these intuitions or traditions as to the intrinsic nature of space, time, matter, and force, and substitute for them a knowledge expressible in terms of the readings of measuring instruments. In considering the relations of science and religion it is a very relevant fact that physics is now in course of abandoning all claim to a type of knowledge which it formerly asserted without hesitation. Moreover, these considerations indicate the limits to the sphere of exact science. We have said that knowledge of the elephant must consist in knowledge of the response of the various objects of the world to its presence ; but this response cannot always be reduced to a pointer-reading or such-like indicator, and the corresponding knowledge is then automatically excluded from exact science. For example, the affection inspired by the elephant in its mahout is one response of the outside world to its presence. A spiritual phenomenon, no doubt, and yet it has the aspects of a physical force, since it causes material objects—sweetmeats—to move in a direction that they otherwise would not have taken. This phenomenon is excluded from exact science not because of any antithesis of nature between the spiritual and the material, but because there is no pointer-reading that can stand for the " likeableness " of the elephant in the way that the reading of the weighing-machine can stand for its " ponderosity."

I venture to say that the division of the external world into a material world and a spiritual world is superficial, and that the deep line of cleavage is between the metrical and the non-metrical aspects of the world.

We may doubt whether there is any branch of knowledge from which exact science is entirely excluded. The modern psychologist is continually devising appliances by which he can read off on a pointer the various differences in our intellectual make-up. In this way he penetrates into the nature of the human mind just as much (or as little) as the physicist penetrates into the nature of the material world. It may be objected that the psychologist is not dealing with the mind but with the material apparatus of brain and nervous system. The distinction seems an idle one. His pointer-readings are symptoms of the activities and limitations of the mind, and they are also perhaps symptoms of material constitution of the brain and nervous system ; the derived knowledge *bears upon* both, but it *is* actually knowledge of pointer-readings. In the same way the physicist's knowledge *bears upon* the nature of matter and ether, but it *is* a knowledge of pointer-readings.

Even as there is no branch of knowledge from which exact science is wholly excluded, so it would seem that there is no branch which exact science wholly covers. There is, however, one exception. The devotee of the physical laboratory or the observatory spends his whole energy in making pointer-readings. Every physical experiment involves readings of a scale or an equivalent estimate made in cruder fashion. (Of course, the proof of this statement requires a survey of the operations of physics far more extended than we can undertake here ; and it requires a strict definition of the type of datum included under the general heading *pointer-reading* ; the student of relativity will be familiar with the argument that every observable result reduces to a determination of the intersections of world-lines.) It is natural, therefore, that the branch of knowledge created on this basis should be wholly covered by exact science. But in most subjects exact science goes a little way and then stops, not because of the limitations of our ignorance, but because we are dealing with something which includes both metrical and non-metrical aspects. The theory of music starts as though we were about to build up a science every whit as exact as physics ; the integral relations of the notes of the scales, the distinction of concord and discord, the time relations of crotchets and quavers, all belong to a metrical scheme. But it is unimaginable that any system of measurements could be correlated to tune in such a way that knowledge of these measurements would be accepted as equivalent to knowledge of tune. That harmony which is metrical and melody which is non-metrical both play a part in determining the pleasing effect of music, suggests that there is no strong opposition between measurable and non-measurable agencies ; measurableness is a specialisation which is relevant when we are studying certain aspects and irrelevant in others.

These considerations also indicate the limits to the method of microscopical analysis so universally employed in physics, except possibly in some of the most recent developments. It is not a microscopic analysis of the entities of the external world, but of the pointer-readings accepted as equivalent to knowledge of these entities. We can see that the equivalence of this substituted knowledge becomes more and more remote and formal the farther the dissection is carried. That is no drawback to its use in physics ; the physicist is concerned only in working out the exact scheme of interconnection of the pointer-readings and is not professionally interested in the entities which these have replaced. When he has arrived at a theory such that all the pointer-readings work out correctly, he has reached the extreme limit of his task.

Perhaps this breakdown of microscopic analysis may be made clearer by an illustration. The operator at a telephone exchange has to deal with a number of entities called *subscribers*. The subscriber is an entity with various aspects ; he is (1) a number, (2) a plug-hole, (3) a voice, and even (4) a human being. In the first and second aspects (which are the aspects with which the operator is most concerned), subscriber No. 1357 may be dissected into digits, 1, 3, 5, 7, or into board 1, section 3, row 5, column 7. This dissection is of importance in explaining some of the mysterious properties of subscribers—for example, why Lady Blank, No. 1357, is so often confused with the chimney-sweep, No. 1397, a phenomenon not explicable by reference to the undissected aspects of these subscribers. Again, it explains why on one occasion the voices for which the first digit is 2 all became silent simultaneously. The telephone operator might well get into the habit of thinking that subscribers were entities composed of four constituents, because this analysis is true of the aspects which he studies ; but we cannot analyse a human being into four parts corresponding to the digits of his telephone number.

The problem on which we may hope to attain some light is that perplexing dualism of spirit and matter which always confronts us when we try to get to the bottom of things. I will state the problem quite crudely in the way it first seems to present itself. The spiritual phenomenon of consciousness is the one thing of which our knowledge is immediate and unchallengeable. It seems to be the most undoubtedly real thing we are aware of. " I think, *therefore* I am." But physics in alliance with common sense brings before us a different kind of reality—a world of matter and electricity, space and motion, which seems to us even more real because it is so clear cut, accurately describable, governed by precise and unfailing laws. Physics does not endorse the beliefs of common sense without some reservations ; it teaches us that our knowledge of this world of matter is indirect and comes to us through very complex channels—is, for example, borne to us from a distance by light-waves and then by some kind of disturbance of the material of the nerves to the brain. The existence of the material world around us is not direct knowledge but common inference ; however, science approves the inference in its main essentials. In this material reality the first reality (consciousness) seems to have no place of its own ; at the most, its existence is grudgingly admitted —a very late arrival after aeons of consciousless past, and occurring only in specks in those strangely complicated mechanical contrivances called brains. The physicist, I suppose, admits consciousness to a place in the world because he cannot very well deny it ; but it would seem that he has no use for it in his scheme. Like Laplace, he has no need of any such hypothesis. The religious mind is naturally jealous of the thought that there can be such a domain of reality pursuing its course independently of all spiritual things. It would welcome an admission from the physicist that his material world is not self-sufficient and would dissolve if it were not sustained by a spiritual reality, which, it is felt, must be deeper than all material reality. But suppose the physicist does see the error of his ways ; suppose he does find it necessary to include an all-pervading spirit among his hypotheses, then even greater apprehension is felt. The physicist is at once suspected of a design to reduce God to a system of differential equations, for it is difficult to see what place in physics there can be for a hypothesis not reducible to this form. We must see whether the recent theories of the physical world help to steer a path between these difficulties. Our discussion has already prepared us to admit that physics (or exact science) can only take within its scope certain aspects of the external world ; and that there remain other aspects which have been excluded, not because they are of less importance, but because they have not the specialised property of measurability. The difficulty does not lie in recognising a wider spiritual reality from which the physical world is a specialised selection. The difficulty is to explain why the physical world, picked out from a more comprehensive world by the criterion of measurability, should be found to constitute a self-contained system ; it operates with so little interference from the rest of reality that we often forget that it is only a part. This problem of the self-sufficiency of the physical world must now be considered.

3. PHYSICAL SCIENCE AS A CLOSED SYSTEM

The central point of Einstein's great theory is a new law of gravitation approximating to but more accurate than Newton's law, and we shall start by explaining exactly the formulation of this law. Our explanation will be more thorough than usual, for we shall make a point of defining each new term that it is necessary to introduce. Probably the effect of giving so full an explanation will be that the reader will not understand the new law any better at the end than he did at the beginning. That does not matter. He is asked to keep his attention fixed on the form of the explanation rather than on the substance of the explanation ; we want to indicate to him the train of ideas that he would have to exhaust if he wished to get to the bottom of the significance of the new law.

Einstein's law of gravitation is a statement that in empty space ten quantities called *potentials* satisfy certain rather lengthy mathematical equations which can be exactly specified. (The term " potential " will be explained presently.) In other words, whereas we might conceive a world in which the potentials at every moment and at every place had entirely arbitrary values, the actual world around us is not so unlimited. The statement that actual phenomena are more limited in variety than imaginable phenomena is evidently equivalent to the statement that the actual world is governed by a law. The next question is, What are the " potentials " which are governed by the law that has been specified ? They are derived by simple mathematical calculations from certain other quantities called *intervals*. If we know the values of the various intervals through the world we can at once find the potentials. What are these " intervals " ? They are relations between pairs of events which are measured by a *scale* or *clock*. Instructions can be given describing exactly how the scale and clock are to be employed, and the interval is merely the scale-reading or clock-reading or a particular combination of the two readings. Next question, What are " scales " and " clocks " ? It would take a somewhat long description to prescribe exactly what constitutes a perfect scale or clock referred to here, but with patience all the requirements can be stated ; we should, however, find it necessary to introduce a new word which ought to be carefully explained—the scales and clocks are made of *matter*. Next question, What is " matter " ? That has often been asked, with many diverse answers ; but here the answer is not so difficult. Metaphysical properties of substantiality have no bearing on the efficiency of a clock as an instrument of measurement, it is only the mechanical properties of matter which concern us here ; and, so far as mechanics is concerned, matter is merely the embodiment of three measurable entities, *mass*, *momentum*, and *stress*. What are " mass," " momentum," and " stress " ? It is one of the remarkable (though comparatively little known) achievements of Einstein's theory that it has succeeded in describing exactly what these are.

They are certain analytical expressions containing various combinations of the *potentials*. What are the " potentials " ? Why, that is just what I have been explaining to you !

The definitions of physics proceed according to the method immortalised in " The House that Jack Built " : *This is the potential, that was derived from the interval, that was measured by the scale, that was made from the matter, that embodied the mass.* . . . But instead of arriving ultimately at " Jack," whom, of course, everybody knows without need for an introduction, we make a circuit back to the beginning of the rhyme . . . " that killed the rat, that ate the malt, that lay in the house—that was built by the priest all shaven and shorn, that married . . ." So now we can go round and round for ever.

But perhaps the reader has already interrupted my explanation of the law of gravitation. When the term " matter " was reached, he cut it short. " You need not trouble to explain any more ; you have at last got down to words I understand ; I happen to know what matter is." Very good ; matter then is something that Mr. X knows. It seems all right—". . . that came from the interval, that was measured by the scale, that was made from the matter, that Mr. X knows." Next question, What is Mr. X ?

The diagram here inserted will perhaps help to keep in mind the essentials of our discussion—

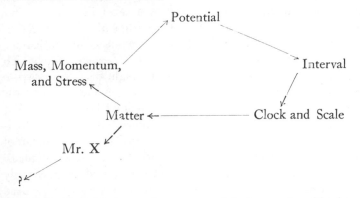

Undoubtedly it is of great importance that there exists this channel leading to Mr. X—and beyond. It is, perhaps, not so simple a channel as Mr. X at first supposed. He " knows " the matter of the scale, but not by a feeler put out from his mind into the scale existing in the external world. Certain radiations proceed from the scale through the external world ; they reach Mr. X's body, which is also a part of the external world ; they cause disturbances of the atoms and electromagnetic fields of his body as the impressions travel along the nerves.   Somewhere there is contact with consciousness ; the mind receives an impression which induces it to create the image of a scale in the external world far removed from the place where the contact occurs.   It is through this contact that man is able to state that he " knows " certain of the entities of the external world which are used as bricks in building up the world of physics.

But theoretical physics turns a blind eye on the track which leads to consciousness.   It would be loath to admit that its edifice of an external world is " The House that Mr. X built."   Mr. X and his colleagues are set down as rather troublesome tenants who have come at a late period of the world's history to inhabit the house which inorganic nature has built.   And so theoretical physics turns aside from that opening and follows the cycle round to the starting-point.

We see the ingenious device of a cycle by which physics has secured for itself a domain of study which is self-connected and independent of the channel leading to the spiritual world of consciousness.   But I do not think we are disparaging the importance of this domain if we doubt whether it can be held to constitute a self-sufficient world in any reasonable sense of the term.   Our consciousness has presented to us for examination a number of apparently disconnected entities, the *matter* which we see and handle, the *stress* which we feel in our muscles, the *interval* of time which we appreciate in our consciousness of the flight of time.   Physics has examined what underlies these facts of consciousness, and has shown how each depends on the other and is definable in terms of the other, reducing all to a unity.   That unity has taken hundreds of years to discover and a very great part of the achievement of physics is summed up in our cycle of definition.   If a subsidiary cycle relating to electromagnetic phenomena were added, practically the whole of that part of theoretical physics which has been reduced to exact order (the so-called *field-physics*) would be represented. The chain of connection of the entities of the world is the province of physics, but the intrinsic essence of those entities is now recognised to lie outside its province.   Micromegas, in Voltaire's fable, promised the terrestrial philosophers " a rare book on philosophy,

telling them that in that book they would find all that can be known
of the ultimate essence of things, and he actually gave them the
volume ere his departure.　It was carried to Paris and laid before
the Academy of Sciences ; but when the old secretary came to
open it he saw nothing but blank leaves.　' Ah ! ' said he, ' this is
just what I expected.' "

When the cycle of physical definition is laid bare in this way,
we can appreciate the following points.

Firstly, the avenue leading *from* consciousness is blocked.　The
working definition of our physical entities makes no reference to
their value for consciousness ; although that would logically be
their most important defining property, since it is because of their
contact with consciousness (near or remote) that we recognise
them and study them.　Theoretical physics substitutes for the
actual entities with mental value symbols with no mental value ;
and this substitution has often misled us into thinking that the
entities of the external world themselves (not the symbols) are of
an intrinsic nature independent of consciousness.

Secondly, working definitions of these entities (or strictly of
their symbols) are secured by connecting them one to another in
cycles so that there is no loose end projecting into the unknown.

Thirdly, the avenue is blocked in the direction leading *to* consciousness, for any properties of the entities by which they could
interact with consciousness have been dropped from the symbols.
The edifice of theoretical physics which has been built up from
these symbols can therefore contain nothing capable of interacting
with consciousness.　In particular, those laws of nature which are
implicit in the mode of construction of this edifice cannot be
interfered with by human free will.

Fourthly, the edifice constructed by theoretical physics in the
territory secured by this device is by no means trivial.　It covers
the whole of " field-physics," to which the most conspicuous
triumphs of scientific investigation belong.　Until recently it was
not recognised that field-physics could not cover the whole subject ;
and even now those who are convinced that its scope is limited are
perhaps in a minority.　Professor H. Weyl, a leading authority
on Relativity, is prominent in advocating the conclusion that the
problems of atomicity and quanta are of a nature which cannot be
brought under field-physics ; but his conversion is very recent—
as indeed is my own.　It is too early to guess whether in this

extended territory physics will be able to maintain its aloofness from consciousness ; it may be that the normal laws are such that they can be set aside by human free will, or it may be that physics has other undetected devices besides the cycle by which it can extend the domain over which it is necessarily supreme.

The exposure of the cycle of physical definition causes a change in our attitude which can perhaps best be illustrated by an example. The nineteenth-century physicist felt that he knew just what he was dealing with when he used terms such as *matter* or *atoms*.   He was ready to admit that much remained to be found out about their structure, but their general nature was definite enough.   The atoms were just tiny billiard-balls—a crisp statement which was supposed to tell you about their nature in a way which could never be achieved for the transcendental entities of the world such as pain, beauty, personality, or consciousness.   Chemical analysis of the brain showed that it was composed of atoms of the familiar elements occurring in inorganic nature.   The unanswerable question was, by what strange means had this collection of billiard-balls acquired the property of secreting thought—a transcendental entity in no way akin to atoms.   But we now see that physics has nothing to say as to the inscrutable nature of an atom ; what it studies is the linkage of atomic properties to other terms in the physicist's vocabulary, each depending on the other in endless chain with the same inscrutable nature running through the whole. *There is nothing to prevent the assemblage of atoms forming the brain from being itself a thinking-machine in virtue of that nature which physics leaves undetermined and undeterminable.*   Because we see that our precise knowledge of certain aspects of the behaviour of atoms leaves their intrinsic nature just as transcendental and inscrutable as the nature of mind, so the difficulty of interaction of matter and mind is lessened.   We create unnecessary difficulty for ourselves by postulating two inscrutabilities instead of one.

It is just here that the physicist's magnifying glass is liable to mislead us.   We have seen that the microscopic view of the world is accepted as the ultimate truth in science because of the exigencies of the methods of deduction used in science.   But the whole truth is not to be seen from any one point of view, and for seeing the connection of mind and brain we must adopt a point of view of less magnification.   I do not suppose that the human mind can be analysed into atoms of feeling in the way that the brain (which includes the physical aspects of mind) can be analysed into atoms of matter. Still less do I suppose that the chemical atoms are, as it were, endowed with tiny elementary minds, which when they get together in certain combinations can build up a complete human intelligence. That would be like believing that each digit of a man's telephone number represents a homunculus, of which four combine to form a man. The kind of view which seems to be required is that in the world which is the basis of both spiritual and material phenomena, the physicist studying certain aspects finds his cycle of entities. In virtue of their cyclic connection they form a domain which can be studied without reference to other aspects. Having selected these aspects and set the rest on one side, we have before us the world of physics. It is after this selection that the magnifying glass becomes useful and the resolution into atoms, electrons, and so forth, is effected. It may be added, moreover, that it is after this selection and with reference only to this selection that *space* itself appears in the scheme, so that magnification would be a metaphor of doubtful meaning if applied outside the selected domain.

4. The Responsibility of Mind

We have left the scheme of theoretical physics maintaining a precarious independence of extraneous support like a serpent swallowing its own tail. It may be expected that such independence will be of a limited character. Everyone will agree that without infringing any law of nature known, or as yet unknown, the world might quite well be different from what it actually is. Let us take two such worlds : A, the actual world, and B, a world which might have been. That is to say, B is ruled by the same laws of nature, but with different and differently distributed stars, planets, mountains, cities, animals, etc. How can a physicist test (by his own resources) that when I am describing the world B, I am not describing the actual world. I refer to a piece of matter of the world B ; it is not real matter, but what right has the physicist to call it unreal ? It attracts every other particle of (unreal) matter according to the law of gravitation, since the usual natural laws are obeyed in B. With my unreal matter I construct unreal scales and clocks which measure wrong intervals between points ; but the physicist cannot say they are wrong unless he has previously shown my matter to be unreal. If once we could demonstrate the unreality of any element in B, the whole structure would collapse ; but we cannot do this so long as we keep to the cycle, because the cycle of unreal quantities is just as perfect as the cycle of real quantities. The unreal stars of B emit unreal light, which falls on unreal retinas and ultimately reaches unreal brains. At last there is a chance to expose the deception, for the next step takes us outside the cycle. Is the brain disturbance translated into consciousness ? That will test whether the brain is real or unreal ; for there is no question about our consciousness being real or unreal—it is just " our consciousness."

Actuality—that which distinguishes this world from many other possible worlds consistent with the laws of nature—is not susceptible of definition without trespassing beyond the frontiers of physics. I fear that the word " actuality " is one of those high-sounding phrases with metaphysical associations obnoxious to science. But most of the terms of physics have metaphysical associations which the physicist must learn to disregard. So I would emphasise that the word actuality is here used with a very definite meaning definable in terms of experience. It is that distinctive property of the world A—the world around us which we study experimentally—which is not possessed by the other worlds which might have occurred consistently with all the laws of nature. And since experience does certainly tell us that we have to do with one particular world and not the whole group of possible worlds, *actuality* denotes something which is significant and detectable by experience.

Actuality is recognised as tremendously important by the experimental physicist. But it does not appear in the scheme of the theoretical physicist. And it is quite natural that it should not appear. The experimental physicist deals with the particular cases ; the theoretical physicist generalises ; he refines away that which is special and particular and seeks to obtain the general laws of nature. So that he eliminates the reference to one particular and actual world and arrives at a theory which applies to all possible conditions that might occur—this, of course, includes the actual world as a special case. The theoretical physicist thus necessarily excludes actuality from his purview, though he arranges that it can be added as an afterthought ; and we can see how admirably the device of the vicious circle of definition is adapted to this purpose, because if actuality is added at any point it runs throughout the whole cycle. If our potentials are actual, then our matter, clocks, scales, intervals, etc., will all become actual.

Theoretical physics leaves room for actuality to be added, but it cannot itself tackle the question. It makes no attempt to define actuality. The experimental physicist, for whom actuality is vitally important, has to turn elsewhere, and he turns to consciousness. He simply accepts as actual that which the mind recognises as actual. He is alert for criticism of the reliability of his scales and clocks, but he has no misgivings as to their actuality. It is, of course, not necessary to appeal to the mind in each particular instance ; when once actuality has been introduced at any point of the cycle it runs through the whole cycle. But to obtain a start we must be given something certified as actual by the mind.

If then we consider a world entirely devoid of consciousness (as we not infrequently try to do), there is, so far as we know, no meaning whatever in discriminating between the worlds A and B. The mind is the referee who decides in favour of A against B. We cannot describe the difference without referring to a mind. The actuality of the world is a spiritual value. The physical world at some point (or indeed throughout) impinges on the spiritual world and derives its actuality solely from this contact.

I think that there is another undoubted fact of experience which is left out in the scheme of theoretical physics ; but in this case I cannot be so sure that the omission is irremediable. In the so-called " four-dimensional " world of the relativity theory the past and future lie, as it were, mapped out along with the near and distant. Each event is there in its proper relation to surrounding events ; but events never seem to undergo what has been described as " the formality of taking place." Here is what Professor Weyl says about it : " It is a four-dimensional continuum which is neither time nor space. Only the consciousness that passes on in one portion of this world experiences the detached piece which comes to meet it and passes behind it as history, that is as a process that goes forward in time and takes place in space." Here you see again the absolute necessity for a reference to consciousness. In a world without consciousness there is no meaning in this flux ; the world is simply spread passively in its four dimensions with the events connected by relations to which we can give numerical measure, but it is by their values for consciousness that we differentiate certain of these relations as *being* and others as *becoming*, certain relations as passive, others as dynamic. That dynamic quality by which nature is not merely something which exists, but is something which becomes, is not in the physical scheme, and must be introduced like actuality by filling the skeleton scheme of physics with things which over and above their physical definition have a value for consciousness, *i.e.*, a spiritual value. As we have said, the non-appearance of " becoming " in pure physical theory may merely be a defect of the present theory which time may remove ; and it should not be so much stressed as the absence of actuality which is evidently inherent in the whole method of cyclic definition. But it is, at any rate, a tempting hypothesis that " becoming " and actuality are spiritual values outside the scope of theoretical physics ; or we may put it in the form that the actuality that must be brought in from outside is not only an actuality of *being* but an actuality of *becoming*.

There is another way in which the mind must be held responsible for the processes of the material world—an intervention which can scarcely be ignored even if our interests are confined to the development of physical science. This intervention may be expressed crudely by saying that " values " are created by the mind. It is generally agreed that aesthetic and ethical values—the beauty of a landscape, the nobility of a deed—belong to a mental sphere ; but it appears also that the value to be attached to physical entities, such as mass and force, is (at least in most cases) ultimately a value for consciousness. We have said that mass, momentum, and stress are certain analytical expressions containing combinations of the ten potentials. Theoretical physics takes the form which it does take, and discovers laws of nature of a characteristic type, largely because it *chooses* to talk about these combinations of the potentials to which it has given the above names ; there are other combinations which it might talk about, but it regards them as uninteresting and leaves them nameless. This choice of subject-matter made at the outset determines the nature of the superstructure. Anyone attempting to construct a theory of the material world *ab initio* —to see how out of a basal relation-structure may be built up a world operating according to the laws of nature recognised by observation—is confronted with the difficulty of justifying and explaining this choice. He can find entities—that is to say, combinations of his symbols—which obey the well-known laws of nature in virtue of mathematical identities ; but he can also find other entities which obey laws unknown in nature. It is not the basal structure but the principle of selection which plays the all-important part in determining whether a law such as the conservation of energy shall take rank as a law of nature.

This principle of selection is partly determined by the fundamental idea of the external world that it shall embody the common element of the experiences of individuals in all possible circumstances. Therefore those entities or symbolic combinations which give greater weight to the experience of one individual rather than another cannot be allowed to appear in it. But after this sifting a further selection is necessary. It has already been stated that physics is content to take as standard the presentation to a normal intelligence, and it does not carry the symposium of appearances further. The selection thus ultimately depends on the contact of normal human consciousness with the physical world ; certain entities outside us awake directly or indirectly a response in our consciousness, and these thereby enter into the subject-matter of physics. Other entities equally substantial in their own right awake no response in consciousness ; no mental pictures vivify them ; they are left out of the subject-matter of physics and degraded to the level of curious constructs of the mathematician.

The principle of selection followed by the mind appears to be primarily a search for the things which are permanent. Just as the eye ranging over the ocean takes no notice of the changing motions of the particles of water but fastens attention on the steadily advancing wave-form, so the mind in its contact with nature ignores the more changeable entities but clothes with a vivid substantiality the things which endure. When we find that a number of the laws of nature take the form that such and such entities are permanent (or in scientific language that there is a law of conservation of mass, energy, momentum, electric charge, etc.), it is fairly safe to say that such laws are due to the mind in this sense. There is no law of government in the external world tending to preserve unchanged specially created entities which occupy it ; but the mind has by diligent search picked out the possible constructs which have this permanence in virtue of their mode of construction, and by giving value to these and neglecting the rest has imposed a law of conservation of the things of value. On the other hand, the mind itself may have developed this tendency through contact with the physical world. Intelligence in man and animals has perhaps developed its idiosyncrasies through the operation of natural selection ; and the dog whose intelligence had not the characteristic of attributing value to permanent things like bones would have short shrift in the struggle for existence.

Finally we come to direct interference of mind and spirit with the course of events in the material world. (To avoid misunderstanding it should be explained that no reference is made to spirit manifestations commonly so called ; provisionally the writer's attitude toward spiritualism is that of a disbeliever.) To-morrow, very possibly, this sheet of paper on which I am writing will, as a crumpled ball, describe a parabolic orbit ending in the wastepaper basket. Does anyone seriously believe that this physical motion is predictable to-day in the same sense that a future eclipse of the moon is predictable ? Will a fuller knowledge of atoms, electrons, and fields of force reveal the springs of an occurrence which I in my egotism attribute to a mental decision on questions of logical coherency and literary expression ? Is the motion of the editor's pencil to grammatically amend the split infinitive in this sentence simply the automatic response under physical laws of a complicated configuration of electrons to the external stimulus of this smear of ink on paper ? Such an extravagant hypothesis might conceivably appeal to the crude materialist who supposes that the world of electrons is the fundamental reality. But we have seen that the external world of physics is in the first place approached by way of consciousness, that it derives actuality and value from consciousness, and that it relates only to certain aspects of the common basis of material and spiritual things. The dance of electrons in the brain is only a partial aspect of the mental states and resolutions occurring, and there is no reason why it should claim to reveal the whole inner constitution by which one mental state leads to another.

Some reference must be made to the time-long difficulty of understanding how a man can voluntarily produce or refrain from producing effects in the physical world without (so experiment teaches) setting aside any of the laws known to govern inorganic nature. The difficulty is undoubtedly a grave one, and we cannot offer a solution of it ; but it is somewhat modified by the newer conception of the nature of the laws governing the physical world. In the present stage of science the laws of physics appear to be divisible into three classes—the identical, the statistical, and the transcendental. The " identical laws " include the great field-laws which are commonly quoted as typical instances of natural law—the law of gravitation, the law of conservation of mass and energy, the laws of electric and magnetic force, and the conservation of electric charge. These are seen to be identities, when we refer to the cycle so as to understand the constitution of the entities obeying them ; and unless we have misunderstood this constitution, violation of these laws is inconceivable. They do not in any way limit the actual basal structure of the world, and are not laws of governance. To quote again from Professor Weyl, " The freedom of action in the world is no more restricted by the rigorous laws of field physics than it is by the laws of Euclidean geometry according to the usual view." You have unfettered freedom to draw anything you like on a flat sheet of paper ; all the same, you cannot draw a circle whose circumference is six times its diameter. But you would not complain that because of this inability to do impossible things your freedom is imperfect. The law of Euclidean geometry is not felt to be a restriction on the freedom of the artist ; similarly the law of gravitation, when the nature of that which obeys it is understood, cannot be regarded as a limitation of freedom. The " statistical laws," including the laws of gases and thermodynamics, are the laws obeyed by crowds independently of the characteristics of the individuals composing the crowds. There remain the " transcendental laws," namely, the laws of atomic structure and of the quantum theory, which so far as we know may be true laws of governance. The quantum theory, perhaps even more than the relativity theory, is a remarkable development of the last twenty years, constituting an amazing breach with the traditional type of physical theory. It includes certain precise laws confirmed by innumerable experiments in all branches of physics, but no one has succeeded in forming an intelligible conception of the quantum processes. One thing is generally accepted, that we here have entered a domain of law of a type to which our experience of the great laws belonging to the first class gives no clue.

Interference of human free will with the identical laws cannot be admitted ; even omnipotence could scarcely set these aside, and free will does not mean omnipotence. It must be the statistical or transcendental laws that are modified when we " make up our minds" to do something. It would be a comfortable theory if we could lay the whole blame of free will on the transcendental laws—particularly on those which have not yet been discovered ! But I fear that there can be no satisfactory theory of free will without admitting an interference with statistical laws. If a human being can produce motion of material objects as the result of a mental resolution—motion which would not have resulted from the automatic interplay of electrons and atoms in his brain and body—it seems clear that those electrons and atoms are for the time not behaving as an ungoverned swarm would do, and some at least of the statistical laws governing random crowds will fail to hold. Indeed, the mind must necessarily have its grip on the crowd rather than on the individual atom or quantum-process, for the contact of matter and spirit is between brain and mind and not between an atom of brain and a (conjectural) atom of mind. If the physical aspects of what is occurring conform to statistical laws the mental resolution itself must be governed by statistical laws, and is therefore not what it appears to be—a simple decision of will—but a conflict of billions of unrecognised mental elements.

The serious difficulty arises that at present no failure of the statistical laws has been detected in experiments made on living organisms, and that the chief of these laws—the second law of thermodynamics—has been verified with some accuracy. Whilst this difficulty is perhaps not insuperable, it must not be minimised.

We have attempted in this essay to show the direction in which, it appears to us, the tendency of modern scientific thought is leading. It differs markedly from the views of thirty years ago. Will the next thirty years see another change ? Perhaps so. Scientific discovery is like the fitting together of the pieces of a great jig-saw puzzle ; now and then we are confident that we have added another piece correctly, and we know that no future wave of thought is likely to call for an alteration. But that technical achievement is not what matters to the philosopher, he wants to know how the puzzle-picture is developing. The scientist has his guesses as to how the finished picture will work out ; he uses these in the search for other pieces to fit ; but his guesses are modified from time to time by unexpected developments as the fitting in of the pieces proceeds. These revolutions of thought as to the final picture do

not cause the scientist to lose faith in his handiwork, for he is aware
that the completed portion is growing all the time. But those
who use these guesses for purposes outside science are on more
perilous ground, and it is with great reluctance and misgiving
that the writer has strayed on to it. Let the scientist stick to his
pointer-readings, is a good rule : and if, like many before us who
have broken it, we have lost our way in the outer fog, we may
perhaps plead that it was necessary to show that students of the
nineteenth and the twentieth centuries have at least different ways
of losing themselves, and the unqualified materialism of the last
century is not to-day the most inviting bypath.

Our thesis has been that the recent tendencies of scientific
thought lead to the belief that mind is a greater instrument than
was formerly recognised in prescribing the nature and laws of the
external world as studied in physical science ; that in exploring
his own territory the physicist comes up against the influence of
that wider reality which he cannot altogether shut out ; and that
by its selection of values the mind may indeed be said to have
created its physical environment. We have spelt mind with a
small " m," for our values are human values ; yet we trust there is
even in us something that has value for the eternal. Perhaps the
actuality of the world is not only in these little sparks from the
divine mind which flicker for a few years and are gone, but
in the Mind, the Logos. " The same was in the beginning
with God. . . . And without Him was not any thing made
that was made."

It will not be expected that science should indicate how this
colourless pantheism is to be made into a vital religion. Science
does not indicate whether the world-spirit is good or evil ; but it
does perhaps justify us in applying the adjective " creative." It is
for other considerations to examine the daring hypothesis that the
spirit in whom we have our being—our actuality—is approachable
to us ; that He is to us the beneficent Father, without which, it
seems to me, the question of the theoretical existence of a God has
little significance. This image of the divine nature is not a convenient fiction for use in workaday life, to be discarded in favour
of a system of equations when scientific accuracy is required. If
the hypothesis is correct, it signifies a direct relation of spirit to
spirit which can scarcely be made clearer by an irrelevant excursion
into the cycle of physical definition where the differential equations

take their rise ; it is more nearly expressed by reference to a relationship of spirit to spirit on the human plane—a relation which
means much more than physical science is able to formulate.   As
to this further question the scientist and the religious teacher may
well be content to agree that the value of any hypothesis extends
just so far as it is verified by actual experience.

MECHANISTIC BIOLOGY AND THE RELIGIOUS CONSCIOUSNESS

BY JOSEPH NEEDHAM

Fellow of Caius College, and Benn Levy Student in Biochemistry,
University of Cambridge

CONTENTS

1. The Problem of Living Matter

It is usually considered in this present age of universal specialisation that the business of men is to speak only about their own affairs, and, if they have any world-outlook, to keep it to themselves. Particularly is this the case with the scientific worker; but he is not alone in his mental prison. There adjoins it another, equally commodious but equally well bolted from outside, which is inhabited by the theologian and the mystic. In fact, there is a whole honeycomb of cells, each containing a section or two of human thought and experience, and the prison is so constructed that whatever opinions the inmates may have about each other, whenever they happen to open their mouths thereon they are miraculously struck dumb.

Yet this was not always so. Those were wonderful days when it was possible for a single mind to run over the whole range of knowledge and speculation. To read only the catalogue of " Particular Histories," or " experiments to be done," which Lord Bacon appended to the " *Novum Organon*," gives an idea of the magnificent impartiality with which a virtuoso of the seventeenth century could discuss Rainbows, Fiery Meteors, Fossils, Human Faculties, the Art of Metallurgy, and the natures of Numbers. Nothing came amiss to the learned of those days, nothing was outside their subject. From the Phoenix to the Mandrake, from the laws of languages to the funerary rites of antiquity, everything interested Sir Thomas Browne ; nothing need lack his learned commentary. But however good those old days were, it is no use regretting the past without facing the future. It is obvious enough that if a seventeenth-century physician had had to learn for his degree half the physiological knowledge that is expected of an honours candidate at the present day, he would have had much less time than he did to think of horoscopes and theological problems. One is sometimes struck with horror at the thought of what human beings will become if the process goes on at the rate at which it has gone on in the last hundred years. Plato's shoemaker, in the

Republic, who is charged to attend to nothing else but the making of shoes, will finally find himself, far from making shoes, occupied with putting the metal ends on to the laces, the shoes themselves being manufactured by ninety-nine other specialists. But the tendency is quite inevitable and can only be partially controlled. It is no bad thing that men should learn caution in speaking of matters which they themselves have not studied. But the ever-rising tide of specialisation has obscured the fact that there are not a few problems, especially in the fields of pure knowledge, which cannot be understood in the terms of one subject. The spectrum of knowledge has been arbitrarily divided up into compartments, whereas the colours really shade into each other quite imperceptibly. Such arbitrary cuttings and slicings have often mutilated the delicate fabric of reality, with the result that there are many questions at the present time most urgently needing the synthesis of two or more illuminations. As an example we might adduce our knowledge of the nervous system of man. It has been studied from three main directions : experimental psychology has examined it, biochemistry has studied its metabolism and its chemical composition, and biophysics has collected data about its electrical phenomena. But no one has yet synthesised these items of knowledge into one unitary whole.

The most outstanding case, however, in which harm has been produced by the superstition that one means of approach and one only is valid, is the subject of this paper, the whole problem of life itself. In ancient times, and in the Renaissance, this difficulty was not felt, for the domain of learning was a unity and everything within it bore directly on everything else. But as a more specialised biology grew up, and as, later still, this science became more and more infiltrated with mechanistic principles, it more and more came to be thought that the full explanation or description of the phenomena of living beings must be given in biological language. Experience has shown, however, that this is not the case. The question, why it is that living animals are different from dead ones and from inorganic matter, cannot be answered completely in terms of biology however physico-chemical biology may have become. Philosophical conceptions must assist in the complete answer. Nor is this because the foundations of the scientific method itself are open to philosophical criticism—as some philosophers would say, the chief business of philosophy—but because in studying life we are studying ourselves, and therefore, in a certain sense, the scientific method has to grapple with the problem of its own existence. Apart from hylozoist speculation, it will be admitted that the main distinguishing characteristic between organic and inorganic matter is that the former, at any rate in its higher forms, possesses mind. Consequently the scientific method, which is after all itself a mental product, is not competent to give us final descriptions of Life, without calling to its aid the other interpretative mental products, such as philosophy.

Yet in the past it has been assumed that the final answer to the problem of life can perfectly well be expected in the language of biology alone. The fundamental postulate of this paper is that scientific methods, even if criticised by philosophy, are not in themselves adequate to answer that problem. It accordingly follows that there is much work to be done by anyone who is prepared to think in terms of biology and philosophy with a view to the synthesis of a satisfactory working synoptic outlook.

The drift of thought from generation to generation is always interesting. The book of which this essay forms part is registering the change in outlook which exists between the Victorian era and to-day, and one of the most interesting passages is that from Zoology to Biochemistry in their influence upon Philosophy and Religion. In the last century it was the zoological conceptions which seemed of paramount importance. Preceded by Lamarck, Cuvier, and Buffon, the zoologists of the early part of the nineteenth century were able to point to a world in which a vast number of species and genera had been classified according to their form, and constituted a static system. Upon this apparently secure basis the evolutionists built up their theory and buttressed it with the evidence from palaeontology and other fields. The opposition which the supporters of the evolution theory met with from the theologians and philosophers did it nothing but good, except in so far as there was a retardation in the appraisement of the theory at its true value. The more misunderstanding there was over the assumed implications of the theory, the more difficult it was to know exactly how it would eventually fit into the general body of knowledge. However, when the excitement died down, it was possible to see more clearly. Modifications in the original theory as set forth by Darwin were introduced and the tide of interest turned in another direction. Physiology, which had had little to say to the evolution theory, since taxonomic classification had been founded on differences of form rather than of function, now began to occupy more and more the centre of the field, and as this process went on it was seen that physiology wore no longer the garments in which traditional teaching had pictured her, but appeared in the breastplate of chemistry, the helmet of physics, and armed with the spear of mathematics. As time went on the hitherto neglected subject of biochemistry became more and more important, so that at the present day zoology has become comparative biochemistry and physiology biophysics. The causes for the change lie deep, but the effect has been a profound infiltration of physico-chemical ideas and terminology into the whole biological field, and this implies a corresponding peaceful penetration of the mechanistic theory of life. This change from comparative morphology to comparative biochemistry is indeed one of the most important factors in the scientific history of the last few decades. It will never again be equalled in importance until comparative biochemistry passes over into electronic biophysics. For it means that we have passed one step deeper into the problem of life—important as the distribution and form of organisms may be, it cannot be so much so as the actual examination of the physico-chemical attributes of living matter itself, of the universal substrate of the innumerable manifestations of living beings. The forms of the different types of sea-urchins are truly most interesting, but they are only the forms taken by the same chemical elements, and in this case as in others the body is more than the raiment.

This profound change in the domain of science has had its effects on philosophy. Whereas evolution was the key-interest of biological philosophy fifty years ago, it is now so no longer, for a more comprehensive problem has supplanted it. The mechanistic theory of life is now the important problem, and the relations of biological science to religion are accordingly altered. Mechanism is a more inclusive conception than evolution, it is deeper, and therefore it more definitely demands the co-operation of philosophy.

But the mechanistic theory of life is not new. On the contrary, it is one of man's earliest speculations. And throughout its history it has had to suffer the opposition of religious thought because it has, as a rule, been linked in thought with materialism or realism. We shall have to discuss in this paper the question of whether this has been or is justified, and to see whether religion and the other realms of human spiritual experience do indeed conflict absolutely with mechanism in biology. The historical alternative to mechanism is vitalism, and we shall have to examine that theory as critically as the mechanistic one. We shall have to see whether McDougall's statement, that vitalism is a form of animism characterised by its neglect of the psychophysical problem, is justified. And we shall discuss a position which seems to fit in with the evidence better than the classical ones and to point the way to a synoptic outlook.

2. The Mechanistic Theory of Life in History

The mechanistic theory of life is not new. Its history as a theory goes back as far as the first speculations on the nature of life and the universe. But it existed only as a theory, which remained a possible opinion and nothing more, until the sciences of physics and chemistry had had time to discard their embryonic wrappings of pseudo-science. Once natural science was clearly founded on such fundamental hypotheses as the belief in the uniformity of nature and such orientations of mind as that which dealt witchcraft its death-blow, then the field was clear for the attempt to see whether living beings would indeed conform to the principles of a mechanistic physiology. In 1527 Paracelsus von Hohenheim, lecturing at Basel, gave biochemistry its charter when he said : "The Body is a conglomeration of chemical matters ; when these are deranged, illness results, and nought but chemical medicines may cure the same." From thenceforward an enormous tract yet remained to be covered before true biochemical researches could begin, for alchemy had yet to yield to iatro-chemistry, and that in turn to the surely built chemistry of the present day. But, nevertheless, since the sixteenth century, the mechanistic theory in biology has been able to point to experimental successes in its support, and indeed, from position to position, sometimes slowly and sometimes with greater rapidity, it has marched forward until it has achieved in the last fifty years its most amazing triumphs. The precise degree of validity of these successes we must reserve for discussion later.

And all through its history it has evoked the condemnation

of the theologians, the mystics, and the idealist philosophers. With remarkable unanimity they have refused to have anything to do with a biology which makes man's body the equal of those of the animals, and his spiritual part a functionless shadow without importance. It will be interesting to compare some of the mechanists in history and place over against them quotations from their antagonists.

We cannot do better than begin with Democritus. One of the Atomistic school of Greek philosophy, born about 440 B.C., he lived at Abdera on the coast of Thrace, and although he left no writings behind him which have lasted to our time, we know sufficiently well what he taught from those of his disciples and from Epicurus, who recognised him as his predecessor. His basic propositions were the indestructibility of matter, the universality of determinism, and the existence of nothing beside atoms. But he paid special attention to the problem of life, and taught that the soul consists of fine, round, smooth atoms like those of fire, very mobile and fluid, permeating the whole body and so causing movement. Such opinions were, of course, only opinions, but it is most significant that Diogenes Laertius has a story to the effect that Plato in later years desired to collect all the works of Democritus and burn them to ashes. Plato's views are only of importance in this connection because they were biologically anti-mechanistic. Moreover, Plato makes Socrates in the " *Theaetetus*" argue against those philosophers who will only believe in what they can grip with their hands. Here then is an example of the conflict.

The next significant contrast is between Lucretius and Tertullian. Lucretius in his great poem, " *De Rerum Natura*," written to propagate the philosophical materialism of Democritus and Epicurus, devoted considerable space to the mechanistic theory of life and, of course, argued in its favour. Although he exercised a great influence on certain minds, notably Virgil, it is impossible to say what effect his writings had upon the apologists on behalf of the Roman " Religion of Numa," a debased form of which was then the predominant cult at Rome, for no priestly writings of that date have come down to us. His poem, by reason of its nature, could never have been very popular, and this probably accounts for the fact that the Fathers of the Church took little trouble to write against his arguments. For them it was not a living issue. But the following lines show the manner of Lucretius' thought :

And this same argument establisheth
That nature of mind and soul corporeal is,
For when 'tis seen to drive the members on,
To snatch from sleep the body and to change
The countenance, and the whole state of man,
To rule and turn—what yet could never be
Failing a contact—Must we not grant they are
Of a corporeal nature ?

Now of what body, what components, formed
Is this same mind I will go on to tell,
First I aver, 'tis superfine, composed,
Of tiniest particles—that such the fact
Thou canst perceive if thou attend from this :
Nothing is seen to happen with such speed
As what the mind proposes and begins, ·
Therefore the same bestirs itself more swiftly
Than aught whose nature's palpable to eyes.

Lucretius differs from Democritus on many points, but, like
him, supposes that the soul, though it has directive power over the
body, is yet itself material subject to the laws governing the atoms
and must perish accordingly with the body. This is different to the
post-renaissance theories, which often admit that the mind is non-
material but deny it any action on the body, treating it as a shadow
thrown off by the body's physical processes, an " Epiphenomenon."
Where Lucretius exactly anticipates the epipheromenalists of
modern times is in his refusal to believe that there can be such a
thing as psycho-physical action. This may show us how inseparable the problem of mechanism in biology is from that of psychophysical interaction. The latter is the real problem, but the former
has its roots in experimental work, and has to be solved first. As
against the mechanism of Lucretius it is instructive to note what
Tertullian says. Strangely enough, Tertullian upheld the corporeal nature of the soul as against Plato, but that did not prevent
him from decrying mechanism in biology. In his treatise " *De
Anima* " he says :

" In the first place there is in the soul some supreme principle
of vitality and intelligence which can be called the ruling power
of the soul—τὸ ἡγημονικόν. For if this be not admitted the
whole condition of the soul is put in jeopardy. Indeed, those men

who say that there is no such directing faculty end by supposing that the soul itself is a mere nonentity."

To Tertullian, at any rate, there was no way of admitting mechanism to be supreme in biology and at the same time giving any validity to spiritual experience.   So the former, being but an opinion of certain philosophers, had to go.

After the patristic period is over, we do not find anything of significance for this subject until the beginning of the sixteenth century.   And now, although very feebly and dimly, there begin to be at work those influences which later on are to bear profoundly on the mechanism problem—namely, those of the experimen'al method.   The early history of Alchemy is not of great interest o us here, but its discipline produced such remarkable men as Abbc Trithemius and Basil Valentine, the teachers of Paracelsus vor. Hohenheim.   This great man, now rehabilitated as a genuine thinker after four centuries of calumny due to the survival of the writings of his adversaries, introduced ideas of the utmost importance into biology.   One would think from the pronouncement of his which has already been quoted, that he was singularly free from the daemonistic and spiritualistic prepossessions of his time.   This, however, was not the case.   Side by side with a peculiarly clear treatment of the chemistry of the period there existed in his mind a hylozoism which led him to a most strange conception of the nature of living matter.   The animal body, according to him, contained, besides its innumerable chemical constituents and processes, an innumerable number of "archaei" or subsidiary daemons which in the last resort were responsible for the functioning of the different parts.   If food was digested in the stomach, it was indeed because chemical processes were going on in it, but these processes were governed, controlled, and perhaps caused by an archaeus.   Paracelsus never very clearly stated that the anima of man was not the sum of the archaei of all the separate organs, but he rather tended to the view that the anima was something quite different from them. His whole pathology was grounded on the view that in the diseased organ the corresponding archaeus was absent or for some reason had let loose the reins of control.   But in spite of these theories, which might have been expected to cripple seriously his experimental work, he brought about a revolution in medicine by abandoning largely the old pharmacopeia with its vast assortment of herbal medicines and by introducing chemical or "spagirical" medicines as they were called, such as preparations of zinc and antimony. To his more rational therapy Erasmus owed a recovery from several dangerous sicknesses.

Thus by one of the most extraordinary ironies of history, the first biochemist was also the first vitalist. For in spite of the gulf between the methods of Paracelsus and those of the present day, there is borne in upon the student of his writings the conviction that had he lived four hundred years later, he would have been eminent in biochemical research. The orientation of mind is the same though the methods are different. And yet, in spite of this, vitalism also has its birthplace with him. It was not until there was any idea of what is meant by experimental science that it was possible to discuss the question as to whether life could be explained solely by its aid, except as a point of speculation. McDougall has pointed out that the ghost-soul of primitive peoples, that half-material, half-spiritual counterpart of man, which arose, as some say, through dreams and images of waking life, or as others would have it, through the remembrances of dead friends, became in the course of history split into two portions. One of these became the basis of the intellect and so the subject of metaphysical discussion, the other became the vital force which it was supposed was needed to assist in the explanation of the activities of the body, and so the bone of contention among physiological thinkers. One of the main points of divergence, of dichotomy of the primitive conception, then, is Paracelsus. Quite apart from the anima, there was to him a vital force which governed the movements of atoms in such a way as to create living beings, so that although the first of biochemists he was no mechanist.

"The business of alchemy," he said, "is not to prepare either gold or silver but to make medicines." This changed outlook took root and the new study of iatro-chemistry flourished for the next two centuries as the real precursor of chemistry. The next important figure in this part of biological history is Jean-Baptiste van Helmont. Like his predecessor Paracelsus, he made several very great advances in what we should now call pure chemistry, such as introducing the conception of enzyme action and the definition of a gas, but he was just as much a vitalist as Paracelsus and adopted his theory of archaei almost entirely. His only difference was that he pictured the archaei as definitely struggling against chemical changes rather than governing and controlling them. Illness resulted from the overthrowing of one or more of the archaei, so that chemical changes could pursue their courses unchecked. This distinction is important historically because researches on the phenomena of autolysis have shown that after death in surviving organs enzyme actions proceed uncontrolled until complete disintegration of the tissue may occur, and this quite distinguished from the action of bacteria, as in putrefaction. Thus van Helmont's notion that chemical processes in the body are withstood by archaei was an interesting forerunner of the modern view that they are limited by the laws of mass action and other chemical necessities.

But a mechanistic influence of enormous importance was at hand in the shape of René Descartes, who in 1664 published the first scientific textbook of mechanistic physiology, the " Traité de l'Homme." Descartes' philosophy in so far as it bore upon physiology was an absolute dualism. He argued strongly for the immateriality of the soul, and at the same time applied the most rigid mechanistic principles to the body. The seat of interaction he placed in the pineal gland, an anatomical structure situated over the brain and now known to be a vestigial eye. He completed finally the separation between the vital principle and the thinking principle by placing the latter in the mind and giving up the vegetative functions entirely to the body and hence to deterministic mechanism. It followed from his theories, though he did not carry them as far as they logically would go, that animals, possessing no soul, were absolutely and completely mechanistic in their operation.

No philosopher has ever exercised so great an influence on purely scientific studies as has Descartes. He influenced the last of the iatro-chemists on the one hand and the first of the iatro-physicists on the other. Franciscus Sylvius of Leyden headed the first mechanistic movement in biochemistry, and wrote in defence of mechanistic notions, accepting all van Helmont's chemistry but rejecting his doctrine of archaei. It is to this Sylvius that we owe the differentiation between acids and alkalies and the building of the first University Chemical Laboratory.

In two other directions did Descartes' mechanistic infl ience extend itself to great effect. Nicholas Stensen, who discovered that the heart was a muscular organ, and early fellows of the Royal

Society, such as Thomas Willis and George Bathurst, owed much to Descartes. And the work of Borelli and Sanctorius, who were the first investigators to apply physical methods of measurement to bodily functions, was also partly inspired by Descartes.

But Descartes' views, however carefully he might leave room for the soul, did not meet the approval of theology. They never penetrated the French or English Universities, and they were successively condemned by the Jesuits and the Oratory. We have already given two instances of mechanistic biology being unacceptable to idealistic philosophy and religion, in the cases of Democritus and Plato, and of Lucretius and Tertullian. We can now give another : Samuel Parker, Bishop of Oxford at the Restoration, wrote voluminously against Descartes and classed him with Gassendi and Hobbes as one of the three most dangerous atheists of the age. In the " Disputationes de Deo," he says :

" Thus from these excerpts from Cartesius I have made it clear that the Mechanical philosophy is quite unfit for solving the problems of phenomena. Cartesius has tried to steer a middle course between Aristotle and Epicurus and has but succeeded in borrowing from both."

But this was simply the reaction of religious opinion. In science itself there was also a reaction. Francis Glisson and Ralph Cudworth, Professors of Medicine at Cambridge and Oxford respectively, wrote against Descartes' physiology. George Ernest Stahl, to whom pure chemistry as well as physiology is much indebted, also took an important step in the other direction. Returning to the conception of the archaei, he rolled them all into one and emerged with the conception of the *anima sensitiva*, itself not a new idea, explicitly distinct from mind or soul. Just as the archaei had been supposed to do, it sat somewhere in the animal body and regulated everything exactly in the same way as a signalman does in a signal-box. When the *anima sensitiva* fell asleep or went on a journey, the art of the physician was necessary.

But this vitalistic reaction did not last long. The influence of Descartes was too deep to be shaken off quickly, and early in the eighteenth century there was a widespread return to mechanical explanations. As typical of that tendency we have the book called " Man a Machine," written by one of the most odd and impish characters at the Court of Frederick the Great, his physician,

Julien de la Mettrie. It is composed in support of a very crude mechanistic view which attributes all thought to brain processes, but it is written in a sprightly style, as the following quotations show :

" The body may be considered a clock and the fresh chyle we may ·look on as the spring of that clock. The first business of nature upon the entrance of the chyle into the blood is to raise a sort of fever which the chemists (who dream of nothing but furnaces) call a fermentation."

" Let us conclude boldly then that man is a machine, and that there is only one substance, differently modified, in the whole world. What will all the weak reeds of divinity, metaphysic, and nonsense of the schools, avail against this firm and solid oak ? "

As might have been expected, an anonymous reply to this work appeared a year or two later. A pamphlet of about the same length, called " Man more than a Machine," was published with an almost identical title-page, " in Answer to a Wicked and a Atheistical Treatise written by M. de la Mettrie." Its style is not so good, but it makes amusing reading, for the author takes all de la Mettrie's points and endeavours to confute them one by one. Here is a sample :

" The physician's ignorance of logic renders him subject to numberless errors which he readily swallows down for want of the art of drawing just conclusions. He observes that a medicine which restores a sick person to health has sometimes the effect that it changes a blockhead into a man of sense. Nothing more is wanting for him to conclude that man is no more than a watch and that it is sufficient that his spring and wheels be in good order to render him reasonable." " Let a man eat and drink as plentifully and as long as he will ; let a new chyle support him for sixty years successively, he will not in this respect be more than a plant or a tree supplied continually with fresh juices."

In this way the polemic was prolonged, on the mechanistic side by d'Holbach and Cabanis, to whom is due the statement that the " brain produces thought in the same way as the stomach and intestines operate in digestion, the liver filters the bile and the submaxillary gland secretes the saliva," and on the vitalistic side by Barthez, Bordeu, and Chaussier. An echo of their contentions is found in the " Religio Medici " of Sir Thomas Browne, though written years before the dispute became general. To deny the action of the soul upon the body, he said, was

" To devolve the honour of the principal agent upon the instrument, which, if with reason we may do, then let our hammers rise up and boast that they have built our houses, and our pens receive the honour of our writings."

Experimental researches during this period were not wanting, and they all tended in a mechanistic direction, though this was not understood at the time. Réaumur in 1752 was the first to study enzymes from the digestive juices outside the body and to show that the processes of life possessed a definite optimum temperature. But the eighteenth century closed with the general acceptance of a mild vitalism, represented by Bichat and Johannes Müller. It was the calm before the storm. As soon as the nineteenth century had begun steadily and without intermission the tide of mechanistic interpretations in biology went forward. The two most important dates in this period are 1828 and 1897, and they are indeed of enormous significance. In 1828 Wöhler carried out at Giessen the synthesis of urea in the laboratory. Before that time it had been generally accepted even among the vitalists that the animal organism was constituted out of the same elements and compounds as those of inorganic nature—though it had required much work on the part of the famous biochemist, Justus von Liebig, himself a vitalist, to convince them of that. At the same time it was generally felt that though the chemical elements inside and outside the animal body might be the same, yet the compounds found in the body could only be manufactured by the body. Such a substance as urea or uric acid, they thought, though capable of ordinary chemical analysis, could never be produced without the intervention of life in some form or other, because for its making vital force was necessary. This whole conception was shattered by Wöhler's synthesis of urea from inorganic substances in the laboratory, for what could be done once could be done again, and all the constituents of the animal body must one day be capable of synthesis in the laboratory. No vital force was necessary. The vitalists had to retire from that position.

But they still possessed the stronghold of the view that the organism is not subject to the laws of thermodynamics. All through the middle part of the century argument was conducted on that indefinite basis, but in 1897 Atwater and Rosa constructed a large and exceedingly delicate calorimeter by the aid of which they were enabled to determine the total amount of energy entering an animal or a man and the total amount leaving him. The error was exceedingly small and their result was that the amount taken in was exactly balanced by the amount going out. *Ex nihilo nihil fit.* And this under all conditions. Accordingly not only was it found that the chemical compounds of which the body is made up were all such as could be studied and synthesised in the laboratory, but also there was no doubt that the law of the conservation of energy held as rigidly for the animal body as it did for inorganic nature. Energy cannot arise out of nothing, nor be dissipated into nothing. The organism agrees to this by not keeping any, and by not producing any.

These, indeed, were the most important of the experimental researches which contributed to the view that mechanistic explanations of animal activity were the correct ones, but there were a thousand others which pointed in the same direction. In more recent times the work of Loeb on animal tropisms, which has provided us with a mechanistic theory of the actions of the lower organisms, the researches of Barcroft and Henderson, which have shown the intricate physico-chemical mechanisms in the blood which tend to keep the internal environment of the organism constant, and the work of Lillie on fertilisation, all point in the same direction ; all implicitly disprove the contentions of the vitalists. One might continue elaborating the biochemical history of the nineteenth century to great lengths ; one aspect more shall be described. In 1812 Legallois located the respiratory centre in the spinal medulla, and much was said at the time about the " vital tripod," the heart, the lungs, and the brain. The *anima sensitiva* was thus beginning to disintegrate once more. When Schleiden and Schwann, ten years afterwards, discovered the cellular nature of living matter and it was realised that the cell and not the organ is the atom of biology, the *anima sensitiva* suffered another dismemberment, for it became necessary to allot a vital force to each cell, because single cells might outlast the death of the whole body for a very long time.

But possibly because of the nature of thought itself, the mechanistic viewpoint was not to be allowed to suppress all other conceptions. There had always, even in the crests of the movement, been a small minority of the older type of vitalists. Very late in the nineteenth century they found a leader in the person of Hans Driesch, and another in that of Haldane, who elevated the banner of a neo-vitalism which has had a considerable number of books to its credit, but few supporters.

At the present day then the situation is in effect the complete triumph of mechanistic biology. It is not alone in the field, because the neo-vitalists do exist as a small minority, but the vast preponderance of active biological workers are mechanists. We have already given four instances of the antagonism between theology and mechanistic biology, and we can now add a fifth. At the Modernist Conference held at Oxford in the summer of 1924 all the speakers on biological subjects were professed and eminent vitalists. Nothing could be more beautifully in line with the traditional manner. But although it is possible to understand the alacrity with which the theological mind greets vitalistic and spiritualistic ideas in biology, yet it may be doubted whether, even from a narrowly apologetic point of view, it was wise to nail the colours of religion to the precarious mast of neo-vitalism.

How far has mechanistic biology really triumphed? Before answering this question we must investigate the fighting power of its present antagonists.

3. A Critique of Neo-Vitalism

The neo-vitalists, although culminating in a metaphysical doctrine, began their speculations from experimental results. In this respect neo-vitalism is superior to the older theories of similar nature, for it does at least start with something definite even though its interpretations of the observed facts may be wrong.

Driesch, while working on certain problems in experimental embryology in which he placed various obstacles in the way of the normal development of embryos, was driven to the conclusion that the effects he observed could never be described in terms of physics and chemistry. Haldane while investigating processes going on in the intact higher organism came to the same conclusion. He was dealing with the delicately adjusted response which the organism makes to increased oxygen-want, and he concluded as the result of direct measurement that the lung epithelium must actively secrete oxygen into the blood. No physico-chemical mechanism could be thought of which would satisfy this demand, so, as Heidenhain had found for the kidney, it was necessary to invoke a vital force. There is an obvious advantage in basing these speculations upon experiments, for there is then something definite to argue about, but there is also the disadvantage that the facts may not be really what they appear, and improved technique may leave the philosophical superstructure in mid-air without any outward and visible means of support. Haldane, however, only based his views partly upon experimental results.

The fact which Driesch found incapable of explanation upon mechanistic lines may be briefly stated as the power which a developing embryo has of three-dimensional regeneration. If an embryo which has developed as far as the blastula stage, in which it is a hollow sphere of cells without any top or bottom, right or left, is then divided into two or more parts with a sharp cut, each half becomes later on one entire embryo. Thus, since there are an infinite number of planes along which the cut might have gone, any one part of the embryo must know what the other parts are going to do, and, moreover, must be prepared to perform almost any function. In other words, until a very late stage in development each single cell must have the potentiality of turning into any other cell, according to the necessity of the whole body. Any one cell might become a liver-cell, a blood-corpuscle, or a constituent of bone tissue according to the demands made upon it : demands, too, incapable of being foreseen, for the plane of the experimentalist's cut is a matter of chance. " A very strange sort of a machine indeed," says Driesch, " which is the same in all its parts." " It is not possible," Driesch says, " to conceive of a machine being divided in any direction and still remaining a machine."

Driesch, as the result of innumerable such experiments, was therefore led to regard the organism as a whole as the only possible biological unit—a conception which Haldane later arrived at independently. There seems to be a kind of autonomy not only in the developing embryo but in all organisms, so that the normal typical form and structure and function come into being whatever the interference, provided that the interference is not too great. There is a certain trend on the part of the organism, and if an obstacle is placed in its way, the organism, quite apart from the attributes of conscious life, seems to try first one way and then another of overcoming it, as if moved on irresistibly by what has been called outside the scientific world, by Bernard Shaw and others, the Life-Force.

Driesch considered the organism as a type of manifoldness which is at the same time a unity, and in which, besides the obvious extensive manifoldness, there was a sort of intensive manifoldness appearing from inside outwards. The cause at work Driesch called the entelechy, borrowing an Aristotelian word for the occasion. Most explicitly he defines this factor as possessing psychoid properties of willing and knowing and as not being conscious, though he is equally sure that it is not material, not a physical thing. It stands intermediate between everything, and it is much easier to say what it is not than what it is. Its mode of operation he conceives of as being the intimate regulation of the physico-chemical processes on the body ; it does nothing active itself but it suspends other processes at one time and releases them at another. For example, transformations of energy-distribution necessitated by differences of chemical potential would be held up by the entelechy until the proper time had come to allow them to go forward.

But Driesch also adds a logical speculative argument. He starts by maintaining that there cannot be more content in the effect than there was in the cause. Therefore, since the predominant attribute of developing organisms is their continual increase in complexity and differentiation, the original cause, the undivided ovum, is insufficient alone to account for the change, and something outside must be postulated.

Haldane, on the other hand, was led to neo-vitalism entirely by experiments on the adult animal. To Haldane, as to Driesch, the functions of separate organs may admit of physico-chemical description, but the body as a whole in all its efficiency of co-ordination and purposiveness cannot do so. No constellation of purely physical and chemical facts can account for the fertility and co-ordinateness of adaptation. The kernel of the nut which physics and chemistry will never be able to crack, lies for him in the continual tendency of the organism to keep its environment, both exterior and interior, constant. The animal body continually tends to maintain the conditions optimum for its own existence, and Haldane cannot conceive of a machine being able to do that. Haldane also considers quite impossible the mechanistic theory of heredity. " On the mechanistic theory," he says, " the cell-nucleus must carry within its substance a mechanism which by reaction with the environment not only produces the millions of complex and delicately balanced mechanisms which constitute the adult organism, but provides for their orderly arrangement into tissues and organs, and for their orderly development in a certain perfectly specific manner. The mind recoils from such a stupendous conception ! "

Haldane also, like Driesch, is not content with arguments of this nature drawn from the supposed insufficiency of mechanism as a working hypothesis, but he also makes use of more metaphysical modes of approach. He points out that Kant created no special category for life, and so in Kantian language the only way of conceiving living beings was in terms of physics and chemistry. On the other hand, Hegel did make a special category for living substance, and Haldane maintains that the biologist should avail himself of this and insist that life cannot be reduced to physico-chemical conceptions. Haldane would say that to take animals to pieces and study separate functions by biochemical or biophysical methods is inadmissible because the essence of life consists of its co-ordination as a whole. He will not allow that we can ever understand the organism by studying one part like a carburettor apart from the rest and then by turning to the cylinders and examining them. The organism is a unit. Again and again he says that since so far no complete mechanistic explanation has been advanced of any one organ, we cannot trust physico-chemical methods to explain the whole.

Another important argument of Haldane's is akin to the criticisms of the scientific method in general which have been so much more common of recent years. He uses the views of LeRoy and Duhem, which logically criticise the whole validity of the scientific method, to support the neo-vitalist position. In scientific thought, he says, we take much of the juice out of reality, we are bound to deal with exsuccous abstractions because in generalising we let the individual escape. We analyse and take to pieces ; we do not look at the object as a whole, but only in bits. We select facts, and abstract from reality itself by focussing our attention upon certain aspects of it. These subjective contingency arguments contain much truth, but they are strange enthusiasms for a scientific worker. Haldane proceeds to apply such conceptions to the biological problem, and says that when we consider a man as a physico-chemical machine we abstract from reality by setting aside his biological and psychological natures. When we regard him simply as a coloured object or a certain weight, we still further abstract from reality, as in the impersonal " Hommes 40. Chevaux 16 " written on French railway wagons. To abstract nothing from reality we must consider him as nothing short of a personality.

To do justice to Haldane's views is difficult, for his arguments are dangerous vehicles, and in following him it is necessary to get off just at the right place. Enough has been said, however, to give an idea of the neo-vitalist position, a standpoint adopted by Arthur Thomson and E. S. Russell, as well as Driesch and Haldane, though with individual modifications. Their views have found very little acceptance among zoological and physiological workers and, naturally, none at all among biochemists and biophysicists.

In the criticism of the neo-vitalist position, the first thing that appears is the insufficiency of the basis which led the neo-vitalists to take up their present attitude. It almost looks, from a psychological point of view, as if, unable to bear the thought of the possibility that biology is really applied physics and chemistry, they had laboriously striven by philosophical discussion to avoid coming to that conclusion.

At any rate it is quite a mistake to suppose that their opinions are in any way new. It is interesting to compare Stahl's writings on the *anima sensitiva* in his " *Theoria Medica* " of 1708 with the description of the entelechy in Driesch. The more the two are compared the more remarkable the resemblance becomes ; each is conceived of as a non-material force informing the tissues of the organism and controlling in a subtle manner all the different chemical processes which are going on in them. It could certainly be argued that there must be something in the idea if two biologists such as Stahl and Driesch, separated by two centuries, could come to a very similar conclusion. But to say that would be to neglect the enormous advances in biological chemistry and physics which had been made between 1708 and 1908, so that whatever praise we allot to Stahl for his theory we must allot much less to Driesch for his, since he put forward an essentially similar conception at a time when it was far less likely Indeed, all the speculations of the neo-vitalists have been preceded by those of the iatro-chemists, with this only difference, that the iatro-chemists were nearer the days of daemonology than the neo-vitalists.

The principal arguments of the neo-vitalists can be stated thus :
(1) the argument from inconceivability, and (2) the " actual wholeness " of the organism. The first of these arguments they are continually using, but perhaps do not realise that it is a two-edged weapon and cuts both ways. As an example of the use of it we have already seen how Driesch refuses to believe that any mechanistic description can be adequate for the facts of development, and how Haldane says the same thing for the mechanisms of adjustment to slightly abnormal conditions in the adult animal. We shall see later whether these are really so inexplicable as they would have us believe. But the fundamental fallacy of the argument from inconceivability is quite a simple one. There are not a few occasions in the history of biology in the last fifty years on which one experimentalist has brought forward a mechanistic theory to account for facts which he has observed, and another has proved that the theory in question is insufficient to account for them. Out of many examples we may take the work of Rhumbler on amoeboid movement. Amoebae, the very low unicellular organisms which live in ponds on dead leaves, progress by alternately putting out and retracting protoplasmic processes called pseudopodia and pulling themselves along. Rhumbler developed a theory to explain these facts which made use of physical conceptions only, such as surface tension. Later, however, Mast, Root, and other biologists in the U.S.A., discovered certain other facts which Rhumbler's theory would not cover, and it had to be abandoned. Naturally the vitalists made much of this failure, and the general assumption was that because a mechanistic theory had hopelessly broken down, therefore no mechanistic theory that might be proposed in the future would ever fit the facts. A most obvious logical error. We do not even know what the face of physics and chemistry themselves may be like in twenty or thirty years—they may even have the same face. How, then, can we maintain that a mechanistic explanation is inconceivable, as the neo-vitalists continually do ? No, all we can do is to express our opinion one way or the other according to what seems to us most likely. Whichever we do, belief will be necessary, and the biologist can either believe that in time physico-chemical explanations—and be it noted, in terms of the physics and chemistry of the period, and not in those of to-day —will be capable of describing all the phenomena of bodily life ; or, on the other hand, he can believe that an immaterial ghost,

distinct from either mind or soul, is present in living matter, eternally watchful to destroy his carefully planned experiments and to escape from his observation.   Moreover, if a graph were drawn having as its ordinate the progress made in mechanistic explanations and as its abscissa the last fifty years, a curve would result unmistakably showing the continual defeat of vitalism.   One would have only to extrapolate the curve to find the date at which complete mechanistic explanation of bodily life should first become possible.   As, however, the shape of the curve also depends on " constraint of Princes, barratry of Master and Mariners, and Acts of God," we shall here decline the task and proceed to consider a few other points relative to the argument from inconceivability.

To return to Haldane's quotation.   " The cell-nucleus must carry within it," he says, " a mechanism by which reaction with the environment not only produces the millions of complex and delicately balanced mechanisms which constitute the adult organism, but provides for their orderly arrangement into tissues and organs." The neo-vitalists are fond of drawing stupendous pictures of the complexity of living stuff, and of inviting appropriate meditations upon it.   But they neglect Poincaré's famous dictum about the hierarchy of facts.   To listen to the neo-vitalists one would think that mechanistic descriptions were useless unless they accounted for the movements of every single molecule in every single cell. The complexity of living cells everyone must admit to be enormous, but it is a belief of the biochemist that there are certain key-factors and vantage-points which enable us to gain a general view over large tracts.   For example, the regulation of the exact intensity of acidity in animal tissues is one of the processes to which the neo-vitalists point as inexplicable ; yet the *Journal of Biological Chemistry* is full of accurate descriptions of the mechanisms by which this is effected.   It is a fact in chemistry that if an acid and a salt are present in concentrations about equal, then the addition of more acid or more base is needed to upset the system than if their concentrations were very different.   This is called " buffer action," and it is one of the key-positions referred to above.   It must play a part in the regulation of numberless systems in the cell. Granted that development and acidity-regulation are extraordinarily complicated processes, nevertheless in biochemistry we are continually coming upon key discoveries which bring at once in their train the explanation of a hundred other facts.   The intensely complex systems to which the neo-vitalists draw our attention are capable of simplification. It is not necessary to know the name of every village in India to understand the shape of its coast-line and the disposition of its cities. A good example from my own work of a key-fact the discovery of which explains many other facts is seen in the phosphorus metabolism of the developing bird's-egg. Inorganic phosphorus is produced from organic phosphorus as it develops : hence calcium is required to form the bones from the shell, hence the shell becomes more brittle : hence carbon dioxide which is produced in greater amount relatively the older the chick can escape more easily, and so on.

By a strange coincidence while preparing this paper such a key-position has become important. E. S. Russell in his book called " The Study of Living Things " supports Haldane's position and makes a great deal of the impossibility of explaining bone-formation on mechanistic lines. Yet the *Biochemical Journal* for 1924 contains an account of Robison's discovery of an enzyme in calcifying bone which transmutes phosphorus in combination with sugar into phosphorus in combination with calcium for bone. The future will see first of all the conditions of the enzyme's working thoroughly understood, next the isolation of the enzyme in a pure state, next its synthesis, and finally its assistance in contributing to a complete mechanistic account of the process of bone-formation.

But the inconceivability argument can very easily be turned against its authors. It is all very well to say that mechanical explanations are inconceivable, but what if someone found the conception of the entelechy quite unintelligible ? As a matter of fact most biochemists do. A directive force, which is neither matter nor spirit, which can act but at the same time cannot think, and which regulates chemical processes perfectly capable of regulating themselves, seems thoroughly inconceivable to the biochemist. "An ' Entelechy,' " as Hoernlé says, " is too hypothetical a creature to command conviction. It is too obviously a stopgap invented *ad hoc*."

The biochemist, moreover, is specially shy of it because his methods, applied with such enormous success since the time of Lavoisier, do not find any traces of the entelechy in practice. The fact that Haldane's speculations are built up upon experiments on oxygen-want is not really to the point, because other physiologists are unable to secure comparable results. It is largely a question of technique, and technique is a dangerous thing on which to build philosophical superstructures. On the contrary, the biochemist has got along very well without the need of the neo-vitalist hypothesis. If he accepts it, it means for him, among other things, that he can never hope to get any approach to controlled conditions in his experiments. The essence of the experimental method is to keep all possible conditions constant in any one experiment, and to vary that one so that its effect unembarrassed by any other effects may be observed. If an entelechy is present in tissues and organs the biochemist can never get controlled conditions, for he has no means of telling what the entelechy may want to do next. But the fact is, however, that by innumerable researches we know results may be repeated any number of times, that controlled conditions can be attained, and that living matter *in vitro* does act as a physico-chemical system. The neo-vitalist retires from this position by pointing out that the entelechy acts only in the body as a whole, and it is to his argument for the "actual wholeness" of organisms that we must now turn.

One aspect of this argument is the assertion that so far no complete mechanical explanation of the functions of any one organ has been advanced. There is very little in this statement, for no organ or cell exists in and for itself; it has relations with all the rest of the body. Accordingly a complete mechanistic description of one unit is impossible until all are so described. It is absurd, as has been said elsewhere, "to expect biochemical investigators to deal exhaustively with the brain or the kidney and then to proceed *en masse* to the spleen."

More important is the contention that the wonderfully delicate regulatory powers of the organism are not seen until the organism is studied as a whole. That is perfectly true, but then biochemists and physiologists do study the body as a whole, and the more those regulatory mechanisms are studied the more clearly mechanistic do they become. The nice regulation of blood acidity is now very fully understood and the processes of metabolism continually demonstrate their dependence on mechanistic principles.

Haldane also asserts that the tendency of the animal organism to maintain its internal and external environment constant is the fact about life which can never be explained on mechanistic grounds. Apart from the implicit argument from inconceivability the fallacy of which has already been pointed out above, this statement neglects several well-known principles in the physics and chemistry of the present day. An obvious illustration is the gyroscope, which when revolving resists strongly any force tending to overturn it, and the facts of buffer action in acid-base systems and poising action in oxidation-reduction systems are obviously of enormous bearing on the point. But to go no further, the principle of Le Châtelier in thermodynamics states that " When a factor determining the equilibrium of a system is altered, the system tends to change so as to oppose and partially annul the alteration in the factor." Surely the tendency of organisms to keep their environments constant is a special case of this thermodynamic principle. As Bayliss says, " The fact that an organism has developed means of returning to the conditions to which it has been previously adjusted may be called ' nostalgia,' but I am unable to see that this makes it essentially different from a physico-chemical system."

But the most philosophical form of the argument from actual wholeness is the one which maintains that to look at an animal as a physico-chemical system is to abstract unduly from reality, since to do so is to ignore the fact that it is a psycho-physical whole. This criticism, when carried far enough, ends in denying all validity whatever to the scientific method, but Haldane takes care to alight at the proper moment. It is certainly undeniable that science abstracts, generalises, analyses, and constructs a picture of reality probably quite unlike that reality itself. In another of the essays in this book it has been clearly shown that theoretical physics is just such a system—its relations with reality are through the human mind, it is a subjective production. But to use this argument as a chastisement for mechanistic biology is inadmissible. It is not sufficient to meditate upon a typewriter if one desires to understand its mechanism ; like a boy with a new watch, one must pry into it and take it to pieces if one really wants to know how it works. That is the method of natural science. It is perfectly true that it analyses and constructs a partial picture of reality, but the process is essential if an intellectual understanding of the substrate is required. Haldane's method is that of the mystic ; not a useless method, but not a scientific method. The attitude of the mystic to the typewriter is to sit down in front of it, until, by a process which psychology cannot define, he feels himself into the typewriter and becomes one with it as a part of the universe. But the scientific method is to take it to pieces, to become familiarly acquainted with every motion in it, and to synthesise it again into a comprehended whole. Exactly similar is the attitude we must adopt to living matter. Neither method, it may well be said, will give us a full understanding of the typewriter, but the second method is the scientific method and as such the biological method. All through the writings of the neo-vitalists one finds an inability to be content with the mechanistic answers to the questions of how the processes in living animals go on. Although it is never explicitly stated, one has a strong suspicion that they want really to ask why living beings should exist and should act as they do. Clearly the scientific method can tell us nothing about that. They are what they are because the properties of force and matter are what they are, and at that point scientific thought has to hand the problem over to philosophical and religious thought.

But even when the arguments of the modern vitalists have been examined and the conclusion has been reached that they are not sufficient to sustain the weight placed on them, there are still other objections to neo-vitalism which cannot be forgotten The first and greatest of these is the pragmatic one that vitalism has been if anything a hindrance to research. Of all the hypotheses put forward to account for the phenomena of life, vitalism in all its forms has been ever the least stimulating. Whereas the mechanistic hypothesis does at least provide definite theories which can be proved, or disproved vitalism simply fills up the gaps in mechanistic descriptions after the fashion of Columbus's map-maker, "Where Unknown, there place Terrors."

But an even more significant fact in the history of vitalism is one which has been referred to above—namely, its constant retirement from one position to another. It is impossible to feel great confidence in a negative theory which has always rested its main support on the weak points of its opponent. Lawrence Henderson, indeed, believes that in limiting the operation of vitalism to entelechies the vitalists have destroyed the distinctiveness of their own case, for, as he shows in his book "The Fitness of the Environment," we have to postulate an entelechy of a sort in the inorganic world to account for the fact that the external world is as adapted to the animal as the animal to it. In this way there is again no difference between organic and inorganic processes. "Vitalism," he says, "disappears in universal teleology. Science has put the old teleology to death, and its disembodied spirit, freed from vitalism

and all material ties alone, lives on.   From such a ghost science has
nothing to fear." Parallel also to the gradual retirement of vitalism
there has gone a continual tendency to set up *ne plus ultra* distinctions, Pillars of Hercules differentiating living matter off from
non-living.   One by one these crumble away and fresh ones are
substituted, each one a little further back.   The conception of
unity in time has played a great part here.   Von Uëxküll suggested
that organisms differed from dead matter by resembling a musical
melody rather than a single note.   Apart from the possibility
brought up by the General Relativity theory, that all events are like
that, the suggestion has some plausibility about it, and was afterwards extended by Bergson, who made the famous remark, " Continuity of change, preservation of the past in the present, real
duration—the organism seems to share these attributes with consciousness."   It was left for Bayliss to point out that inorganic
systems, especially in the colloidal state, can show similar phenomena.   A silicic-acid gel behaves quite differently according to
whether it has been previously exposed to a high or low concentration of water vapour.   An earlier *ne plus ultra* distinction was the
simple one of primitive man into things which moved and things
which did not, and most recently there is Haldane's tendency
towards optimum conditions.   All these have gone the same way.

Neo-vitalism as well as vitalism, then, is unsatisfactory, and we
are left with the conclusion to which we were brought from the
historical evidence—namely, that at the present day the triumph of
mechanistic biology is undoubted and it has no serious rivals.   But
is it capable of criticism from other directions ?

4. A Critique of Mechanism

We have seen so far that throughout the history of science
there has been mechanistic biology, and that it has always been
allied to materialism in philosophy and censured by theology and
the mystics.   We have observed that in the last century and a half
the theory which before had had little to support it beyond the
opinions of certain philosophers has rested upon a sure basis of
experimental evidence.   We have also concluded that its triumph
at the present day as a discipline and a method is complete, since
the neo-vitalist position is thoroughly unsatisfactory.   Before proceeding to the question of whether the theological aversion to
mechanistic biology has been justified, however, we must see

whether the mechanistic theory of life is as strong on the philosophical side as it is on the experimental.

As has been shown in one of the earlier essays in this book, naturalism gained ground by immense strides during the first seventy-five years of the nineteenth century, but came to a climax about then, and has been undergoing severe criticism ever since.

In the first place the general acceptance of the evolution theory had vastly different effects from anything that Huxley and Spencer could have conceived. It affected the philosophers profoundly, for apart from raising difficulties over the question of how mutations and the production of new species could possibly follow from mechanical laws, how qualitative transformation could result from quantitative permanence and determinism, it led also to a subjective position represented later by many minds. Naturally enough, if man had been evolved in the struggle for existence, as the evolutionists said, then his mind also must be conceived of as the product of such a struggle and could therefore hardly be fitted for the grasping of absolute truth. "The forceps of our mind are crude," said Bergson later, "and they crush the delicacy of reality when we attempt to hold it." This argument from evolution was also applied in the physiological world by Poincaré to the genesis of our sense of space.

More important for our purposes are the criticisms of the scientific method which were made by Mach, LeRoy, and Duhem. Mach pointed out that science has a biological end; it is a kind of shorthand, it guides man through an impossible maze of facts, and without it he would be lost. But in doing so it necessarily abstracts from those facts and gives him a sketch, not a complete picture. Mach distinguished three periods in scientific thought, the first experimental, in direct contact with reality, the second deductive, not so much in contact, and the third theoretical or formal, entirely subjective. Scientific descriptions, mechanistic descriptions, according to Mach, are "quite fictitious, though still valuable modes of describing phenomena, and to place the laws of physics actually in external nature is to hypostatise an abstraction of purely human origin." In his constructive suggestions he was not perhaps so happy, for, as Aliotta says, he replaced "a mechanical by a sensorial mythology." Boutroux, anticipating Bergson, maintained that the scientific method takes us farther away rather than nearer to the nature of reality, because it is forced to omit consideration of what is most real in things, their qualitative aspect, their incessant transformations and their individuality.

LeRoy, much influenced by the anti-intellectualism of Bergson, also pointed out many things about the scientific method which compel agreement. Whereas the older positivism of Comte went into ecstasies over the "fact" which it failed to distinguish from pure data, LeRoy sees in the fact an unconscious product of spiritual activity directed without knowing it towards a practical end. The very name of "fact," says LeRoy, should put us on our guard against believing that it is something outside ourselves—on the contrary, that which has been made, *factum est*, cannot be made an immediate datum. There is no such thing as an isolated fact, but everything flows into everything else, and to dissect out facts from the body of reality is a proceeding that may be very useful but cannot be ultimately valid. Isolation, fragmentation, analysis, these are the real watchwords of the scientific method. There is, of course, below these isolated facts, a mysterious residuum of objectivity, but science cannot take this into account, and according to LeRoy intuitionist philosophy is the only thing that can.

Future work in philosophy will probably not confirm all the views of LeRoy, though as one of the sanest members of the intuitionist school he will live in the future. The important part of his philosophy for us is that there is a profoundly subjective factor in science—quite unrealised by men such as Huxley and Tyndall. The scientific man plays an active part in the selection of the facts before him, and his selection of those facts is determined by the construction of his mind.

Duhem continued the thought of LeRoy and pointed out that when a phenomenon is observed it is never observed purely but always with a certain interpretative infusion. A law of common sense being a general agreement may be either true or false, but a law of natural science can be neither true nor false, because it is fundamentally a symbol, and of symbols it can only be said that they have been more or less well chosen. Duhem's arguments undoubtedly show that physical law cannot be said to describe absolute reality, but at the same time they do not disprove that it contains a certain amount of truth.

These philosophers and many others have shown quite conclusively that the methods of science are inadequate for a complete picture of reality. This opens the door wide for the advent of a " synoptic " philosophy as pictured by Merz and Hoernlé, for as long as scientific men were prepared to assert that the scientific method alone could provide a valid approach to reality, it was impossible to hope for any common ground for discussion. Writers on the scientific side in the last century such as Clifford never realised that because of the very methods of science it has its definite limitations, not in subject-matter, but in technique. Word-symbolism, averages, approximations, statistical data, general laws—in every application of the scientific method the individual always escapes and we construct a world corresponding only very inaccurately to the world of reality. We " fit the world on to the Procrustean bed of our own intelligence." In order to correct the distortions of vision which we must of necessity suffer when we apply the scientific method, we must have recourse to the other methods of human perception, we must philosophise, appreciate beauty, and make use of our faculty for mystical experience.

C. D. Broad first applied these criticisms to mechanistic biology. If we accept the view that the scientific method does not give an absolutely true picture of reality, and that the form of scientific theories is almost entirely the creation of our own minds, then we cannot possibly extend the sway of physics and chemistry to mind, for their essence is mechanistic and we should then be describing mind in terms of an emanation from itself. It is as if we followed the practice of patients suffering from certain types of mental diseases who are so much bound up with the happenings of their dreams and fantasies that they interpret all their fully waking experience in terms of their imaginary life. The creature would thus sit in judgement upon the creator, and the substance would be interpreted in the language of the shadow.

Moreover, the mechanistic conception of the universe is almost patently stamped with the evidences of mental origin. The more one thinks about it the more one feels that whatever may be the objective substrates of external things, it is only due to the configuration of our minds that we conceive of matter and energy in mechanistic fashion. Our minds are like templates in engineering, they necessitate the corresponding flexion of the universe, and before we can understand any set of phenomena they have to be made to fit. " In a sense we are always anthropomorphic," says James Ward, " since we can never divest ourselves of our consciousness; hence not only spiritualistic intuition but the very mechanical interpretation of the Universe, which in the last analysis derives its concepts from our human experience, is of an anthropomorphic nature." The statements of the optimistic advocates of nineteenth-century materialism seem crude and gross when made to submit to tests of this kind. It is not as if the mechanistic world-view came into our knowledge as something from outside, something given, written on tables of stone and possessing immutable authority; on the contrary, it is a product of our own minds and bears deeply impressed upon it the marks of its origin. Mind, therefore, and all mental processes cannot possibly receive explanation or description in physico-chemical terms, for that would amount to explaining something by an instrument itself the product of the thing explained.

This criticism has shown us, therefore, that whereas on the physical side mechanistic conceptions are perfectly adequate, they cannot without grave logical difficulty be extended to cover the sphere of mind. It is at this point that we realise the profound truth of McDougall's dictum that vitalism is a form of animism characterised by its neglect of the psychophysical problem.

Once again we find ourselves back face to face with the problem of interrelation of the material and spiritual part of the organism. But we have assuredly cleared away a considerable mass of debris around the base of the matter. The triumph of mechanistic biology has indeed been a real one, for it has succeeded in abolishing the vital force in living things which so unnecessarily complicated the whole question. We are back again with the concept of the undivided anima, and the ground is perfectly clear for philosophical and psychological discussion as to the psychophysical problem. It is in this that the achievement of physico-chemical biology is to be found.

The name which must command our chief respect accordingly is that of Descartes, who first saw clearly that the body was really a machine governed not by any vital force but by the soul or mind or whatever the non-material part of man may be called. It is needless to say that we are not tied to any of the details of his philosophy or his physiology; indeed, both of them have for two centuries been of merely historical interest. Nor are we in the least compelled to accept his absolute dualism of matter and spirit; indeed, in our concluding section I hope to show that this view is quite compatible with a relative dualism of a Spinozistic type. It is, of course, the common-sense position. And our return to it through centuries of speculation is not the first time that a common-sense view has been proved the most acceptable in the long run, nor will it be the last.

5. CONSTRUCTIVE THOUGHTS

In returning to the biological philosophy of Descartes we are making use of a conception which now possesses experimental evidence, though in his time it was only the brilliant guess of a philosopher. The following quotation from the " *Traité de l' Homme* " is unavoidable :

" All the functions of the body follow naturally from the sole disposition of its organs, just in the same way as the movements of a clock or other self-acting machine or automaton follow from the arrangement of its weights and wheels. So that there is no reason on account of its functions to conceive that there exists in the body any soul whether vegetative or sensitive or any principle of movement other than the blood and its animal spirits agitated by the heat of the fire which burns continually in the heart and which does not differ in nature from any of the other fires which are met with in inanimate bodies."

Is there then at the present time any theory of life which will be both philosophically and biologically adequate ? What we have seen above points the way to it. The legitimacy of physico-chemical explanations in the realm of physical life we have seen to be well grounded, but we have also found that as far as mental life is concerned biochemistry and biophysics have no authority. The opinion, therefore, which seems to me to be most justifiable is that life in all its forms is the phenomenal disturbance created in the world of matter and energy when mind comes into it. Living matter is the outward and visible sign of the presence of mind, the splash made by the entry of mental existences into the sea of inert matter. We must observe, however, that there appear to be certain conditions which are necessary for the action of mind in this manner. Biochemical speculation regards the most important of these as the properties of the element carbon. By whatever fundamental characteristics of the electron it comes about that the carbon group in the periodic table is the only one the elements of which possess the power of combining with themselves, one thing is certain. No other element but carbon, and in a much lesser degree silicon, possesses the power of combining with itself to form long chains of atoms. If it were not for this power, which ensures the formation of the enormously complex molecules of organic chemistry, life as we know it would be quite impossible. The second conditioning factor for the appearance of living matter is the colloidal state. People who have no intimate acquaintance with biochemistry have no idea of the importance of the colloidal state of matter in life. Thomas Graham in 1862 first recognised the fact that solutions of substances in each other may be of two kinds, crystalloidal or homogeneous, and colloidal or heterogeneous. An ordinary solution of salt in water is homogeneous because the dissolved molecules are so small as to have no surface in the real sense of the word, but a solution of a fat in water is heterogeneous because the molecules are collected into molecular aggregates, too small indeed to be seen except with the ultra-microscope, but large enough to affect profoundly all the properties of the solution. So different, as a matter of fact, are colloidal and crystalloidal solutions, owing to the enormous increase of surface in the former by thousands of times, that they form, as Graham said, " two quite different worlds of matter." Now colloidal solutions do occur in nature among inorganic systems to a certain extent and may have played a great part in geological processes, but their association with carbon compounds is what is pre-eminently characteristic of living matter. Thus physical and chemical processes, though obeying fundamentally the same laws both outside and inside the organism, appear different to us simply because they are taking place on surfaces in a colloidal system nothing very nearly analogous to which exists in inorganic nature. Johann Christian Reil, a German physiologist, had the remarkable intuition to grasp this fact long before anything very exact was known of colloidal solutions. In an extremely interesting and rather rare article published in 1796, called " *Ueber der Lebenskraft,*" he discusses the various theories, vitalistic and mechanistic, of living beings, and finally comes to the conclusion that the physical and chemical processes of the animal organism are identical with those of inanimate matter, save that they are conditioned by the nature of living stuff.

"We have for the Existence of Vital Spirits, no knowledge through Experiment," he says. ' In the Composition and Form of

Matter there lies the Ground of Physical Phenomena of Nature in general and of Animals. The Foundation of the Regular Formation of Animal Bodies has its Origin in the actual Nature of Living Matter. The Forces of the Human Body are also Properties of its Matter and its Special Forces result from the special characteristics of its Matter."

If now we substitute for Reil's word "Form" the term "Colloidal state" we see how nearly he came to the present view. But he went further, and his guess came even more miraculously near the conclusions of modern biochemistry, for he thus defined the word "Form" : "The Form of Matter is a Result of the Manner of the Aggregation of its Constituents." It is possible that he meant the structure and disposition of organs rather than any more intimate molecular arrangement. But even if so, he was not on the wrong line ; he simply failed to go far enough, since it is the molecular structure and not the morphological structure which is here in question. There can be no doubt that mechanistic biology is quite capable of describing physical life, as far as anything can be described by the scientific method. Bergson's opinions on the mind-body problem fall well into line with these views. He speaks of the brain as the "organ of the insertion of the mind into things," and uses Descartes' own words in saying that "the body is utilised for the ends of the mind."

But if we adopt this view, that living matter is the result of the impact of mind into the world of mechanics, we shall not be able to go the whole way with Descartes. For he would have said that nothing was produced by that impact, rather bodies acting mechanically were produced by necessity in the world of mechanics and into one type of them and one only "God breathed a living soul." Descartes was led to this position by various now obsolete arguments of a psychological nature which tended to show that no consciousness could be attributed to any animal except man. Comparative psychology of the present day would not admit his conclusions for a moment : so our conception, though owing a great deal to his, is necessarily much broader. For although all living organisms are to be considered as physico-chemical systems, yet at the same time they are, as it were, musical instruments, the keys of which are in all cases played by something however meagre in mental development it may be. This form of animism is in every way compatible with physico-chemical research, for although nobody denies that man is a thinking, willing, feeling creature, yet that does not hinder the mechanistic explanation of such things as the laws of growth, and the process of acidity-regulation of his circulatory fluids.

On this point Merz has an interesting remark. He reminds us that in some types of book-keeping the ledgers show all the transactions of a complicated business yet disclose nothing of the names of the persons involved and the purposes of the operations. In other words, the process of oxidation of lactic acid during muscle activity will be just the same in two cases though the purposes for which the organism set the muscles in action may be entirely different. Accordingly, we may agree with James Drever, who in a recent paper said, " The behaviour of the living organism as such it is not the physiologist's business to study. His task begins and ends with the functioning of the individual mechanisms."

According to this theory, then, it is the physical functions of life that physics and chemistry are competent to explain, for such questions as the distribution of animals and the general theory of evolution, which obviously involve the consideration of conscious striving, do not come under their entire dominion. McBride in a recent essay has spoken of evolution as a vital phenomenon, but, from his actual words, this means no more than that evolution is in part a mental or psychological phenomenon, and in this respect we may fully agree with him.

Again we see how the whole subject hangs round the problem of psychophysical interaction. There is no space in this paper to go into the theories which have been advanced to give a good account of this, and the reader who is anxious to follow up this aspect of the problem must be referred to the writings of William McDougall. It will be sufficient to say that the work of Lotze, Clerk-Maxwell, Poynting, Boussinesq, and Lotka have shown how psychophysical interaction may be conceived as possible.

It will have been observed that, however we phrase it, we are left with a complete dualism of matter and spirit. Whether we remain at that point or proceed further by the adoption of a relative dualism will depend upon our personal philosophical predilections. For my part I prefer to adopt a relative dualism the way to which was shown by Merz. It is a modification of Spinoza's. If we do take this step we may also think it possible that laws may some day be discovered capable of explaining both the mechanistic world of physics and chemistry and that other world of mental phenomena which is studied by the psychologist. It is important to distinguish this view from the psychophysical theory described by McDougall as Phenomenalistic parallelism, and originally put forward by Spinoza and Kant. According to their opinions, there was no causal connection between mind and body, but both were the shadow thrown by some underlying reality, just as two shadows are often seen thrown by the same object when two lights exist on the other side of it. This may be represented by the following diagram :

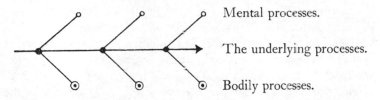

Mental processes.

The underlying processes.

Bodily processes.

Against this there are rather unanswerable arguments to be adduced, and I should prefer to confine the two-aspect view to the metaphysical field and allow that psychophysical interaction does go on. In other words, it is not so much body and mind that are two aspects of one underlying reality, but matter and spirit. This view can be represented by the following scheme :

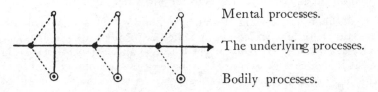

Mental processes.

The underlying processes.

Bodily processes.

The philosophy of Theodore Merz is most helpful in the discussion of this question. The quotations are taken for convenience from Jevons' appreciation of him. Merz considered that the history of British philosophy during the seventeenth and eighteenth centuries was one of the most important phases of human thought. " Berkeley finally dropped the idea of matter as unnecessary, Hume showed that there was no foundation for the idea of a spiritual or thinking substance." The classical school of Philosophy thus evacuated itself and scepticism supervened, at first unrecognised but eventually thoroughly conscious.

Merz attempted to continue the classical tradition, and felt that it led not to emptiness but to a very real constructive result. He accepted all the reasoning of Berkeley and Hume, only he broke with Hume on one point—namely, that although Hume analysed consciousness, he omitted to note that consciousness must first be there to be analysed. In other words, Hume made exactly the same mistake in the psychological world as the nineteenth-century mechanists did in the physiological world. " The inner life of man is as a matter of fact a connected totality," said Merz, and to see it so was to take what he called the " Synoptic view of the Inner life." So Merz was led to regard the object of introspection as the " Firmament of Thought," using thought in its widest sense. " Disrupting the firmament of thought, which is one, into two worlds, matter and spirit, which are different from one another, has for one consequence the impossibility of putting together again the worlds thus sundered. It hypostatises the external world, which at times it regards as alone real, or as supereminently real. It also does the same for the internal world." It introduces the insoluble enigmas of object and subject. And so Merz proceeded to develop his conception of the unitive nature of the ground of our consciousness with many illustrations drawn from psychology and other domains. Although he never developed at length a psychophysical doctrine on these lines, it obviously follows from his position that we are to regard the idea of the body and idea of the mind as two of the chief constellations in the firmament of thought.

" There is a certain cluster of sensations," he says, " which is always there and which accompanies us through life—that is our physical body. We cannot get rid of it and a general sensation of it is always with us forming a more or less prominent feature in the flow of our thoughts and feelings. And on the firmament of consciousness we observe other clusters of sensations similar to what we call our body and we infer that these are connected in a similar way with similar firmaments of experience."

Moreover, these ideas are not severed from each other there, they inextricably intertwine, and their separation, like all disruptions in that sky, brings confusion in its train.

In addition to discussing a possible biological philosophy which unites biology and philosophy in a synoptic whole, I have tried to show in this paper how mechanistic biology has arisen from being at first the speculation of a few philosophers, till it stands at last on a firm basis of experimental evidence and cannot be said to be in danger from neo-vitalism and similar opinions. I have hoped also to show that although mechanism in biology is perfectly justified and indeed essential, it cannot be applied to psychology. Lastly, I have pointed out how mechanistic biology has ever been regarded with aversion by theology, mysticism, and idealist philosophy. Democritus and Plato, Lucretius and Tertullian, de la Mettrie and his anonymous antagonist, René Descartes and Samuel Parker, and finally the Oxford Conference of 1924, all exemplify that statement. The earlier mechanistic biology before the era of experimental science was indeed somewhat incompatible with religion, because it did not know its own limitations, nor did these become apparent until quite recent times. But now that the assumptions on which the triumph of mechanistic biology in the last century is based have been well examined, it is seen that for its own sphere it is a real triumph, but, at the same time, its jurisdiction over other fields cannot be admitted.

The biochemist and the biophysicist, therefore, can and must be thorough-going mechanists, but they need not on that account hesitate to say with Sir Thomas Browne, " Thus there is something in us that can be without us and will be after us though indeed it hath no history what it was before us and cannot tell how it entered into us."

THE SPHERE OF RELIGION

BY JOHN OMAN

Principal of Westminster College, Cambridge

CONTENTS

I. Definition Difficult but Necessary

Because the world is one and known to our minds as one universe of discourse, no subject of study has absolutely determined frontiers. We have to draw them to meet the needs of our limited minds. We ought to do it according to real differences, but as there is no ultimate separateness in things, or in our experience, we are apt to leave matters out in a way to make our study one-sided, or to include what is alien and to make it confused. Even a subject so well defined as Physics has been shown in our day not to have escaped either danger ; and in a subject like religion, enormously varied in its manifestations, both in respect of outward forms and of inward manifestations, and more widely concerned with the world as a whole and the mind as a whole, the difficulty is manifestly greater, and in practice the results have been more misleading. Some writers, in consequence, have abandoned the hope of finding any mark which shall be common to all religious phenomena yet distinguishing them from all else. Thus Professor Runze, in a recent book on the psychology of religion, after passing in review a long list of definitions of religion, concludes that no definition or description of religion can include all the manifestations of it, without being so general as to be utterly useless for distinguishing them from other phenomena as specially religious. Instead of attempting such a task, he proposes, as the better way, that we find guidance in the right kind of interest. The one requirement, he says, is to have a soul at peace with itself, so as to be responsive to the great things in life. Then, without being able to define its sphere, we shall have sufficient practical acquaintance with religion to know when we are within its special territory and when we are wandering into other fields. This may seem vague guidance, but every other central human interest, he says, is in the same position. And, moreover, he takes it to be a happier position than might appear. Natural science, for instance, can no more be defined, so that everything belonging to it shall be included and all else excluded, than religion, but, if we have a scientific interest and a scientific habit of mind, we have no difficulty in distinguishing between what does and what does not belong to science. And, in like manner, if we have a religious interest and a religious attitude of mind, we shall know what belongs and what does not belong to religion.

This view contains at least an important truth. Our particular departments of study are determined rather by our particular interests than by any rigid divisions in the universe : and, therefore, if we ourselves are without the right kind of interest, we shall certainly lack an essential kind of guidance for determining them. Practically, moreover, the value of this criterion is seldom questioned, except in respect of the one subject of religion. It is not expected that anyone without scientific interest and a scientific attitude of mind can have much to say of value about the sphere of science, while it is fairly confidently assumed that, if he have these qualifications, he will not readily mistake for science anything outside its territory. Nor do we expect a valuable discussion on the sphere of art from anyone who is interested in it only as creating articles for sale at a profit or as a means of advertising. The significant facts in any subject cannot be discerned without the right kind of interest, however great labour be devoted to search for them : and that is quite apart from the difficulty of pursuing the study of any subject without interest.

Religion, more than any other subject, claims interest as its due, and more definitely affirms that it cannot be found or understood without something like enthusiasm for it ; and practically it would seem to be even more dependent than other subjects upon interest for discerning its facts and carrying on the right kind of study of them. But this view is far from receiving universal acceptance. While students of other subjects are approved for regarding their facts as certain and important, interest in religion is frequently, forthwith and without further discrimination, identified with bias. Thus, not merely complete lack of interest, but a positive distaste for the whole business has at times been put forward as a necessary qualification for uncorrupted inquiry. Should the student affirm that he wishes to know the truth about religion precisely because it is to him of supreme interest, and to be rid of unreality because he knows by experience its essential reality, he would be in great danger of being regarded as a hopeless obscurantist. Instead of interest in religion to sustain his labours, he is expected to work with interest in the curiosities of history and the aberrations of the human mind.

As these interests are unfortunately more easily satisfied by what we may call the psychological imagination than by patient objective investigation, those who work with them are certain to concern themselves more with the abnormal than the normal, and to feel themselves more helped by the clever than the conscientious labours of previous inquirers. The result is too frequently on the same level of intellectual achievement as some studies of the mind of Germany during the war, for which it was a disqualification to have had experience of Germans by living in their country, or sufficient interest in their minds to have mastered their language.

In the study of religion, as in all other subjects, as a wise Greek has said, " Not to know what was done in the world before we were born is always to remain a child." In this also, as in all other subjects, lack of bias is not to be won by the easy method of lack of interest. Lack of bias is not an absence of interest or even of experience, but a very active interest in truth, which requires so high a sense of the value of the subject that no labour or cost can be esteemed too great a price to pay for knowing the truth about it. Lack of interest, moreover, in a subject which deserves interest is itself bias and is sure to overlook or distort the facts to be considered.

Some religious people, it is true, have too frequently given cause for thinking that interest in religion is mere prepossession. They fail to realise that truth is the supreme religious interest, and they even seem at times to treat religion as a sort of germ which would die in the sunlight. But this does not disprove the fact that we cannot know an environment without interest in it, and we cannot know it is a reality without that interest being concern to know the truth about it. Moreover, a study which lacks interest in its own sphere exposes us to the still more serious danger of confusing the subject with the things in which we are interested, because, not being able to occupy ourselves long with what does not interest us, we must introduce what does, however irrelevant it may be. Thus persons who lack interest in poetry treat it as epigram or rhetoric or philosophy. And, in the same way, persons not interested in religion treat it as a kind of science, or as a popular philosophy, or as a useful buttress of morality, or as a bond of the social order. This is no rare occurrence, and few other causes have introduced more confusion into the study of the subject. Thus there is a sense in which we could ascribe to lack of the right interest nearly all the mistakes about the sphere of religion.

Even for practical purposes, nevertheless, it does not suffice to say : Have a soul at peace with itself and be responsive to the high things of life, and you will know. It does not suffice for two very practical reasons. The first is that no one can determine when this condition is fulfilled ; and the second, that, in actual discussion, we could not bring our differences to the test of this criterion, even if we had it. Moreover, the history of past discussion shows very plainly that the workers in this field are not agreed about what they mean by religion and that the matter cannot be so easily determined.

Nor is the difficulty of riding the marches so great, either theoretically or practically, as Runze affirms. It is true that there is only one world, known in one experience. But it is equally true that, the more fully we recognise the world as one, the sharper are the distinctions we draw in it and the more we see the reality and significance of things by themselves ; and that, the more we bring it within the unity of our thought, the more the nature of our minds compels us to concentrate on one aspect of this experience at a time, and, the more we do so, the more sharply we distinguish one part of our knowledge from the rest. Thus all advance in knowledge has meant discrimination and differentiation.

Religion is no exception, for it has, with the process of time, been more clearly distinguished from other concerns in practice as well as theory. Thus, in primitive beliefs and practices, it is extremely difficult to say what is religious, and still more what is not : while, as we advance, it becomes ever plainer that religion has its distinctive sphere, for, though it touches ever more widely all aspects of human life, it does so in a way which is quite distinct from the ways of science or social custom. But difficulty does not save us from the necessity of trying to distinguish even primitive religion from primitive science, or magic, or social custom. On the contrary, the greater the confusion and the more difficult it is to distinguish, the more the attempt is necessary. And, supposing that the confusion were throughout so great that it seemed, from first to last, impossible to discover any mark by which we could define religion so as to include all its phenomena and exclude all else, a discussion of the problem would be all the more necessary, because, on matters on which we are apt to err and on which we differ because we are not all considering the same object, the mere discussing of our differences may be valuable, even if the result should still leave much to be desired.

Of this we have an example in the recent discussion of the sphere of Physics. Though it seems to the superficial observer a definite enough subject, the problems of whether it works with facts of nature or ideas of mind, and of what is meant by its abstraction from mind and from changing incidents in nature, are far from having been finally determined. Nevertheless, the discussion of them has cleared away many errors which have sometimes been elevated into dogmas. And if the sphere of religion is less definite than the sphere of physical things and the study of it touches many wider interests, and if this makes its sphere more difficult to determine than the sphere of physics, so much the more imperative is it to distinguish as clearly as we can, and to discuss the difficulties which hinder our further progress in definiteness.

Runze is so far right that, if we look at theories of religion historically, we can usually see that they have been largely determined by other interests than religion. As they were produced by intellectual persons by the process of argument, this interest has usually been intellectual, with the result that religion has been conceived as a kind of reasoning. Thus the Rationalist view of religion, as concerned with proofs about God as the maker of the world, providence as the direction of it, and immortality as compensation for its injustices and imperfections, and as mainly a matter of "evidences," was due to preoccupation with scientific discussions which had determined the interests and temper of the age for the religious as well as the non-religious people. But discovery of the influences which have affected the theory does not deliver us from the necessity of discussing whether religion is of this intellectual quality or not. The value of such a discussion appears in the work of the greatest sceptic of the time—David Hume. The rational element, he pointed out, is a very small part of religion as it has appeared among men. Most of the rest he regarded as superstition, judging it very much after the fashion of his time ; but he also saw that religion was life, and that it was so much the true greatness of man that, without it, man would scarcely be human. And one of the chief causes of the barrenness of the study of religion for so long was that this suggestion fell at the time on barren ground, so that there are many who to this day continue to treat religion as though it were purely an intellectual inference from the visible world to an invisible, or supernatural information made known by certain revelations in the past. But, if this be wrong, no account of the causes which introduced it will spare us the necessity of giving a better account of what religion is and what part it has played in human experience.

A consideration both of what religion is and what it has done is necessary. We may not ignore its manifestations in history, for they may correct and enlarge our conception of religion. Yet without any idea of religion to determine what are manifestations of religion, we shall not know what part of history is concerned with them. Nowhere is this plainer than in what has sometimes been offered to us as presenting, in purely objective form, the simplest and most unquestionable elements of religion—the study of primitive religion. Little discrimination being used, religion is sometimes regarded as including every outlived idea, though plainly many of them are science and many ethics, none the less so because they are not our science or ethics. Justification might be offered for identifying outgrown ideas with religion in the fact that primitive science and custom took to themselves religious sanction and with it entrenched themselves against progress. Then religion is taken to be essentially conservatism and reaction, a view which may not have been often formulated, but which has been the fundamental assumption of many discussions of religion.

It might be possible to show that such a view of religion springs from lack of interest in the higher concerns of the human spirit, but it is more profitable to consider why religion is thus conservative, and to take along with that the other question of why it is also the most revolutionary of all forces. In history the latter aspect has been at least as prominent as the former, because it is religion which has produced the faith and courage and self-sacrifice which have combated traditional ideas and customs, and dared, in face of every kind of social ostracism, to stand alone in defence of what seemed truer and higher. And this raises a larger question : Why is religion the chief, if not in the end the only, power in the might of which man has denied self for goods the self may never realise ? And this question also we cannot answer without considering the nature and sphere of religion.

While there are still persons who regard religion as an intellectual phenomenon, there has more recently been a tendency in the opposite direction. It was not left to our time to discover that the proper study of mankind is man, but, in our time, the conception of this study has altered. The notion of normal human nature has retired into the background and man is studied as a creature of life-impulses, instincts, and complexes. This has tended to confirm a treatment of religion which is by no means new, which ascribes to religion in particular much that is due to human nature in general. And this is particularly easy to accept, not only because it is the same human nature which works in religion as in all else, but because religion tends to magnify its defects as well as its virtues.

This, too, is an error we might explain by saying that we are not at peace with ourselves and responsive to higher things. But, if we left the matter there, we should miss some considerations of the greatest importance for the study of religion.

In religion, as in all else, we ought to try to distinguish what belongs to it as such from what is merely imported into it by imperfect human nature. Mass opinion, for example, has often assumed the authority of religion, and even cruelty has invoked its sanction. But we ought to be able to distinguish religion as such from mass opinion and cruelty, just as we ought to be able to distinguish government as such from graft and wire-pulling. In a general study of the subject we have to conceive religion widely enough to include both St. Francis and the Grand Inquisitor as religious men, just as, in a general study of politics, we must include Abraham Lincoln and Boss Croker as politicians. Yet we ought not to regard devotion to the Church as a state, which is not really different from devotion to any other social unit, as belonging to religion in the same way as devotion to the poor and ignorant, any more than we should regard political corruption for party or private ends, which is essentially the same as in the other kind of selfish business, as belonging to the conduct of government, in the same way as courageous devotion for patriotic ends. Yet it is most necessary to remind ourselves that it is the same human nature, with all its errors and imperfections, with which we have to deal in religion as in all else ; and that, therefore, there is bad religion as there is bad business or bad science or bad politics or bad morals. Forgetfulness of this fact and the expectation that everything offering itself as religious ought to be admirable merely gives an air of unreality to the whole subject. A vast number of things profess to be religion, and our conception must be wide enough to include consideration of them, just as a vast number of doubtful doings profess to be politics, and our study of politics must not be too prudish to admit them. But we ought also to have some standard of what is genuinely and normally and rightly religious, just as we should have a standard of the ideal originally expressed by the word " politics." Or if a standard be too exact a measure to obtain, we must at least discuss what religion ought to be as well as merely what it is.

For all these reasons, therefore, we must consider the theories of religion, and not be superior to any serious thought upon the subject.

2. Religion as Belief in Gods or Observance of Cults

Theories of religion may be divided according as they seek the essential distinguishing mark in its outward beliefs or practices, or in its inward faiths or emotions. Thus one is more historical and the other more psychological ; one considers what men worship, the other how they worship ; one what they believe, the other how they believe. It will be convenient, even though it cannot be done with absolute definiteness, to divide theories accordingly, and to consider these types in succession, beginning with the former, which emphasises gods or cults.

Probably the view which has found widest acceptance is that the distinctive mark of religion is the belief in gods. This is taken to belong to all religions and to belong to them only : and, in that case, it would be what we need for marking off the sphere of religion.

It cannot be questioned that this belief is a very prominent element in most religions. But, if we keep strictly to the idea of gods as personal beings, there is at all events one religion without it. Primitive Buddhism replaced at least all effective idea of gods by a rigid law of requital ; and we may not exclude a religion which has claimed so many adherents for so long a time. Nor can we include all the objects of worship in other religions under the conception of personal gods or even of their dwelling-places.

But, on the other hand, should we define gods more vaguely as unseen powers, while our definition would then cover all religion, it would include much else. Magic is also belief in unseen powers, and magic has been sharply distinguished from religion by the most profoundly religious persons, such as the Hebrew prophets. Further, there is a wide range of belief in vague unseen influences, such as has recently been called the " numinous," which may be merely the " spooky " and have no necessary connection with religion.

More recently the observance of some kind of worship or cult has been regarded as the distinctive characteristic of religion. For example, it has been argued that there is no common element in all forms of Christianity except that Jesus has been the centre of all forms of its cults, and that, so long as this continue, it will remain, in spite of all its variety, one religion. And this importance of the ritual could be maintained with still more certainty for other religions, such as Confucianism or Brahmanism.

But, even if the cult could be regarded as the mark of a particular religion, it could not, by any narrowing of the meaning of the word, be made to exclude all that is not religious. There are elements in many cults which are mere social traditions, and not in any strict sense religious. Still less can it, by any stretching of the meaning of the word, be made to include all that is religious. There have been beliefs which have been the more religious for remaining a secret of the heart, except in so far as they may work a visible change in the believer ; and there are practices which have been the more religious for turning attention from public ceremonies to common human relations. The most conspicuous example in history is the religion of the Hebrew prophets, who constantly declared that a religion marked only by the cult was mere profane trampling God's courts, and who made no attempt to replace the existing cult by a better, but declared that true religion was to do justly and love mercy and to walk humbly with one's God. Nor, though Jesus visited the synagogue and the temple, can it be said that his religion had much to do with either. In face of these examples to the contrary, it cannot be, as has been maintained, that what makes doctrines religious and not merely philosophical, and practices religious and not merely ethical, is their relation to the cult.

3. Religion as a Special Type of Thought or Feeling or Acting

More recently the tendency has been to define religion, not by the object, but by the manner of its belief; not by its cults, but by its piety. The reasons given are, first, that such inward marks of it are simpler and more certain than any attempt to combine the multitudinous outward forms ; and, second, that the special quality of religion concerns a person's faith or piety and not the objects of his belief, which may be merely accepted from tradition.

The first reason, however, does not seem to be justified by experience, because there never has been any agreement even on so broad a question as the department of mind to which religion is to be assigned. If the marks are simple, this question ought to be elementary. Yet the answers given to it by the profoundest thinkers have radically disagreed. Kant held religion to be essentially belief in the reality and sovereignty of the moral order, and, therefore, to be dependent, in the last resort, upon a right attitude of the will. Schleiermacher denied that such an appendage to morality was of the nature of real religion at all, and found the sphere of religion in piety, which he described as a feeling of dependence that is absolute because it places us in immediate relation to the absolute, universal, final reality. Hegel rejected both views and regarded religion as intellectual exaltation into the region of eternal truth. Thus Kant placed religion in the sphere of will, Schleiermacher of feeling, and Hegel of reason. Such wide divergence between thinkers so serious and profound does not encourage the hope that the essential mark of religion will be easier to discover in the peculiar quality of religion in the soul than in its manifold outward manifestations ; and, in point of fact, the question of what belongs to religion in history has never received quite such divergent answers as the question of what belongs to religion in psychology.

The second argument, that the essential quality of religion belongs to the soul that cherishes it, rests on the fact that no kind of religious belief would be of any religious value unless it were entertained by a conviction of a peculiar quality, and that no rite is truly religious except as it is done with piety. And, without doubt, when personal belief and reverence are wanting, religion is an unreality : and our chief difficulty in studying the religions of the past is that their monuments embalm only their outward forms, while the spirit has fled.

But that would not be in any sense a distinctive mark of religion. Nothing is really truth for us except as it is our own conviction, or beauty for us except as we truly perceive and feel it, or goodness except as it is good to our own insight. Truth, without our conviction of its truth, would be mere facts in an encyclopaedia ; and morality, without our own conscience of right, mere rules of good form. Nevertheless, the special quality of truth is to be objectively valid and of goodness to be concerned with the actual moral order. And, in the same way, the special quality of religion is to be concerned with what is regarded not merely as real, but as the ultimate reality ; and this is in no way altered by the importance of our personal relation to it.

This, as a matter of fact, is the only point on which Kant, Schleiermacher, and Hegel are agreed. The difference in their opinions about the seat of religion in the soul is as complete as the possibilities admit, seeing that there is only intellect, feeling, or will to which it could be ascribed. But they are at one in seeking religion where they think they discern the creative element in experience. Their real divergence does not concern religion, but has to do with the point where ultimate reality touches the human spirit, because for all alike the intercourse with the universe which creates all our experience is, so to speak, a religious intercourse.

Schleiermacher definitely held this view. The universe is a great aesthetic unity all of which touches us in the creative moment before intuition divides into thought and feeling. We may call this intuition feeling, because feeling is the stem, yet it is not feeling in the sense of conscious emotion, but is that moment before consciousness divides into thought and action which is the contact between the universe as one and the soul as one. This is so essentially a religious intercourse that religion would naturally develop out of it alongside of the reality which comes in by the channel of it, were not the progress arrested by false worldly prudences. To say generally that for Schleiermacher religion is feeling is to miss his central conviction that its source is the peculiar feeling or intuition which is the contact with the universe that creates all experience of reality.

Hegel, though denouncing Schleiermacher's view of religion, as confusing it with mere personal emotions, does not really differ from him in his way of relating it to the creative element in experience.   For Hegel this is reason, as the channel of the universal reason, which thinks in us and through us.   Philosophy is the highest and purest manifestation, but religion also is philosophy, even if it be in popular and picture form : and its task, too, is to emancipate the spirit from the merely individaul, and to show, amid the changing shadows of time, the calm and steady sunshine of the eternal light.

Kant is somewhat less definite in stating this relation of religion to the creative source of experience, but it is quite as deeply embedded in his theory.   The necessary forms of the Theoretical Reason, he held, are imposed by itself, and, therefore, may not be valid beyond its own ordering of phenomena.   The real world is the world of freedom, which approves itself to us as we deal with it in freedom by obedience to our own moral reason.   And to this world of reality, this realm of free moral ends, religion belongs, and indeed its reality is one with the existence of such a realm.

All these theories, therefore, though ascribing radically contradictory origins to religion in the mind, agree in seeking them where reality manifests itself to us.   Their views of what religion is also differ with the seat to which they ascribe it, yet all agree that it is, or ought to be, victory and peace through providing for us a right relation to the ultimate reality.   For Kant this reality is the moral order, for Schleiermacher the artistic harmony of the universe, for Hegel the cosmic process of reason ; but, for all, it is that which is absolute in its claim, and, for all, religion is the recognition of this claim and, through it, is emancipation from the fluctuating values of sense and victory over all that is changing and accidental.

These three theories having exhausted the possibility of finding a special aspect of mind which would be the characteristic mark of religion, several more recent writers have maintained the view that the mark of religion is the absence of limit either in the activity of our minds or in our dealing with all reality.

Thus James defines religion as our total reaction to reality. In a sense this is true, but it is not true in any sense which would mark off religion from other experiences.   Each of us might be summed up as our total reaction to reality : and from this relation to ourselves our religion does not escape any more than anything else which belongs to us.   We may go still farther and say that religion is the spring of all efforts after harmony both in our souls and in our conscience. Yet ever this would not be of any value as a means of distinguishing religious from non-religious phenomena. Religious phenomena are not, as a matter of fact, all reality, but the very special and limited part of it which we call sacred ; and, moreover, we respond even to that by a very specialised kind of reaction. Finally, in any case, it is not a test we could apply to anyone's religion except our own ; and it would require a self-knowledge few possess to apply it even there.

The other form of this generalising view of religious faith is that it is the harmony of all our powers. Though different in form, this theory is an attempt to express the same truth about religion, that it is very widely concerned with experience and touches our minds in many ways. Both theories are probably rather judgements of what religion ought to be than definitions of what it is ; and this latter view in particular is the expression of minds more anxious to shun excess than to understand enthusiasm. As a psychological mark, who is to say when the powers of mind are in harmonious balance ? And if we succeeded, would not a vast amount of very vital religion be excluded ? And with this care about the balance of our powers, would what remained be particularly religious ?

Probably both theories are determined by the same idea, which is not so much to find a mark of religion, as to discover a standard of validity. Thus, they are rather theories of knowledge than theories of religion, or only theories of religion in so far as they agree with the theories discussed above that the source of religion must be one with the source of the knowledge of reality. What the theories really set forth is the view that we have a right to believe in anything which has on its side our whole experience and which we have tested with all our mental powers. This is important in its own place, but it is not a mark by which we can distinguish religion. It is rather a confession of inability to find any special aspect of mind which would serve as such a test, and it ends, as the other theories do, in directing attention to the objective reality with which religion deals as the essential mark of religion.

4. RELIGION AS A FORM OF ILLUSION

A still newer type of theory claims to determine the whole character of religion psychologically by denying its validity. It does not deny that this objective reference belongs essentially to it, but it denies all reality to the reference, and professes to explain, from the mind itself, how this peculiar kind of illusion has arisen, and to make psychology in consequence sole arbiter.

On this point all forms of the theories seem to agree. But it is precisely on this point that all need to be questioned. Illusion is not confined to religion. Therefore, if all religious beliefs were proved to be illusions, this would not, in any case, make illusion a distinctive mark of religion, but the distinctive mark would still be in the objects about which the illusion exists. And, further, the reality or unreality of its objects can no more be determined purely psychologically in religion than, say, in commerce. For psychology an object is real when it is regarded as existing outside of the mind ; and the determination of whether it is actually real or not is a matter of evidence and not of psychology. The judgement that the object of religion is an illusion is merely a negative conclusion about the existence of an outside reality, and must go as much beyond mere consideration of purely mental states as the most positive.

As a matter of fact, there is no psychological difference between the theories of religion as concerned with illusion and the theories of it as concerned with ultimate reality, for we can divide them in exactly the same way. Thus we have (1) theories of the Hegelian type, theories which ascribe religion to intellectual aberration ; (2) theories of the type of Schleiermacher's, theories which consider religion a delusion of feeling ; (3) theories of the Kantian type, theories which regard it as a practical prepossession. The sole difference concerns validity, which quite clearly is not a matter of psychology : and, in point of fact, the actual reasons for the different judgement about reality are not psychological, but are drawn from physical science or empirical philosophy.

(1) Of the theories of the Hegelian type, that most akin to Hegel's is one which regards religion as an illusion due to a peculiar mechanism of the human mind, because it is just the process of mind that Hegel makes the measure of the universe.

This theory of religion as illusion from a necessary mechanism of mind is taken to be the most radical way of determining religion by psychology. But that is quite obviously itself an illusion, because, just as Hegel's postulate that the process of mind is the form of the process of reality is not psychology but metaphysics, so is the view that it is a mechanism which necessarily leads to illusion, with this difference, that if error can be a part of the mind's normal functioning, there seems little use discussing metaphysics or anything else. More particularly illusion would then in no way be the special mark of the sphere of religion, for what could we assume to be excluded from its scope ?

If, however, we consider the Hegelian form as including the whole intellectualist type of explanation of religion, there is a theory of religion as illusion of this form which has been much more widely accepted and has had much more to say for itself. On this theory, religion is a primitive, anthropomorphic kind of science. The general type is fairly well represented by Comte's view of the order of human progress. First, when the happenings of the world were thought to be purely accidental, they were ascribed to the caprices and interferences of personal beings like men themselves, only more powerful. Religion is thus a theory of gods which marked man's earliest study of his environment, but based on his thoughts about himself. Second, after the idea of some kind of order had arisen, the religious stage was followed by the metaphysical, which explained the world on abstract mental and rational principles. Finally, with the discovery of the fixed sequence of events, metaphysics gave way to science, which offers the only valid explanation by mechanical sequence, and which, having reached the final method, is the final stage.

So far neither religion nor metaphysics has departed before science as darkness before the dawn, but both continue to ask whether reality, in the last resort, is rational or merely mechanical, and whether even scientists could get along without the freedom and purpose they find it convenient to ignore.

The theory has been many times criticised as a whole, especially as a theory of knowledge, but the only point which concerns us here is whether religion is merely outlived science, or whether science is just science whatever be its conclusions, and religion something other than a graveyard in which to bury its dead. True, the theory leaves nothing at the end, save a world of mechanical sequences in which religion could have no place and admits no mind that could have any concern in it. But it only does this by making the method of physics the measure of all reality, while we are left with the question of whether even the method of physics could have any value, if mind were merely an accidental equipment of a particular biped, like, for example, a smooth skin.   And this again is a metaphysical question not to be evaded by turning a convenient abstraction from mind into bad metaphysics.

(2) Of the type akin to Schleiermacher's theory, the best-known is Feuerbach's, which not only resembles Schleiermacher's view of religion, but was in fact based on it.   Religion is for Feuerbach illusion caused by feeling.   Feeling in this case has no longer any relation to reality, but is pure wandering desire.   Man's gods are the mere emotional reflexion of what he himself would like to be, the mere projection of desire by fantasy.

Once again it is plain that the essential religious part is the objective reference, and that the ground on which reality is denied to it is not any kind of psychology.   So far as psychology goes, there is no reason why the "infinity, perfection, might, holiness we seek in ourselves and have not" should not have a reality corresponding to them.   The true ground for the denial is empiricism, the denial of any kind of knowledge except what comes through the senses or is inferred from their data.   The professed rejection of metaphysics does not alter the fact that this is merely a very questionable metaphysical conclusion.   Moreover, it is a conclusion which turns a great deal more than religion into illusion, for, if desire of every kind is, as Feuerbach maintains, pure egoism which stains our whole life so that it becomes a desolating hypocrisy, can we rely even upon our senses, seeing that the use of them also depends upon our interests ?   The observed phenomena of the senses do not enter our minds as water by a pipe into a cistern, but become conscious knowledge as we think them ; and we think them as they are of value for us.

(3) The more recent theories of religion as illusion are mostly of the Kantian type.   All of them profess to settle the matter on psychological grounds alone, but all of them, once more, make it plain that religion is a reference to an external environment, and that this reference remains characteristic of religion whether the environment be real or imaginary.

Of this type there are two distinct forms, one ascribing religion mainly to the struggle for survival, and the other to the requirements of society, but both making it essentially an affair of will.

Leuba's theory we may take as an example of the first type. As with Kant, the central place in the creation of experience is given to will, though the reason for it is different, being determined by the Darwinian theory of evolution by the struggle for survival. Religion is a way of asserting this will to live. Though very different from Kant's will to live well, religion would still, as with Kant, be connected with will as what is primary in experience. And, if the struggle for survival is the principle of evolution, what the will proceeds upon seems to be as real at least as anything else with which we have to deal. Religion too for Leuba, as for Kant, is essentially belief in a personal order, and, as he seems also to hold with Kant that it is by purpose that we deal with reality, even if it be only the purpose to survive, it is difficult to see how he escapes Kant's conclusion that a realm of purpose is the most real. But to Leuba science proves this personal order to be non-existent. Yet belief in it persists, and it does so because it is a useful illusion in the struggle with environment. Environment apparently is wholly mechanical uniformity, but to conceive it in that way would crush man's spirit. Therefore, he cherishes the illusion of a being who gives him companionship and backing in the battle of life ; and this is of the utmost value for bucking him up in the struggle for survival. Further, the idea of having to deal with spirits and not with mere dead things stimulates intelligence and feeling, while the sense of superiority from associating with superior persons creates an optimism and confidence of high dynamic value.

Here again it is apparent that the essential religious element is an objective reference. The unreality of this reference Leuba professes to determine psychologically. But, as a matter of fact, on his theory the personal order, which he says religion affirms, has every possible support from psychology ; and it is on the ground of physical science, not psychology, that Leuba rejects it as illusion. But, in that case, it cannot be religion alone that is thereby called in question, for if our knowledge is all developed in the struggle for survival, and if illusion will work better for it than reality, we have not even a pragmatic test of reality. Real knowledge we might perhaps not hope to obtain with powers which have been evolved for so purely practical ends, but if we could believe, as might seem natural, that success in the struggle would be determined by the extent to which our real environment was accepted, and that illusion about it would be the most certain of all causes which blot the living creature out of existence, we might have assumed that the processes of our mind, even if they did not rise to the level of knowledge of reality, must run an effectively parallel course with it. But if a vast illusion about it prove to be the most effective way of dealing with our environment, even this confidence is baseless.

Apart from this idea of the unreality of its reference, Leuba's theory of religion is not very different from Ritschl's view that the beginning of religion is a distinction in value between personal beings and extended things, and that its concern is to secure this worth in face of the mechanical forces of nature or society, or, in other words, that it is essentially personal victory over the mechanical world. And it is certainly not any kind of psychological argument which would prevent us from concluding with Ritschl that, if this victory is possible, it can only be because there is a reality in the world and above it akin to the personal.

The second form of this theory of religion as an illusion of the will ascribes religion to man's social consciousness. Leuba also adds that the ideals of the community are unified, socialised, consolidated by being embodied in gods. This is, however, only a slight extension of his theory, for society is considered by him mainly for its value as support in the struggle for survival. But the French anthropological school of which Durkheim is the best-known representative, makes the authority of the social group itself the source of all religion.

Religion, Durkheim says, has been too enduring and dominating a factor in human history to be regarded as a mere mental illusion. Some objective reality, he thinks, it must have. This he finds in the sanction of the social group. The authority of the group is what makes anything sacred, and so distinguishes its sanction from all other sanctions of various degrees of force.

But, first of all, a social sanction is not the kind of sanction which religion itself claims, and in point of fact a social sanction is not by itself more sacred than a personal one, nor is it recognised, at least by any advanced religion, as being so. This theory, therefore, would seem to reduce religion to illusion quite as much as Leuba's.

It also quite as definitely raises the question why such an illusion should have wrought so long and so effectively. If there is actually a sacred world and man belongs to it, human relations may be sacred and sacred obligation be the pillar and ground of them ; but if society is merely an extension of the herd instinct, the idea that its relations are sacred is an illusion, the rise of which is difficult to explain and the obligation of which all progress in understanding must undermine.

The recognition of the sacred as the religious element is important, but it is precisely this sacredness which is, on the theory, illusion. And the question is how such an illusion could arise out of mere mass feeling, and still more, how it could later develop into the only sanction which could be set up effectively against the mass mind. If the sense of the sacred were already there, it would naturally attach itself to the society in which we live and by which we live ; but how, out of mere social, variable, and comparative values, could the idea of an absolute value, in the might of which man can stand alone over against his whole society, ever arise ? Nothing is more certain than that the sacred claims to have its sanction in itself and to be corrupted when it is accepted as submission to public opinion.

All these theories, therefore, direct attention away from merely psychological marks of religion. Quite as clearly, by regarding it as illusion as by regarding it as the ultimate reality, they show that the essential quality of religion is the claim to deal with a special kind of environment, which has its own particular sanctions. If this environment do not exist, religion has no basis. And, even so, it would not be a mere psychological state to be described as illusion, but would be a wrong objective reference, due to misunderstanding, not about our own minds, but about our environment, so that it ought rather to be described as delusion. Wherefore, any theory of religion as illusion also brings us back to the view of religion as essentially a dealing with an unseen environment of absolute worth which demands worship. If this environment were proved to be non-existent, religion would be shown to be baseless, but its essential character would still depend on this supposed objective reference and not on some peculiar quality of belief, or pious feeling, or practical trust. And, as it is the same human nature which deals with all environment, if the environment do not exist, we should the less expect anything peculiar in man's way of dealing with it, because, while every real higher environment stirs higher faculties and affords larger opportunities for displaying them, an imaginary one cannot be the source of such a development as the sense of the sacred.

5. THE FACTORS OF EXPERIENCE

Our discussion so far has tended to show that, whether this
environment be real or not, religion is an affirmation of what we
may call broadly the supernatural, and that its quality is determined
by this outward reference and not by any particular kind of
subjective feeling or attitude, while its validity wholly depends on
whether such an invisible world exist or not. Now this would
seem to bring us so near to the Rationalist view of religion, as a
matter of evidences for the existence of God, providence, and
immortality, that the difference might not seem worth discussing.
Even where difference does exist, the advantage may appear to be
on the side of a theory which states what its supernatural is and
establishes the existence of it by inference from the natural. And
undoubtedly we have in its insistence that the essential question
about religion concerns its truth, the reason why the rationalist
view of religion has been so widely held and why it endures to this
day, for unless its object is real, nay, the ultimate reality, religion
is a vain and most unnecessarily distressing illusion. Moreover,
Rationalism was right in insisting that this question may not be
evaded, and also that we may not escape the demand to answer it
for ourselves.

But, while men are religious according as the world which
religion affirms is, by their own knowledge, the ultimate reality for
them, it is equally certain that religion is not a matter of evidence
from nature, or life, or moral principles, and that men are not
religious as they reason or even reason cogently. Most religions
have held some belief in God, but the religious element in the
belief has not been an inference from the order of the world ;
usually they have believed in a providential order, but the religious
element of it has not been a deduction from the happy ordering of
our existence ; with few exceptions they have held the hope of
personal immortality, but never, religiously at least, on an argument
about a juster reward than this world provides.

Rationalism proceeded on the assumption that the world with
which religion was concerned needed to be proved, and this by
evidence not depending on itself. Religion came so badly through
the test that the supernatural seemed reduced to the shadow of
a shade, leaving naturalism triumphant through pure lack of a
rival. Then naturalism was taken to be unchallenged as the

only self-consistent, scientific, and comfortable theory of the universe.

Yet the theory was plausible only to those who overlooked the fact that the natural had been subjected by Rationalism to the same test, and that its reality had been left in even greater dubiety. From Descartes onwards the task was attempted of proving the existence of a material world by other evidence than the way it environs us. The result of this test was certainly no more reassuring for the reality of the natural world than it had been for the reality of the supernatural, and the questions raised were even more embarrassing. The natural world is also known by feeling and value, and surely that has even less to do with the reality of a material physical world than of a metaphysical, which might be of that mental structure. If we are not content with the meaning and order of experience, and try to get behind it, we find nothing but a stream of impressions, amid which knowledge and reality are indistinguishable from dream and fantasy.

This sceptical conclusion was as inevitable in the one case as in the other, and in both for the same reason, which was neither remarkable nor recondite. It is simply that we cannot prove the reality of any environment while omitting the only evidence it ever gives of itself, which is the way in which it environs us. If this count for so little to us that we need to have its existence proved, it would not seem to matter much whether it exist or not : and, in any case, no environment presents further testimonials besides its own witness. So far is reality from feeling obliged to meet all our objections that it only dimly unveils itself to our most sympathetic and far-reaching insight.

It is an inadequate statement of the position to say that such methods of proof left men's belief in the visible world no more certain than their belief in the invisible, because, when we betake ourselves to this kind of proof of reality, the world of the senses is necessarily called in question earlier and more radically than the world of the mind. All things, even though known by the senses, are known only in thought, whereas thinking is at least a direct experience. Hence, for many centuries, the Indian philosophy, making use of this method, has denied all reality to the world of the senses. Its only external reality is a sort of nightmare of Brahma, and the witness of our senses about it is *maya*, illusion. Yet, with all this scepticism about the natural world of the senses, the existence of a great spiritual, unseen reality, both without in the universe and within in the soul, has never been so much as questioned.

To us practical people it may seem impossible that any sane person should regard the visible world as more unreal than the invisible, but the fact remains that there are such persons and that their conduct proves this estimate to be no pretence.   As practical people we give a practical reason for our conviction.   We go about our business in the world sensibly, and that leaves us in no doubt about the world's reality.   Were we asked to explain why the Indian is not equally convinced, we should say that, having withdrawn from the world, he has deprived the world of the power to witness to itself by its uses.   That is to say, we take the reality of the visible world along with the employment of its natural values, and do not go on to ask for some reason outside of what it means for us whereby to establish its reality.

But while we accept in this way the natural world, it seems reasonable to many to require a quite different kind of proof of the supernatural.   Instead of asking, what is the relation of this environment to us and our relation to it, which is the essential religious question, it is thought necessary to require evidence of it quite apart from considering whether it does any business in life. What is new never comes in, however, in any other way than by making a difference to our environment, and we cannot discover it by reasoning from something else.

At the same time no environment comes in as mere crude importation like our furniture, or, indeed, by any mere impact or impulse.   All environment deals with us and we deal with all environment as meaning, and for that our thinking about it is of the utmost importance.   We know a reality not, as some seem to suppose, when we do not think about it, but only when we think about it rightly, which is when our meaning corresponds to its meaning.   Thus a vast amount of thinking and valuing, which is a kind of science, is embedded even in our perceptions.   And, in the same way, a vast amount of thinking and valuing, which is a kind of theology, interpenetrates our higher intuitions.   For this reason we can argue ourselves out of any experience and, without right thinking, we cannot rightly receive the plainest facts.   This is sometimes obscured by the difference between our speculative and our practical thinking.   Just as we may be sceptics with regard to the material world in profession while all our actions in it prove our theory to be mere intellectual gymnastic, so we may be materialists in theory while we show that our real faith is of quite a different quality. But this does not make theory of no importance, because it always in time works back into our experience and comes to determine the kind of experience of which we are capable. If we are not continually seeing our theory through our experience, we shall come to see our experience through our theory. Thus the theory of the Indian about the world of the senses being illusion, makes the world to him in time a dream and paralyses his practical dealing with it. In the same way, what we may call our theology is of vital importance, for though our practical spiritual world may long continue very different from our theoretical, the theoretical will gradually bring it to its own level, so that, as a matter of fact, nothing has more determined the history of the race than men's conscious, though not necessarily their formulated, theologies, meaning by that their ideas about the supernatural. Thus, even for seeing the highest, we may say that the greatest need of every age is a true theology.

Yet, while we cannot have a true experience without thinking rightly, we cannot have a new experience by any kind of thinking. Therefore, the idea that theology is religion merely puts all religion in the air. Like every other science, theology is never more than the interpretation of what is otherwise given. It must, to be of profit, be science within experience and not instead of it.

Here we have the other side which gives interest and some appearance of truth to the subjective theories of religion. Religion does not deal with its environment by way of metaphysical inference, but by way of feeling and value. From this it is concluded that the main question must concern our feelings and practical purposes themselves. But they are not more subjective in religion than they are in our dealing with the visible world.

It is plainly not possible to go with any fullness here into a matter which would involve us in a whole theory of knowledge, and it must suffice to make some statements which may seem to be no more than assertions. We know all environment, not as impact or physical influx, but as meaning : and this meaning depends on (1) the unique character of the feeling it creates ; (2) the unique value it has for us ; (3) the immediate conviction of a special kind of objective reality, which is inseparable from this valuation ; and (4) the necessity of thinking it in relation to the rest of experience and the rest of experience in relation to it.

In all experience these four aspects are indivisibly joined in one, and each loses its significance in isolation. The feeling depends on the value, and the value on the feeling ; the conviction of reality is not an additional inference, but the valuation depends on the conviction of reality, and the conviction of reality on the correctness of the valuation ; the thinking of it in its place in our whole experience is not after we have received it, but is necessary for receiving it, and essential to the conviction of its reality. These elements are the same for the experience of things physical as for the experience of things spiritual. What does distinguish religion from all else is the unique quality of the feeling, of the valuation of the nature of the object, and of the way of thinking things together.

There is, however, a constant necessity to distinguish what we may not divide, nor is it specially difficult with the world of religion, because, as with every other environment, there is (1) a reflection of it in a feeling of its own special quality ; (2) an immediate judgement of worth of a kind different from all others ; (3) a conviction of a peculiar kind of reality; and (4) a special way of thinking it all together as one experience. For the first two I propose to distinguish two words which are only vaguely distinct in our language, and, as is often necessary in the use of terms for more technical purposes, to differentiate them somewhat more precisely than is done by common usage. These words are the " holy " and the "sacred." The "holy" I propose to use for the direct sense or feeling of the supernatural, and the " sacred " for its valuation as of absolute worth. The special object I shall call " the supernatural," and the thinking together "theology," both words, however, having a somewhat more definite meaning than they have in popular usage. By the sacred, in particular, all religion is distinguished, and all religious thinking is right thinking as it is about what is truly sacred. The supernatural is not a further inference from it as from effects to a cause, but is felt and valued in it ; and, when separated from this manifestation, it is without content and deprived of all reality, because it no longer deals with an environment, but is mere abstract argument about the universe.

6. THE SENSE OF THE HOLY

Holy and sacred are only vaguely distinguishable in ordinary usage, and that rather by some difference in the feeling associated with the words than by any clear difference of application. But here, as has been explained, it is proposed to use them more definitely, making the sense of holiness apply to the special feeling of awe or reverence which certain ideas or objects evoke, while excluding from its meaning the valuation of them as of absolute worth, for which the term sacred is reserved.

In our language the " holy," used by itself, would mean something which stirs moral reverence. But, in such expressions as the " holy edifice " or the " holy sacrament," it is still used to express a vague feeling of an awe which is not of an ethical quality : and the history of religion shows that this is its original meaning. Even a " Holy God " did not originally mean a " God of purer eyes than to behold iniquity," but an awe-inspiring being, with the sense of holiness not unlike the feeling evoked by countless material objects. These different types of feeling may be distinguished as the " awesome holy " and the " ethical holy."

The more primitive form of the sense of the holy is here called the " awesome holy," because it is an awe so near akin to fear as to give colour to the theory that fear was the source of all religion, that, according to a very ancient theory, *timor fecit deos*. What is at least most immediately obvious in it is dread of some mysterious dangerous force, though a closer study shows that this is only the negative side of the sense of it as exalting, stimulating, re-enforcing. But even this seems to be conceived almost as a material fluid, and to have no spiritual and at least no ethical significance. In view of this there are writers who maintain that this primitive awesome holy has no connection with the ethical holy : and there are some who regard them as distinct to the end. This awe, which is held to be quite apart from moral reverence, is then taken to be the distinctive religious feeling. In this way, we are told, we keep religion and ethics to their own departments.

That they ought to be kept to their own departments might seem to be shown by the unfortunate history of their amalgamation, for religion has been made to depend upon ethics and ethics on religion in ways which have wronged both. Religion has been made a mere sanction of morals, whereupon it ceases to be religion ;

and morals a mere announcement of commands of the Deity, dependent on the blessing and ban of religion for its sanctions and motives, whereupon it ceases to be morals. Religion, if it be worth anything, must stand in its own right ; while good is good to be done for its own sake and not because an omnipotent person has laid down rules and will maintain them by rewards and punishments.

But, though this is true, it is far from being the end of the matter. A religion which is not ethical is in danger of being superstition and not religion ; and an ethic which has no appeal except to the visible and the useful is business, not morals. Historically, too, the religious sense of the holy becomes an ethical feeling. On the one hand, the natural evolution of the awesome holy is into moral reverence ; and by that very thing we measure it as progress. On the other, morality has always been a religious development, directly related to the sense of the holy, and a real moral feeling can never be wholly divorced from something at least akin to its awe.

Professor Otto, more perhaps than any other writer, has put the emphasis on the awesome holy as the essential religious character, and he divides it entirely from the ethical, which he regards as a quite separate development alongside of it. Yet so undeniable is the close and apparently necessary connection, that, after distinguishing them sharply, in the interests of his theory, he maintains, in the interests of experience and common sense, that they are related *a priori*.

Such a position hardly needs refuting, and would not have been taken up had it not been necessary, in order to afford support to a non-ethical and non-rational view of religion, without denying, as a consequence, the dependence of all higher religion upon both ethics and reason. But how two quite separate developments should be connected *a priori* is difficult to conceive, for it does not seem to be in accord with any known form of development. In every development, it matters not what may be added in the course of development, when we look back, we can detect the germ of it long before it appeared in separate, clearly distinguishable form. And, when we thus look back on this evolution of the sense of the holy, it is not difficult to discover, in every stage of it known to us, the germ at least of the moral development. What, but something akin to our ethical feeling, distinguishes the sense of holy awe from mere fear ? We may, it is true, fail entirely to discover as yet our particular ethical ideas and ethical values, but, if the feeling of the holy is a sense that man stands in presence of a reality before which he may not seek his own pleasure or walk after the imaginations of his own heart, has he not in that the well-spring of all ethical progress ? For this reason, holy awe, even when most akin to abject fear, is never utterly abject, but, if it crush man with the sense of being the creature of a day, it also speaks to him of the eternity " God has set in his heart," so that the most primitive man who responds to it could say with the poet, " I felt myself so small, so great." And, just as there is in the poorest awe a certain quality of moral reverence which distinguishes it from fear, so, at the other end, there is in the highest moral reverence an element of awe which distinguishes it from a purely intellectual judgement. At the lowest stage the object of this awe may be so confusedly conceived that we may discern little but crude dominating feeling ; at the highest, its object may be so clearly conceived through the true, the beautiful, and the good, that Kant could regard it as delivering us from the domination of all feeling whatsoever. Nevertheless, the feeling throughout has its own essential quality, and affects us quite differently from any other series of feeling ; and there is no break anywhere in the evolution. Being original, it is not to be described by something else, but, being the same feeling throughout, all the stages of its progress shed light on each other.

Professor Otto, on the other hand, divorces the sense of the holy from any sense of an environment which is becoming for man an ethical reality, and relates it to what he calls the " numinous." The mark of the holy, he says, is throughout the sense of a mystery at once tremendous and fascinating, the " numinous " being this kind of half-lit shadow, at once forbidding and attractive.

Three points may at once be conceded. First, the earliest religion was, probably enough, largely the sense of mysterious moving things in the world about one. Second, this feeling is common and exercises a powerful influence in all primitive forms of religion. Third, there is a sense in which a living nature must remain the basis even of the highest religion.

Of this highest stage of the sense of the " numinous " we cannot find a better description than Wordsworth's :

A presence that disturbs me with a joy
Of elevated thoughts ; a sense sublime
Of something far more deeply interfused,
Whose dwelling is the light of setting suns,

And the round ocean and the living air,
And the blue sky, and in the mind of man,
A motion and a spirit that impels
All thinking things, all objects of all thought
And rolls through all things.

To this feeling or mood or intuition the sense of the holy is
certainly akin, and there are times when they are practically one.
Yet this aesthetic sense does not necessarily have religious quality,
nor has the religious sense necessarily aesthetic quality.   As mere
feelings, however, they would be difficult to distinguish, and an
account of the difference would be impossible to give.   Both are
exalted responses to what is taken to be more than a mechanical
environment.   But the real difference is much less in the mere
feeling than in the quality of this reference, much less between an
artistic and a religious feeling than between the artistic and the
religious valuation.

And if it be difficult, as mere feeling, to distinguish rigidly
between the higher aesthetic sense of the numinous and the higher
sense of the holy, it is still more difficult to distinguish, purely as
feeling, the awed sense of the holy from the lower type of numinous
dread.   That they are quite distinct is plain.   No sense of the
holy is ever the merely shuddery, spooky feeling.   This latter is
the basis of magic, but not of religion : and at all stages the feelings
connected with religion and magic are distinct.   Yet, if we confine attention to the feelings themselves, the distinction is almost
impossible to see and quite impossible to describe.   Both are vague,
awed feelings, and both accompany what Leuba calls an anthropo-
pathic view of the world, but which, in its numinous form at least,
is also theriopathic, and, in all forms, is something more immediate
than anything to be described as a view.   Views might only be
wrong inferences, but this is the practical sense by which apparently
life has always conducted its business of living : and just for that
reason it is difficult to draw distinctions in it, and they would be
impossible to convey to others.   Ideas we can explain more or less
successfully by other ideas, but feelings are more direct experiences
and are not to be described from other feelings.   Yet we are not,
for this reason, incapable of speaking about them.   Only we must
speak about them through the values they attend or the objects to
which the values are referred.   There is little success in describing
feelings, because, the moment we start, we are dealing with ideas,

not feelings. But, when we speak of an object which makes a unique impression, we have common ground in our feelings about it for mutual understanding. Now the sense of the holy at every stage is peculiarly easy to distinguish in this way, because it is stirred only by what is valued as sacred. From this sacred or absolute valuation it has its special quality as feeling, a certain absolute quality of awe or reverence, which at once distinguishes even its lowest forms from the merely uncanny or magical. The feelings both of the uncanny and of the magical are attached to our fears and wishes, and are to be subjected, as best we can, to our uses ; whereas the holy is a feeling neither to be run away from nor to be put in subjection. Thus, if the feeling is attached to a sacred value, then it is the sense of the holy ; but if to one of merely comparative value as it satisfies our desires or suits our convenience or our profit, the feeling with which we respond to it cannot be so described.

This valuation, we shall see later, is not necessarily a moral valuation, but may be of a curiously material quality, so that there is a material and moral sacred, which reflects the difference between the awesome holy and the ethical : and we shall also see that, just as the holy, in the sense of exalted moral purity, is continuous with the holy as the sense of awe akin to dread, so is the ethical sacred continuous with the material.

7. The Judgement of the Sacred

The sense of the holy, we have seen, has its own peculiar quality as feeling, being a direct response to a special kind of environment. But we have further seen that it goes inseparably with the valuation of this environment as sacred, and that the feeling can only be described through the values to which it is attached, the unique character of the feeling being made plain only by the absoluteness of the sacred with which it is bound up. The sacred, as used here, means this valuation as of absolute worth, and not anything less, being that which may not be brought down and compared with values of pleasure or ease or any visible good.

The interaction between this sense of the holy and this valuation as sacred is not all in one direction. On the one hand, the valuation may immediately follow the feeling, or, on the other, the feeling may immediately follow the valuation, though it is not, in either case, mere sequence. We value things because they appeal to our feelings, but we also feel about them largely as we value them. Yet, more frequently perhaps than any other feeling, the sense of the holy follows and depends on its value ; and, on the whole, this becomes increasingly the case as the mind develops. We might even regard it as at least one mark of progress, that while the more primitive the life, the more the feelings determine the value; the more advanced the development, the more the values determine the feelings.

The sacred, as defined above, might seem to afford a very exalted test of religion, entirely different from the feelings which mix themselves up with all kinds of crudities. But, unfortunately, history is far from confirming this expectation. Even as an absolute valuation, such as we have defined it, we still find that it includes the most weird and even debased objects, and, moreover, to such an extent that even the problem of the most dread sense of the holy is easy, compared with the problem of the grossness of the sacred. The task of conceiving how absolute value should have been ascribed to birds and beasts and creeping things, even by the most primitive minds, entirely baffles, not merely our knowledge, but our imagination. Of how the vault of heaven and certain aspects of the spirit of man should be sacred we have some understanding, because, with Kant, we revere the starry heavens above and the moral law within, and that because they speak to us by what cannot be measured by mathematics or the categorical imperative. But, for the very reason that we have attained so exalted an idea of the manifestations of the sacred, we have difficulty in understanding how it could be embodied and expressed in cows and cats.

This inability to explain why the sacred was embodied in such strange forms should not, however, blind us to the enormous significance of the entrance into human life of a valuation not to be weighed or bargained with, a valuation which spoke to man of another reality than that he knew by his senses and judged by his appetites.

But the problem of these queer, gross sacreds still remains, and it is impossible to be satisfied with the usual explanation that the whole scale of values of primitive man was different from ours. As the surest measure of progress is the higher quality of our values, this is doubtless part of the answer. But it cannot be the whole, because, on the one hand, primitive man had much more reverence for the higher things of the spirit than the material forms of his worship would show, and, on the other hand, as mere material objects, his reverence for his sacred things does not seem to have been much greater than ours.

The reason for their sacredness was quite apart from their actual value even for him. What he valued them for can be explained by a quasi-material presence, and the explanation would be right enough, because the mark of the primitive mind is inability to think except in material forms. But, if that were all, we should have expected him to see it only in the highest material forms. We have to ask why the objects might be at once trivial and yet so sacred as to be valued above life itself. Only the sense of a higher world could have required from him such surrender of what embodies all natural values. This must have meant intense and deep experiences. But he embodied them in such crude forms, because, as a matter of fact, they came to him in this context of strange objects. Even in our own better ordered minds, our deepest feelings and our highest thoughts are often stirred by the trivial and not infrequently by the repellant, and are by no means rigidly reserved for sublime occasions. The experiences of primitive man apparently were much more accidental, sporadic, unarranged and uncriticised even than ours : and to the extent in which this was so, the difference in his view of the sacred depended on different experiences. Yet it was only to this extent. The real difference was not due to anything in the experiences themselves, but to the absence of power to deal freely with them. The main reason why his higher experiences remained embedded in crude material things is simply that, lacking free ideas, he was unable to separate any part of his experience from the whole context in which it happened to him. Our emancipation entirely depends on this freedom, which enables us to set our ideas at liberty from their accidental associations. Without this power, we too should have had few sacred things free from bizarre material associations, and even as it is, we are, perhaps, not quite so superior to the savage as we imagine. But the lack of this power of free ideas, this power of selecting from his experience, and thinking it as his own generalised thought and finding what is to be revered in it apart from its material embodiments, is precisely what makes man primitive. His experience, being as it were solid with its context, was necessarily material in form. Moreover, this form was cherished, because his sole method of seeking to revive his experience of higher reality was to return as much as possible to the material conditions in which it first came. This explains not only why primitive religion has many crude sacred objects, but why it is so much occupied with particular places, marking them with pillars or stocks or such-like. It was in order to return to the exact spot and thereby to revive the presence of the sacred formerly felt in it. Our imagination may still remain baffled before its amazing pantheon, not only of the sky and the hosts of heaven and of river and mountain, but of birds and beasts and creeping things ; yet, when we think of the way of arriving at it, we should not be wholly without understanding. But, above all, we ought to see that the experience may concern high matters which are really and truly sacred, while the embodiment of it is, so to speak, rather gargoyle than seraph. And with that should go his queer and, to us at least, absurd and irrational taboos, for they are all ways of respecting the presence of sacred powers, of powers not at any cost to be brought down to the convenient.

This limitation, which tied his conception of higher ideas to material objects, is not at all confined to religion or to ideas of the sacred, because primitive man could no more conceive sharpness apart from a cutting instrument than sacredness apart from material embodiment. Yet as he knew, in spite of that, what sharpness meant, so he knew also what sacredness was. Therefore, if the absence of free ideas left the sacred unemancipated from a sporadic and unreasoned and material experience, we ought not to conclude that there was nothing in it besides the accidental and material. On the contrary, the recognition of anything as sacred, as of an absolute value above desire and even above life, was the well-spring of all endeavour after emancipation from a material world merely appealing to his appetites, because this alone in his life was not measured by them. Manifestly, therefore, he was finding a higher power which made this victory possible, and this he made plain by revering it above all might of visible things and obeying its requirements at all cost of loss or hazard.

This valuation as sacred, therefore, we ought to esteem as the spring of all self-mastery and all mastery over the world, as the sublime attainment by which man became truly man. Man with a taboo, which he would not break for any earthly gain or even to save his life, was no longer a mere animal whose only inhibition was the threat of suffering or the fear of death. He might still fear what could only kill the body and his judgement of sacredness might still relate itself to that fear, but if there was something in his experience more sacred than life, the fear of death as the final ill was conquered in principle : and this victory is the condition of all progress, for there is no real spiritual good possible at lower cost than the hazard of our material life, nor any impossible at that price.

This relation of the judgement of the sacred to human progress is obscured by the frequent use of its sanction to defend reaction. A belief or custom is fixed with all its present material associations by being regarded as sacred. Then it becomes a sort of fenced city from which it is hard to escape and which can resist attacks both of right and reason. Instead of leading men into a world of free ideas in which the sacred liberates itself from material bonds, sacredness is invoked on behalf of these associations. Thereupon, we have an idolatry which is the worst form of reaction and a " yoke of bondage."

But men can misuse anything, and the possibility of good is usually the measure of the possibility of evil. Moreover, it is on the steepest road that the temptation to make our progress the justification for resting where we are is strongest. Wherefore, the misuse of the sacred to arrest progress is no disproof of its importance as the spring of the specially human evolution. Nor does the fact that reaction is mainly a return to its material form, or at least a maintaining of it when greater freedom offers, disprove the importance even of the material sacred as a necessary stage of progress, because influences are like persons who have the more power to arrest progress if they have been effective to advance it.

Both results we can see plainly in the religion of Israel. The prophets, just because their higher truths were sacred and required all their devotion, emancipated religion from material associations, in a way unparalleled elsewhere. These associations, which were sacred in the popular mind and were defended as such, the prophets denounced as idolatry, and found it the chief hindrance to the discernment of spiritual progress and what they regarded as the true sacred : but, nevertheless, even the prophetic religion had itself travelled through a stage at which the judgement of a sacredness above life had been embodied in material objects like the ark.

The ark is a specially interesting example of the material sacred. It stirred an awed sense of the holy which made the touching of it sacrilege ; and yet part of its contents could be destroyed when it became itself an object of worship.   It represented a value which was above life and killed the profane person who would steady it as though it were a mere box, yet the natural life alongside of it was also becoming sacred and that through the religion embodied in the ark.

This singular connection between sacredness and life, so that to be above life in value is the measure of sacredness, while at the same time life itself becomes sacred, is only a material form of the singular relation to our own souls which goes with every valuation as sacred.   This also could only be conceived materially as the life. Yet it is, in its way, a manifestation of the claim of the sacred by a worth within us which belongs to us, and which we only win by being ready to lose it.   And even life was at first too immaterial an idea.   Wherefore, the blood was taken to be the life, and was esteemed sacred.   Other things, and above all the peculiar physical impression made by blood, and especially on primitive minds, went to intensify the experience, but that does not hinder the fact that in its sacredness was felt something of higher meaning and value than can be explained by mere blood, something which is the real explanation of the blood-sacrifice, the whole impression and valua-tion of which is not explicable by rational arguments about totem-animals or feasting with the god, or even upon the reasoned idea that life is the noblest gift of the gods and must be offered them again.   None of these explanations suffice for a sacredness which is raised above all comparison.   Above all a sacredness felt in the blood, and not the mere blood, is needed to explain human sacrifice, which confers sacredness on human life as well as sacrifices it to the god.

Later, man conceived this sacred nature in himself in the form of a soul, a half-material, vaguer, swifter, smaller image of himself.   This again was necessary because of the inability to think without material association ; but again, though there was more of argument and inference here, such reasoning does not account for the peculiar feelings about the soul or for the value set upon it, a value which, in its rudimenatry way, is of the same quality as the estimate that it would not profit to gain the whole world and lose one's soul.

If this be a right account of the material sacred, there is no more difficulty than with any other higher development in explaining how it passes into the ethical sacred, which also had a long progress before it could be summed up as the absolute value of the true, the beautiful, and the good. The rudimentary presence of the higher in the lower form is not more difficult to discover, nor are the stages of the evolution of the lower into the higher less closely linked than in any other kind of human progress. First, the most primitive and material valuation of anything sacred manifests the three abiding forces of ethical advance : (1) the affirmation of a reality of absolute value ; (2) the subordination of all else to it ; (3) a tendency to regard its nature less materially. Therefore, ethical quality was there from the beginning. And, second, in ethical progress we have in all history a singular insistence that nothing is ever new, that it is in man's world and man's heart already, something he has always been rejecting and not something only recently brought to his notice. The prophet in all ages speaks as though he were merely reviving an old religion, and the more ethical the newness is, the greater is the assurance that it merely comes out of the old. Nor is this either convention or historical illusion, because there is no sacred which does not have the values in which the ethical is potentially present.

This is not hindered by the fact that it may, besides being material, also be irrational and immoral, because a possibility of good is, in all human uses, always a possibility of evil. And in this case we have an explanation in the very close dependence both of reason and conscience upon the sacred. This would require a fuller justification than can be given here, but how can we conceive them developing with no restraint upon desire beyond fear of consequence ? And if that be so, religion could not use reason and conscience at the start for determining its character, but had to develop them in the process of exploring its territory.

Everything that is sacred is in the sphere of religion, and everything in the sphere of religion is sacred. Unless dogmas express beliefs valued as sacred, they are mere intellectual formulas ; unless rites are the worship of a power valued as sacred, they are mere social ceremonies ; unless God Himself embody all we value as sacred, he is a mere metaphysical hypothesis. Only when the valuation as sacred accompanies the sense of awe and reverence have we the religious holy, and only a reality having this absolute value is the religious supernatural. Therefore, if there is any one mark of the sphere of religion, it is this valuation of everything within it as sacred.

8. THE EXISTENCE OF THE SUPERNATURAL

If, as has been maintained, everything sacred is within the sphere of religion, and everything within the sphere of religion sacred, and this valuation interacts with a peculiar type of feeling to be described as the sense of the holy, we should seem to have discovered a mark by which the sphere of religion could be defined so as to include what belongs to it and exclude all else.

On that view, if, as has been further maintained, moral reverence is continuous with material awe and what we may call the ideal with the material sacred, when we speak of the sacredness of truth and beauty and goodness, we are, whether consciously or not, putting them into the sphere of religion. And there must be a sense in which this is right, because we cannot by any building up of natural values arrive at anything of absolute worth, and it is the sacredness of truth, in itself and for our own loyalty, which distinguishes it from mere facts in an encyclopaedia, while by the same mark beauty is distinguished from prettiness, and goodness from merely useful behaviour.

But, while the sacred to which they appeal and the reverence they stir are from the world of religion, it is vital to any right interest in them that each should be in a world of its own. We have the study of their norms or standards in logic, aesthetics, and ethics. Thus, on the one hand, even if their sacredness be in the same sphere as religion, they carry on their business in independence of it ; and, on the other, religion is not a mere combination of them, nor yet something merely alongside of them. In seeking truth, we may not be influenced by religious considerations, but must regard only the reality we would know. And beauty, too, must just be beauty, and goodness goodness. If religion try to control such judgements, it corrupts them and is itself corrupted. Wherefore, while we cannot separate true thinking, feeling, and acting from religion without losing the absolute worth by which alone they can be valued, it becomes necessary to distinguish the business of religion from the business of logic, aesthetics, and ethics as sharply as we can.

The distinction, however, depends neither upon the feeling of holiness nor the judgement of sacredness, but upon the reality to which these belong—the existence of the supernatural. The supernatural is the special concern of religion, and nothing else is concerned with it in the same way as religion.

As here used the supernatural means the world which manifests more than natural values, the world which has values which stir the sense of the holy and demand to be esteemed as sacred. This is the only way in which the distinction can be drawn, but in this way we draw it quite simply every day. We cannot distinguish the natural as the mechanical and the supernatural as the free, for we do not know how much freedom there is in the natural or how much law in the supernatural ; nor can it be divided as between the ordinary and the miraculous, for nature is sometimes the more miraculous, and the supernatural the common stuff of our daily experience. The two are not in opposition, and are constantly interwoven, and there may be nothing wholly natural or wholly supernatural, but our interests in them are perfectly distinct, and very definitely distinguish aspects of our experience. Part of it is natural, in the sense that its values are comparative and to be judged as they serve our needs ; and part of it supernatural, in the sense that its values are absolute, to which our needs must submit. We know the supernatural as it reflects itself in the sense of the holy and has for us absolute value, directly and without further argument, and henceforth we are concerned with its existence and its relation to us and our relation to it. We can make no more out of arguing abstractly about it than we should out of arguing abstractly, as men long did, about the natural. The supreme task, the task which has, more than any other, marked human progress, has been to discover the true sacred, and that means again to exercise the true sense of the holy. And, only on the basis of the right judgement inspired by the right feeling, can religion with profit ask : What is the sacred reality and how is it related to us and we to it ? Thus there is only one sound reason for saying it is personal, and this is, that, the more we have stood on our own feet and thought and felt and acted for ourselves, the more the whole universe has responded to us. In the same way, there is only one sound reason for saying the supernatural is in front of us and not something merely in the making, and this is that the sacred requirement is ever in front of us, something not existing yet always there to be realised.

Thus the awareness of the reality of the supernatural is not something added to the sense of the holy and the judgement of the sacred by some kind of argument, say from the natural world. The fatal misrepresentation is that, at this point, religion is identified with theology, and theology is hung up in the air without any world of its own to work in, so that it is expected to be its own reality, instead of being, like other sciences, the study of a reality already given.

It is here that we must recall that, though we may analyse them, we may not separate the elements of our experience. The awareness of the supernatural is not given apart from and in addition to the sense of the holy and the judgement of the sacred, but in them, because they are the experience of it as an actual environment. And in this it does not differ from the natural world in its way of manifesting itself. We know the natural world too as it reflects itself in feeling and has meaning for us by its values. But forthwith we are interested in it in itself and the world becomes an objective concern for us, its existence being itself the assurance of all values. And so it is with the supernatural, which must be inquired into, like the natural, as a world in which we live and move and have our being, if it is to be inquired into at all.

Nor can we so easily separate the reality of the natural world from the reality of the supernatural as we imagine. The reality of the former is not proved merely by the violence of its assault on the senses. The difference between us who take it to be the most solid reality and the Indian to whom it is *maya* is no mere matter of the senses, for the witness of the senses is the same for him as for us. The difference concerns a different valuation of the world the senses reveal and a keener response to it in feeling. And these valuations are not, argue as we may, exclusively by natural values, but consciously or unconsciously by a different sense of their place in our higher life, being far more a difference in our religion, and the place the natural world plays in it, than in our science. Did we betake ourselves to the same kind of religion as the Indian, we also should live in the world as in a vain show, and no kind of physics could in the slightest degree make the world appear less of a dream. But the existence of the supernatural world as a real world no more proves that we may not be misled by illusions in it than the existence of the physical world guarantees us against mistake about it. This, too, is a world in which we may err and which we may misuse, and indeed it is only in this world that error and misuse become graver matters than mistake, and can be spoken of as falsehood and sin.

The last factor, which I have called theology, we cannot enter upon here, because it raises the whole question of how we are to think within this sphere. But it must not be forgotten that none of these experiences are apart from thinking them in relation to all other experiences, and all other experiences in relation to them, and that it was religion, and not science, which first inspired men to try to unify all their experiences, and that it is religion still which alone seems to unify all experience—the corporeal and the mental, the inward and the outward, the ideas of value and the facts of existence, the events of time and their significance for eternity.

RELIGION AND PSYCHOLOGY

BY WILLIAM BROWN

Wilde Reader in Mental Philosophy in the University of
Oxford ; Hon. Consulting Psychologist and Lecturer on
Medical Psychology, Bethlem Royal Hospital, London ;
Psychotherapist to King's College Hospital, London.

CONTENTS

I. PSYCHOLOGICAL METHODS IN THE STUDY OF RELIGION

IN considering how far psychology can throw light upon religion, it is desirable to set out from some general conception of what Religion is. Religion itself is a state of mind, a mental attitude towards the universe : it is an attitude which we take up towards the totality of existence. Now there are many different attitudes with which we may face existence. We may meet it with a question, as we do in asking what it is, what is the universe and what are we as parts of the universe. We may endeavour to get to know the universe, and in some mysterious way we do succeed to some extent in understanding it, as a general system of physical and mental forces. Or again, we may enjoy the universe as a work of art or a collection of works of art. We may appreciate the beauty of the scenery and other things about us. We may deplore ugliness which we find intermingled with that beauty. Thirdly, we may face existence from the point of view of duty, of what should be done, or more adequately, in the light of the idea of the Good. There are, then, these three general all-inclusive attitudes towards the universe : (1) a cognitive attitude, based upon the desire to know ; (2) an aesthetic attitude, based upon the desire to appreciate, to do full justice to the beauty of existence, and perhaps to play some little part in adding to that beauty, if the individual is an artist ; (3) an ethical attitude, based upon the desire to achieve the highest good possible in individual conduct.

Is there a further general attitude remaining over after these three attitudes have, I won't say received adequate satisfaction, but at any rate have discovered their appropriate fields of activity ? There seems to be such a field in the experience of personal relationship towards the universe as that upon which we completely depend. That is, there is an attitude of complete dependence upon the universe which is distinct from the cognitive, aesthetical, and ethical attitudes. This attitude was first singled out by Schleiermacher as the essential element in the religious conscious-ness. But if we analyse the situation psychologically, we find that there are other forms of experience in this attitude besides the experience of complete dependence, and these additional forms of experience have been well analysed and described by Professor Rudolf Otto in his recent book, " The Idea of the Holy " (" Das Heilige "). He shows very clearly that the feeling of dependence which is characteristic of the religious attitude is not one of merely causal dependence, not the experience of being a link in a series of causal processes, just a link on the chain of causation, but something still more thorough-going, the experience of what he calls creature-hood, that " It is God that hath made us and not we ourselves." We have been made by Him and so we are completely dependent upon Him in that sense, made by Him and therefore entirely in His power. And then there are the further feelings called out in our mind by that idea, the feeling of His infinite power, the feeling of the tremendous, of complete otherness, something entirely different from ourselves, the feeling of mysteriousness, of majesty, and of fascination in which fear and attraction are blended.

I am taking this particular line of approach to the problem, because it seems to me that in this way one can avoid so much of the arguing in a circle that is to be found in the historical approach, which is the usual so-called scientific approach to the question of the religious sentiment. Usually, we find introductory chapters on lower forms of religious observance, and we have explained to us how, in the course of evolution, there must have been a pre-religious state in which magic figured largely. In magic the individual attempted to get his own way with the powers around him by spells and incantations, and then later, as a result of failure, relative or absolute, of these spells, the individual turned from the attitude of magic to the attitude of prayer or supplication, and at the same time passed from polytheism to a form of monotheism. Along this line of thought, according to this natural history of religion, one is given the impression that the higher forms of religious feeling and religious insight are simply products of lower forms of mental activity : religion has grown out of forms of consciousness that could not themselves be called religious. In a similar way, attempts have been made to explain knowledge as a development out of mental processes that are not themselves knowledge, the sense of duty as a development out of simpler mental processes not themselves involving the feeling of obligation, the appreciation of beauty as a development out of forms of mental experience not themselves involving beauty, but merely sensations of pleasure and displeasure. Such an approach to the problem of religion is inadequate, if not positively misleading. In considering the subject, we need to take a broader view. At the commencement, at any rate, we must start from a philosophical outlook rather than a merely psychological one. What is first in philosophy is last in science.

For the merely psychologically minded, progress in the science of knowledge, and in the other mental sciences too, might be presumed to mean a greater and greater restriction of the field of religion, and to some minds, at any rate, an ultimate explaining away of religious experience. It was fear that in the beginning of things created the gods, and through knowledge the scope of that fear has been ever more and more reduced. But what has really happened is rather this. Starting with a general attitude towards life, in which these various values of experience were not distinct from one another, where science and religion, ethics and aesthetics, were all mingled together, the development of knowledge and civilisation has brought about a gradual separating out of these attitudes—each attitude, as I said at the beginning, has achieved its own general sphere of reference and of fact—and yet we find, after the claims of what may be called the profane sciences have been met, that there is something left over—namely, the distinctively religious experience itself.

It is true that this religious experience has been specially closely associated with ethical experience in the course of mental development in the individual as well as in the race ; forms of worship and religious appreciation have been linked up more and more closely with moral valuations, so that in the higher religions it is impossible to think away moral predicates from the conception of the Divine. Yet there remain non-rational in addition to these rational moral predicates, characteristics of the Divine which we can merely indicate in words—non-rational types of feeling, such as the feeling of dependence, of otherness, of the mysterious, the tremendous, etc., already referred to. These have their lower as well as their higher forms. In lower forms they appear in various species of superstition, fear of ghosts, the feeling of uncanniness, the otherness of the miraculous or the supernatural. These feelings gradually alter under the influence of increased knowledge, but do not disappear entirely. They are purified and pass from a lower to a higher form, and so in spite of all the progress of scientific thought there remains this particular mental attitude which has been called by Professor Otto the " numinous," (from the Latin word *numen*, divinity), and he claims, and I think rightly, that in this attitude we have a definite form of experience and a definite way of experiencing reality ; not just a feeling that may vary from one person to another, that may come and go and perhaps disappear entirely with further mental development, but a way of experiencing reality on the same level with the cognitive attitude—the attitude of knowing reality—and the other attitudes which I have enumerated. The task of Psychology is partly to do full justice to this mental attitude by analysing it in as detailed a way as possible, partly to link it up with other forms of experience not generally recognised as religious.

A great deal of work has been done by the method of the questionnaire, in which the investigator sends out a series of questions about their religious feelings to a large number of people. One of the first to adopt this course was Professor Starbuck in America, and in the first great book on the psychology of religion, by Professor William James, Professor Starbuck's results were largely used. James here marshals the evidence, and sums up the characteristics of the religious life (independently of the discrepancies of creed) as including the following beliefs : " (1) That the visible world is part of a more spiritual universe from which it draws its chief significance ; (2) That unison or harmonious relation with that higher universe is our true end ; (3) That prayer or inner communion with the spirit thereof—be that spirit ' God ' or ' law '—is a process wherein work is really done, and spiritual energy flows in and produces effects, psychological or material, within the phenomenal world " (" Varieties of Religious Experience," p. 485).

It also becomes clear from the evidence that the phenomenon of *conversion* is a fundamental process in the religious life. Conversion may be defined as a change of general mental attitude from the merely naturalistic attitude towards life to a definitely spiritual attitude. The individual finds the world so full of strange and wonderful things that his mind is at first mainly occupied with getting to understand and appreciate it in a profane way, but he discovers that this is not sufficient to give him true happiness. In spite of his most earnest endeavours to adjust himself to his physical and social environment and to be true to an ethical ideal, a feeling of insufficiency weighs upon his mind, and produces depression from which he struggles to free himself. Peace may come in one way or another, and the process of passing from such a state of conflict and strain to a state of harmony and peace is the process of conversion. Among certain religious sects conversion is striven after along definite lines. The sense of insufficiency and sin is emphasised in the prospective convert. He is encouraged to struggle hard against his difficulties, to face them, and to realise them as fully as possible. He passes through a state of intense mental anguish, and then suddenly reaches a state of calm and peace. But in another class of individuals who take religious life just as seriously, such sudden conversion may not occur. Yet I do not think that we can say that conversion as such is absent, and I am inclined to believe that conversion in its general sense of turning from the merely naturalistic attitude towards life to a more spiritual attitude occurs in every case, but in many cases it may occur slowly and gradually, as a process of healthy growth. Cases of sudden conversion are often to some extent pathological. I do not mean that the conversion itself is pathological, but that the conditions and consequences may be in part pathological. The strain and stress of mental conflict may produce temporary disturbance of functioning of the nervous system, and in that way give rise to experiences that are not in every respect normal religious experiences ;— depression, hallucinations, and even temporary delusions that show very close resemblance to the depression, hallucinations, and delusions met with in mental patients quite independently of their religious life.

The feeling of peace and relief may be partly explained on the psychological side as a transition from a state of division of the self, where one part of the self is fighting against another, to a state of unification and harmony. In this transition from division to unification a certain amount of energy is liberated which as a surplus allows all mental processes to occur more readily and freely, producing a feeling of happiness. This is an extremely crude theory, in terms of physiology and psychology, and certainly cannot be accepted as a fully adequate account of the process. The truth is that, so long as we speak merely as psychologists, we are tending to leave out the truly religious attitude altogether. Again, I can only illustrate by the analogy of knowledge. So far as we treat knowledge psychologically, we describe what goes on in the individual mind as a sequence of individual processes which if taken by itself would actually explain away knowledge. It would leave us without that conviction of the *validity* of our knowledge which is such an essential part of it. And so it is with religious experience. Psychologically, in the very effort that we make to describe religious experience as a sequence of mental processes in the individual's mind, we are invalidating that experience. We might, indeed, say that we are making an experiment, we are seeing how far we *can* explain the religious experience of the individual in terms of that individual's own antecedent experience without reference to anything beyond, that we are for the time being putting aside transcendence, because directly we assume that the individual is in touch with an existence outside him, we are passing beyond psychology. All that psychology does is to describe as accurately and fully as possible what goes on in his mind.

Moreover, psychology, like other sciences, is committed to the principle of parsimony, the principle of "Occam's razor," to use as few hypotheses as possible and to explain experience as fully as possible in terms of the most general hypotheses ; and this brings me to the use made of the doctrine of the subconscious or subliminal self, and in more recent years to the doctrine of the unconscious, to explain or explain away religious experience. Following up the hints of resemblance of certain startling religious experiences to certain pathological experiences, the attempt was made by James to fill up the gap, or to soften down the suddenness of the transition in the individual mind from the state of depression and sinfulness to a state of redemption, by an appeal to processes assumed to go on below the threshold of consciousness, in the subliminal. In the case of sudden conversion, for example, the theory was that the individual's consciousness seemed to remain on a merely naturalistic plane of existence, with a naturalistic outlook on life ; in the depths of his mind, however, a change was going on, other considerations were being weighed, other motives were getting their way, a subsidiary self was being developed, a set of mental tendencies which gained in strength and at last broke through into consciousness, and just before breaking through produced a feeling of intense strain and depression. When, however, it had broken through, it was able to combine with what it found there, modifying it, transforming it entirely, so that the individual felt a new man, as if he were born again. James himself goes further, and suggests that it may well be that the individual conscious mind comes into relation with the Deity through the intermediation of the subconscious mind. The changes in the conscious mind, in the direction of a more satisfactory religious attitude, may be produced through the intermediation of the subconscious, and in this way prayer may receive its answer. Influences may reach us through the dreamy subliminal which in the hubbub of waking life might pass us by.

From the scientific point of view, one would criticise such a theory as this, because it is not thorough-going enough. If you bring in the conception of the subliminal, and use it as an hypothesis, it is your duty as scientists to press that hypothesis to the utmost. Although James did not do this, it has been done by later writers, and in modern times we find a number of enthusiastic psychologists who look to the unconscious for an explanation of all these phenomena, but who, one cannot help feeling, have at the back of their minds the idea that they can only truly rely upon religious experience if it proves recalcitrant to this method. On the one hand, they will reject the supernatural, in the sense of the belief in a spiritual universe as distinct from the ordinary universe in space and time, because all the possibilities of explanation in terms of what goes on in the individual mind have not been exhausted, and yet, on the other hand, they are quite certain that these possibilities of explanation will never be exhausted. To all intents and purposes they are sceptics with regard to the validity of religious experience. The present situation of the psychology of religion is very similar to the situation as regards knowledge at the time when Locke, Berkeley, and Hume were writing. They were endeavouring to get to know what knowledge meant, their aim was to understand knowledge, to know about human understanding, but they used a predominantly psychological method, and although that psychological method increased their knowledge of psychology, it only made the central problem of knowledge more apparent, and it remained for Kant to show how completely they had failed to do justice to the science of knowledge. In the same way, at the present day and during the last twenty years, psychologists have approached the question of the validity of religious experience along psychological lines, not always realising that, by the very method they have adopted, they are challenging or denying that validity. In other words, just as psychology as such cannot do justice to the validity of knowledge, psychology cannot do justice to the validity of religion. Of course, it is open to every one to pass beyond the psychological to the philosophical line of explanation, and it is just as essential to do that in the problem of religion as it is in the problems of ethics, aesthetics, and epistemology.

Having emphasised this side of the question, we can with a clearer conscience proceed to apply psychological methods and observations to religious experience, although at every step in our argument we shall find it necessary to supplement psychology with philosophy. I am thinking at the moment of the attempts made by certain members of the psycho-analytic school to explain away the main facts of the Christian religion in terms of concepts borrowed from pathological psychology. One continental writer, who does not himself belong to the Christian faith, explains the central or main tenets of the Christian doctrine in terms of "projection" and "regression." He contends that the Christian attitude towards life is an infantile attitude that arises as a result of the individual's complete failure to grapple with the mystery of exist- ence. The individual tries to face the facts of reality, fails, and regresses towards more infantile modes of adaptation. Not being able to see adequate security among the forces of nature around him, he steps back to the mental attitude he had when a young child, of implicit faith in the power and goodness of his parents, in the modified form of a belief in a beneficent Deity. His belief in the Divine is simply this infantile feeling, which may surge up even in spite of himself. Again, his intense desire to conserve or preserve his values, logical, ethical, and aesthetical, all those things that make life for him worth living, may be so strong that it pro- duces a sort of hallucinatory fulfilment. It produces a feeling in him that it is fulfilled, that everything is all right, that we are safe in God's hands. Just to illustrate the kind of explanation proffered nowadays, we may mention that another psycho-analyst undertakes to explain the feeling of original sin in terms of the Oedipus complex. The individual has a bad conscience because in his childhood he felt a strong affection for one of his parents, and hatred and jealousy towards the other, which he repressed, and, as a result of repression, there arose feelings of sympathy and bad conscience. These were projected outwards and formed the basis of the systematic doctrines of the Fatherhood of God, the Atonement, etc.[1]

We can meet these arguments in two ways : one theoretical and the other practical. Theoretically, we can say that they are guilty of what Aristotle called a μετάβασις εἰς ἄλλο γένος,— the fallacy of explaining the facts of one science in terms of the concepts of another—of explaining the normal mind in terms of the abnormal, without first giving an adequate theory of the distinction between normal and abnormal. An analogous situation exists in the neighbouring science of physiology. No one would explain physiological change in terms of pathology. Physiology benefits by knowledge gained from pathology. Pathology also clearly gains enormously from the knowledge of physiology. But the two sciences are quite distinct. Clearly pathology is in the main subsidiary to physiology. The second line of attack is the more satisfactory one of actual experience. According to one's experiences of the pathological processes of projection and regression and the influence of the Oedipus complex in a patient, these are usually diminished or eliminated by a course of psycho-analysis. If, therefore, the typical religious attitude towards life is explicable in these terms, the religious consciousness would be altered by analysis in the direction of elimination. One would expect, according to this theory, that deep analysis would leave the patient less religious than he was before. My own experience has been the exact opposite of this. After an analysis (for scientific purposes) by a leading psycho-analyst extending over ninety-two hours, my religious convictions were stronger than before, not weaker. The analysis had indeed a purifying effect upon my religious feelings, freeing them from much that was merely infantile and supported by sentimental associations or historical accidents. But the ultimate result has been that I have become more convinced than ever that religion is the most important thing in life and that it is essential to mental health. The need of forms and ceremonies is another matter, far less fundamental. In many patients whom I have myself analysed I have found a similar result. Although mere

---

[1] Although psychological factors of this kind, among others may contribute their share to crude religious emotion, to use them to explain away the essential characteristics of religious experience would be to " pour away the baby with the bath-water."

emotionalism and religiosity is diminished, the essentially religious outlook on life remains unimpaired.

2. SUGGESTION AND FAITH

We may now consider in more detail the psychological factors at work in bringing us into relationship with the Divine, and there occurs at once to the therapeutic mind the problem of the general nature of faith, and its relation to suggestion. The modern psycho-therapeutic doctrine of suggestion was a direct development from the rather extreme views of Christian Scientists of thirty or forty years ago. So-called faith cures were produced by Mrs. Eddy and her followers supported by the enthusiasm they had for this line of thought, and many medical and other psychologists who investigated the matter came to the conclusion that, for the most part, the cures could be explained in terms of suggestion. It therefore behoves us to understand as clearly as possible what is meant by suggestion and the theory and practice of suggestion-treatment, and the bearing it has upon faith and other forms of religious experience. Suggestion may be defined as the acceptance of an idea by the mind, especially by the so-called subconscious mind, independently of adequate logical grounds for such acceptance. It is an instance of ideo-motor action. The idea is placed before the mind, or rather, aroused vividly in the mind, when the mind is in a state where opposing and conflicting ideas have no chance of making themselves felt ; whereupon this implanted or elicited idea tends to realise itself. It takes a certain time in doing so, known as the " latent period." In a simple case of suggestion, then, the mind of the individual is in a passive state, free from contradictory or conflicting ideas, receptive, ready to allow the suggested idea or ideas to be aroused in full force. The idea has a tendency to pass over into action, to bring about its own realisation, in so far as it is not interfered with by conflicting ideas. Favouring factors in suggestion are a state of general passivity, muscular as well as sensory, combined with concentration upon some neutral idea. We find in psycho-therapeutic practice, when we wish to produce benefit by suggestion, that our best results are obtained if we get the patient into a passive state, when the muscles are relaxed, a state not so much of attention as what is called by Baudouin *contention*—a state of concentration without effort. We eliminate effort by requesting the patient to relax his muscles, and we encourage concentration by giving him something to concentrate upon. The mind, although passive, is not in a state of distraction. It is narrowed down upon some very general idea, preferably upon the idea of sleep, and if in that state an idea is aroused in the mind, an idea of some change in the patient's bodily and mental condition, that idea tends to realise itself to its utmost possible extent. A convenient time for giving suggestion is before rest at night. At that time the patient has relinquished all his interests in matters of the day, he is more able to get really peaceful and relaxed, and the background of his mind, the so-called subconscious mind, is more accessible to outside influences. In referring to the subconscious in this way, one seems to be speaking rather metaphorically, as if the subconscious were a sort of occult force. It is not exactly that, but rather a class concept, including mental tendencies which are not clearly present in consciousness. Indeed, it is those tendencies not clearly present in consciousness that are most important in suggestion treatment, because those which are clearly conscious have appropriate ideas linking them up with other conscious tendencies. The mind, so far as it is conscious, is alert and acts therefore according to more or less rational motives. Suggestion to the conscious mind has usually little effect—it is transitory if it takes effect at all. Persuasion, which uses rational arguments, is the more appropriate and effective influence in this sphere. Suggestion is a kind of affirmation, it is rightly addressed to the subconscious, to the fundamental tendencies of the mind that are not directly represented in consciousness.

The question then arises, What is the relation between suggestion, as we have thus explained it, and faith ? The following example may throw some preliminary light upon this problem. A year or two ago I was treating a boy of thirteen for some disturbing nervous symptoms which interfered with his life at school, and which he was most anxious to get rid of, by means of suggestion (after a preliminary analysis of the conditions in which the illness began). The first two or three hours of suggestion treatment, during each of which he lay passive on a couch, receiving suggestions from me every five minutes or so, seemed to produce very little if any effect, till about the fourth treatment, when he suddenly burst into tears, and said in a voice charged with emotion, " Now I really do believe that it is going to be all right, I feel absolutely certain about it." From that moment his symptom (enuresis) disappeared, and he became permanently well. In this case we have an interesting illustration of a transition from suggestion to a state of faith. In suggestion the mind is passively stimulated to produce an idea, and then this idea in its turn realises itself, because it has no competitors, it works automatically, by its own momentum as it were. In faith, on the other hand, one finds a state of mind which is essentially active ; as William James said, there is a will to believe, it is a definite assertion or affirmation of an active mind. The whole mind is active and the experience is accompanied by an emotion which is something of the nature of volition, a determination to give oneself up completely to the idea for some reason or other. It may be just in order to get rid of a symptom, or for the sake of higher development of the mind—a belief in the possibility of such higher development.

Intermediate between suggestion and faith is auto-suggestion, where the individual gives suggestions to himself. In auto-suggestion he is passive, he thinks of sleep, he gets for a moment or two into a comatose state, almost free from all activity and yet in a state of concentration, and then, in some wonderful way, he is able to present to himself the idea, or bring up before himself the idea, of what he wants, the change he wishes to bring about in his mind or body. He, as we say, affirms this idea to himself, that *e.g.* at night he will sleep well, and wake up feeling much better and free from the stammer, or nervousness, or difficulty of concentration, or whatever it may be, that he will be able to concentrate well, to remember well, to feel cheerful and happy ; and experience shows us that beneficial results definitely follow. By perseverance in the use of this method the patient can often transform his whole outlook upon life. I look upon auto-suggestion as a bad term. It is really something more akin to faith than to suggestion. It is the cultivation of a special active attitude of mind, an assertion of health and of faith in its possibility—a particular kind of healthy-mindedness. If you treat yourself by auto-suggestion, you get benefit so far as you can make it depend upon the extent to which you can really believe and affirm to yourself the gospel of health, that health is more real than disease ; that so far as the will of God goes, He wills health rather than disease. With such a crude belief results actually do follow.

In dealing with these problems, which are, of course, really extremely difficult, it is necessary to take facts first and look for theories afterwards. We can say as a fact that suggestion produces results, that auto-suggestion produces still more permanent results, and that, if genuine faith is aroused, the most astounding results of a permanent nature may be produced. In this sequence, looked at psychologically, we see that the transition is from passivity to activity, that faith as such is a form of volition, and that auto-suggestion as such is not in conflict with volition, as M. Coué and his followers have wrongly contended ; it is simply a completion of volition. The so-called law of reversed effort, which Coué and his followers have made famous, may be expressed in this form: "When the will and the imagination are in conflict, the imagination always wins." The conclusion would seem to be that imagination is stronger than will ; but in the French the word *vouloir*, though sometimes meaning will, often means wish, and, so far as one can make out in Coué's own brief writings, he is thinking really of wish rather than of will. If there is a wish on the one hand and imagination on the other, the imagination-result is more likely to occur than the wish-result ; indeed, the situation is one of frustrated will. The process of wishing is on the road towards volition or will, but it has not yet reached the final stage of volition. In that transition from wishing to willing or volition, the imagination, lighted up and intensified by fear or some other disturbing emotion, slips in as it were, gets the lead, and prevents the wish becoming the will. Imagination then wins because the will has not been completed. On the other hand, that which has been called auto-suggestion, and which I think is a definite attitude of mind akin to faith, is a process of complete volition, turning mere wish into will by adequate control of the imagination.

This will become clear if we take an example. A patient suffering from a fear of open spaces, called technically agoraphobia, may be unable to walk a hundred yards down a wide street by himself or to cross it. As soon as he attempts to start on his journey, his heart palpitates, he becomes breathless, tends to hug the wall, becomes less and less able to move, is glued to the spot, and has to give up and return home. Such a patient may be encouraged by his relatives and friends to pull himself together and to make a real effort, and may be told that if he makes an adequate effort he will succeed in getting over this difficulty. But he finds, on the contrary, that the greater the effort the worse the situation becomes, the harder he tries the less he succeeds. This seems to be a situation akin to that summed up in Coué's law of reversed effort ; on the one side, the will to walk alone, on the other side, the imagination, the fear, that he will not succeed ; and in this conflict imagination wins. But, on looking more closely into the situation, one realises that there is no complete volition here. The patient is ill, his mental processes do not enable him to will completely in this particular situation. Why, is a matter to be discovered in other ways, through deep analysis— deep analysis will show why he is unable to will to cross the street. In his attempt to will to walk along or to cross the street, the feeling of effort becomes more vivid and more intense, but it remains a mere wish or suggestion. Opposed to this effortful wish to cross the street, one finds the idea or suggestion of failure accompanied by the fear of failure. In this conflict the suggestion of failure accompanied by the emotion of fear ob- viously will win, as against the suggestion, unaccompanied by any strong emotion, that he will cross the street. This so-called law of reversed effort is thus merely a simple illustration of conflict between one suggestion and another, or between one " imagina- tion " and another. If this is so, what do we mean by will ? We mean a wish or desire, accompanied by the judgement, affirmation, or belief that we shall fulfil the desire from our own resources, so far as in us lies,—that we shall realise the desire because we desire it. In cases like that of agoraphobia [1] the object of the psycho- therapist is to train the patient's will, so that one disagrees with Coué, and, instead of saying that a re-education of the will is useless, one rather points out that the patient has not achieved complete volition in this situation, and that he has to learn to will, after first discovering the cause of his incomplete volition by self- analysis or (much more effectively) by deep analysis carried out by the physician. In these cases mere suggestion as a passive thing is extremely ineffective. One may produce temporary alleviation by calming the patient's mind, and discouraging spasmodic effort and diminishing the tendency to intensify the symptoms by effort ; but the patient quickly falls back to the original state, because the cause is still there. The truth is, he has no faith in that particular treatment, nor in his power to cross the street, and there is reason for this lack of faith. In some cases one finds deep down in the

---

[1] So far as the agoraphobia is a manifestation of " anxiety neurosis " it is physically caused, and is to be treated by advice on sex-hygiene.

mind a fear of fainting ; he has fainted on some previous occasion, and so he has lost confidence in himself ; he feels he will be right away from all aid, so the mere sight of an open space arouses this subconscious idea, his heart beats rapidly, and the initial stages of a fainting attack set in with this feeling of anxiety, a feeling that he is " glued to the spot."

If, then, suggestion and faith are distinct, in what way can we indicate their relationship more clearly than we have already done ? From the theoretical point of view, I think we can say that suggestion is ultimately always dependent upon some form or other of faith, and not conversely. The patient may not be conscious of faith, he may respond to suggestion, and suggestion may be given in a mechanical way. He may have no conscious faith in the method, but he finds that the method benefits him. If one analyses him, however, one discovers that in his subconscious mind there is faith. The relationship between suggestion and such a general (often subconscious) background of faith is similar to that between the empirical investigation of nature by scientists, and the general metaphysical principle of the uniformity of nature, within the domain of knowledge. A scientist would not be able to make a single step forward in his investigations or theories about the universe unless he had that belief in the uniformity of nature—that A remains A unless and until it is altered by some other factor, that if A becomes B there is some reason for it in the intrusion of further factors. Unless he holds this metaphysical belief in the uniformity of nature, he is unable to form hypotheses, and by their means advance in scientific knowledge. His individual generalisations from facts of experience are based upon this belief. Similarly an individual benefits by suggestion treatment along special lines because of his more general belief or faith in the universe. The individual may not consciously hold such a faith, but somewhere in his mind there is that faith, the belief in a friendliness somewhere, and if he is completely lacking in it, then he will be completely inaccessible to therapeutic suggestion. Actually, in the case of everyone, there is the tendency, the readiness to believe in friendliness outside—based upon early childhood experiences and inherited tendencies. This again brings us back from the point of view of suggestion and faith to the more fundamental problem of " deep " analysis.

Some psycho-analysts consider that the facts of suggestion, of faith-healing, etc., are explicable in terms of early experiences within the bosom of the family, in terms of the Oedipus complex and psychological reactions thereto. The theory is a very complicated one and cannot be dealt with in detail here.[1] One may, however, consider it in its most formal aspect, and point out that the whole question of faith in terms of infantile experience is based upon an original postulate. It is not necessarily based upon facts at all ; facts may later on be discovered to support the special details of the theory, but the general theory has its real basis elsewhere, in the *postulate* that whatever is in the mind can be explained in terms of previous experience. It is the postulate of determinism. Some psychologists may think that determinism is on the road to being proved through the further development of psychology. That, of course, is reasoning in a circle, because what we do in psychology is to look for causes of the various effects that we see, on the basis of the postulate of determinism. In philosophy there is the fundamental principle of sufficient reason (Leibnitz), the principle that there is always a sufficient reason why anything should happen rather than not happen. Determinism looks for the sufficient reason in any particular case always in what has already occurred. We therefore know beforehand, however rapidly deep analysis may develop—and it is developing rapidly every year now—we know beforehand that it will seem to restrict ever more and more the doctrine of the freedom of the will. The further psychology advances, the less will the idea of freedom, or of spontaneity of the mind, be apparent. But the very fact that we can predict this shows that it is not the result of psychological advance. Psychology cannot either prove or disprove determinism.

More cautious psychologists adopt the doctrine of self-determinism. They must adopt some form of determinism if they are to be psychologists at all, in order to link up and co-ordinate mental events within a wider system. But they take as their system not the antecedent processes of the mind only, but the entire mind right up to the present moment. The test of a determinist doctrine is the power of prediction, and, in the case of mental process, prediction is impossible unless we know every moment of the person's life right up to the moment when the action which we are supposed to be predicting occurs. The act is then completely

[1] See especially S. Freud : *Totem and Tabu, Group Psychology and the Analysis of the Ego*, and *Das Ich und das Es*.

determined because it is determined by his entire self. This is a doctrine of self-determinism, rather than determinism, because it is determinism within a self which is growing, and which acts as a whole. What we mean by freedom is the power of the mind of the individual acting as a whole. A person is free and is acting freely when he is most himself in carrying out an action. The kind of action that to us seems impulsive action, where we feel out of ourselves, out of our mind, and we wonder later on however we could have done such a thing, such action is not free. So far as conduct is the outcome of the whole mind working in its unity, so far it is self-determined, and free in the only sense in which we can understand freedom.

Although one may seem to have deviated along another line of thought, and to have left the question of faith, it is of significance for the problem of faith, because faith is such an affirmation of the entire mind. Someone has defined faith as a readiness to trust and to follow the noblest hypothesis ; it is an act of self-assertion, one decides to be on the side of the angels, takes one's side in the battle of existence, for battle it is. Ideally at least, it should represent an attitude of the entire mind, but it may often be not so complete. It may often be rather a momentary mood, and so far as it is that, it may be followed by a relapse. Here the vexed question of spiritual healing arises. The process of spiritual healing is a process of arousing faith, the faith state, and that faith state may have different degrees of rationality which is the same thing as saying that it may extend over a smaller or larger area of the self, and if it is limited to a small part of the self, it may mislead the individual instead of helping him. One reason why many of us are very doubtful of the wisdom of spiritual-healing services is that, for many who attend such services, it is an appeal to superficial emotion and to primitive credulity. There is the tendency to intensify that hysterical condition of mind from which many of the patients are already suffering. In some cases there may be a disappearance of hysterical symptoms and apparent cure, but only at the expense of replacement by another symptom—namely, reliance upon a quasi-miraculous possibility, the expectation of getting something for nothing, as it were, of getting direct gifts without full appreciation of corresponding demands upon personality. Mass-suggestion may produce startling results of a temporary and superficial kind, but individual treatment is more likely to produce deep and lasting benefit.

The whole question of spiritual healing is one of extreme difficulty, and awaits further medical and psychological investigation. But among its more obvious dangers we cannot overlook the danger of intensifying the hysterical or the infantile attitude towards life that many neurotic patients have, and the danger of disappointment and of a set-back to their faith in the case of those who receive no benefit.

3 MYSTICISM

We now come to a consideration of what is probably the most important form of religious experience—namely, mystical experience—to which all other religious feelings seem to lead up. The mystical experience is an experience of apparently direct union with the Divine. It is a form of meditation which leads the soul up to divinity. In this mental state the person may lose the feeling of individuality, and may seem to pass beyond the limitations of space and time. When he endeavours to describe his experience he can only express it in negatives. He can say what the experience is not, but he is quite unable to say what it is. One of the greatest authorities on mysticism is Saint Theresa, and her own experience and general theory are summed up in that important book, " The Interior Castle," in which she describes various stages of union with the Divine. In almost every form of religion in the world we find similar experiences described, although there are individual differences. Leaving aside these differences, we find quite enough identity to convince us that, just as religious feeling itself is a special mental attitude towards life and a sort of knowledge of reality, so here in mysticism we have its central core, the most characteristic way in which our religious knowledge comes to us. If only it were universal, there would be no further trouble about the matter. Unfortunately, so many people protest that they are unable to verify the occurrence of mystical experience in themselves ; this is a serious difficulty in the way of its significance or validity, though not destroying its interest for psychology.

Before considering this matter further, it would be well to mention certain types of experience that are analogous to the mystical experience, but that otherwise are not regarded as of special religious value or importance. In the first place, there is the peculiar feeling of joy, exultation, or rapture that may accompany certain sensory experiences. Certain bars of music and phrases of poetry seem to have a quite irrational appeal that cannot be explained in terms of the actual associations of the sounds or meaning of the words, but apparently touch some hidden chord in the mind, and thereby stir the soul deeply. Muscular and kinaesthetic sensations sometimes arouse a similar feeling. Well-ordered muscular activity may often induce a feeling of unity with nature. On a beautiful spring morning, when away from one's fellow men in the fields, one may be suddenly overtaken with a feeling of the direct continuity of one's own life with the life of nature. One looks with different eyes upon the scenery and welcomes it as a part of one's self, or rather, as something infinitely greater than one's self in which one is merged. This feeling may be intensified in special circumstances, as *e.g.* when riding, in which no doubt sympathy with the horse as well as the muscular exercise play their part. We might perhaps explain these, often extremely pleasant, experiences as a sort of reversion to an earlier and more primitive form of consciousness, when we were less aware of our own individuality and its problems : when we were more in touch with the animals and plants around us, and felt our kinship with them more vividly. Since it is not an experience constantly present, when it does come it comes with a special vividness, as intensified pleasure, which is not surprising ; it is normal and healthy, not pathological. Communion is in general a healthy form of experience. It is the feeling of isolation from nature, animate and inanimate, which is the terrible thing, and which we find in such pronounced form among some of our mentally deranged patients.

Secondly, there are the mental states sometimes produced by anaesthetics—the so-called " anaesthetic revelation." Under the influence of alcohol, ether, chloroform, and especially of nitrous oxide gas, many people get extraordinary feelings of deepened insight into the meaning of things. They may come out of the anaesthetic with the conviction that they have solved the riddle of the universe, and suffer great disappointment because all they can find in their minds at the moment of awakening are some doggerel rhymes that have no significance whatever. Then again, a similar mystical experience can come over one in conditions of self-hypnosis. If one lies passive on a couch with the eyes closed and all voluntary muscles relaxed, and breathes slowly and deeply in order to increase that relaxation, one may feel oneself slipping away from the world of clear consciousness, losing the feeling of orientation and of sensitivity in the limbs. The body seems to be floating in the air, and later on one may feel that one does not possess a body at all. In this state, one seems to become depersonalised, as it were, absorbed in the " all," into the soul of the universe. One attains to what has been called cosmic consciousness.

Now can we find any identical factor in these various experiences ? In all except those accompanying muscular exercise, in the anaesthetic revelation, auto- and hetero-hypnosis, etc., one characteristic seems to be the abolition of the motor tendency. In a normal man who goes about his affairs with eyes wide open and mind alert, there is a definite adjustment of muscular activity to the needs of the situation. His muscles are tense and always ready to come into action, and his experience is essentially sensori-motor. It is probably this motor aspect of experience that intensifies the feeling of personality, and if it is brought into abeyance with anaesthetics or special artificial modes of relaxation, the sense of personality disappears with it. The individual is less conscious of the dividing lines between himself and the rest of the universe.

It is clear that, in mystical experiences proper, we ought to allow for the possible admixture of such experiences as these and discount them ; although it is more than doubtful whether we can say that all religious mystic experience should be explained in terms of such cruder experiences. Some scientists tend to criticise all these experiences as abnormal, because they involve a disturbance of the sensori-motor attitude towards life. But this would be to make a very great assumption, an assumption analogous to the one we have already discussed in connection with determinism. Such scientists map out a general system of explanation, and everything they find in that system they call scientific. Everything not explained in terms of that system they attempt to explain as pathological, and in calling it pathological they deny the validity or importance of it.

An alternative explanation would be the following : it is very obvious that experience, as we know it, occurs and comes to us under the forms of space and time, because we are embodied minds, because we are limited, finite parts of the universe, and yet we have in us powers that can in some way lift us beyond these limits. It seems quite clear that one such power is that of thought : another is the direct insight of aesthetic appreciation ; and religious experience in its mystical form may prove the greatest power of all in this direction. When, in the mystical experience, we have the feeling of timelessness, it is quite conceivable that we *are* passing beyond the limits of time, and proving, to ourselves at any rate, that time is appearance and not reality, and that immortality is not something we have to wait for at the end of this life, but something we can and do achieve in varying degrees while still living this life. That has been the view of leading philosophers throughout the ages. We find Aristotle urging his readers, ἐφ' ὅσον ἐνδέχεται ἀθανατίζειν, to be immortal as far as possible, even in this life.

Thus we come to the tremendous metaphysical problem of the reality of time, which is, perhaps, the greatest metaphysical problem of the present day, and especially important to our point of view of personality. So long as we consider time as one of the conditions of individual experience, we are tied down to a certain theory of personality, which may easily be the wrong one. All psychological theories of personality, of course, are of this nature, and, to a great extent, they are for that reason rather depressing, because they emphasise the limits that we are all aware of. But in emphasising these limits they tend to make them much more complete and ultimate than they really are for us. Again, if we take physiological modes of thought in considering psychological problems, we are impressed by rates of rhythm of physiological processes. As physiological psychologists we may be impressed by experiments which show that estimation of time is most accurate with a certain rhythm and less accurate with shorter or longer rhythms, or again, that experience of succession has a lower limit of causation. In the background there may be the unspoken but fallacious assumption that the experience of succession is the same as, or at least runs parallel with, a succession of experiences; and again the further assumption that a succession of experiences runs parallel with a succession of physiological changes somewhere or other in the organism. It is easy to show by metaphysical argument that the conception of time as something ultimately real leads us to definite antinomies or contradictions, from which we cannot escape unless we agree to regard time as appearance and not reality. But we still find it extremely difficult to understand most aspects of experience, unless we do regard time as real. If we consider experience in detail, we see how much time contributes to the quality of that experience. So impressed was Bergson by this fact that he has taken time as the very stuff of which reality is made. He speaks of *durée réelle* as something which is ultimate, although he regards the time of mathematical physics and the other physical sciences as spatialised time. Of course, many of the goods and pleasures of life seem to be bound up with the time function. Time is essential even to such a good as the ethical good, the good will. A good action is one which is definitely and deliberately intended and carried out, and can only be carried out in the course of time. If one imagines time transcended, it is difficult to imagine any strictly moral action, or indeed any action at all. It is difficult to attribute the characteristics of morality, which is one of our three general values, to a timeless experience. In transcending time, one seems to transcend morality as such. In aesthetic experience timelessness seems to be more possible. When we enjoy a picture, for the time being we feel ourselves out of time ; its artistic meaning is timeless. But then when we turn to music, another form of art, time appears to be of its essence, though even here we should not be too certain of this. We know there is an anecdote about Mozart, who, in speaking of one of his compositions, explains how he first had it in his head before he wrote it down. He heard all the notes together—*zusammen.* That was a wonderful experience, he said, the like of which he never heard again. In music there is a degree of transcendence of time : chords occur one after another, yet they have to combine in some way to give a feeling of harmony and melody, and one is conscious of what has gone before and what is about to come. One sees more meaning in the production the second time than the first, because one knows what is coming. So that one might say, with regard to music, that although the possibility of musical experience, and of the training of the ear, is bound up with the conditions of temporal sequence, yet the ultimate outcome when the trained ear appreciates the true inward meaning of music is something that is already on the way towards transcendence of time. As regards truth, it is quite clear that time is transcended—once true, always true. Although the proving to a class of school-boys that the three angles of a triangle are equal to two right angles takes time, and individual boys take varying lengths of time in gaining an adequate insight into that geometrical truth, once they have acquired the truth the insight is beyond time. Moreover, it was true before they began to consider it, and it will remain true after they have ceased to think of it. Truth, as truth, is certainly beyond time.

Finally, as regards religious experience, one feels that it is essential to this experience, if to any, that it should be beyond time. Although it may be conditioned by time, in that one gains a deeper and deeper insight into its truths through an experience that comes to one in the course of days, yet the experience itself takes us out of time and enables us to attain to a mystic attitude towards the universe, beyond any opportunism that acceptance of the reality of time can give. If we assume that time is completely real for us, that we are bound down in a time process, and that we do not transcend it at all, then our ultimate outlook upon reality is very depressing and unmeaning. Despite temporary improvements in the conditions of human life and the advance of physical science, this earth will eventually become uninhabitable, degeneration will come sooner or later to the race, to the physical side of things, so that in terms of matter and material change and temporal process there seems little room for ultimate hope. The life of the human race would really be " a tale told by an idiot, full of sound and fury, signifying nothing." But all the meaning we find in life is on the way towards a transcending of time. When we look towards a future life, we look not so much towards a life at some future time that some enthusiasts would like to prove and even describe for us, but to a life eternal, in which we pass beyond the conditions of the merely material, which of course is the temporal and spatial. We mean by matter something such that two portions of it cannot be in the same place at the same time—that is probably the best definition of matter which we can give. We can only think of matter in terms of space and time.

It is very significant that these various experiences that appear to transcend time, and also perhaps space, accompanied by disorientation in space and time, bring with them a diminution of feeling of individuality, so that at the end it looks as if we shall have to dismiss individuality with other aspects of existence as appearance and not reality. It is very doubtful whether we shall be able to preserve individuality as an ultimate value in the scheme of things ; it is a stepping-stone, no doubt, and, as far as we can see of existence in this life, there is a parallel process of individuation and inter-relation going on, so that really great individuals, great person-alities, are those who have individualised their lives so that they are in closer communion with their fellows, rather than in isolation from them. In a way this is an absorption. The great statesman, the great man of action, the great scientist, is the person who is able to suppress his mere individuality in order that he may get a wider personality of the group or nation to which he belongs. The great statesman speaks for an entire nation, because he is able to understand the various needs of the individuals in it. He does not lose his personality thereby, he does not efface it, he makes it all the more real. On the other hand, the self-centred paranoiac who has to be shut up in an asylum is convinced of his own greatness, believes himself to be a reincarnation of Napoleon or of the Messiah, or even God himself, and, corresponding to his intense feeling of individuality and difference from others, we find a depressing bankruptcy in his mental make-up. The great scientist is he who keeps clear of fanaticism and crankiness by continuous moral effort, by effacing his own peculiarities, wishes, desires, and interests in the matter, in order to get as unbiased a view as possible of the facts. He has the greater task of effacing, not only the individuality of nationality, but of humanity itself, and yet in that process we cannot say that he is losing personality in the true sense of the word. Personality, then, ought to be distinguished from individuality. Individuality is a mere difference from others. Personality is a process of development, in which we have parallel processes of individuation and assimilation. The man of personality gives out to the world around him and also absorbs it in himself, identifying himself as far as possible with others and sympathising with their aims. Yet, in the end, even personality must go, because in the universe there is no room for merely separate persons. Ultimately there can only be one complete person, he who is completely self-sufficing, and he can only be completely self-sufficing if he has complete knowledge and power over his environment, and therefore he must extend throughout that environment, and must be the totality of Reality itself. The only complete person is the Absolute or God, and progress towards personality in individuals seems to be intellectual, along the path of reason. One can see it as a union, ever closer and deeper, with the spirit of the universe, as identification to a greater and greater extent with all that is highest in the universe, and that is the intellectual counterpart of what we mean by the mystical experience.

One might perhaps do more justice to this problem of the mystical by admitting that there is a lower and a higher form of mysticism. The lower form is on the plane of immediate feeling, unmediated by thought. Such is the experience of the athlete, the drug-addict, the devotee of self-hypnosis, the primitive artist in man. Here is an experience of direct union on a lower plane of feeling. Then thought discriminates, distinguishes subject from object, objects from one another, holds the mind apart from its object, and yet, in that process, links it up more and more closely with its object until, when its work is done as far as it can be done, again there arises a communion, a feeling that the subject-object relationship is being transcended, and this is the true, the highest mystical experience. It will include various types of experience. We will not identify it with religious mystical experience because we have already marked and separated that off from our other general attitudes towards the totality of things—the intellectual, the aesthetic, and the moral attitudes, and in each of these attitudes we find the higher form of mysticism. There remains the mysticism which may truly be called religious. But even that does not completely satisfy us, since we are left with four distinct things which we feel must in some way be unified. Actually, of course, they are unified in an all-inclusive experience, which is the real higher mystical experience, the mediation by thought of all the other attitudes, including the religious, so that just as the race began life in a primitive religious way, likewise at the end, after science and philosophy have done all that they can, the fundamental attitude is once more a religious attitude. An individual who is unable to get that attitude at all is to that extent incomplete. We sometimes find that such an individual is mentally sick, suffering from repressions which cut him off from it. With the removal of these repressions by analysis the experience may become once more possible to him.

It is only fair to mention here that one school of thought explains all these mystical experiences in terms of what is called Narcissism. In such experience there is a turning inwards of the mind upon itself, a drawing in of libido, a concentration of libido upon the self. An increase of Narcissism under certain conditions may bring with it a feeling of intense pleasure and of liberation, transcending time and space, although it is really a set-back, a regression, to an infantility of an extreme type. The actual evidence in support of so extreme a theory is quite inadequate, and against it may be set the general arguments of pp. 309, 318 above. But we should not overlook the rôle played by Narcissism in some forms of religious experience.[1]

[1] See, *e.g.*, Ernest Jones, " The Nature of Auto-suggestion," *British Journal of Medical Psychology*, vol. iii, 1923.

SCIENCE CHRISTIANITY AND MODERN CIVILISATION

BY CLEMENT C. J. WEBB

Oriel Professor of the Philosophy of the Christian Religion
in the University of Oxford.

CONTENTS

1. Secularity in the Modern World

It will be generally admitted that our civilisation is strikingly distinguished from that of earlier ages by what may be described as its essentially secular character. Religion, which was once regarded as the very foundation of the common life of men, is looked upon to-day as a matter left to individual choice or even caprice ; as something which does not, or at least ought not to, enter into political arrangements or affect the freedom of economic, scientific, artistic, or general social intercourse, whether of citizens of the same State among themselves, or of the citizens of one State with those of another. Religious communities may no doubt often be wealthy and powerful, the statesman or student of affairs will no doubt allow for religious affinities as an actual factor in his calculations, just as he will allow for ties of kinship between ruling families or for similarity of tastes or of educational tradition between politicians ; but it is scarcely regarded as permissible to appeal to them in justification of public action. The hesitation in recent years of British Governments to base their policy with respect to victims of Turkish oppression on any special sympathy due to a common Christianity is an obvious illustration of this point. Health, comfort, leisure, peace, the gratification of a taste for beauty or for knowledge, these are ends which it is taken for granted or all hands may reasonably be pursued, and the attainment whereof in any measure is considered a natural subject for congratulation. On the other hand, to presume an interest in religion is dangerous, and may easily lead to an offence against good manners ; and while a man or a woman may indeed choose to sacrifice such good things as I have enumerated for the sake of religion, we have no right to expect such a sacrifice from anyone who has not by some overt act (such as entering the ministry of some Christian Church) expressly declared himself concerned in the cause.

It is indeed easy enough to exaggerate the extent to which other centuries were truly " ages of faith," while underrating the influence of religion where its profession is no longer a point of social obligation ; to overlook, for example, the participation of medieval Christian and Moslem in a common inheritance of culture ; or again, to ignore the economic and political motives of movements which, like the Crusades or the Reformation, were superficially in the main religious.   Still, it is true that in the past religion was recognised as the chief principle alike of union and of division among men, and religious sanctions of conduct were everywhere acknowledged ; now, we are often as it were shy of referring to these, and cannot consistently with politeness assume their influence in the case of any unknown neighbour ; and to insist upon differences due to creed alone is to be immediately suspected of narrow-mindedness and bigotry.   Despite a widespread reaction in certain quarters—the natural sequel of the Great War—against the nationalism which occasioned it, self-denial for a patriotic end is not only generally approved but commonly expected, and its absence readily censured ; while self-denial for a religious end is regarded as purely optional, and in any extreme form is apt to be looked upon as eccentric or even morbid.

Those who have reflected upon the features of modern civilisation which I have just been endeavouring to describe, and who have learned from Hegel to expect the philosophy of any epoch to reproduce the outlines of the experience which the human spirit has lived through in the period now drawing to its close, will not be surprised at the appearance in our day of a system of thought—that of Signor Benedetto Croce—which denies to religion a place of its own among the " real kinds " of spiritual activity, and sees in it no more than an immature form of philosophy, destined ultimately to disappear when all that has been hitherto symbolically or imaginatively adumbrated in religion shall have received an adequate expression in the philosophical language appropriate to a more advanced stage of culture.

It is not because I underrate the importance of the issue thus raised that I content myself here with the bare mention of it, but because the plan of the present volume appears to imply a view different from that of Croce, and also more in accord with my own convictions ; a view which would allow to religion a permanent sphere of its own in human life, wherein it cannot be replaced by anything else, even by philosophy.   Indeed, if we accept what Hegel says in the context of the observation to which I have just referred, we shall expect the appearance of Croce's account of religion to herald the end of the period whose experience it reflects ;

and there are, perhaps, facts in the present situation of the world which point in the same direction. I have especially in mind the antagonism of Bolshevism to religion, as the grand obstacle to its destructive policy, on the ground of that very "transcendence ' of the earthly life, on account of which it is also, from a different point of view, dismissed by Croce as incompatible with a genuine comprehension of the meaning of history. For this suggests that religion, as commonly understood, is more intimately involved in the fabric of civilisation than is altogether consistent with our modern way of treating it as a matter of merely private concern.

But, if religion has thus a part to play in modern civilisation—which is itself essentially *one*, and which, through the continual improvement of the means of communication, is continually (if less rapidly than is sometimes supposed) carrying out a progressive unification of humanity—it is clear, both on general grounds and in view of the obvious and notorious hindrance to its efficacy presented by the internecine warfare existing between different religions and different versions of the same religion, that it cannot, if it is to play that part effectively, acquiesce in this warfare as necessary and permanent. The problem of the unity of religion thus becomes of supreme importance for all who recognise religion as an essential factor of human life.

2. A Universal Religion

There are fewer nowadays than in the seventeenth and eighteenth centuries who will be disposed to look for a solution of this problem in a call to dismiss as comparatively unimportant the distinctive features of the historical religions and to concentrate on certain great doctrines—such as those of God, Freedom, and Immortality—as the essentials of a religion natural to all men and defensible by arguments which, properly handled, would win universal assent. Our increased knowledge of the religion of primitive peoples on the one hand, and on the other the damaging criticisms brought by philosophers and men of science during the last two hundred years against the old " rational " theology with its " proofs of the existence of God," have antiquated a type of view which appeared reasonable to some of the greatest minds of an earlier age. It will probably now be considered a more hopeful task to inquire whether some one or other of the historical religions may not claim either, if rightly understood, to be already or at least to have the capacity of developing into a universal religion adequate to the needs of modern civilisation.   It is the purpose of the present essay to discuss the qualifications of Christianity for the discharge of this function.

The ideal of a universal religion may be presented under two distinct forms ; and, under each of these forms again, either after a pictorial or after what we may call a philosophical fashion.   The two forms in question are perhaps best represented by the points of view characteristic of Hinduism and of Christianity respectively, and may be discriminated by the different attitudes taken up by these two religious systems towards history.

To certain minds there is a singular attraction in the belief that there exists a secret tradition, handed on from age to age by adepts, equipped with an occult knowledge of spiritual powers which confers upon them the control of natural forces, who communicate so much as they think fit of the mysteries in their possession to different peoples at different periods under various symbols, the inner significance whereof is nevertheless always one and the same. This belief, sometimes entertained by scholars in the infancy of historical and philological criticism, now exercises its influence only over those who are, in this field at any rate, imperfectly educated ; but among these it is the backbone of doctrines of the kind that, passing under such names as Esoteric Buddhism, Theosophy, and the like, appeal to widely spread prejudices by their parade of out-of-the-way information, their comprehensive eclecticism, and their claim to bestow extraordinary powers upon their votaries.   It may, however, serve as a pictorial representation of a faith which commends itself to many who could not accept the hypothesis of a secret doctrine, literally understood.   To this faith Hinduism among the great historic religions of the world is perhaps the nearest akin. With its traditions of periodically repeated incarnations of the Deity in the most diverse forms, its ready acceptance of any and every local divinity or founder of a sect or ascetic devotee as a manifestation of God, its tolerance of symbols and legends of all kinds, however repulsive or even obscene, by the side of the most exalted flights of world-renouncing mysticism, it could perhaps more easily than any other faith develop, without loss of continuity with its past, into a universal religion, which would see in every creed a form, suited to some particular group or individual, of the universal aspiration after One Eternal Reality, to whose true being the infinitely various shapes in which it reveals itself to or conceals itself from men are all alike indifferent. It is not, however, upon the special possibilities of Hinduism as the nucleus of such a universal religion that I desire now to insist, so much as upon the fact that the ideal of a universal religion may be conceived in this form of a mutual agreement by the professors of all religions to acknowledge in all others an equally valid expression of an aspiration common to humanity and transcending all distinctions due to difference of historical context. The negative attitude towards the notion of historical development herein implied may be illustrated from the records of all the great religions, though it is perhaps peculiarly congenial to the temper of Hinduism.

In marked contrast with this form of the ideal of a universal religion stands that which is especially associated with Christianity. This, like the other, may be presented in a pictorial guise. It is so in the familiar scheme of a historical process which, starting from the creation of man, his temptation and fall, leads, through the selection and discipline of a peculiar people from whom the Redeemer should in the fullness of time proceed, to the redemption of the whole race by Jesus Christ, the incarnate son of God, and the offer of a share in this redemption to all mankind through the missionary activity of the Christian Church ; and culminates in the second coming of Jesus Christ in glory, to exercise the final judgement of God upon every individual human being. This scheme, which satisfied the imaginations of Augustine and of Dante, of Milton and of Pascal, it is not indeed possible for us to accept as more than a symbolic picture. It is too late in the day to rehabilitate the credit of the book of Genesis as a faithful record of the origin of the world and of mankind, or that of the New Testament eschatology as an accurate forecast of their future destiny. Nor can those whose conception of the extent and duration of the physical universe and of the process of evolution whereof human nature and human civilisation are the outcome has been moulded by the scientific discoveries of the last four centuries be content with an account of the world's history which presupposes the cosmology of an age in which these discoveries were undreamed of. But the traditional picture which has so long been associated with the Christian religion may suggest an ideal of a religion for all mankind, capable of being expressed in terms that do not presuppose obsolete beliefs, much in the same way as that in which the theosophical fancy of a secret doctrine suggests the ideal already described as congenial to the spirit of Hinduism. Such an ideal would take account of the actual history of religion as something more than a record of the infinitely various masks worn at different times and on different stages by the one eternal Actor, and would see in it rather the story of a single incarnation of God in humanity, culminating in the life and death of Jesus Christ and in His risen life, whereof the Christian Church is the organ and vehicle, with the capacity eventually to assimilate and incorporate the whole religious experience of mankind. But the further elaboration of the nature of this ideal must be postponed until we have considered an important preliminary objection which may be and has been brought against the whole conception of such a universal religion based upon historical Christianity.

The objection which I have in mind has been lately urged in a very striking manner by one of the most eminent of recent German theologians, the late Ernst Troeltsch, in a lecture written for delivery at Oxford, which, however, in consequence of his lamented death on the eve of departure for England, he never actually delivered.[1]

Some years previously, in a work called "*Die Absolutheit des Christenthums*," he had pointed out that the Christian religion was singular in claiming for itself an unqualified validity, not merely as, at least by implication, all religions initially do, in that they ignore other revelations than that which they themselves mediate, but as an essential article of its characteristic creed, in full view of the diversity of traditions among the peoples brought into mutual relations by modern civilisation. Subsequent consideration had led him to modify this view. He had been more and more impressed with the importance of the distinct *individuality* belonging to different civilisations and to the religions associated with them : and, while recognising that the supersession of inferior systems of culture by more advanced must involve a corresponding prevalence of the religious expression of the deepest convictions of the latter over that connected with the lower culture which it had superseded, he came to believe that we could not reasonably anticipate

---

[1] It has since been published in this country, along with other lectures, intended for other English audiences, in a volume entitled *Christian Thought, its History and Application* (University of London Press, 1923).

any replacement of one of the great historical religions by another. If the range of Islam and of Buddhism is limited by climatic and racial conditions, Christianity also must not be expected to make itself at home except in the atmosphere created by the tradition of Graeco-Roman culture. In fact a universal religion is an impossibility. The apparent unity of modern civilisation is after all in the main restricted to the material setting of human life. Even in the region of exact science men think less alike than we are sometimes inclined to suppose. And the further we go from this region of abstractions the greater the variety that we encounter. In politics, morality, art, religion, it is vain to pretend that all men are even on the road to unanimity. Nor is it in reality desirable that they should be. Individuality, whether in a single human being, a nation, or a school of thought, is what we value most of all ; and reverence for individuality encourages the cultivation of what is most distinctive and characteristic in each individual. What unites us is, as a celebrated jest of Goethe's reminds us, not what is *distinguished* but what is *common*. It is in the dissimilarity of the *dramatis personae* that the interest of the action lies, whether in private life or on the larger stage of universal history.

The conclusion to which Troeltsch thus came was strikingly similar to that reached a few years previously by an English philosopher whose thought, like his, had been concentrated on the problem of Individuality, and whose death, as it chanced, almost coincided with his own. " A number of great systems," writes the late Mr. Bernard Bosanquet, " very profoundly differing in life, mind, and institutions, existing side by side in peace and co-operation, and each contributing to the world an individual best, irreducible to terms of the others, this might be (I do not say, must be) a finer, higher thing than a single body with a homogeneous civilisation and a single communal will." But the two thinkers differed in their estimate of the place to be assigned to history in the philosophical interpretation of experience ; and Bosanquet, for whom in the last resort full individuality belongs to no finite system, but to the one eternal Absolute alone, would not, I think, have been ready to follow Troeltsch in holding not only culture, but truth itself to be, as he expressed it, " polymorphous." It must be allowed that this theory unquestionably suggests itself when once we have admitted that a variety of points of view in philosophy does not involve the erroneousness of all but one, but rather is necessary to the full exhibition of what is thus variously apprehended ; but, as expounded by Troeltsch, it certainly tends in the direction of a general scepticism, and, in respect of religion in particular, of the doctrine, already hinted at by Schleiermacher, of " one man, one religion." Thus Troeltsch himself not only denies to the great historical religions a common nature sufficient to render possible an ultimate synthesis, but, even within Christianity itself, can find in the religion of the Eastern Church no genuine identity with that of the Western ; so that the union of Christendom must have become for him as idle a dream as a universal religion for all mankind. In fact, his doctrine of polymorphous truth, although it had its origin in emphasis on the lessons of history, ends by completely dissolving the unity of the historical process.

If, however, we persist in regarding the history of civilisation as a unity, we come to recognise that the Christian Church occupies a central position in the development of religion, analogous to that occupied by Greek speculation in the development of science and philosophy, or to that occupied by the Roman Empire in the development of political organisations. It cannot seriously be disputed that the philosophical and scientific development which is central for universal civilisation is that which originated among the ancient Greeks. The existing political system of the world traces its descent from the Roman Empire. Even a people like the Japanese, with a civilisation that has grown up independently of Greek and Roman traditions, has therefore only been able to find its opportunity of participating in the task of universal civilisation by means of its entry as a national State into the community of commonwealth which inherits the traditions of the Roman Empire, and by means of the association of themselves by its men of science with the European " republic of letters " which traces its descent to Hellas. This must remain true, however vigorous the new blood thus infused into the old stock, and however great the part— even though it should ultimately be a predominant part—which Japan or any other Oriental nation may come to play in the future development whether of polity or of science. Like England or France or Germany before it, it will only have been enabled to play that part by incorporation with the stock whose roots are in the civilisation which sprang up in the centuries preceding the Christian era in the peninsulas that project into the Mediterranean Sea south of the Balkans and of the Alps respectively.

The case of religion appears to me to be parallel to those of science and of polity. I remember being much struck nearly twenty years ago by the confirmation of this view afforded by an article contributed to the *Hibbert Journal* of 1905 by a distinguished Japanese, Mr. Anesaki, who, though not himself a Christian, admitted that the religion of the future must be Christian, even though, having been profoundly modified by the accession of the Buddhist tradition, it might be in consequence very different from the Christianity of to-day. Probably even among those who look forward to the evolution of a universal religion which, owing to the abandonment of the distinctive dogmas of traditional Christianity, might seem no more like it than like others of the great historical religions at present existing, many would, notwithstanding, allow that they would expect this religion of the future to be, as an institution, and also in its modes of worship and in the general framework of its theology, continuous rather with Christianity than with any of the faiths which are now its rivals.

3. The Historical Element in Christianity

Now this prerogative position among the world's religions, as their historical centre, Christianity owes in great part to the peculiar importance attached by Christians, as compared with followers of other faiths, to the historical element in its doctrines. At the same time, to the very same characteristic of Christianity is due the fact that it is less readily universalised, not only than Hinduism with its characteristic indifference to history as mere appearance, but than Buddhism, which, despite its attachment to a historical personality, is rooted in the same unhistorical view of the world, and even than the faiths more closely akin by descent to itself; than Judaism, the more conservative offspring of its own parent religion, and than the more remotely related system of Islam. For, if Judaism can pass the bounds of the sacred people, it must also be able to dispense with the ritual law ; and its historical element would be reduced to the acknowledgment (in which Christians could join) that Israel has been, in the words of Athanasius, " a school of the knowledge of God to all nations." In Islam, indeed, the personality of Mohammed takes a more important place than that of any human teacher in Judaism ; but not comparable to that of Jesus in Christianity ; and it is the unique position assigned in the latter religion to its Founder—a position the abandonment of which would transform it beyond all recognition—which is the great obstacle to its absorption in a religion, such as Kant sketched in his " *Religion innerhalb der Grenzen der blossen Vernunft*," which should teach none but moral truths which appeal to the universal conscience of mankind, independently of all circumstances of time and place. Yet not only, as I have already said, is the more intimate implication of Christianity with history the ground of its prerogative position as the historical centre of the religious development of mankind, but (if I may quote words of my own written elsewhere) " the importance of the historical element in Christianity—and its importance there is greater than in any other religion—though it of course exposes it more than any other religion to that particular kind of doubt which we call historic, yet does not stamp it as a less philosophical religion than those which are not so much exposed to this sort of doubt. Rather it stamps it as a more philosophical. For the problem of the relation of abstract or universal significance to concrete or historical fact is a question in fighting shy of which philosophy does but refuse, so to say, to take its last hurdle, and surrenders the hope of winning its race. Religions which remain in the region of the universal and treat the individual and the historical as something illusory may seem to afford to the philosopher a quieter shelter than Christianity ; but only at the cost of abandoning the supreme venture to which, as a philosopher, he is committed—that of understanding not merely universal principles rapt away into a solemn rest ' above the smoke and stir of this dim spot which men call earth,' but the real world of historical individuals, in which alone these principles can live and move and have a genuine existence." [1]   The philosophy of the present day in particular, in Bergson, in Croce, in Troeltsch, in Alexander, in Whitehead—among all the differences which divide these thinkers from one another, and whatever their own quarrels with Christianity—will certainly, by insistence on duration, on history, on the indissoluble union of time with space, on the event as the true unit of reality, discourage him from being content to pay this price for an inglorious peace. A religion which does not see in history a mere symbol or illustration of eternal truths, but the genuine manifestation of God, is better adapted to

[1] *Philosophy and the Christian Religion*, Oxford, 1920, p. 17.

express the deepest convictions of an age like our own than one which cannot take history thus seriously.

But if the emphasis of Christianity on history is after all congenial rather than otherwise to the spirit of the present day, this would by no means qualify it to play an important part in the civilised world if it led to a mere uncritical adherence to historical tradition ; if it made Christians intent only on guarding a dogmatic deposit, and not on seeking to apply the principles of their creed to the changed and changing conditions of the human race. But one who looks below the surface of the religious life of our time, among ourselves at least, will find something very different from such mere conservatism. He will find a spirit of independent and active criticism of tradition alive among the very people who are most vigorously engaged in presenting Christianity to the world as a rule of life—for example, in the Student Christian Movement, and in the mission field. He will find a real advance toward mutual understanding between members of different Christian denominations, which has already made a reunion of the Churches on a scale scarcely dreamed of within living memory, although doubtless an ideal which no prudent person expects to see realised in the near future, still a matter of practical politics, in a sense in which it was not such in the youth of men who are not yet much past middle-age.

4. Christianity and Scientific Civilisation

A contrast especially notable to those interested in the general subject to the consideration of which this volume is devoted is that between the attitude to scientific views which challenge Christian tradition adopted by Christian theologians half a century ago and that of their successors to-day. No such outcry as that with which the theories of Darwin were received has been aroused by those of Freud, although the latter might well seem fraught with far more danger to the ordinary Christian's religious life than the former. On the contrary, the reception accorded by the religious world to the speculations of the psycho-analysts is chargeable rather with undue precipitation than with excessive suspicion or distrust. The change of which this is a particular instance is intimately connected with a revolution—for it is no less—in the view taken of the Bible by educated Christians generally. It is not merely that they have abandoned belief in its verbal inspiration ; it is that recognition of the supreme religious value of the teaching to be found in the Bible is no longer felt to involve the assumption that, because something is in the Bible, it must be in some sense true and important, or that something is lacking to what is otherwise true and important until sanction for it can be found in the Bible. Even quite orthodox and earnest teachers of religion do not scruple to express disagreement with a sacred writer ; and feel no temptation to force upon scriptural texts by ingenious devices, of allegorism or the like, meanings which one might wish them to bear but which are clearly quite remote from their obvious primary intention. No doubt there are many circles still little, if at all, affected by this reaction from the old veneration of the books which were formerly held, in the phrase still officially used by the Roman Church, to " have God for their author " ; no doubt that Church itself, the most numerous of Christian communions, continues (although the close observer will not be inclined to think it in fact untouched by the new spirit) to affirm unchanged the traditional estimate of the Bible. But, when all allowances have been made, the fact that a revolution is in progress in this matter can scarcely be denied by any candid student of the religious situation. Great as the change made by that revolution promises to be, however, it has not the appearance of heralding the disappearance of Christianity. A religion which in its cradle survived the disappointment of those confident hopes of a return of its Founder within the lifetime of the generation that had seen Him in the flesh, which seem to have loomed so large in the minds of the first disciples, has shown from the first a wonderful capacity of retaining an unmistakable identity through changes of a very far-reaching kind. In such changes as have actually taken place we have, indeed, to note loss as well as gain. Thus, when critics of the Reformation in the sixteenth century speak of it as " deformation," or critics of the revival in recent times of Catholic ideas and practices in the Churches of the Reformation describe it as " reaction," their strictures are not altogether without justification. Yet in either case we may observe a combination of reversion to type (*e.g.* to primitive simplicity or to primitive sacramentalism) with an appropriation of new elements belonging to the contemporary civilisation (*e.g.* nationalism or romanticism) which gives evidence at once of essential stability and of vigorous vitality. In comparing Christianity once more with Hinduism, which also has for ages preserved a certain identity of theory and temper while exhibiting an immense receptivity, we see, as has been suggested above, that the former faith distinguishes itself from the latter, and from all the forms of theosophy which find their inspiration in Indian ideas, by an historical outlook and by a characteristic ethical standard of its own, which, if hard to define, is not so hard to recognise, and which is bound up with the unique place occupied by Jesus in the devotion of Christians. It can scarcely be disputed that neither a comprehension of history nor an ethical standard is to be looked for from the scientific factor in modern civilisation. It is of the essence of science, as we now commonly use the word, to abstract from the human and ethical element in the world which it surveys ; and while it is beyond question that scientific research is a school of many virtues (including some which religion in general and Christianity in particular have not always promoted), the act of valuation implied in calling them virtues is one which science by itself cannot explain or justify. The ethical standard of the modern world has, as a matter of historical fact, been in the main fixed under Christian influence ; and this remains true, even when we have made full allowance for its purification in the predominantly secular atmosphere of recent times from defects which had been fostered by theologians and ecclesiastics. This purification itself can be welcomed by Christians as a legitimate stage in the development of their religion and one consonant with certain aspects of its original character, while they can claim that, in its fundamental principle of love to God and man, together with its fundamental creed that the manifestation of God in humanity centres in the movement of which Jesus, as portrayed in the Gospels and as present by His Spirit in His Church, is the founder and the guide, it can supply to the modern world the religious motive, inspiration, and consecration without which science is in danger of becoming but a powerful instrument in the hand of passions and interests to which scientific men, trained under Christian traditions, would be as unwilling as any to entrust the future of civilisation.

CONCLUSION

BY WILLIAM RALPH INGE

Dean of St. Paul's, London

IT has been my privilege to read all the essays in this volume. I hope the critics and the public will endorse my opinion that they reach a high standard of excellence, and deal in a masterly manner with questions of the greatest interest and importance The instructions of the editor were that the essays should be solid, but not too technical for the general reader. These conditions have, I think, been observed admirably.

It was also stipulated that the essays should not be directly apologetic in tendency. The book is neither a defence of Christianity nor a criticism of it. Its object is to make clear what the present state of the relations between religion and science actually is. This restriction also has been observed, but the writers have quite rightly not contented themselves with a colourless presentation. The book, after all, has a practical object, that of indicating possible terms of peace, or a *modus vivendi*, between religion and science. The writers are not all agreed as to how this is to be brought about ; but the differences between them are, in my opinion, less remarkable than their general harmony. After reading the whole volume, one is inclined to feel confident that a reconciliation is much nearer than it seemed to be fifty years ago.

My task in summing up the work of the essayists—it is not a debate, for the contributors have not seen each other's work—is very difficult. There are some subjects dealt with in the book with which I have only a superficial acquaintance ; and there are others which I should myself have treated somewhat differently. I have thought myself bound not to depart from the rules laid down for the essayists, and in particular not to turn all their arguments into an apology for the Christian faith. A certain degree of neutrality is, I think, imposed upon me by the task which I have accepted, of attempting to sum up and bring together the contributions of the different writers. And yet I have felt that a mere *résumé* is not what is desired from me. There may be one or two gaps which I should try to fill. The position of one writer may satisfy me better than that of another. If, on reading the whole book, a clear notion of acceptable terms of peace has suggested itself to my mind, it will be desirable that I should say so, and that I should not shrink from ruling out suggestions which seem to me impossible.

For instance, I have rejected with decision that kind of agreement which rests on a delimitation of territory. Some recent writers have said that there can be no conflict between religion and science, because they never meet. They move on different planes. To this way of thinking belong all such bisections of the field of experience as those which oppose sharply to each other fact and value, reality and appearance, the knowable and the unknowable, the visible and the invisible, prose and poetry. To acknowledge such distinctions, and rest an agreement upon them, assigning all on one side of the line to science and all on the other side to religion, is at best a proposal for an armistice; it can lead to no permanent peace. I shall give my reasons later for dissenting from a solution of the problem which is favoured by one or two of the essayists and rejected by others. A religion which does not touch science, and a science which does not touch religion, are mutilated and barren. Not that religion can ever be a science, or science a religion ; but we may hope for a time when the science of a religious man will be scientific, and the religion of a scientific man religious.

I have not concealed the fact that I write as a Christian. It would, I hope, be absurd for me to do so. But I have treated the religion of Christ as one of the permanent achievements or acquisitions of humanity like Hellenism and the Roman science of law and government. There are few scientific men, in this country at least, who would not allow so much as this, though the question remains how much of traditional Christianity is essential, and how much an accretion or an accommodation to transient conditions. This question will not be dealt with directly in this essay, though I shall not hide my conviction that some parts of the tradition are not integrally connected with the kernel of Christ's religion.

Following the usual practice now, the editor has divided the subject into two parts. The first part of the book is historical ; in other words, it treats religion as a branch of anthropology. By usage, anthropology has come to mean chiefly the study of the backward races, though there is nothing in the name to exclude the social history of civilised man. In this section, the relations between religion and science are brought down to recent times, and thus a transition is made to the second part, which may be called, in the broadest sense of the word, philosophical. The importance thus given to history will be generally approved, though it has its dangers. It is right that we should remember that we stand in the middle—or perhaps nearer the beginning than the end —of a long evolutionary process, and that our thoughts and beliefs are determined by the period at which we live. Our civilisation has its distinguishing characteristics, like the civilisation of classical antiquity, or of the Middle Ages. We are what the past has made us ; and if we can trace certain changes slowly at work in the period preceding our own we may be able to predict with some probability that these changes will continue, for some time at least, to operate in the same direction. The study of early history is certainly far more instructive in religion than in science. The rudimentary science which may be discovered even among savages is not interesting or important to modern research, which discards obsolete hypotheses without scruple or sentiment. The case is very different with religion, if we allow the word to include myth, ritual, and magic, through which religion has maintained its position as a social force. Religion is a powerful antiseptic, which preserves mummified customs that have long outlasted their usefulness, and otiose dogmas that have long lost their vitality. The history of customs and beliefs which have been put under the protection of religion is very instructive. It explains, as nothing else can, the vast quantity of mere survivals which encumber modern life. Even outside religious sanctions the race has contracted habits which seem to be hard to eradicate in proportion to the length of time during which they have existed. These habits have become, as the proverb says, second nature. Rapid changes are impossible ; even slow changes are exceedingly difficult. Nature, or habit, reasserts itself, though it has been expelled with a pitchfork. Religions, in the same way, tend strongly to revert to type. Stolid resistance to innovations is a policy which often justifies itself.

These are only some of the lessons which we may learn from history. But historicism, as we may call it, has been responsible for many errors and fallacies, especially in the most recent times. The tendency to judge movements of the human spirit by their roots instead of by their fruits is widespread, and in all the higher activities of mankind it is far less illuminating than the Aristotelian canon that the " nature " of a thing must be sought in its completed development, its final form. There have been writers who have treated all existing forms of religion as survivals of barbarous beliefs and customs.   The error is no doubt associated with a very recent tendency to regard myth, ritual, and magic as the kernel instead of the husk of religion.   If the essence of a religion were sought in the devotional life of its followers and in its influence upon the thought and action of the peoples among whom it flourishes, there would be less disposition to seek for explanations of it among the primitives of the past and the savages of the present.

Anthropologists of this type may learn something from the analogy of biology.   The fact that gill-slits and a tail exist in the human embryo tells us something about the remote past of humanity, but nothing about its present or its future.   It tells us nothing about Newton to know that he once had a tail.   Religion in the higher sense, which alone seriously concerns us, is a phenomenon of civilised humanity.   We do not care much how it began ; we want to understand it as it is or may be.

An even more serious objection is suggested by the extreme uncertainty of historical and anthropological records.   In this field, if in any other, " nothing worthy proving can be proven, nor yet disproven."   Laborious compilers may collect instances given by travellers of this or that quaint tribal custom, found in different parts of the world ; they may make ingenious theories as to the inner meaning of sacrifices and sacraments ; but can they really enter into the mind of the savage, and interpret his thoughts to civilised Europeans ?   The savage, we may guess, could not explain himself if he would, and would not if he could ; for he is a shy person, imbued with the notion that certain things are not to be talked of to strangers.   Some learned anthropologists have never seen a savage, and would be much alarmed if they met one ; others have travelled in barbarous countries, but have failed to master the very complicated native languages, which are not the same in any two tribes.   There have been instances when the natives have wilfully made game of the investigator, whose motives for inquiring they cannot be expected to understand.

Consciously or unconsciously the champions of the historical method are often the victims of the great superstition of the last century, the belief in a natural law of progress. This delusion has been lately revived in a curiously crude form by the Italians who claim to represent the *dernier cri* in philosophy. When we find savagery called " primitive," and a sort of assumption that the later in time is always the better, we may suspect a survival of this superstition. Nobody treats the history of art and poetry in this way, but the delusion has not been completely abandoned in the case of religion. We have discussions on what is supposed to be a serious difficulty in the way of accepting Christianity—that on the Christian hypothesis the highest revelation came to mankind nearly two thousand years ago.

The truth is that the great religions—Buddhism, Christianity, and Islam—date from the millennium which ends with the career of Mohammed ; and all of them were at their best when they were fresh from the mint. It is quite possible that religious genius culminated at that stage in human history. Our species has been in existence for half a million, perhaps for a million years. The changes in bodily structure which differentiate man from the other Primates belong to a vast period of which there are few records. Mental evolution seems to have checked the progress of physical changes, and the use of tools seems to have brought to an end the growth of the human brain. Intrinsic progress there has been none, or very little, for twenty thousand years. The vast accumulation of knowledge, and of mechanical appliances, which we call civilisation, may not be very favourable to religious insight. Industrialism has been very injurious to art ; may it not have injured religion also ? There are reasons for thinking that civilisation has been biologically a retrograde movement, which by no means implies that it was not inevitable, or that a return from it is possible. Man the tool-maker has made " inanimate instruments " (as Aristotle says) do his manual work for him ; he is now trying to make them do his mental work for him. Nature has no objection —at a price. The price may be the progressive deterioration of our faculties. Our brains may follow our teeth, claws, and fur.

The temptation to confound accumulated knowledge and experience with intrinsic progress is almost irresistible ; but it must be resisted. It is quite unnecessary to go to Australia or Central Africa to find the savage ; he is our next-door neighbour. The mentality of the stone age exists on our platforms and in our pulpits.

There is no superstition too absurd to find credence in modern England ; fetishes and tabus dominate London drawing-rooms. Dr. Malinowski's sojourn in Melanesia has convinced him that the mental processes of the South Sea islanders are very like those of Europeans. It is probably only politeness that prevented him from adding that a return to civilisation has convinced him that the mental processes of Europeans are very like those of Melanesians.

The belief in a law of progress, which is the soul of historicism, is a form of Millenarianism which constituted the secular religion of the nineteenth century. It was, of course, taken over by Christian progressives, who tried to find some warrant for it in the New Testament, where its only analogue is the apocalyptic Messianism which we find St. Paul and the author of the Fourth Gospel cautiously discarding. It is, however, very undesirable that Christianity should make friends with science by annexing a superstition which has nothing scientific about it. What we call progress is a biological episode which other species, such as the bees and ants, traversed long ago. The age of turmoil and experiment ended for them in the establishment of a stable civilisation, after which any further innovations have been severely and successfully discouraged. It is more likely than not that our species will come to rest in the same way, unless our present habits end in mutual extermination.

Dr. Malinowski's article shows the extreme importance of a distinction which is not always drawn, and the neglect of which has led to great confusion. Science is one thing, philosophies built upon science are another. The statement sometimes made, that mythology is primitive science, is an example of this error. Mythology is an attempt to account for facts in the natural order ; it is more like primitive philosophy than primitive science. It is not true that the savage knows nothing of natural laws, or of the sequence of cause and effect. He has his own traditional lore which teaches him when to plough and sow, how to make weapons, boats, and tools, and whatever else belongs to the stage of culture in which he lives. In these essential matters the savage reasons and behaves very much like a civilised man.

And yet it is true that magic plays a large part in his life. It is resorted to in difficulties, and in connection with mysterious and awe-inspiring events in the life of nature and of human beings. Magical rites gather round puberty, marriage, birth, death, and the corresponding processes in the vegetable world. Magic is an attempt to set in motion laws which the savage does not understand.

On the much-discussed distinction between magic and religion Dr. Malinowski seems to me to be right in rejecting the theory that magic is a private affair, while religion belongs to the community. There is much corporate magic, and much individual religion. The distinction is rather that magic always aims at producing some definite result, while primitive religion gives expression to mental states, such as sorrow, hope, and despair, without pursuing any practical aim. The separation cannot be made precise, for the cult of spirits, demons, and mythological personages has undoubtedly a practical object—namely, to placate these unseen but powerful beings, to avert their wrath and win their favour. Prayer has a practical object, though prayer is not a magical act. But the distinction is none the less valuable.

Dr. Malinowski emphasises the pragmatic and unspeculative character of religion among backward peoples. The savage (like the civilised man !) appeals to his gods and his priests when he finds himself in a hole or a quandary. The practical advantage of organised cult and sanctified custom is to stabilise valuable results already won. Innovation is made artificially difficult ; but most innovations, like most mutations in a species, are deleterious. Tribal law also keeps a social aggregate together, which gives it a great advantage in lawless societies, where raids and wars are even more frequent than under civilisation. But though the survival value of cohesion may be the real explanation of tribal ritual and custom, that is not the conscious motive of the discipline. It is honestly believed that the transgression of custom, the mishand ing of ritual, and the commission of acts which shock the conscience of the community, will call down upon the tribe collectively the vengeance of the higher powers. It is a great mistake to suppose that beliefs which have, or which once had, a survival value, are adhered to because they are known to have a survival value. They are maintained with equal zeal when they are manifestly disadvantageous, when, for example, they prescribe painful and even dangerous operations as part of the ceremony of initiation into full membership of the tribe. The answer, " It is the custom, ' is final for the savage, as for the lady of fashion. There is no other reason why they behave in a certain way, so it is useless to push further inquiries.

The statement that myth is not a speculation, nor the result of contemplation of nature or of the desire to explain natural phenomena, but rather a historical record of an important event, out of which a ritual act has been born, is manifestly true only of one class of myths. The savage is not without curiosity ; he is a natural "animist," and he enjoys poetical and picturesque descriptions. His cosmological myths may be described as poetical nature-philosophy ; they have no close connection with his tribal customs and disciplines.

Before leaving this subject it is worth while to notice that belief in the supernatural presupposes a belief in natural law. Where there is no law, there is no miracle. The savage dislikes the idea of a lawless universe ; and when he sees countless things happening of which he can give no rational explanation, he assumes that there is another causative principle, besides the natural order on the regularity of which he counts in sowing his fields. Having once restored his belief in law and order by this hypothesis, he is content to ascribe wind and rain and everything else that seems irregular to supernatural agency, and then to speculate whether this power is in any way amenable to control. Rain-making is an almost universal industry among savages, and we are told that twenty years ago there were still old women in the Shetlands who made a livelihood by selling winds to seamen. It is a slow process to find out the limits of the possible ; the principle of causation is fully realised, but its operation is unknown. Lubbock gives an example of a Kaffir who broke a piece of a stranded anchor and died soon afterwards, upon which all the Kaffirs looked upon the anchor as alive, and saluted it respectfully whenever they passed near it. We behave in the same way when our science is at fault. A house in which there have been two deaths from cancer is not easily let. The savage eats a tiger, or a slain enemy, to make him fierce ; the British parent stuffs his boys with roast beef to make them strong. There are to this day, I believe, remedies in the *materia medica* which have no origin except sympathetic magic.

Dr. Malinowski sums up magic as " pseudo-science," and yet feels bound to find a justification for it and a value in it. It represents, he thinks, " the sublime folly of hope," which has encouraged men to face life with courage, and therefore with some chance of success. Without disputing this, we must remember that the ' false science has been the deadliest enemy of the true. Religion is the guardian of all the higher values ; but magic is a will-o'-the-wisp which tempts men to their destruction. We have only to think of the resort to magic in modern times, to stop an epidemic, to cure diseases, to protect soldiers against bullets, to wash away sin, and to predict the future, to realise that we are dealing with an evil thing, a genuine survival of savagery. True religion and science have here a bond of sympathy—they have a common enemy to destroy.

The next essay, by Dr. Charles Singer, takes us into the heart of the subject, the relations between religion and science, treated historically. It should be supplemented by the two brilliant contributions of Dr. Singer to " The Legacy of Greece," in which justice is done, almost for the first time, to the achievements of Greek science in the classsical period. The subject is an immense one, too great, as the writer would admit, to be summarised adequately in one essay, while a summary of a summary, in this concluding paper, would obviously be worthless. Accordingly, I shall not attempt to make any comments on the relations of religion and science in antiquity, nor shall I discuss the causes why science decayed and died under the Roman Empire. The Dark Ages, and even the Middle Ages which followed them, are to the scientist a melancholy chapter in human history. I shall confine my remarks to the modern period, beginning with the revival of learning in Italy. It should be said that Dr. Singer treats the period between Newton and our own day very slightly, leaving it to be dealt with, from a rather different point of view, by Professor Aliotta.

Dr. Singer " omits any discussion of the revival of learning as irrelevant " to his subject. His reason is that the scholars of the Renaissance were antiquarians rather than researchers, and confined themselves chiefly to unearthing the remains of the science of antiquity. It is not easy to see what else they could have done. Greek science had done wonderful things, and had then perished and been forgotten. To disinter what could be found of these treasures was an indispensable preliminary to a new advance. And the great name of Leonardo da Vinci shows that the Italians were ready enough to turn their new knowledge to practical discoveries.

The truth is, I think, that the Reformation not only checked but obscured the scientific progress which had begun in the century which preceded it. The Reformation and Counter-Reformation were, from the point of view of secular culture, a retrogression. The Humanism of the fifteenth century was more literary and artistic than scientific, but it was ready to welcome scientific research, and would in a short time have freed itself from the ecclesiastical shackles which hampered its development. But the outbreak of fierce religious war in the sixteenth century destroyed the hopes of the humanists. It is useless to ask whether the Catholics or the Protestants were the most guilty of this set-back to civilisation. It was not Catholicism or Protestantism, but the state of war between them, which had this evil consequence. Christianity, when unmenaced, is no enemy to culture ; but as soon as war is declared, every nation or institution must subordinate all other considerations to the necessity of victory. It must curtail liberty of action, speech, and thought. It must devise and publish a fighting propaganda, in which the claims of truth and fairness are cynically disregarded. It must rest its claims on very clear and simple issues, which all can understand. When two religions are at war, there is no call for deep philosophers or subtle theologians. Both sides will rest their case on some external authority ; their dogmas will be coarsened and materialised ; they will both, while the struggle lasts, become religions of a narrow and brutal type.

It was, I believe, the terrible Wars of Religion that made the fatal rift between religion and science which we are now trying to close. It was a really disastrous accident that the greatest problem which the Christian Church has ever had to face was thrust upon it when it was distracted by an internecine conflict. That problem was the destruction of the geocentric view of the universe by the discoveries of Copernicus and Galileo. The momentous consequences of these discoveries were not at first apparent. Copernicus had no wish to provoke a battle with the Church, and his writings were not published till after his death ; Galileo was intimidated and persecuted. This was only to be expected ; but the Church of the Roman Renaissance would probably have withdrawn from an untenable position. Not so the Church of the Spanish Inquisition, of Luther and Calvin. Catholic and Protestant vied with each other in denouncing the new theories. Nor has this disaster ever been retrieved. By degrees the Copernican astronomy has passed into the region of common knowledge ; and though Rome put it under the ban, the devout Romanist is no longer expected to assert that the earth is the centre of the universe. But the retreat of Church authority has been gradual and, as usual, unavowed ; there has never come a time when it seemed urgently necessary to consider the new situation created by the revolution in astronomy. The task has been put off from generation to generation, and to this day little has been done to relieve the strain upon the intellect and conscience of the Christian world. Those Churchmen who airily declare that there is no longer any conflict between Christianity and science are either very thoughtless or are wilfully shutting their eyes. There is a very serious conflict, and the challenge was presented not in the age of Darwin, but in the age of Copernicus and Galileo.

The discovery that the earth, instead of being the centre of a finite universe, like a dish with a dish-cover above it, is a planet revolving round the sun, which itself is only one of millions of stars, tore into shreds the Christian map of the universe. Until that time the ordinary man, whether educated or uneducated, had pictured the sum of things as a three-storeyed building, consisting of heaven, the abode of God, the angels, and beatified spirits ; our earth ; and the infernal regions, where the devil, his angels, and lost souls are imprisoned and tormented. The mystics had been allowed to hold and expound a more spiritual philosophy ; there was never, I believe, a time when the saying that God has His centre everywhere and His circumference nowhere was condemned as unorthodox. But most certainly heaven and hell were geographical expressions. The articles in the Creeds on the descent of Christ into Hades, and His ascent into heaven, affirm no less ; and it is obvious that the bodily resurrection of Christ is intimately connected with the bodily ascension. The new cosmography thus touched the faith of the Creeds very closely. That the Church interpreted these doctrines literally is shown by the Anglican Articles of Religion, which declare that Christ ascended into heaven " with flesh, bones, and all things appertaining to the perfection of man's nature ; and there sitteth." Transubstantiation was denied on the ground that the body of Christ is in heaven, and that it is contrary to the properties of a natural body to be in more than one place at the same time.

The Copernican astronomy, and all the knowledge about the heavens which has been built upon this foundation, leave no room for a geographical heaven. Space seems to be infinite, or as some prefer to say, boundless—a distinction not very intelligible except to the mathematicians ; and among all the stars, planets, satellites, and nebulae which are sparsely scattered over its vast empty distances we can hardly imagine that one has been chosen as the abode of the Creator and the site of the heavenly Jerusalem. The belief in a subterranean place of punishment, which has not been disproved by astronomy, seems to have faded away without making any commotion, though I am told (I speak under correction) that the law of the land is still committed to it. If I buy a square mile of ground, I become the proprietor not only of 640 acres of the earth's surface, but of a cube with this base reaching " from heaven to hell."

There are also difficulties about time, but these are less serious, because though the Church rejected the belief, held by most of the Greek philosophers, that the universe had no temporal beginning, there is no reason why creation in time should be erected into a dogma. Few would say that this is a vital question. Nor does the doctrine of evolution cause any serious difficulty to Christians who have rejected verbal inspiration. It was a shock to many to hear that the human race has developed out of non-human ancestors ; but the question is only about the methods of creation ; Darwinism has inflicted no injury upon the Christian faith.

The older problem, however, is still shirked. A short time ago I reviewed a book by a writer whom a popular vote would probably choose as our foremost theologian. I found there a statement that Christians are no longer expected to believe in a local heaven above our heads. In reviewing the book I welcomed this rejection of a geographical heaven as significant, coming as it did from a pillar of orthodoxy. To my surprise, the writer complained that I had injured his reputation by suppressing part of his words. Of course, he said, he believed in a local heaven, only not above our heads. And yet he must know that the earth rotates ! Another distinguished theologian, in discussing the ascension of Christ, said that the words " into heaven " might be taken symbolically, but that we must believe that the physical body of Christ was raised to a considerable distance above the ground.

Nothing is further from my intention than to speak with disrespect of the religious convictions of any man, least of all of two of my friends. I would as soon laugh at a man's wife. But I do ask with all possible earnestness, is this kind of shuffling any longer

tolerable ? Is it not essential that the Church should face this
problem, which for four hundred years it has kept at arm's length ?
Do Christians accept those verdicts of astronomical science which
seem to be surely established, with those modifications of traditional theology which they imply, or do they not ? To juggle
with words, letting I dare not wait upon I would, can satisfy
nobody.

There are at least three positions between which the Church
may make its choice. It may condemn modern astronomy as
impious and heretical, as the Inquisitors and the Reformers agreed
in doing. Luther denounced Copernicus as a fool who dared to
contradict the Bible, " an upstart astrologer who dared to set his
own authority above that of Holy Scripture." Melanchthon
thought that those who set forth such theories must have no sense
of decency ; and Calvin asked, " Who will venture to place the
authority of Copernicus above that of Holy Scripture ? " The
Roman Church has lately condemned the doctrine of evolution in
terms not less stringent than these. This is one possible policy.
It declares that there can be no truce between science and religion
till science has renounced its errors and accepted the authority of
the Church.

A second policy, equally open to the Church, is to admit that
these traditional doctrines do not belong to the natural order with
which science deals, but to claim that they possess a higher truth,
to which science cannot reach. This may be done by regarding
these and other dogmas as symbolic of eternal truths, aids to the
imagination in forming clear conceptions of revealed truth in a
region beyond the compass of our senses. The apologist for tradition who takes this line will not be content to justify the use of
symbols. He will point out that science itself is an imaginative
construction ; that the supposed laws of nature are not derived
directly from our observation of the behaviour of atoms and molecules ; that what are called the assured results of science are the
work of the mind upon an abstract view of reality, which neglects
the values and qualitative properties of things, and attempts to construct a universe out of mathematics and chemistry. This dis-
paragement of science as incapable of forming any adequate
synthesis may be pushed so far as to reach what is called acosmism,
the theory which denies the objective existence of the world or
universe. The conclusion will then be, that though the dogmas

in question are symbolic, they are much nearer to truth than the scientific laws which pronounce them to be impossible.

The third policy is to recognise that all theological doctrines which rest upon the geocentric theory must be recast, inasmuch as the results of science are, within their own sphere, unassailable. I do not think I underestimate the seriousness of this step, nor the great difficulties in taking it. But anything, I believe, is better than trying to conceal an open sore which destroys our joy and peace in believing. If we adopt this third policy, we shall be driven to think of God less anthropomorphically, and of heaven as a state rather than a place—a state, too, which is eternal in a deeper sense than that of unending time-succession. But I cannot pursue this subject without transgressing the limits set for writers in this volume.

If I had any doubts that the religion of Christ can and will weather the storm, if I had any doubts that it is entirely independent of any false opinions about the nature of the universe, my readers may be certain that I should not have spoken as I have done. If I believed that Christianity stands or falls with a Ptolemaic universe, I should be obliged either to take the painful course of confessing that I have believed and taught all my life a creed which is as outworn as Paganism, or I should do like thousands of others —I should hold my tongue. But I am quite confident that this crisis will be surmounted if the Church has the faith and courage, and, above all, the common honesty, to face it candidly. Only let us hear no more of clergymen thanking God that theology and science are now reconciled, for unhappily it is not true.

The next essay, that of Professor Aliotta, leads us on to a new field. In the last paragraphs we have considered science as a steadily advancing army of ascertained facts, with which religious tradition is often at variance, and with which it must come to some sort of agreement. Professor Aliotta shows us science on the defensive, science divided against itself. In his famous book, translated into English under the title of " The Idealistic Reaction against Science," he has brought together the very various hostile forces which are assailing the fortress of Naturalism from different sides. He finds that the dominant tendency in modern philosophy is a reaction from " intellectualism." " The ruined shrines of the goddess of reason are invaded by the rebel forces of feeling, will, imagination, and every obscure and primitive instinct." The blind power of impulse has been exalted, and the guidance of the intellect abandoned. Theosophy, occultism, magic, and spiritualism have returned to the places from which they seemed to have been finally banished. The Professor traces for us the causes and progress of this astonishing revolt against the view of the world which not long ago seemed to be triumphant.

Even Kant, while discerning beyond the realm of mathematics and physics that of ethics and aesthetics, considered these as outside the pale of true knowledge, which belongs to mathematics and physics alone. Hence arose the agnosticism of writers like Du Bois-Reymond, Huxley, and Spencer. But Spencer in his language about the Unknowable was approaching the mystics without knowing it. Since his time reflection has shown clearly that mechanism and evolution are two concepts which do not agree together. Mechanism asserts quantitative permanence and determination by mathematical law ; evolution asserts qualitative transformation which cannot be calculated mathematically. The doctrine of evolution rehabilitates history, and destroys the rigidity of the mechanical method. In practice it is associated with a valuation for which mathematics can find no place. A still harder blow was dealt when science itself began to be treated historically as a mental habit in process of evolution, the direction of this evolution being determined not by correspondence to external truth, but by practical human needs. This is the genesis of pragmatism, which disintegrates the whole structure of science, and incidentally bids every superstition which seems to work, to take heart of grace.

The varieties of Voluntarism, which starts with Kant's primacy of the practical reason, but carries this doctrine much further, cannot here be discussed. On the other hand, the general tendency of Hegelianism is to regard the world, both as given by experience and as constructed by science in its concepts, as an illusory appearance of a deeper reality, to the understanding of which we are led by speculative philosophy. The Hegelians, however, though their audacious claims for dialectic as the revealer of reality may make them impatient of laborious research, are not such enemies of science as the other schools enumerated by Professor Aliotta. In this they resemble the school of Plato, which allowed science to die, but welcomed its rebirth at the Renaissance.

There is a French school which strikes at Naturalism by

affirming the contingency of natural laws. This is the thesis of Boutroux ; Bergson seems to reduce the universe to a stream of forces flowing in no definite direction, a shoreless river deriving the strength for its renewal from some blind and unintelligent impulse. " With all his metaphors," says Aliotta, " Bergson fails to convince us that continuous creative activity can give birth to practical discontinuous activity, and this activity in its turn to the objective world with all its determinations." A more fundamental criticism is that a philosophy which has no place for the intelligence is a contradiction in terms.

In the last part of his book Aliotta discusses the influence of new mathematical theories as shaking the foundations of a materialistic philosophy. I must leave this topic to those who are qualified to deal with it. It is the subject of Professor Eddington's essay, which follows that of Professor Aliotta. I will only say that an outsider like myself feels a strong suspicion that the new instrument with which Einstein has presented the mathematicians is being put to uses for which it was never intended. I cannot see how a purely mathematical theory can either prove or disprove materialism. In fact, I am still unconvinced that it has much importance either for the metaphysician or for the theologian.

It appears to me that Professor Aliotta might have kept further apart the philosophical revolt against intellectualism and the revolt of biology and psychology against mechanism. The former belongs to epistemology, the theory of knowledge, the latter belongs to pure natural science. The reaction against intellectualism is, on the whole, hostile to the claims of science ; the revolt against the tyranny of mathematics and physics is justified by the fact that these sciences have not succeeded in explaining the phenomena of life ; it is suspected that they are not, as was once supposed, universally valid principles. Thus we find some of our leading biologists inclining to some form of animism or vitalism, without showing the slightest tendency to disparage the claim of natural science to interpret the truth of phenomena, or to follow the pragmatists in denying the possibility of a disinterested and successful pursuit of things as they really are. The anti-intellectualist movement seems to me to lead to sceptical subjectivism. It discredits the authority of science, but it is equally damaging to religion, or at any rate to Christianity. For Christianity aims at nothing less than absolute truth. The Christian God is not only relative to human needs ; He is not only the ideal of human efforts. To put it technically, Christian philosophy cannot dispense with ontology ; the modern division of philosophy into the theory of knowledge, psychology, and ethics cannot be a philosophy of the Christian religion. If this be granted, the metaphysics of science needs rather more consideration than it has received in the body of this volume, and I propose to offer a few additional considerations on this subject.

It is a common error to speak of the doctrine of science when what is meant is Naturalism, which is a philosophy advocated by many students of science. Much confusion would be avoided if it were realised how little of what is called Naturalism depends directly on the results of nature-study. Let us then consider what Naturalism means.

It arose as a protest against supernaturalism, and as such has existed from the atomistic theory of Democritus to modern materialism. We find it opposing all mythology and miracle, insisting that throughout nature there runs a constant association of cause and effect, so that whatever happens could be explained simply and adequately if we knew its natural antecedents. As knowledge advanced, the hope was strengthened that all things would be found to be bound together in a uniform and necessary system. In almost all naturalistic theories we find an aversion from the idea of purpose. Teleology is banished as well as supernatural intervention. The machine of nature must somehow run by itself.

Now we have to distinguish between two widely different developments of Naturalism. One of these tends to an apotheosis of nature, as the life of a world-soul, which may become the object of religious reverence. Instead of ending in atheism, Naturalism may end in pantheism. This has been one of the most important lines of human thought. It is well represented in Greek philosophy, and has been the creed of many great men in modern times, of whom Goethe may serve as the type. As an example of this kind of Naturalism, " touched with emotion," I will quote some beautiful but little-known lines by Constance Naden :

> Yes, thou shalt die ; but these almighty forces,
> That meet to form thee, live for evermore ;
> They hold the stars in their eternal courses,
> And shape the long sand-grasses on the shore.

Be calmly glad, thine own true kindred seeing
    In fire and storm, in flowers with dew impearled ;
Rejoice in thine imperishable being
    One with the essence of the boundless world.

It might be better not to call this pantheistic creed Naturalism, reserving the name for the belief that the whole system of nature is calculable in terms of mathematics and mechanics. This is a clearer and more exact theory than the other ; for pantheism is generally a conglomerate of animism, poetical fancy, and mysticism; it soon leaves the domain of exact science. True Naturalism is determined to keep within this domain, and to reduce all phenomena under a few simple, easily formulated laws. All must be measurable and ponderable.

With this object Naturalism selects as the normative sciences mathematics, physics, chemistry, and mechanics. All the phenomena of life and change, all the operations of the human mind, in spite of their apparent freedom and independence, must be theoretically capable of being reduced to problems in physics and chemistry. In its desire to find a quantitative calculus for everything alike, Naturalism divests life, whether physical or spiritual, of all that separates it from the inanimate and inorganic. So far from deifying nature, like pantheism, it devitalises it. Pantheism is romanticist, Naturalism is positivistic. Clear-sighted pantheists have expressed a strong dislike to Naturalism.

But though these two developments are antagonistic, the popular mind easily and frequently confuses them. The same persons who speak of men as mere machines, the cunningest of nature's clocks, will try to bring down will and instinct into the lowest stages of existence. They do not realise how much they are borrowing, quite illegitimately, from idealism, poetry, and religion, and while they profess to build upon Naturalism an edifying and attractive philosophy of life, they disguise from themselves and others the bare and abject poverty of the scheme which alone can be supported by their primary hypothesis. One might go further and say that even materialism could not exist if there were nothing real except matter and energy.

The method of Naturalism is simplification. Its ideal is to find one simple law under which everything may be brought and explained. This law can only be purely quantitative, and since qualitative differences are incommensurable, they must be neglected altogether. This arbitrary rejection of all the "imponderables," which in philosophy as in politics are the most important factors of experience and determinants of action, is an even more comprehensive error than the omission to consider the fact of consciousness, which has so often been brought home to Naturalism. It is, however, this latter mistake which has caused the revolt against Naturalism within the ranks of science itself. Naturalism is driven, by its passion for simplification, to assume that all mental processes are the accompaniments of material changes, and that the material changes are the causes, while the mental processes are inert consequences, mere "epiphenomena." Thus the broad and deep gulf which, in our experience, divides the living from the dead, the organic from the inorganic, is obliterated ; the inanimate is made the norm by which the animate is to be explained. The method of simplification demands an even greater sacrifice. Physics and chemistry are theoretically capable of reduction to the fundamental laws of movement in general ; the end of the simplifying process is a statement of the nature of reality in mathematical symbols, which are valid whether there is anything corresponding to them in nature or not. And so the philosophy which professes to be grounded on the solid rock of observed phenomena, severely rejecting all subjective human valuations, ends in pure mentalism, which is independent of the existence of any external world whatever.

It is thus plain that the instinctive repugnance of the religious mind to Naturalism, however clumsy the expression which it has sometimes found, is not the wilful blindness to ascertained truth which the scientific controversialists of the last century often assumed it to be. These doughty champions of nature study, who had, we must not forget, a good case against the theologians who wished to forbid their investigations and discredit their conclusions in advance, were in the habit of saying to the defenders of religion, " Leave us alone, and we will leave you alone. Leave us the knowable, and keep the unknowable for yourselves. Our province is realities ; yours is dreams, and you are welcome to them." This delimitation of territory was absolutely impossible, because both sides claimed to have an interpretation of existence as a whole. Naturalism is not science, but a jejune and self-contradictory philosophy. Its outcome is not to leave religion alone, but to destroy it, along with the other interests of the human spirit which

we have agreed to call the highest part of our nature.   That the
controversial Naturalists were themselves high-minded and cultivated men is not disputed ; but their devotion to the good, the true,
and the beautiful was built not on their philosophy but on their
self-denying labours and pure unselfish lives.   It is perhaps fortunate
that the philosopher is the reverse of audacious, except in speculation.
His books generally end in a *salto mortale* which lands him in very
familiar and conventional morality.

The aim of every intellectual construction of the universe—
of every world-view, as the Germans call it—is to find universal
law, to comprehend all experience in a closed system.   An exception does not (as a mistranslated proverb states) prove the rule ; it
disproves it.   If there are phenomena, whether biological, psychological, or religious, which cannot be made to fit into the framework
of Naturalism, Naturalism as a philosophy is overthrown.   Biologists,
among others, now assert that there are such phenomena.   There
are some religious minds which rejoice in this new proof that
Omnia exeunt in mysterium.   It pleases them to find that the closed
system is not closed, and that " contingency is brought into the heart
of things."   I am not in entire sympathy with this feeling, though
I agree with Plato that " only that which is perfectly real can be
perfectly known," and that the impasse into which Naturalism
falls is an indication that the perfectly real is spiritual.   But
those who take refuge in gaps find themselves in a tight place
when the gaps begin to close ; and those biologists who join the
idealists in exposing the limitations of Naturalism are themselves in search of a wider Naturalism which will find room
for life, mind, and spirit within the scheme of nature.   The
inexplicable is for them, as for the naturalists of the last century,
a scandal, or at least a problem.   Perhaps the most fruitful
line of thought, in view of the present situation, is to consider
briefly the problem of teleology, the possibility of purposiveness
in nature.

It has been pointed out lately (by Mr. S. A. McDowall) that
organisms are not closed systems.   The general tendency to the
degradation or dissipation of energy is balanced, for a time, by
a building-up process in the cell and in the organism.   In this
building-up process we seem to see signs of purpose, and this purpose
is clearly not only individual but racial.   Although many writers
speak of unconscious purpose in the sub-human and even in the

vegetable world, this, he thinks, is an unintelligible idea. Purpose is the prerogative of personality, and since it exists in ourselves, we may infer the existence of a personal Creator.

Now it is certainly true that we are convinced of the existence of a self-directing purposive activity in ourselves. The *onus probandi* rests with those who ascribe to delusion one of the primary characters of our nature, as it is known to ourselves. A theory which denies the truth of one of our fundamental convictions about our own minds must have very strong evidence from other quarters to make it credible. Nor do I dispute the validity of arguing by analogy that the Creator must possess *per eminentiam* the highest qualities with which humanity is endowed. But personality is obviously a matter of degrees. The argument which I have recapitulated implies that there is somewhere a line which divides the personal from the infra-personal, and this line can nowhere be found. The evidence seems to me to point to a purposiveness running through all nature, sleeping in the stone, dreaming in the flower, and partially awake and conscious in man, a single purpose which points to a God who is both immanent and transcendent. This view, as I shall presently show, is in harmony with the doctrine of evolution, but not with the Naturalism which is logically bound to deny evolution.

I would rather emphasise what Professor Arthur Thomson has said of the organic world, only extending it to the inorganic world as well, since I believe that here also there is no rigid line of demarcation, but a transition, in accordance with universal law, from the inorganic to the organic, from the inanimate to the living. This has not yet been definitely proved ; but it is possible, as Professor Moore has suggested, that the colloids, or giant molecules, may supply the link which is still missing. Professor Thomson says : " Only a system with order and progress in the heart of it could elaborate itself so perfectly and so intricately. There is assuredly much to incline us to assert eternal providence and justify the ways of God to man."

If the whole of nature is purposive, it is not likely that we can discern special purposes operating in particular cases. The laws of nature are, on this hypothesis, purposive laws, like all other laws ; and if they are the laws of an omnipotent and omniscient Being, we should expect them to act regularly and uniformly. A machine that needs tinkering is a faulty machine, but a machine that has no intelligence behind it can hardly be called a machine at all. All that science has done to establish the uniformity and regularity of nature's operations tells heavily in favour of the existence of a single creative intelligence, and tells with equal force against the non-Christian hypothesis of a plurality of gods, against the Manichean theory of a good and an evil spirit contending on nearly equal terms in the arena, against the hypothesis of an inert and yet intractable " matter," and against any other theory which makes God a spirit among other spirits, struggling with only partial success to enter into His kingdom. It is against this dualism or pluralism that scientific men, and many others who cannot claim to be men of science, protest when they reject the vulgar conception of miracle as the suspension of a lower law by a higher. They find no valid evidence for such suspensions ; but they also feel that the classification of events as natural or supernatural withdraws the natural order from the immediate jurisdiction of God, and virtually hands it over to some lower principle, or to blind and unintelligent " necessity."

Naturalism declares that neither purposes nor ideas are to be found anywhere in nature, neither in the whole nor in the parts. They are driven to this, not by dislike of the idea of an intelligent Creator, which does not interfere with the freedom of science in any of its branches, but by the attempt to reduce everything to the quantitative formulas which are used in physics, chemistry, and mathematics. There must be nothing in the consequent which was not in the antecedent. The Naturalist is bound by his theory to deny all real change. Evolution, if he uses the word, is a mere mechanical unpacking of what was there all the time. There is nothing in this theory of mechanical unpacking which necessarily conflicts with Aristotle's theory of entelechies. Aristotle taught that the perfect " form " of everything was implicit in it from the beginning, and determined the course of its development. Naturalism, however, rejects this theory because it implies a kind of vitalism or panpsychism, an inner unconscious will residing in the developing organism, or, if this is not asserted, it merely describes what happens, and gives no explanation of it. This dispute does not concern religion, which needs only to assert that, however evolution is effected, a divine purpose is being realised in it. Religious teleology is belief in an eternal purpose. Every additional proof that the world is a closely interwoven system of means carries back the evidence of purpose to the mind of the Creator Himself, and so assists religious belief. The religious difficulty in welcoming this proof arises from a different source—namely, from our moral valuation of the natural order. This belongs to a later stage of our discussion.

Here, however, it is necessary to point out again that Naturalism and Darwinian evolution do not agree together. There is, of course, a vulgar Darwinism which is exactly the jumble of Naturalism with pieces of other and incompatible philosophies already mentioned. Darwin himself no doubt accepts the naturalist philosophy as true within the sphere of his own studies ; he took no interest in metaphysics. He denies purpose as a factor within nature. Natural selection is for him a sieve through which those forms of life which happen to be adjusted to their environment pass. In theory, all valuation is excluded. There is no reason why the better should survive, even if the words better and worse had any relevant meaning. But several expressions in Darwin's writings leave us in no doubt that he shared the confidence in progress which, arising from very unscientific sources, dominated the minds of his generation. And if natural selection leads to the survival of the better or more valuable stocks, it is difficult to attribute so beneficent a result to blind unconscious forces with no intelligence behind them.

The legacy of Darwin is now in a state of chaos. Some reject natural selection and the struggle for existence altogether as explanations ; indefinite variation is opposed by orthogenesis, slight variations by saltatory mutations. There are neo-Lamarckians and neo-Vitalists. But besides this, reflection on Darwinism proper, when treated as a philosophy, shows that its outcome is not Naturalism, but something more like sceptical pragmatism. The common notion is that Darwin teaches that all history is development towards a goal, and that therefore the strongest must be the best. So, I suppose, the ideas which prevail must be true. But although Darwin may have held this comfortable opinion, it is no part of his system. All he has a right to say is that the ideas by which humanity has progressed so far are called true, and that while using the same ideas there is some probability that we shall continue to go on in the same direction. The true idea is the idea which prevails ; truth, in this system, can have no other meaning. As Bradley says, " The one criterion for Darwinism is the abstract success or prevalence of whatever happens to prevail, without any regard for its character. And this leaves us in the end with no criterion at all." Darwinism, in fact, is a fruitful theory of the means by which nature works. It cannot be made the basis of a philosophy, and it has no vital connection with religion.

I have spoken of Naturalism as a poverty-stricken and ultimately self-contradictory philosophy, which is now being dethroned by its own subjects. But it is wise to be cautious in condemning views and systems which are now out of fashion. We have to understand what made them plausible, and to remember that the errors against which they were a protest—for an *-ism* is always in opposition—are probably raising their heads again now that their adversary is in retreat. And so I will make use of a review by Professor Wallace of Lord Balfour's " Foundations of Belief," in which Wallace earnestly deprecates the modern tendency to disparage reason. Naturalism, he reminds us, was in its origin a protest, not against the supernatural in itself, but against a supernatural conceived as arbitrary, incoherent, and chaotic ; it was a protest against the idle profanity which thinks it has explained an event when it has said that it is the work of God, as if anything were not the work of God. The world which reason claims is one where she may go on and never die ; a world where nothing can be called unknowable, though much may remain for ever unknown ; a world where, as man accumulates more and more his intellectual and spiritual capital, we shall move about more and more freely and wisely. The world which the genuine Naturalist desires is not different. It is a reign of law ; but may not the reign of law become the kingdom of the spirit ? " To assault Naturalism and Rationalism is to strike at Nature and Reason ; it is to support supernaturalism and the materialism of authority."

Professor Wallace is attacking what I should agree with him in thinking a dangerous tendency, but what he calls Naturalism at its best is not consistent Naturalism. The passage which I have summarised shows how alarmed a Hegelian may be by an assault upon the authority of science. We have now to consider, assuming that the attempt to reduce life, mind, and spirit to the quantitative categories of physics, chemistry, and mathematics has definitely failed, what philosophy is likely to commend itself to thoughtful students of nature, in the place of what we have called Naturalism.

Of one thing we may be certain. Science will never renounce the attempt to bring everything under a single system of laws. Science must be monistic, for under any other dispensation science could not exist. The dualism of nature and supernature is intolerable to science. And therefore, since the attempt to explain mind materialistically and life mechanically appears to have failed, nothing remains but to explain nature spiritually. Even the partition of the world into the animate and the inanimate is distasteful to science, which dislikes any lines that cannot be crossed.

There are many signs that this solution will be attempted. Professor J. S. Haldane says, " It was formerly assumed that as we trace life backwards to its simpler forms, we are tracing it towards a primitive world of physical mechanism. This is not the case. We are really tracing life into what we had wrongly assumed to be a world of physical mechanism. It may be many years before the significance of the phenomena of life for our conceptions of visible reality are generally understood ; but assuredly this general understanding will in time be reached." How far this movement towards panpsychism has already gone may be realised by the following words from an essay by Professor Carveth Read : " It is reasonable to suppose that every cell that goes to constitute the body has its own consciousness, of which we are never distinctly aware, though each cell may contribute something to our total subjectivity ; and even in the central nervous system, with its prepared lines of connection, it is only in the cortex that consciousness becomes identified with ourselves, and only in the focus of attention that it becomes clear and coherent." On this theory we are literally nations of living individuals. And if such tiny entities as the cells of the body are to be regarded as having their own life, and the germs of consciousness, it seems likely that some thinkers will go back to the speculations of Fechner, a very remarkable philosopher whose works are now receiving much attention on the Continent, though they have unfortunately not been translated into English. Like the later Platonists and many others in antiquity, Fechner regards the earth and the other spheres as animated beings of a highly spiritual kind. As the spirits of men, with all the life in the earth, are comprised as moments in one conscious earth-spirit, so the earth-spirit is included with all the other sidereal spirits in one conscious spirit of the universe, God. I am not defending this theory, which to many will seem fantastic.

There is something absurd in the idea that a vast aggregation of incandescent gas must have a soul of a dignity proportioned to its bulk. But it is surely significant that panpsychism is once more being taken seriously. And with panpsychism comes teleology, and perhaps, as some think, the admission of freedom and contingency. What we call mechanism may be the teleology of the inorganic world.

If Fechner is ever studied in this country, he will be found to have laid down with great power and insight a spiritual philosophy which may be acceptable to a speculative student of nature. To the sceptical biologist or pragmatist who undermines our faith in the objective truth of our convictions, he replies with much force : We should not need religious faith if its objects did not exist. For if man has made belief in those objects because he needs it, he did not create the circumstance that he needs belief in them for his continuance and welfare, and is therefore obliged by that necessity to make it. The production of this faith by man must therefore be based on the same real nature of things which produced man with his needs. It would be to impute an absurdity to the nature of things, and it would be contrary to experience, so far as we can speak of experience in such a matter, to say that nature has constituted man in such a way that he can only prosper while he cherishes a belief in a thing that is not. We may hope that what Fechner calls the Day-view of the world (in contrast with the Night-view which he rejects) will dissipate the mists of the scepticism which would cut us off from any real knowledge of things as they are.

I have written at some length on the philosophy of science, because science, no less than religion, aims at formulating a general view of reality, within which its more abstract investigations may be set. Neither science nor religion can claim less ; both involve a philosophy. There is, in my judgement, something of a gap between the scientific essays in this book ; the philosophy of science is not adequately dealt with. I could have wished that the filling of this gap had fallen into more competent hands ; but I thought that the book would be incomplete without some such discussion as I have tried to supply. If I am right, the materialistic monism of the last century is giving place to a spiritualistic monism which is still in a very tentative stage. The whole problem of the interplay of the psychical with the physical is very far from settled, and the difficulties seem to be extremely formidable. It is, however, obvious that any theory which finds room for mind and spirit as essentially parts of the field of inquiry must be far nearer to the religious view of reality than the Naturalism of the last century. To the religious view of the world we must now turn.

Perhaps the first caution which we shall do well to bear in mind is that religion is not always true or good. As Dr. Oman has said, we are dealing with human nature when our subject is religion, just as much as when we are discussing art or politics or social life. There is much bad and false religion, which we shall discard, just as we should discard bad and false science. We wish to take both religion and science at their best, and to consider how they stand towards each other.

We have said enough about the religion of the backward races. Let us consider religion as we know it in civilised modern Europe. We shall find it full of distortions and corruptions which explain, if they do not justify, the hostile attitude which some reformers take to religion, at least in its institutional forms.

Alienists tell us that the highest of our mental faculties are the first to yield to morbid conditions of the brain. Decadent races or individuals will have a decadent religion. The close connection between religion and morals is loosened ; the religious conscience, except in relation to some tradition of the elders which has no real ethical sanction, becomes blunter than that of the respectable man of the world. The happy and joyous temper, which characterises a fresh and confident faith, degenerates into moroseness, or into the vapid hilarity of the seminary. Religion relapses into mere cultus, which is the husk of religion ; its genial symbolism petrifies, and offers a stolid opposition to the best-established secular knowledge. In order to retain the allegiance of the masses, it stoops to fraud and deception, and endeavours either to impede education or to control it. A decadent religion does far more harm than good in the national life. If we blame the pioneers of modern science for the acerbity of their language about the religion of their day, we must in justice remember that the religion of their day contained much rotten material.

Next, we must remember that religion, like some chemical substance, is never found pure, and it is not at all easy to isolate it in order to learn its properties. We have seen in the earliest part of this book how difficult it is to separate religion from magic in the beliefs and practices of savages. The difficulty is not less among civilised peoples. Religious beliefs always impinge upon natural science. They may at first have been myth, symbol, or poetry, since primitive man does not distinguish clearly between these and the field of strict science ; or they may once have seemed probable explanations of phenomena ; but it is far more difficult for religion to correct its mistakes than it is for science. A doctrine which has acquired a mysterious or sacramental value is too precious to be sacrificed ; its place cannot be taken by a new symbol manufactured for the purpose. Pieces of obsolete science, imprisoned like a fly in amber in the solid mass of a religious creed, may have become the casket in which the soul keeps her most valued treasures. They are defended fiercely by believers, not because as brute facts they have much value for religion, but because they have become charged by association with spiritual values which " must be given through something." Religion clings like a climbing plant to extraneous supports of many different kinds ; the supports may become rickety, but the vine has grown round them and entangled itself with them.

There is so much even in the highest religion that seems archaic and obstructive, that some thinkers, like Comte in the last century and Croce at the present day, can make out a case for treating religion as half-baked philosophy, and predicting its disappearance. There are, however, no signs that this is likely to happen ; and if we examine religion as we know it, not only in its first beginnings but in its fullest maturity, we shall understand why neither philosophy nor science can take its place.

Religion for most of us, I think, is born in the antithetic consciousness of alienation from, and of communion with, the unseen power which surrounds us. The sense of alienation begins with the mere feeling of impotence in face of an indifferent or friendly world. Then our dissatisfaction turns inward, and becomes a sense of guilt. We realise that it is our self-centredness which puts us at enmity with our surroundings, and in the sacrifice of self-will we find our peace. The sense of communion with God is equally important as an element in all religion. It finds ritual expression in most religions, but its own language is prayer, which is the pulsation of the heart of religion. We need not trace the evolution of prayer from a half-magical incantation to the sublimation of petition in " Thy will be done," and the " prayer of union " of the saintly mystic. It is only necessary to say that the consun-mation of communion with God coincides with the final resolution of the sense of estrangement from Him. In both aspects of religion there is a spiritual death and resurrection to a higher life, in which the " I yet not I " of St. Paul is no longer a contradiction.

A similar antithesis is that between the two processes of expansion and sinking deeper into ourselves, which mark the progress of the religious life. The expansion movement throws out what Carlyle calls organic filaments into our environment, enlarging our personality by establishing new affinities and sympathies with our fellow-men, with nature, and with God. This enlargement of sympathy is so far from dissipating our personality, that it deepens and intensifies it. It is only by going forth out of ourselves that we can attain to a really personal life. Here again we see that two apparently divergent movements meet at the top. Those who are willing to lose their " soul," their separate individuality, in larger interests and self-forgetting activities, can hope to find it unto life eternal.

At the present day, when psychology attracts so much more attention than metaphysics or dogmatic theology, the old question whether the organ of religious faith is the intellect, or the will, or the feelings, is much debated. Some of the disputants are in great danger of falling back into the discarded faculty-psychology, which treats our undivided human nature as if it were a bundle of separable forces or attributes. In particular, a large school of thought cherishes a curious animus against what it calls intellectualism, and argues as if it were possible and desirable to banish reason and logic from religion altogether. I shall follow Dr. Oman in discussing this question of the faculties which religion uses, but I shall take my own line in developing the argument.

But before weighing the claims of the intellect, the will, and the feelings in the production of religious faith, there is a preliminary truth to which I attach the greatest importance. We have spoken already of the quantitative and qualitative differences between things, and have rejected the attempt of Naturalism to reduce everything to quantitative terms. To do this would be to rule out all valuation, if it were not true to say, as I shall argue presently, that the rigid order and uniformity at which Naturalism aims is itself a value. The whole case for a spiritual interpretation of the world rests on the belief that the tendency to attach values to all experience is not only a psychological necessity which we cannot escape, but an avenue leading to objective truth. I do not think that any religious view of the world, or any genuinely religious conviction, is possible if we do not believe that value is as objective as existence, and inseparably connected with it. I am not afraid to say that there can be no existence without value, and no value without existence. I know well that in putting forward this claim for our value judgements we are in danger of an intractable dualism, which we must not seek to escape either by reducing the world of becoming to a mere appearance, or the eternal world to an unrealised ideal. We cannot solve the problem by setting an imperfect world in the present against a perfect world in the future. As I have said elsewhere, we cannot levy unlimited drafts on the future to avoid bankruptcy in the present, like the belligerents in the late war. If the world of becoming is unreal, the will is an illusion, and time, space, and moral choice disappear with it. If, on the other hand, the ultimate values have no objective existence, but are merely regulative ideals on which we are to model our conduct, we have no absolute standard left, and are abandoned to subjective and fluctuating valuations. My own conviction, if I may quote from myself, is that " reality is neither mental nor material, but a realm in which thought and thing, fact and value, are inseparable, neither having any existence apart from its correlative. The real world is a coherent organic unity, space-less and timeless, but including all happenings in space and time in their proper relations to itself—that is to say, *sub specie aeternitatis.*"

The attributes of ultimate reality are values ; and we may follow the usual classification by saying that the ultimate values known to us are goodness, truth, and beauty. Windelband even says : " There can be, as regards content, no further universal values beyond these three, because in these the entire province of psychic activity is exhausted." We are nearest to God, and to knowledge of the world in which His attributes are reflected, when we can see and feel these ultimate values without us and within.

Science is not, as some have erroneously supposed, a description of fact without valuation. Such a description would be utterly impossible, and it should be superfluous to point out how widely the world as known to science differs from the final analysis of material objects into electrons and protons. The mind of the scientist constructs its own world, in which certain values alone are looked for—those of coherence and uniformity and commensurability. It seems that at present observation gives only approximate or average regularity. This may or may not be philosophically important. But it is most important to realise that physics and chemistry aim at only an abstract picture of the world. All that falls under the heads of goodness and beauty is omitted. And yet, if we are right, these are just as real as those aspects of existence which can be weighed and counted.

This theory of ultimate values is at the root of all that I have to say about religion. It follows that I am opposed to what may be called psychologism, the theory that we cannot get beyond the study of mental states as such. I believe, on the contrary, that our knowledge of the ultimate values, so far as it goes, brings us into touch with the truth of things, with the mind and will of the Creator. I accept Plato's well-known canon that only the perfectly real can be perfectly known; and perfect knowledge is no mere intellectual process, but an enhancement of the whole personality till it becomes capable of " knowing even as we are known." The unity of knower and known, through the love which passes knowledge (but which has not passed by knowledge), is the ideal consummation of spiritual growth.

In saying this, I have in part anticipated what I have to say about the place of intellect, will, and feeling respectively in the life of faith. But my criticism of what seem to me one-sided views will be better understood if my general standpoint is known.

There have been many who have found the source and the essence of religion in pure feeling, which they have tried to isolate from thought and will. It would be a mistake to place the mystics in this class. Emotional theism is not the same as mysticism, which is an intensely active inner life, usually involving a strenuous exercise of the will, and often profound thought. The exaltation of a religion of feeling was naturally popular among the romanticists, among whom Schleiermacher was the most famous theologian. He found the origin of faith in an undifferentiated feeling of the Infinite and Eternal. Some, like Jacobi, have claimed that faith is its own evidence ; that as we can say with Descartes, " Cogito, ergo sum," so we can say, " I pray, therefore God is." This kind of apologetics admits of no refutation and carries no conviction. Immediate and infallible revelation of this kind is not given to man.

But Schleiermacher's plea for the trustworthiness of the emotions cannot be so summarily dismissed. The life of devotion does carry its own evidence with it. We must only demur to its being called pure feeling. There is nothing intrinsically good or bad about feeling. Flowers and weeds bloom there side by side. We cannot even speak of truth of feeling, unless we extend feeling to include the formation of ideas. I do not think religious feeling is ever aroused, except by ideas of objective truth and value ; but these ideas are certainly not generated by feeling.

It is not to be denied that the stimulation of violent emotions may leave permanent traces on the mind. This was doubtless discovered empirically, and orgiastic worship was practised with this end. The undifferentiated, inchoate religious sense is thus intensified and fixed, to the great and lasting injury of the spiritual life. The fruits of emotional revivalism, if they are permanent, are chiefly bad.

This is, perhaps, the best place to mention the concept of " the Holy," which since Otto's famous book has been given a new importance in English books on the psychology of religion. The idea of holiness has its history, like other religious ideas, and the history is not edifying. The holiness of Jehovah, as exemplified by the death of Uzzah for touching the ark, was much more like electricity than any moral quality. The whole history of taboo might be introduced here. But Otto is right in emphasising the feeling of awe, dread, and fascination as an essential part of religion. It is generally mixed with superstitious elements, and should never be the dominating feeling in the approach of the Christian to his Father in heaven. " He that feareth is not made perfect in love." The impression made by Otto's book may lead to this feature being somewhat over-emphasised.

Another school, which is well represented in our day, makes faith an affair of the will. It is pointed out that people in general are not convinced by pure reasoning, but that they believe what they wish to believe. Hobbes declared that even the axioms of Euclid would be disputed if men's passions were concerned in them. But the question is not whether men do actually form their opinions in this way, but whether they ought to do so ; and the answer to this question depends on whether we have any confidence in human reason or not. The primacy of the will over the intellect goes with sceptical empiricism. It is the root of the philosophy called pragmatism and of the revolutionary movement in the Catholic Church called modernism. It is not possible to discuss either of these in this concluding essay.

The word intellectualism, used in a disparaging sense, occurs in one of these essays. It is in common use among the opponents of speculative idealism, especially when the Hegelians are being attacked, and also by modernists in attacking the Catholic system of dogma, based on the " Summa " of St. Thomas Aquinas. It is a matter of faith with Catholics that " the one true God can be known with certainty by the natural light of reason." This, it will be observed, is quite different from the " ontologism " of Jacobi, mentioned above. The knowledge of God's existence, for the Catholic, is of the nature of a valid inference. The rationalistic proof of religion may take several forms. Paley's argument is well known : " The marks of design are too strong to be gotten over. Design must have a designer. That designer must be a Person. That Person is God." To this section would belong, if there were room to discuss them, the famous four proofs of God's existence—the ontological, cosmological, teleological, and moral arguments, with which Kant dealt very roughly. The ontological argument has no doubt been often formulated faultily ; but it seems to me a fair argument to say that the conception of God can hardly be a purely subjective notion. A mystic might go further. The intellect is trying to formulate and explain an actual experience, the essence of which is that it is known or felt not to be purely subjective. The cosmological argument, as restated by Lotze, is not concerned with a Prime Mover but with an immanent ground of the World. There must be an ever-present energy, which is the source of all cosmical movement. The teleological argument, which Kant treats with respect, has since his time been repudiated by the majority of scientists. But though the simple teleology of Paley is out of date, we must protest against the assumption that uniform law and order are incompatible with the idea of purpose. 1 am inclined to think that the very conception of law implies purpose. These arguments are sometimes called proofs, though they are not demonstrations ; they are, however, closely inwoven with the texture of rational experience.

Intellectualism, in the disparaging sense, may take the form either of pantheistic naturalism or of speculative idealism. The rationalism of the deists lost sight of the meaning of faith ; it ended

in a " common sense " attitude, from which the religious valuation
of the world has quite disappeared. Its practical outcome was
utilitarianism, which, though philosophically weak, provided many
excellent men with a calculus of personal conduct and of social
reform. I shall not attempt any description or criticism of speculative idealism, as expounded in the numerous disciples of Hegel.
The tide is running strongly against this type of philosophy. But
I agree with Sir Henry Jones, that " the intellectual ardour of the
world cannot be damped, far less extinguished, by any theory,
blindly advanced in the interests of religion, of the radical insecurity
of knowledge, or of the incompetence and untrustworthiness of
human reason."

The special quarrel of the modern schools with the idealists
is connected with the repudiation by the former of " absolutism."
Here I must take leave to paraphrase from what I have already
written (" Faith and its Psychology," 1909). To give up the
conception of reality as a single system would be to give up both
philosophy and science. If the world is " wild," as William James
thinks, only wild men, whom we do not permit to be at large, would
be at home in it. " And yet so great is the fear engendered by the
conception of a cosmos which shuts man up in an iron framework,
that we find Lotze reducing natural laws to mere conceptual
generalisations ; we find Ritschlians warning the intelligence away
from the domain of religion ; we find Professor James and his
followers constructing the universe of enigmatical atoms dignified
by the name of persons, and rushing into polytheism."

We cannot regard particular facts as real, and the laws which
connect and regulate them as only subjective. " Mere ideas "
cannot bind together " real objects." Or if the objects also are
said to be subjective, everything disappears at once into dreamland,
including the reasons for doubt. The sceptic cannot throw his
opponent if his own feet are in the air.

We pursue the absolute, not because we are " intellectualists,"
but because we must. The opponent of absolutism generally sets
up an Absolute of his own without knowing it. Even the principle
of relativity has become, with some of its defenders, a kind of
absolute.

The objection to intellectualism loses its force if we use intelligence in the Platonic sense, not of the logic-chopping faculty, but
of the whole personality become self-conscious and self-directing,

under the guidance of its highest part. In my other books I have attempted to show in detail how the spiritual life is or should be a harmonious development of the whole man, passing, as Clement of Alexandria says, from faith to knowledge, and from knowledge to that love which " unifies the knower and the known." In this state of enlightenment there is no more discord between the will, the intellect, and the feelings, and the objects of our reverence— the True, the Beautiful, and the Right—are more and more blended, like a triple star.

It seems strange that a warning should be necessary to take our religion seriously. But we cannot look about us without noticing the extraordinary frivolity of much which passes for religious interest. In Southern Europe, especially, religion is largely a social diversion, a spectacular performance, an artistic enjoyment. The attitude of our own public towards popular superstitions, half belief and half make-belief, is too common among church-goers. The scientific man cannot understand this playfulness where matters of the highest moment are at stake. Nothing repels him more from the worship of the churches. It is difficult for a student of science to realise how weak the love of truth is in the majority, and how widespread the mistrust of reason. The real sceptic does not write books on agnosticism ; he never thinks at all, which is the only way to be perfectly orthodox.

It is, I think, a valuable reflection of Otto that much injury is done to the cause of religion by separating the question of human immortality from the truth or falsehood of the religious view of the world generally. It is of the essence of religion, in its higher forms, to distinguish between the transient, unsatisfying flux of things, and the permanent, satisfying reality which lies behind it. This distinction has been embodied in countless mythologies and eschatologies, but the conviction which creates them is funda- mental. So long as we discuss immortality merely as the question whether the individual continues to exist as a conscious being after his death, we have taken it out of its religious context. For religion this question is significant only as a part of the much larger convic- tion that the true nature of things lies behind their visible appear- ances, and beyond time and space. The mere question of survival in time, and for a time, is almost frivolous to the religious mind. What is essential is the conviction that, in the words of Plotinus, " nothing that really is can ever perish," or, as Goethe puts it, " all that is transitory is only a symbol." I honestly believe, as Otto does, that the destruction of the supramundane physics of the Middle Ages by the discoveries of astronomy will be found to have done a good service to religion, by forbidding it to seek its treasure and its everlasting home in space and in time. I have not room to follow Otto in his penetrating analysis of our conceptions of time and space. As he says, the arguments of which Kant was the pioneer, though they do not remove the curtain which separates being from appearance, at any rate force it to reveal itself as a curtain.

The religious conception is made up essentially of a belief in the pre-eminence of the spiritual world over the natural, and rejects the common scientific view that " mind is but a kind of *lusus* or *luxus naturae,* which accompanies it at some few places, like a peculiarly coloured aura or shadow, but which must, as far as reality is concerned, yield precedence to 'Nature' in every respect." And although it is certain that when religion is in any way complete, it includes a belief in the everlastingness of our spiritual nature, and its independence of fleeting phenomena, it is a mistake so to isolate the question of survival that opponents may dictate both the questions and their answers. If this pre-eminence and autonomy of the spiritual be not granted, it is misleading to use the word God at all, and those who do so are open to F. H. Bradley's gibe that they call the Unknowable God only because they don't know what the devil else to call it.

The naturalist arguments against a spiritualistic interpretation of nature are certainly formidable. Briefly, the best answer to them is to remind opponents that without the free and creative activities of the mind there could be no naturalism. Further, it is legitimate to point out that if the spiritual faculty is given fair play, and suffered to develop normally, suspicion and distrust of it must disappear. We do not disparage the results of science, or throw doubt upon them, when we affirm that they are the creation of the free spirit which finds in nature those laws which their and our Creator has planted alike in the conscious and in the unconscious world. " The world we know, the world of sound, light and colour, of all properties whatsoever, of the ugly or the beautiful, of pain and pleasure, is in the most real sense the product of consciousness itself." The spirit is never dumb, and it speaks a different language from that of mathematics or physics.

I pass to the psychology of religious belief as it has been studied from another side. The literature is abundant ; a satisfactory survey of the subject is Professor Pratt's " Religious Consciousness." This writer makes a useful fourfold classification, which we may call either four aspects of religion, or four temperamental kinds of religion. These are : the traditional, based on the authority of the past ; the rational ; the mystical ; and the practical or moral. These four aspects are to be found in every genuinely religious person ; but in varying degrees according to circumstances, temperament, and, not least, according to age.

Wordsworth's well-known line, " heaven lies about us in our infancy," can hardly be accepted without qualification. The child's mind is a garden where flowers and weeds grow together. The perverted ingenuity of the psycho-analysts has laid bare the roots of unpleasant vices even in the apparent innocence of the nursery. The child believes in God because he has been told that He exists, and probably imagines Him as resembling in character one or both of his parents. He readily assimilates the supernatural stories of the Old Testament, and it is a serious problem how to teach him without making him believe many things which he will afterwards learn to be untrue. It is not easy for his elders to know what really goes on in the mind of the child. Much of the religiosity which unwise parents delight to observe in their children is pure imitation or innocent hypocrisy. And on the other side, the child's inner life is often a turmoil of terrors and anxieties of which his parents know almost nothing. And yet we must always remember that young children not infrequently have an exquisitely beautiful saintliness of character, " walking with God " in a simple directness of realisation which is rare in adult life, except among the highest saints. Sometimes when a child is called early from this world, the experience of sickness seems to accomplish in a few months all that a lifetime of devotion and sustained moral effort could have produced.

The period of adolescence has engaged the attention of many researchers, especially in America. It is said to be a time of storm and stress, of repressed cravings, morbid brooding, and alternations of communion with and alienation from God. The ages between eighteen and twenty-five are the usual time for what is called con-version. The subject has been investigated in America by means of the questionnaire, a method which, in my opinion, is unsafe if much reliance is placed upon it. It selects those who are willing to answer such questions and omits the large number of those who refuse to answer them. It assumes a power to analyse one's own heart and motives which is by no means common. It does not allow for the great influence of suggestion, especially in such matters as instantaneous conversion. There are some Christian bodies in which the young are taught to expect a sudden turning to God, and in these bodies it is reported as a common experience. Roman Catholics and Anglo-Catholics do not expect it, and for them it is an unusual event. John Wesley believed that it is almost universal, and reported that " in London alone I found 652 members of our society who were exceeding clear in their experience, and whose testimony I could see no reason to doubt. Every one of these, without a single exception, has declared that his deliverance from sin was instantaneous, that the change was wrought in a moment. As I have not found, in so long a space of time, a single person speaking [of a gradual change], I cannot but believe that sanctification is commonly, if not always, an instantaneous work." A living Wesleyan minister of large experience has told me that among modern Methodists instantaneous conversion is very far from being felt by all.

There is also a danger of overestimating the " storm and stress " of adolescence. Very many persons develop healthily and happily without it. The special psychical disturbances caused by sex are no doubt very common, but they have been greatly exaggerated by Continental writers, unless we may flatter ourselves (and I am not sure that we may not do so) that a much larger proportion of young people in England preserve their innocence than in other great countries.

In middle life we have come to take ourselves for better and for worse. We have learned that there are some things which we are good for and others that we are bad for, and we no longer kick against the pricks. We live in our work and in our affections and ideals ; we are what we are interested in. We have given up our claim to " unchartered freedom," and are beginning to understand that our perfect freedom consists in service and submission to God. As I have said elsewhere, " Lucan speaks of :

Libertas, cuius servaveris umbram
Si quidquid iubeare velis.

But in religion it is the substance, and not the shadow of liberty, which is gained in this way." In middle life, petition forms a smaller and smaller proportion of our prayers. Our creed is simplified, and intensified. God becomes for us less an object than an atmosphere.

Dr. Brown, like all modern psychologists, attaches the greatest importance to the mystical experience, the essence of which is that the soul believes itself to have come into immediate communication with a spiritual power or presence above itself. It may be hoped that we shall have no more attempts, like that of Murisier, to prove that all mysticism is pathological. If the student chooses to take for his examples only the extreme types of ecstasy, it is no doubt easy to show that the subjects of these trances were often in a morbid state of the brain or nerves. Even among visionaries, however, there have been many men and women of robust health and keen intelligence. But if we realise, as is certainly the truth, that what is called mysticism is only a further development of a universal religious practice, that of prayer, we shall put aside these attempts to discredit religion at its base. It is the conviction of all religious people that in prayer we are speaking to One who hears us, and this is the strongest argument that the religious quest is not vain. Dr. Brown mentions that many persons fail to achieve anything like the mystical experience, and regards this as an argument against the value of the mystic's testimony, except to the psychologist. But, so far as we can judge, very many persons are religiously ungifted, just as many are indifferent to music. They may be excellent people, but they are, so to speak, deaf on this side. There are many also who have never given long and concentrated attention to the unseen world ; they do not " practise the presence of God." Such persons do not receive the mystical experience, because they have not earned it. They have not even attempted to climb a mountain which, as all who have climbed it testify, is long, steep, and difficult. There are specialists in the spiritual life, as in other things. Their testimony is of supreme value in their own sphere ; and it is an error to say that what they have seen and felt is valid only for themselves, because others cannot share it. It is not thus that we treat the authority of genius in other subjects.

But there is a question of special interest in the study of mysticism, to which Dr. Brown calls attention. The mystic nearly always describes his initiation into the higher mysteries as a progressive simplification, in the course of which he closes one avenue after another through which ideas might reach him from the world of sense, and at last reaches a point where time and space and individuality drop away from him, leaving him "alone with the Alone." The interesting question is whether in this experience of simplification and nakedness the soul really has an intuitive perception of the Unity which lies behind all multiplicity, of an eternal mode of existence which transcends time and space, or whether this is an illusion and not in reality a deeper experience than the definite and brightly coloured images of the normal consciousness.

The question is very difficult, especially when we remember that we have not ourselves enjoyed this ineffable experience, and that those who have had it agree that it has been the culminating point of their life of devotion.

It is well known that the Vision of the One forms the apex of those systems of philosophical mysticism of which the scheme of Plotinus is the type. He was led to his doctrine of the super-essential One by three distinct paths. His dialectic led him to acknowledge in the real or intelligible world a unity in duality, a complete correspondence between thought and its object, which nevertheless remain two in one, not simple unity. The same method of rising from multiplicity towards unity which he had used in all his philosophy, compelled him to take the last step, and postulate a final and complete unification in the Absolute "beyond existence." It is part of his greatness to realise that without some duality of thought and its object, there can be no existence ; and that yet this duality cannot be absolutely final. Secondly, he feels that the soul cannot be in bliss unless it has something above itself to worship and aspire to, "always attaining, and always striving on." "All things pray, except the First Principle," as Proclus says. Thus the Absolute gives him an object which the beatified spirit can adore. And thirdly, he has experienced the blank trance, and he thinks that in those moments he has risen even above the spiritual world, and been merged in the immediate presence of the Absolute, the First Principle.

Many who have followed the mystics so far will shrink back at this last claim. How can any finite spirit so transcend the conditions of its existence as to share, even for a moment, the life or consciousness of the Absolute ? And if this belief is illusory, are we not thrown back upon the full and rich life of the spirit among other spirits as the highest state which man can attain ? Some who have been repelled by the bleak isolation of the mystic's final climb might welcome this conclusion. Dr. Brown emphasises the transcendence of space and time in ecstasy as perhaps an important experience. But in fact much of our higher life is timeless and spaceless ; it is not only in ecstasy that we rise beyond these forms of thought.

The last essay in the book deals not with religion in general but with Christianity in particular. What is its position among other religions ? Is it, in any real sense, unique ? Can we expect that it will ultimately conquer the world ?

These questions cannot be answered without a clearer defini-tion of what we mean by Christianity than Professor Webb's essay contains. The future of Christianity as an institution—the fate of the Churches—is, from the point of view of these essays, not a matter of supreme importance. It is even possible to speculate (though I should not go so far myself) whether the religion of Christ might not be a greater power in the world if its professional custodians were removed. As a great historical institu-tion, Christianity can be characterised only as the religion of the white race. Although it arose on Semitic soil, it had made its choice between Europe and Asia long before the end of the first century. The Jews would have none of it, thus transformed ; the Asiatic Christians made a poor fight against a genuinely Oriental religion, that of Islam. From the second century till the present day, Christianity has been the most European and the least Asiatic of religions. Its great expansion in modern times has been due to the unparalleled expansion of the white race. It has made no triumphs worth boasting of among the brown, black, or yellow peoples. The gospel itself, no doubt, may exercise a wide influence upon Buddhism, Hinduism, and Mohammedanism. There is a cult of Amida in Eastern Asia which is said to be not unlike the Logos-Christology of the early Church. But the European nations, arrogant, domineering, and rapacious, have done little to recommend the name of Christianity in Asia and Africa ; and it is hardly probable that the European Churches, which have formed their customs and forms of government to suit Western conditions, will impose their organisations upon the immemorial religious traditions of the East. That the Gospel of Christ will one day " convert the world "—that is to say, the religiously minded in all nations—is not beyond the possibility of hope ; but an universal institutional Church is as chimerical an idea as an universal Empire.

It is not scientific to pick out all the superiorities of Western civilisation and put them down to the credit of Christianity. European civilisation has been, like Hellenism, a permanent enrichment of humanity, and the religion of Europe has borne many exquisite flowers. But unless, like the Roman Catholic Modernists, we assume that every transformation which helped the Church to survive and prosper was a legitimate development of the original design, we shall not find it easy to affiliate Hildebrand, Oliver Cromwell, and Cardinal Manning to the Gospel as it was preached to the fishermen of Galilee. Organised religion is not, in modern times, one of the strongest forces in human affairs. As compared with patriotism and revolutionary aims, it has shown itself lamentably weak. The strength of Christianity is in transforming the lives of individuals—of a small minority, certainly, as Christ clearly predicted, but a large number in the aggregate. To rescue a little flock, here and there, from materialism, selfishness, and hatred, is the task of the Church of Christ in all ages alike, and there is no likelihood that it will ever be otherwise. To many the most pressing question is whether the Churches will ever make it easier for students of science to profess themselves churchmembers without doing violence to their scientific conscience. What the institutions will decide is quite uncertain. But there are already large numbers of Christians who find it possible to follow Christ while accepting the conclusions of science and the scientific attitude of mind. These are far more important than their isolation from ecclesiastical life might lead us to suppose. It is to individuals that we must look for encouraging signs, not to institutions. Science has learned this lesson in its own sphere ; it must look at religion in the same way. The right note was already struck at the Renaissance. Leonardo da Vinci exclaims : " Let bigots talk at leisure and heed them not. The study of Nature is well-pleasing to God, and is akin to prayer. Learning the laws of Nature, we magnify the first Inventor, the Designer of the world ; and we learn to love him, for the great love of God results from great knowledge. Who knows little, loves little. If you love the Creator for the favour you expect of Him, and not for His most high goodness and strength, wherein do you excel the dog, who licks his master's hand in the hope of dainties ? But reflect how that worthy beast, the dog, would adore his master if he could comprehend his reason and his soul." Whether our dogs would respect us more if they knew us better may be seriously doubted ; but I think we may say of natural science what Bacon said of philosophy, that while a little knowledge often estranges men from religion, a deeper knowledge brings them back to it ; though we ought to add that the religion to which deeper knowledge brings us is not the same as that from which superficial knowledge estranges us.

INDEX